D0771744

"Hal Wright successfully tackles a daunting
children with disabilities prepare for their futu
passionate about serving and enriching the live
needs community. Illustrative and practical, this guide is imperative reading for
families and professionals who are driven to make a difference. Well done, Hal!"

—*Peter J. Wall, Vice President and Trust Officer, Colorado State Bank and Trust*

"The transition into adult life for an individual with a disability and his or her
family is often incredibly stressful and overwhelming. Hal's book provides real
answers to real questions for real people. It is comprehensive in its approach. I
anticipate that it will not only help families create a plan that works for their
unique set of dreams and needs, but will also provide families with a sense of
hope for a beautiful future."

—*Julie Dani, MS Education, Special Education Consultant*

"Parents of children with special needs and their advisors will return again and
again to *The Complete Guide to Creating a Special Needs Life Plan* when sorting
through the maze of thorny issues they face. Hal Wright weaves together diverse
and inherently complex areas of planning with the expertise of an experienced
practitioner and the compassion of a loving dad."

—*Hartley Goldstone, JD, co-author of* TrustWorthy: New
Angles on Trusts from Beneficiaries and Trustees

"This comprehensive book offers a plan for the maze of life that families of
children with disabilities travel through. Specific and well-written information
on challenging issues such as finances (including advice on Special Needs
Trusts and Supplemental Security Income), insurance, guardianship, and estate
planning provides excellent guidance for these families."

—*Fran Hickey, MD, Director of the Sie Center for Down
Syndrome, Children's Hospital Colorado*

"Hal's book is the most comprehensive, easy-to-read book on living with and
helping those with disabilities that I have ever read or imagined. It's a book you
can (and should) read from cover to cover as well as a resource you can go back
to as needed. It answers every question I can think of and so much more. It's
a resource for those just starting their journey and those already well on their
way. Highly recommended!"

—*Ally Bailey, parent of a daughter with an intellectual disability*

"This book is at the top of my list for families and professionals that are touched by someone with special needs. As an attorney with over 30 years' experience, my practice focuses on elder law and special needs planning. Hal provides advice that is practical, comprehensive, and easy to understand. I give *The Complete Guide to Creating a Special Needs Life Plan* my highest recommendation and applaud Hal for his insight and mastery of a multifaceted subject."

—*Bradley J. Frigon, JD, LLM, CELA (Certified Elder Law Attorney), CAP (Council of Advance Practitioners)*

THE COMPLETE GUIDE TO
CREATING A SPECIAL NEEDS LIFE PLAN

of related interest

**Guiding Your Teenager with Special Needs through
the Transition from School to Adult Life**
Tools for Parents
Mary Korpi
ISBN 978 1 84310 874 0
eISBN 978 1 84642 727 5

Life After High School
A Guide for Students with Disabilities and Their Families
Susan Yellin and Christina Cacioppo Bertsch
ISBN 978 1 84905 828 5
eISBN 978 0 85700 302 7

Divorce and the Special Needs Child
A Guide for Parents
Margaret "Pegi" Price
ISBN 978 1 84905 825 4
eISBN 978 0 85700 284 6

Adults on the Autism Spectrum Leave the Nest
Achieving Supported Independence
Nancy Perry
ISBN 978 1 84310 904 4
eISBN 978 1 84642 870 8

The Complete Guide to Getting a Job for People with Asperger's Syndrome
Find the Right Career and Get Hired
Barbara Bissonnette
ISBN 978 1 84905 921 3
eISBN 978 0 85700 692 9

**Employment for Individuals with Asperger Syndrome
or Non-Verbal Learning Disability**
Stories and Strategies
Yvona Fast
ISBN 978 1 84310 766 8
eISBN 978 1 84642 015 3

THE COMPLETE GUIDE
TO CREATING A
SPECIAL NEEDS
LIFE PLAN

A COMPREHENSIVE APPROACH INTEGRATING LIFE, RESOURCE, FINANCIAL, AND LEGAL PLANNING TO ENSURE A BRIGHTER FUTURE FOR A PERSON WITH A DISABILITY

HAL WRIGHT CFP®
FOREWORD BY JAMES FABER

Jessica Kingsley *Publishers*
London and Philadelphia

Figures 1.1 and 1.2 have been printed with kind permission from Inclusion Press.

First published in 2013
by Jessica Kingsley Publishers
116 Pentonville Road
London N1 9JB, UK
and
400 Market Street, Suite 400
Philadelphia, PA 19106, USA

www.jkp.com

Library of Congress Cataloging in Publication Data
Wright, Hal, 1948-
  The complete guide to creating a special needs life plan : a comprehensive approach integrating life, resource, financial, and legal planning to ensure a brighter future for a person with a disability / Hal Wright CFP ; foreword by James Faber.
    pages cm
  Includes bibliographical references and index.
  ISBN 978-1-84905-914-5 (alk. paper)
  1. People with disabilities--Care--Planning. 2. People with disabilities--Finance, Personal. I. Title.
  HV1568.W75 2013
  362.4'048--dc23
                            2013012242

British Library Cataloguing in Publication Data
A CIP catalogue record for this book is available from the British Library

ISBN 978 1 84905 914 5
eISBN 978 0 85700 684 4

Printed and bound in the United States

To Eleanor
My spouse, companion, and helpmate of 40 years

To David
Who has a special relationship with his kid sister

To Rebecca
Who has had to patiently wait for Dad's attention

And to Meg
Who has made me a better person by being the person she is

CONTENTS

PART 4
LEGAL PLANNING: PROTECTING YOUR VISION
AND YOUR CHILD

PART 5
SPECIAL CIRCUMSTANCES

FOREWORD

Finally someone has created a much-needed resource to help families, care givers, and anyone else navigate the maze of special needs planning. This book is an invaluable resource in showing how to create a person-centered life plan that focuses on an individual's abilities, not his or her disability. Hal Wright has done the nearly impossible and created a comprehensive guidebook that crosses several disciplines to build a roadmap for special needs life planning. I particularly like the practical checklists that follow every section making the process of life planning achievable for everyone regardless of resources or family situation. Guidance on how to develop a life plan is a critical need in the disability community. Done well, it can open doors to a joyful and meaningful life and allow individuals to make significant contributions in our communities. Hal has taken a very difficult process and made it manageable with a simple vision: to create the best possible life for an adult with a disability.

The author is a parent of an adult daughter with Down syndrome and brings the hard-won experience of a parent to explain special needs planning in clear and practical terms. As a Certified Financial Planner, Mr. Wright has an uncommon breadth of knowledge in all aspects of special needs planning. He has a family perspective observing that the needs and goals of all family members must be considered. He notes that fairness to all of the children can be one of the more difficult questions financially constrained parents will face. Hal writes that his family has been a part of the community of special needs families for 27 years and they have benefitted from the emotional support, advice and experiences of so many. He has much to be thankful for and uses his lessons learned and wonderful expertise to "give back" to our families and the disability community.

I was struck by his forthright articulation of the civil rights of people with disabilities. He makes this statement in the book's Preface: "A person with a disability has the right to a joyful and meaningful life, the right to an appropriate place in the community, and the right to determine the nature and quality of his or her life to the extent capable. I strongly believe these rights are universal…" I share Hal's vision and this is exactly what the disability community advocates for every day. He is a firm advocate of person-centered planning focused on capabilities, not disabilities. We should never underestimate the ability of people with a disability and I am convinced our society is failing to recognize a vast amount of human potential. This book is aimed at breaking down barriers and helping our communities maximize everyone's abilities.

Hal Wright breaks new ground in special needs planning in three areas. Typically special needs planning focuses on taking care of needs related to the disability. Mr. Wright asserts that we must focus instead on the person's capabilities. The former approach is minimal and limiting. The latter is enabling and empowering. Second, Hal explains how to explicitly link a financial plan to a life plan by developing a resource plan (the life plan's enablers) and an estimate of the financial support needed to pay for the resources. Third, he shows how to address the entire life span of the person, including how to ensure the continued care and support of a child who significantly outlives his or her parents.

The book is full of practical guidance. I found especially helpful the four case studies that provide real-life illustrations of what a life plan looks like for persons with different abilities, challenges, and in different economic circumstances. I think you will find yourself personally caring for these four individuals as I did. Literally they are fictional characters but at the same time they are real people. We have met these people; we just know them by different names.

So, in the strongest possible terms I commend this book to you. I know it will change the way you see special needs planning and it will help you take control of creating a better quality of life for your child or loved one.

James Faber
President
The National Down Syndrome Congress

ACKNOWLEDGMENTS

Special needs planning spans many professional disciplines and no one can be expert in them all. I am deeply grateful to the professionals who have reviewed the manuscript for accuracy and soundness of concept to assure that readers of this book are well served. I thank Carolyn Ajie and Scott Quicke of the Mile High Down Syndrome Association's Alive! Program; Bob Ward and Jenny Jordan of Developmental Pathways; Carol Meredith of the Arc of Arapahoe and Douglas Counties (Colorado); Laura Thompson of the HERO Alliance; Cara Brennan George and Alison George of ABC Investments Team at RE/MAX Professionals; Melinda Borchardt of Borchardt Senger & Associates, Public Accountants; Pete Wall and Carrie Steinert at Colorado State Bank & Trust; Loyce Forrest, family law attorney; and elder law and trust and estates attorneys Nancy "Susie" Germany, M. Kent Olsen, Bradley Frigon, and Eric Solem.

I wish to thank consultants who helped with the case studies: Margie, Mae, Libby, Jeannine, and Angela of the Federation of Families for Children's Mental Health on the Henry Lowenstein case study; Bettie Lehman and Jill Baldauf of the Autism Society of Colorado for the Mike Olmstead case study; Jon Vigne of the Colorado School for the Deaf and Blind, and Julie Deden and Bart Batron of the Colorado Center for the Blind for the Noelle Williams case study.

I found out as a first time author that writing a book is not as easy as I thought it would be. The professionals at Jessica Kingsley Publishers have been wonderfully supportive: Emily McClave, Commissioning Editor; Victoria Nicholas, Production Editor; and staff in the Philadelphia office—Laurie Schlesinger, Anthony Schiavo, Carolyn Busa, and Katelynn Bartleson.

There are many people who have supported my family and our daughter over the years but I want to specifically mention Linda Barth, the founder and for 20 years the executive director of the Mile High Down Syndrome Association, and Julie Dani, a most extraordinary special education teacher and founder of the ASPIRE Club.

I must acknowledge Anna and John J. Sie and Michelle Whitten of the Anna and John J. Sie Foundation and the Global Down Syndrome Foundation for their passionate work and generous support helping people with Down syndrome to a better life.

PREFACE

I am a retired Certified Financial Planner (CFP). Most of my planning clients were parents of children with special needs. The focus of my practice was very personal. I am a parent of an adult daughter with Down syndrome.

Meg was born on December 23, a Wednesday afternoon. The doctors hadn't told me and Eleanor that our third child would be born with Down syndrome though they had told us she had duodenal atresia, a telltale indicator, and would need major surgery to survive. She was a tiny, beautiful baby but we didn't get to hold her. She was quickly whisked away to a local children's hospital where she underwent a six-hour operation to construct a functional digestive system. Back in the delivering hospital, over an hour passed before the obstetrician came to the post-delivery room to tell us our baby had Down syndrome and would be "mentally retarded." I don't remember anything of the conversation after the "mentally retarded" part. I remember it wasn't handled well, though in fairness to the doctor this can't be a comforting conversation.

Forty hours later, I was home on Christmas morning trying to make the best Christmas I could for an eight-year-old son and a four-year-old daughter, with my wife in one hospital and our baby in the infant intensive care unit of another. About ten o'clock the phone rang. The caller said, "Hal, my name is Debbie Hauserman. I'm with the Mile High Down Syndrome Association. I'm calling to ask how you're doing and if there's something I can do to help." I will never forget that phone call.

Within a couple of weeks, MHDSA assigned a volunteer couple who had a son with Down syndrome to help me and Eleanor through our first year as special needs parents. We joined a parent support group. We went to educational programs and events where we met children with Down syndrome and their families. A lot of people helped us in that first year gain the strength and determination to be good parents for our new child. I can't repay them for what they did for us. But it's like baby clothes. You don't return the baby clothes to the parents who gave them to you. You pass them on to someone who can use them. That's why I wrote this book, to pass on what I have learned to you. I write first and foremost as a parent with experience planning for my daughter's future. I also write with the expertise of a Certified Financial Planner who practiced in the field.

What is special needs planning? When someone asks me and Eleanor what we want for Meg, we reply: "After her special needs are met, we want her to have friends, a job and a home, and to have what she wants for herself. We want her to be safe and happy when we're not here to protect and support her." This is what special needs planning is all about.

As a financial planner, I am well aware of the marketing slogan used by life insurance companies directed at parents: "What will happen to my child when I'm gone?" I have learned to be wary of insurance and investment professionals who see their commissions before they see my child, and so should you. But the slogan reflects a truth. "What will happen to my child when I'm gone?" is a very big fear. I have felt that fear as a parent, and behind that fear I have felt the worst fear of all: "Will my child, someday, be left alone?" This is what lends compelling urgency to do special needs planning and do it well.

I can tell you as a parent that special needs planning is not easy. When my wife and I started planning for our daughter's future, we found no one who could explain how "the System" worked, how to put things together, where to go for help, or what we had to do. People could explain their part of a fragmented and disconnected system but couldn't show us the whole picture. It was like trying to put together a jigsaw puzzle without the picture on the box. There were other challenges. We had to go on a scavenger hunt for puzzle pieces. When we got home, we found some were missing, some didn't fit, and every now and then someone came by and took some of them away.

How do you put a jigsaw puzzle together? You start with the picture on the box. Then you locate the major pieces—corner pieces, border pieces, and pieces that make up prominent features. Gradually, you fill in the areas of the puzzle. I wrote this book to show you the picture on the box. It identifies key puzzle pieces. It will help you take control of planning for your child's future. I hope to do for you what I wished someone could have done for me and Eleanor.

There are two core values that guide what I have written:

1. *A person with a disability has the right to a joyful and meaningful life, the right to an appropriate place in the community, and the right to determine the nature and quality of his or her own life to the extent capable.* I strongly believe these rights are universal, as well as the rights to comfort and freedom from fear, neglect, or harm.

2. *We must take a person-centered approach to planning, focusing on the individual's capabilities and not their disability.* I believe we underestimate the ability of people who are cognitively impaired to speak for themselves and participate in decisions about their lives. We tend to assume an individual's expressive skill is indicative of his or her receptive skills. This assumption can be very wrong. I am convinced that as a society we

may have underestimated the human potential of a vast population of people thoughtlessly labeled "mentally retarded."

My daughter has taught me that she understands her situation better than I sometimes realize and has hopes for her future beyond what she can express without help. Our challenge as parents is to give our children opportunities to express their hopes and dreams in whatever way works for them. Our responsibility is to listen.

I intend this book to be helpful to families who have loved ones with special needs regardless of the nature or severity of the disability. I address the needs and opportunities of people with intellectual disabilities, mental illness, and seriously limiting physical disabilities such as sensory or mobility impairment. It will help parents of children who are mildly, moderately, or severely challenged. This is a wide span of circumstances to cover. Most material in this book applies to people with a moderate intellectual disability but there is material here for a broader population. This book is not just for parents. I also write for relatives, friends, advocates, and for people with disabilities who can take control of their own lives.

Deliberately I write also for financial advisors because the special needs community is woefully underserved by my profession. I hope to encourage more advisors to practice in this specialty. I want to help my colleagues understand the profound, aching hope of parents to create a better life for their children and how to help them fulfill that hope. This book is also intended to be useful to attorneys, special education teachers, social workers, and others who serve the special needs community.

I want to comment on the terminology you will find in the book. When I use the term "child," I use it in terms of a familial relationship such as the child of their parents regardless of age. Usually I am speaking about an adult child. When it comes to age, I use the terms "minor" for someone under 18 and "adult" for someone 18 or over.

I also need to comment on "people-first language." In a conversation about writing this book with an executive director of a non-profit organization, she urged me to use people-first language, which means use of language that respectfully puts the person before the disability. "If you don't know what it is, Google it," she said. So I did. I found by reviewing several search results that there is commonality in the philosophy of people-first language but not on specific language. I found across the different domains of disabilities that there is little agreement on terminology. One advocate for the blind, who is blind herself, told me, "I don't like the term 'a person with blindness.' It separates the condition as if it's something different from me. I am a blind person. Blindness is part of who I am." I had a conversation with a fervent advocate for the rights of people with disabilities, who uses a wheelchair, in which I expressed my dissatisfaction with the word "disability." She replied, "I don't see the problem you have with that. It's what we are called. If you disparage the word, you disparage the people referred to by the word." The internet search and those conversations have me worried that some wording in this book will offend someone. I ask you to see the substance and not the syntax.

That said, I despise the word "disability." To me, "disabled" evokes an image of a car broken down beside the road waiting for a tow truck. According to the *American Heritage Dictionary of the English Language: New College Edition* (Morris 1981), the prefix "dis-" means "1. Negation, lack, invalidation or deprivation." I prefer the word "impairment." One definition of impairment is "a lessening." Impairment does not mean the lack of something like disability does. We all have impairments, some more significant than others. I am hearing impaired. I wear hearing aids. I hear but I hear less. I cannot avoid the word "disabled" because it is such a widely used term, especially in law and in services for people with disabilities. Nevertheless, I limit its use. I prefer the words impairment, special needs, or challenges to avoid what I consider an unhealthy emphasis on a person's limitations implied by "disability." I also avoid the word "developmental." Some people become impaired as adults through brain injury or disease so "cognitive" or "intellectual" are words more specific and accurate. My daughter has a cognitive impairment. She does not have a developmentally disabled personality. Compassion starts with a care for accuracy.

Some public policies are set by the Federal government and some are set by states. Federal laws and regulations apply nationally by definition. Important Federal domains are the Internal Revenue Code, Social Security, Medicare, Federal housing, and Medicaid policy. The states pass laws and set policies in domains reserved to them by the United States Constitution, by law, or by legal tradition. These domains include probate law, trusts and estates law, guardianship, family law, divorce law, and Medicaid administration. It is impossible to describe the laws and regulations of individual states so I will sometimes use Colorado's for illustration because that's where I live. You need to be knowledgeable in the laws and regulations of your state or consult with professionals in the relevant domains.

Dollar numbers from government laws and regulations are for calendar year 2013 unless otherwise stated. I note those that are indexed for inflation.

There are four case studies in this book. These case studies present the life, resource, financial, and legal plans of four individuals in different circumstances to illustrate the principles, concepts, and approaches to special needs planning. The case studies give you a practical sense of what a plan looks like and how you might prepare one.

This book is organized into five parts. Part 1 covers life planning. Part 2 addresses resource planning. Part 3 describes financial planning. Part 4 explains legal planning. Part 5 deals with special challenges such as divorce with a special needs child in the family. The scope of special needs planning is too vast to cover in detail; individual and family circumstances vary widely and there is no "one size fits all." Nonetheless, what I have sought to do is to give you a picture of what comprehensive special needs planning looks like, how to go about it, and where to go for additional help or information.

INTRODUCTION
WHAT IS SPECIAL NEEDS PLANNING?

What is special needs planning? The term has different definitions for parents, educators, care planners, attorneys, financial planners, case managers, and so on. It seems to be defined by one's experience or responsibility. This is how I define it:

> *The purpose of special needs planning is to assure an adult with a physical, cognitive or mental impairment a place in the community appropriate to his or her needs, capabilities, financial resources, and wishes for the nature and quality of their own life. A comprehensive special needs plan integrates the life, resource, financial, and legal plans into a complete and practical plan of action.*

The elements of special needs planning and their interrelationships are depicted in Figure I.1.

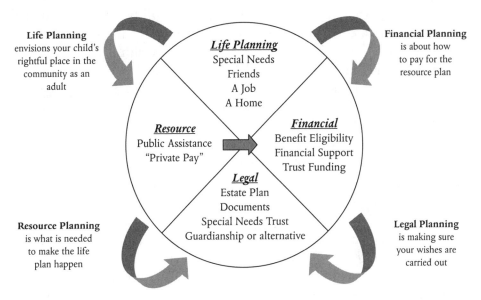

FIGURE I.1 THE ELEMENTS OF COMPREHENSIVE SPECIAL NEEDS PLANNING

Life planning envisions a desirable quality of life for an individual. What do any of us want from life? We want security, independence, dignity, and the ability to do what we want to. We want to know that we have significance in the eyes of others. We want to be loved. The hopes of a person with special needs are the same as the hopes of any human being. How these hopes are realized will be different from those in the "typical" population, but their hopes are human hopes. My daughter never aspired to be a musician like her brother but she very much wants a job and is proud of the one she has. Life planning addresses a person's physical, mental, and psychological needs, personal protection, circles of support, spiritual needs, friends, job, home, and independence to the extent of his or her capability.

Resource planning identifies the necessaries for a good life. I'm not talking about money. I'm talking about enablers for health and safety, social relationships, employment, and a desirable and safe place to live. The enablers for health and safety include healthcare, personal care and supervision, therapy, service management, and assistance with daily living. Those for an active social life include relationship skills, participation in activities, and opportunities to be with friends. The enablers for employment include secondary education, vocational training, job skills coaching, personal aids, and transportation. The supports for a desired residential situation include the skills for living with others or independently, assistive technologies, and human supports. Resources come in two "flavors"—government assistance to the extent a person is eligible and "private pay" to the extent a family can afford.

Financial planning is about how the resources will be accessed and paid for. It starts with a cost estimate for a desired life situation. The estimate will determine if the family has the necessary income, wealth, and insurance to implement the life and resource plans. The plan should recommend measures to improve outcomes if less than desired. Effective accumulation and management of family wealth will increase the available lifetime support. Consequently a financial plan usually includes an investment strategy. There are goals in life you save for and events in life you insure against. A plan should address the adequacy of health, life, disability, and long-term care insurance. Arrangements must be structured to provide support without causing the child to lose his or her eligibility for government assistance. This often entails funding and managing a special needs trust. Financial documents should be reviewed and updated to ensure conformity with estate plans. A financial advisor or qualified person should trace the distribution of property and money at the death of either or both parents to verify that the estate plan executes as intended and that the child does not receive an inheritance that causes him to lose eligibility for government assistance. The life and resource plans must be affordable and so there are often two financial plans, one for the child with special needs and one for the family to verify affordability.

Legal planning is about protecting the person with special needs and ensuring that the plans made by parents are implemented as intended. The essential legal documents include wills, trust agreements, appointment of agents with power of attorney, and healthcare directives. Appropriate protections for the individual with special needs must be established, such as an appointment of a guardian, conservator, or an agent with power of attorney, or execution of privacy waivers to empower advocates.

There are different approaches to special needs planning. Unfortunately, the most common seems to be the "*que sera, sera*" approach. The parents' circumstances, particularly income, at any point in time determine the quality of life of their child. The attention is on the immediate situation and solving the problems of the day. Little consideration is given to the future except wishful thinking. The "*que sera, sera*" approach isn't planning at all. Absent family wealth or good luck, there is a danger that the child will experience a diminished quality of life, perhaps a future of poverty, neglect, and loneliness. Such a life will be an unhappy and fearful life. The result may ultimately be a shortened life. The outcome of the "*que sera, sera*" approach, or the failure to plan, can be tragic.

A common misconception is that a special needs plan is the preparation of legal documents. However, the preparation or update of legal documents is the closing step in comprehensive special needs planning. Legal documents direct the actions that need to be taken in the event of your death or incapacity. When I was in active professional practice and told someone at a social gathering what I did professionally, they would quickly assure me: "Oh, I've done special needs planning. I set up a trust." I realize this is the defensive reaction of someone afraid they are going to get hustled for life insurance but it's frightening if they believe it. This misconception can lead to serious gaps in the future. If you think you did special needs planning because you set up a trust, you are as naïve as an aspiring cook who thinks that because she bought the pot, she has cooked the meal.

There is no template for special needs planning, because families and circumstances are unique. However, there are general approaches defined by the type of disability, the life stage of the individual, and the potential for independence. These factors are shown in Figure I.2.

Disabilities are categorized as physical, cognitive, or behavioral (mental illness). The life stage of an individual refers to minor, adult, or senior. The potential for independence is a continuum of needs and capabilities. On one end of the continuum are those who need continuous care and supervision. At the other end are those capable of independent living. In between are those capable of living in the community if they have adequate support. It is this spectrum, ranging from managed care to full independence, that is the most important determinant in special needs planning. Where an individual falls on the continuum will be determined by the severity of the disability. One can't generalize from the type of disability to the potential for independence.

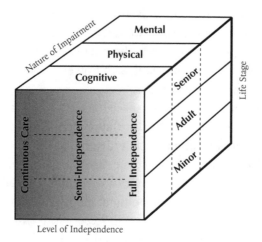

FIGURE 1.2 THE THREE DIMENSIONS OF SPECIAL NEEDS PLANNING

I have found from years of experience that many people—lay people and professionals—approach special needs planning from the wrong direction. I have learned the two most important questions to ask at the beginning of a planning engagement are:

1. Is your loved one capable of living on their own perhaps with help?

2. Is he or she capable of holding a job, either full or part time?

The answers to these two questions and the family's financial resources will determine the possibilities that will be addressed. A potential quality of life is not defined by an individual's disability; *it is defined by his or her capability!* There is a caveat. It is the parents of an adult child with a moderate cognitive impairment, trying to create and maintain a life of supported independence, who will likely face the toughest challenge, the greatest financial burden, and the highest risk of failure.

Planning solutions may be limited by parents' wealth. I find with affluent and upper-middle-class parents that the child's capability will be the limiting factor. With working-class or lower-middle-class families, affordability will likely be the constraint. There is obviously an area in between where the most good can be done by shifting the focus from constraints to possibilities. The art of special needs financial planning is creating the best possible outcome with the resources one has to work with. Affordability is a poignant limitation. It means that our society has left someone behind, someone who will not achieve her full potential through no fault of her own. I long for a society where the verse in Paul's Epistle to the Romans has true meaning: "And since we have gifts that differ according to the grace given to us, let each exercise them accordingly" (Romans 12:6). Our society bestows inadequate grace on individuals with special needs.

Another complication of special needs planning is the fact it crosses so many professional disciplines—medicine, social work, education, psychology, law, finance, and accounting. Parents know from experience how hard it is to assemble and coordinate a multi-disciplinary professional team. There are few generalists in this field.

Special needs planning is not something you do once; it is an on-going process. You will address different issues in different life stages. An intuitive planning approach sees life unfolding in five phases. The first phase is the minor child in the care of his parents. The second phase is the adult child living at home. The third phase begins when the adult moves into an external living environment, either a government-provided or a "private pay" residence. The fourth phase starts, often without warning, when a parent passes away or can no longer care for his child. The fifth phase comes with the death or incapacity of the second parent. The supports needed, particularly financial, will increase as one moves from one phase of life to the next, often significantly. A transition is not without risk and a plan should identify, for each transition, what must be done to assure the outcome is a stable, desirable situation. Typically we give much attention in special needs planning to the next life phase.

The challenge in planning for the fourth and fifth phases is uncertainty when death or disability will occur. Many families have inadequately prepared for these events. They lie, hopefully, far in the future and most people don't want to think about them until they have to. But we must plan for the possibility of an unexpected tragedy to mitigate the risk that a person with special needs will be left not only without parental support, but with no support at all.

Let's Meet Four People and Their Families and Friends

It is time to meet four special people: Angel Herrera, Mike Olmstead, Noelle Williams, and Henry Lowenstein. These individuals will be the center of the four case studies in this book. Their life, resource, financial, and legal plans will be described to illustrate the principles, concepts, and typical approaches in special needs planning. Each has "gifts that differ." Each has different needs. I hope their stories will give you an idea of what life is like for them and the challenges facing their parents, or in Henry's situation with no family, the people who try to help him.

Angel Herrera

The Herreras live in Colorado. Angel was born with Down syndrome. Now 20 years old, she will "age out" of public school after finishing the fall semester. She is in the low range of cognitive ability for someone with Down syndrome. Her

IQ was tested and she scored 65. Given her age and health, her life expectancy is estimated to be in the mid-60s. Like many people with Down syndrome, she is gregarious, trusting, and eager to please. There are no mean people in Angel's world. Her parents, John and Michelle, have never been able to teach her "stranger danger." She can use public transportation but will never be able to drive because of her slow processing of sensory inputs. She can manage time but has limited skills for managing money. She has a good memory to compensate for her lack of cognitive skills and once she learns a routine she will conscientiously follow it. She does not have abstract or generalized reasoning skills. She can read but can't do arithmetic except with a calculator. Her favorite social activity is going to movies. She has a volunteer job as a food assistant at a local senior center arranged by her special education team through the school's School to Work Alliance Program. To the surprise of her Transitions Program teacher and the delight of center staff, Angel connects well with the seniors.

The key people in her life are her immediate family—her parents, older sister, and older brother. Angel's father John is a corporate mid-level executive with salary and incentive compensation and excellent employee benefits. He is 51 and plans to retire at 65 when Medicare eligible. Angel's mother Michelle is the director of development for a small non-profit organization. She is 50 and wants to retire when family finances permit. John and Michelle don't know when that is because they don't know what will be needed to take care of Angel. They are very concerned about cutbacks in Social Security, Medicare, Medicaid, and state disability services and don't want to leave their daughter reliant on government assistance. Their gross income is over $300,000 and their net worth is about $1.6 million. John and Michelle have no family in Colorado. They are second-generation immigrants. John's parents live in Tucson, Arizona, in modest circumstances. They are retired, working-class people. John is the most economically successful of his siblings. Michelle's parents live in Bakersfield, California, and are also retired. Unusual in Hispanic families, she is an only child. They met when John was in his senior year of college, Michelle in her junior year.

Josephine, or Jo, Angel's big sister, is 26 years old and lives in Portland, Oregon. She is an accountant with a regional accounting firm. She is engaged to be married. Angel's brother Paul is 23. He lives in Dallas and is a property and casualty insurance agent for a national company. There has always been a special relationship between Paul and his kid sister. Angel worships the ground he walks on. Paul promises his parents that he will always be there for Angel. They believe him but know that he and Jo have lives to lead and may someday have children of their own. They want Jo and Paul to be involved in Angel's life but not have to sacrifice their opportunities for her.

Angel has a circle of friends with special needs in their late teens and early twenties who are children of families comprising an intentional family group. Her best friends are Sarah and Tracy, two young women her age with Down syndrome in the group.

Angel is a welcome member in her faith community. She has no concept of theology but has an acute sensitivity to a welcoming and loving environment. She loves to go to church. She was told that God really, really loves her and that's good enough for Angel. She wishes she could meet Him.

Mike Olmstead

Mike Olmstead is a teenager, slender, with appealing facial features, reddish hair, big ears, and a tentative smile. Mike's mother, Sharon, sensed he was different at an early age but since he seemed precocious she wasn't concerned until problems developed in elementary school, notably after her divorce. Mike hated school. He was moody, withdrawn, and resistant to direction. His elementary-school teachers didn't know how to work with him. Punishment proved futile. Recess was a nightmare for him. Small for his age and socially awkward, he suffered teasing and bullying by his schoolmates. When he was nine, a sensitive teacher had him evaluated for autism and Asperger's syndrome. He was diagnosed as having Asperger's. Concurrently, he tested above average in intelligence. Now 19, he is in his school's Special Education Bridges Program.

His mother Sharon, 44, is an associate librarian employed by the county library system. Her income is $16.77 per hour or $27,905 per year for a 32-hour work week. She has group health insurance, $50,000 in term life insurance, and a 401(k) retirement plan. She does not have disability or long-term care insurance or individual life insurance.

She and her husband Frank divorced when Mike was seven. Frank is a production control supervisor with a manufacturing company in another city. The divorce was not hostile but Frank and Sharon are estranged. Frank pays child support regularly ($750 per month) but otherwise takes little interest in his son. Frank remarried and there are three children in the second marriage. There are no other children from Sharon and Frank's marriage. Sharon is an only child. Her parents both live in modest circumstances in Florida. Confined by the demands of raising a child with special needs as a single mom, Sharon does not have a large circle of friends but, as a librarian, she is skilled in research and finding information relevant to Mike's needs and hers.

Things improved somewhat for Michael as he moved through middle school and into high school. With a diagnosis, he could access needed services through special education. Particularly helpful was a social skills class. Sharon paid out-of-pocket for therapy in behavior management. His middle-school teachers were better trained in student diversity and different teaching methods. However, Mike's academic progress has been quite uneven. He is strong in math, computers, and science lab, but weak in reading, writing, and language. He is resistant or indifferent to schoolwork in subjects in which he does poorly but immerses himself in subjects where he is proficient. Mike needs to have expectations and routines set for him. He needs his environment organized, stable, and predictable. He is poor at multi-tasking and organizing complex tasks. He hates unfinished tasks and refuses to leave them until finished to his satisfaction. He is highly sensitive to noise, especially sudden, loud noises. Harsh, chaotic, dissonant noise disrupts his ability to function. Most noticeable about Mike is his lack of normal social skills. He has little interest in social activities. He has no close friends, certainly no girlfriends, but is accepted by some classmates, usually non-conforming themselves, with similar interests such as computers. His interest, almost to the point of obsession, is computers. Surprisingly he has no interest in computer gaming but loves compiling hardware and software technical specifications, test reports, and product reviews. He wants to own the latest technology. He spends hours in chat rooms with other computer geeks. He owns several computers, primarily purchased with money from newspaper routes.

In his sophomore year of high school, Jack Carmody, a math teacher who also runs the school computer lab, took an interest in Mike. Jack would let Mike assist him setting up for classes. He introduced him to the school district's IT staff who found the boy to be quite interested in their work. Jack connected Mike with a computer users club, attending a membership meeting to introduce his young friend. Jack, probably without conscious intent, touched Mike's unexpressed and unfulfilled need for self-esteem and understanding. The special education staff found Mike a trial job at a small computer shop that repairs and upgrades computers and sells used and reconditioned equipment. The shop owner, Mr. Allen, has indicated that he might offer Mike a job when he finishes the school program.

Mike will age out of school next year and Sharon faces a difficult decision. She desperately hopes that Mike can be self-supporting and independent as an adult. She wants him go to college and get a degree in information technology or computer science so he can have a well-paying job. There are many obstacles. She can't afford a private school or a major state university and a scholarship is out of the question. A student loan is risky if he fails college or doesn't get a job after graduation. She worries about whether Mike can cope in a college environment with academically demanding courses. She knows Mike wants to work at the computer shop. Sometimes she thinks the best possibility for Mike is working at the repair shop but it offers no employee benefits or health insurance, which will be a problem when Mike reaches age 26 when her employer group insurance will no longer cover him as a dependent. She doesn't know what to do and feels she needs a plan for her future and Mike's.

Noelle Williams

Noelle Williams is age 16 and blind, not visually impaired but totally blind. She was born in a public health hospital in rural Mississippi with congenital cataracts that were not properly diagnosed or treated. As the condition developed through the first couple of years, surgery was attempted but the outcome was poor. By the age of five, Noelle had lost her vision. Her parents, Robert and Dorothy, frustrated by the lack of services where they lived and concerned about the quality of local schools, moved to the mid-west when Noelle was in second grade. Despite their efforts, Noelle's learning is delayed. This is not uncommon with childhood onset blindness. Without specific and effective intervention strategies and technologies, the child's development and academic achievement lags behind her innate capability because she can't see.

Robert, Noelle's father, is a process operator at the county water treatment plant. He has worked there for 15 years and has reached the highest rung on the union scale, making $23.55 per hour. With overtime, he makes about $56,000 per year. He works a four-squad shift schedule, 12 hours per shift, three days on and three days off, changing from night to day shift on the seventh day. Rotating shift, common in the chemical and water treatment industries, is hard on the body and difficult for the family. However, it pays well by blue-collar wage standards. The union contract includes paid health insurance and a pension plan. Dorothy, Noelle's mother, works as a part-time office assistant at the church her family attends, the Full Gospel Baptist Church. She took the part-time job because her employment prospects were limited and because she wanted to care for her daughter's needs. She makes about $8400 annually; the job offers no employee benefits. Noelle's younger brother, Robert Jr., is a typical 13-year-old, loves sports, is average in school, and spends most of his time "hanging out" with friends. Like many young children, he cannot grasp the significance of his sister's blindness. The two have a brother–sister love but their lives move down different paths.

Robert, like many men who have found opportunities in life denied him because of his lack of education, feels it is highly important for his children to go to college. He demands they apply themselves in school. Dorothy, also with a limited education, works hard to help her daughter progress academically. She faithfully attends school meetings with Noelle's teachers and is always pressing the special education staff to show her how she can work with her daughter at home.

Noelle is intelligent and capable. She is outgoing, exuberant, and has many sighted friends. Very religious, she accepts being blind without complaint. Denied access to a visual world, she fully enjoys an auditory one. Music is her passion. She plays piano proficiently and sings in the church choir. She has a rich mezzo-soprano voice. Lacking voice training, she will never sing opera professionally. She prefers gospel music anyway. Robert and Dorothy have great hopes that she will eventually have a good job and be independent. If she can't support herself as a musician, perhaps a career in some aspect of the music business is possible if she can get a college education.

They debated over the years whether Noelle should be mainstreamed in school or go to the state school for the blind 60 miles away. At this point, she lives with her family and attends the local high school. She struggles academically because the school district lacks the resources to effectively teach a child with total loss of sight. The school for the deaf and blind has skilled teachers and the best tools and technologies but it's a closed social environment. Robert and Dorothy don't want their daughter to leave home but they are willing to put aside their emotional preference if they could believe that the distant, specialty school is best for their daughter. Noelle does not want to leave home and her friends either. This is but one example of the cruel dilemma so often faced by special needs parents. They must choose a path for their child without being able to predict or control its outcome, and without knowing where their own hopes stop and their child's life begins.

Henry Lowenstein

Henry Lowenstein is in his early thirties. His father died when he was seven. Behavioral problems became evident when he was ten. His mother struggled to cope and his brother distanced himself, not wanting his friends to know his brother was "crazy." He had difficulties in school and no real friends. Things boiled over in Henry's junior year of high school when he assaulted a boy who was taunting him in the school cafeteria. The teachers saw an opportunity to rid themselves of this difficult student and called the police. Henry was sent to the state reformatory for boys. At the reformatory, a psychiatrist noted in the file that Henry likely had a personality disorder. He completed his high school education at the reformatory. After his release, he enrolled at the state university intending to pursue a degree in political science and public policy. (Henry's father worked in public policy research and was well known locally as a liberal activist.)

During Henry's freshman year he experienced a major manic-depressive episode. His residence hall neighbors, alarmed that he might be suicidal, contacted the campus medical center. Brought to the center by campus security, he was diagnosed as having Type 1 bipolar disorder. He was also assessed as "comorbid," a medical term meaning the co-occurrence of two or more psychiatric problems, in Henry's case co-occurring borderline personality disorder (BPD).

Bipolar disorder affects about one person in 50, much higher than the incidence of autism or any other cause of a developmental disability. In its Type 1 form, it is characterized by a manic cycle, which typically runs for three to six weeks, followed by a depression that can last for several months. In the manic state, the individual experiences a euphoric mood, decreased need for sleep, grandiosity about one's talents or prospects, a hyperactive mental state, distorted perception, impulsive and reckless behavior, and problems dealing with others. The depressed state brings feelings of hopelessness, worthlessness, apathy, guilt, and a diminished ability to make decisions. Suicidal tendencies are not uncommon. The cycle repeats with irregular and unpredictable frequency and, if the condition goes untreated, the cycles will accelerate in frequency and severity. The problem lies in the biochemistry of the brain, a poorly understood interaction between genetic, physical, and social factors. A mood disorder cycle can be triggered by high stress. Substance abuse can both aggravate the condition and be caused by it. One of the more frustrating obstacles in treating the condition is denial by the individual affected; they often discontinue their medication after the depression cycle has passed. Medication is the primary method of treatment and control but for many individuals psychotherapy is essential. Borderline personality disorder is characterized by intense and unstable relationships, manipulative and aggressive behavior toward others, impulsive and reckless behavior, and difficulty controlling one's anger. Those who assume the individual should be able to act with logic and discipline, and can be helped with good intentions, patience, and calm counsel, are naïve. The individual needs psychiatric help. Without medication, psychotherapy, and social support he is incapable of rationally or willfully controlling his behavior.

Henry tried to find jobs but employer and co-worker fear of mental illness is an almost insurmountable obstacle. With the help of a mental health social worker, Henry applied for Social Security Disability Insurance (SSDI) benefit as an adult child on his father's record, Supplemental Security Income (SSI), and Medicaid. He moved into low-income housing with rent assistance from the local housing authority.

Attempting to leave poverty, Henry enrolled in a teaching certification program with a well-known, for-profit, national education company. It took advantage of him, accepting his payment of tuition and fees for two years and graduating him a degree in education, knowing full well that he would not find employment in a school system with his criminal record and medical history. He was crushed by the rejection of his many job applications and sank into depression. During this period, Henry had difficulty controlling his condition. He was erratic taking his medications. He was lax in following his mood-management techniques. Throughout his lifetime, Henry had paid little attention to physical fitness. He was overweight, smoked, and consumed too much alcohol. These factors likely led to a serious mood disorder episode in which everything fell apart. Impulse control is weakened in the manic phase of bipolar disorder, especially with co-occurring BPD, and Henry was arrested for shoplifting as he was leaving a department store. Seriously psychotic, he was routed from the criminal justice system to the state's ICF/MI hospital (Intermediate Care Facility for Individuals with Mental Illness). After several months in a psychiatric ward, his mental condition was stabilized with medication and he was discharged.

Henry returned to his old apartment building. He was taking a mood stabilizer, an antidepressant, and an atypical antipsychotic drug. This time Henry stayed with his medication and his self-help routines. He was capable of normal daily function and managing his affairs. Finding himself in a stable situation, for a while at least, Henry began to look for ways to create a better life for himself. He volunteered with a non-profit mental health advocacy and support organization. He took a position on the crisis management hotline, frequently working the night shift because he tends to have a day-sleep cycle. Personally experienced and quite perceptive, he is an effective counselor, very aware of what the desperate callers on the crisis line face, including the suicidal ones.

Henry's part-time position pays $10.00 per hour. He works on an as-needed basis, averaging 20 hours per week. He receives no fringe benefits. Henry's mother died while he was in the state hospital. She left a small inheritance to Henry, about $50,000, in a trust with his brother Alan as trustee. His pay is below the Social Securities income limit of $1040 to qualify for disability income so he retained his SSDI. His brother drifted away long ago. However, a small circle of friends has formed around Henry in the apartment building— Craig, Lucy, Jose, and Adam. Craig took the lead in trying to help Henry as a friend, counselor, and advocate. He is a building maintenance engineer for the property management company. Most people find Henry to be a difficult person to befriend, so why did Craig take an interest? Craig saw something most people had never bothered to see. Henry is well informed, culturally literate, and has a sharp sense of humor. He can be fun to be with out for an evening on the town (as long as he and Craig avoid bars). Craig saw something else, a human being trying hard to better himself and help others despite the obstacles that will always diminish his hopes and opportunities for a normal life—the social stigma of mental illness, the criminalization of abnormal behavior, the lack of public services, and the high cost of therapy and medication which impoverishes individuals and families.

PART 1

LIFE PLANNING

YOUR CHILD'S PLACE
IN THE COMMUNITY

CHAPTER 1

START WITH A LIFE PLAN

A life plan envisions a good life for your child and what it will take to get there. It is the guide-star and foundation for the other three elements of special needs planning—the resource plan, the financial plan, and the legal or estate plan. These three plans implement a life plan and are not separate, stand-alone actions. They work together to make a good life possible. Life planning is not something you do once. Creating and sustaining a good life is a lifelong process.

After you finish reading this chapter, I want you to take away four key thoughts:

1. Planning for someone with a disability should always be person-centered. Help your child participate in the planning process and allow him to make decisions about his life to the extent he is able to do so.

2. A life plan has three aspects:

    (a) the vision of a good life

    (b) accomplishments or resources to make it possible

    (c) annual plans to make steady progress toward your goal.

3. There are useful models, such as PATH, that provide a disciplined framework for creating an annual Individual Life Plan (ILP).

4. Always have a plan to take care of your child if something happens to you and your spouse.

Life Planning is Like Taking a Family Automobile Trip

A family automobile trip is three things: a destination, a route to get there, and stops along the way. When you plan a trip, you choose a destination, plan the route you will take, and break the trip into manageable days. You have decisions to make while en route, such as where to stop for gas or meals or where to spend the night. You may decide to take a side trip to see something interesting or stop at tourist attractions. You may encounter problems such as an accident or road construction. If you plan well and manage things along the way, you should have a good trip and reach your destination.

The metaphor of a family trip offers some insights into life planning. One, a trip can be safer and more enjoyable traveling with others. Two, you should plan your route and start out and stay headed in the right direction. Otherwise you waste time and energy, perhaps getting lost and never arriving at all. Three, organize the plan into manageable projects, like the driving days on a trip. Four, you can't plan everything in advance. There are decisions to make as you go along and you may encounter unexpected opportunities and difficulties. Five, if you want to arrive on time you need to start on time or face some long days and hard driving to recover.

Applying these lessons to life planning, consider the following:

1. Life planning is challenging and it can be hard going it alone. There are many people who may help you on your trip. Other parents who have similar dreams and common experiences can become treasured friends and invaluable companions.

2. Your vision of the best possible life for your child is the destination. Have a plan to get there and start out in the right direction.

3. You don't have to do everything at once. Do annual plans, setting goals each year and actions to reach each goal. This is how you make steady progress.

4. You can't anticipate nor control all of the things that will happen in your life or your child's. You will need determination and persistence and flexibility to adjust to changing circumstances and unforeseen problems or possibilities.

5. The earlier you start to plan, the better. Get serious about planning when your child is entering her early teen years if you haven't started earlier. Otherwise you probably have some catching up to do.

A Life Plan is a Vision of the Future, a Plan to Get There, and Steps along the Way

Life planning operates on three levels: vision, plan, and action. The top level is the vision of a good life. It defines the qualities of that life and pictures what it will look like as-lived. The second level is a long-range plan. A long-range plan includes the projects and accomplishments that create the foundations for a good life, such as an education or training for employment. The third level is a set of annual goals and actions. The vision and the long-range plan should be updated periodically as things change in your life, the life of your child, and the lives of others in your family.

Defining what makes a good life is a process of asking and answering questions, questions that should be carefully formulated. Good questions challenge unexamined assumptions and vaguely defined goals. Consider Andy, who is profoundly challenged, and Ruth, his mom. "What would a good life for Andy look like?" is a good start. This is a visionary question. Visionary questions should lead to more specific and practical questions. A chain of questions prompts a set of answers that defines the best possible life and how to make it happen. I stress the word "possible." The dream must be within reach, perhaps not immediately but someday.

What is a good life? Ruth, Andy's mom, says, "I want Andy to be happy." What makes him happy? "Happy" for Andy, who is profoundly challenged, is defined differently than for someone who is mildly impaired. This is one reason why we do person-centered planning. "Happy" to Andy is comfort, physical care, emotional security, and kindness. Comfort is in the moment, being adequately fed, a pleasant room, a nice day, pleasurable sensory stimulation, and being free from pain and fear. Physical care deals with proper nutrition, alleviating pain, personal assistance, hygiene, and medical care. Emotional security is freedom from anxiety about having his needs met, worry of being left alone, or fear of being threatened or hurt by someone. And at some instinctive level, emotional security for Andy is knowing that his care givers care about him and are not merely doing things to him. Kindness may be a smile, a gentle touch, or a friendly tone of voice. Andy is primarily emotional in dealing with his world. If you are impatient or angry with him, it makes him sad and anxious. If you are warm and friendly, he is happy.

Person-centered planning for someone who is as profoundly challenged as Andy is more difficult than for individuals with a higher level of functioning. If a person is non-verbal and can't communicate by sign language or writing, our ways of knowing what he wants and needs will be indirect. A casual acquaintance or stranger may not be able to read the clues. One of the challenges in developing Andy's life plan will be "hearing" him in his way of communicating. One person who does hear him is his mother. But who hears Andy besides Ruth, or who will hear him when she is no longer there? Ruth must teach others to hear Andy, and leave them guidance on what she has heard. In Andy's situation, it is obvious that good care givers will be crucial to his happiness. How can Andy's mom find those care givers? Can she afford to hire and pay for them herself? Probably not. Only the wealthy can do so. If Andy is going to be in a government-provided residence where she can't control the staffing, will she be able to monitor the adequacy of his care? If Andy is unhappy, what are her options? How should she respond if the state agency restricts her access to her son because she is too demanding about his care? (This happens.) And after Ruth dies, who will be Andy's protector to make sure this very vulnerable human being is not abused or neglected?

The Four Elements of a Life Plan are Social Life, Vocation, Home, and Special Needs

As I said in the Preface, when someone asks me and my wife what we want for our daughter, we tell them: "After her special needs are met, we want her to have friends, a job, and a home." Segmenting a life plan into the domains of social life, vocation, home, and special needs is a useful way of organizing the plan, as shown in Table 1.1. Vocation is a broader category than job. A vocation is a calling. It can be a job or a personal business. It could be a self-advocate position on the board of directors of a non-profit organization serving the special needs community.

Table 1.1 The components of a life plan

Social life and community access	*Vocation*
Family, friends, and companions	Employment, personal business, or volunteer position
Life skills	
Spiritual life	Skills coaching, vocational training, or secondary education
Daily, weekly, and monthly routines	
Entertainment, recreation, and hobbies	On-the-job training and assistance
	Earnings and employee benefits
Participation in organizational activities	Transportation
	Social Security TTW*, TWP**, or PASS***
Travel	
Pets	*Ticket to Work
Transportation	**Trial Work Period
Circles of support	***Plan for Achieving Self-Support
Home	*Special needs*
Type of residence	Medical, vision, dental, medication
Housemates and in-residence care givers	Speech, occupational or physical therapy
Location	Psychological or behavioral coaching
Property management	Guardianship or other protections
Furnishings and amenities	Government programs for income, healthcare, and disability services
Independence or semi-independence	
Cost of rent or mortgage including taxes, maintenance, and insurance	Care management, case management
	Dietary needs
Human supports	Hygiene
Assistive technologies	Personal fitness
Home modifications	Day programs
Transportation	Respite care
	Management of medical, financial, and legal affairs

Developing a Life Plan

Those experienced in project planning understand the advantage of using a back-planning approach, starting with an outcome and tracing the necessary steps backward to where you are today. Planning is also done top-down, breaking large projects into manageable ones. In a top-down process, you define each element of a good life, addressing social life, employment, residential situation, and special needs. There are subsidiary goals in each domain and lower-level goals under them. For each goal at each level, you define the success criteria to complete each goal. Your annual plans are the steps to reaching each incremental goal that supports the ultimate goal of a good life.

You don't do life planning, then resource planning, then financial planning, and then legal planning. There will be a lot of concurrency and overlap. You will have multiple balls in the air at the same time. Some steps will be repeated. Some will need reinforcement, update, or refinement. Occasionally, something won't work and you will need to back up, reassess, and revise your plan. You may discover an opportunity or decide to add, drop, or replace a goal. But always, always keep your vision in mind and have a sense of direction and what you need to do to reach your objective.

Not all elements of a plan will be addressed with equal emphasis at all points in time. Different elements will be emphasized to different degrees in different life stages. In the child's pre-teen years the focus will be on social life and special needs. Planning for employment should begin in the early teen years. Planning for an external residential placement probably should start when the person is in his or her early twenties, perhaps after successfully reaching the goal of employment. The various aspects of the plan should converge to a comprehensive solution as the child moves into adulthood and toward a permanent, stable life situation.

Developing an Annual Individual Life Plan (ILP)

Parents of special education students are familiar with an Individualized Education Plan (IEP) and an Individualized Transition Plan (ITP). One of the shocks faced by parents when their child ages out of school is the realization that they are now on their own planning for their child's future. After our daughter aged out, I found I missed the annual IEPs and ITPs with the school's professional staff to review our daughter's needs and develop an education plan for the coming year. It occurred to me that my daughter, as an adult, needed an annual Individual Life Plan (ILP). It now falls on my wife and me to assemble the team and manage the process. An ILP fits the concept of life planning quite well. Each annual plan is a stepping stone toward a hoped-for future. A long-term plan is a strategic look three to five years in the future or to the next major life transition. Tactically, you want an action plan for each year. An ILP is a tactical plan.

Team planning is a facilitated process where family, friends, and professionals come together to set annual goals and actions. There are several models used to create annual plans. Social scientists love constructing models, but no model guarantees success. At its best, a model provides a proven process and a framework for organizing one's efforts. Once you understand the concepts, common sense and experience will take over. After your first planning session, you will see things that worked, things that didn't, and things you wished you had done differently. We learn by experience. It's not as important which model you use as much as it is to get started, enlist the right participants, set goals, develop a plan of action, follow through, *and keep doing it!*

A commonly used life planning model is "Planning Alternative Tomorrows with Hope" (PATH). An advantage of the PATH model is the body of books, manuals, forms, and templates to guide how it's done. (See the resource box at the end of this chapter.) There are other models that may be used in your community or supported by a government agency or non-profit organization. Although different approaches are used by different models, they all have the same desired outcome—an action plan. Figures 1.1 and 1.2 give you a glimpse of the PATH approach. Figure 1.1 is a schematic of the template and the steps in its preparation. Figure 1.2 briefly describes the information that goes on the completed form.

An annual PATH session is done in the following steps:

1. Form a team.

2. Determine the desired outcome of the session.

3. Obtain a facilitator (highly recommended).

4. Assure participation of the person whose future is being planned.

5. Hold the session.

6. Follow-up.

PATH
(Planning Alternative Tomorrows with Hope)

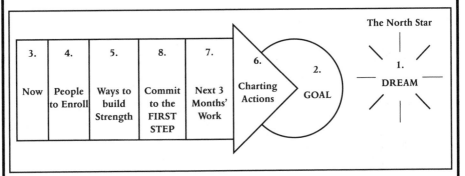

YOUR PATH
A focused Planning Process

Steps

Situate yourself in a very positive future, picture it clearly, then think Backwards.

1. Touching the Dream (the North Star).

2. Sensing the Goal: Focus for the next year.

3. Grounding in the Now: Where am I/are we?

4. Identifying People to Enroll on the Journey.

5. Recognizing Ways to Build Strength.

6. Charting Actions for the Next few Months.

7. Planning the Next 3 Months' Work.

8. Committing to the First Step (the Next Step).

(Including a Coach to Support your First Step.)

© Inclusion Press   J. Pearpoint, J. O'Brien, M. Forest 1991

FIGURE 1.1 THE PATH TEMPLATE AND STEPS TO COMPLETE IT

PATH

Planning Alternative Tomorrows with Hope by Jack Pearpoint, John O'Brien & Marsha Forest
© Inclusion Press

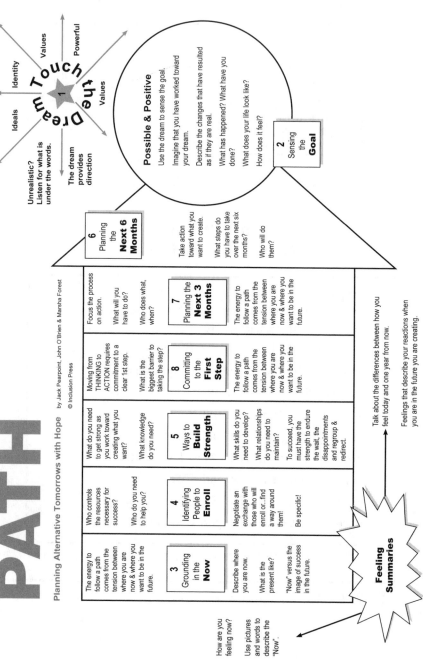

Touch the Dream — 1

Ideals · Identity · Values · Powerful · Values

Unrealistic?
Listen for what is
under the words.

The dream
provides
direction

Possible & Positive

Use the dream to sense the goal.

Imagine that you have worked toward
your dream.

Describe the changes that have resulted
as if they are real.

What has happened? What have you
done?

What does your life look like?

How does it feel?

2 — Sensing the Goal

---

6 — Planning the Next 6 Months

Take action
toward what you
want to create.

What steps do
you have to take
over the next six
months?

Who will do
them?

7 — Planning the Next 3 Months

Focus the process
on action.

What will you
have to do?

Who does what,
when?

The energy to
follow a path
comes from the
tension between
where you are
now & where you
want to be in the
future.

8 — Committing to the First Step

Moving from
THINKING to
ACTION requires
commitment to a
clear 1st step.

What is the
biggest barrier to
taking the step?

The energy to
follow a path
comes from the
tension between
where you are
now & where you
want to be in the
future.

5 — Ways to Build Strength

What do you need
to get strong as
you work toward
creating what you
want?

What knowledge
do you need?

What skills do you
need to develop?

What relationships
do you need to
maintain?

To succeed, you
must have the
strength to endure
the wait, the
disappointments
and regroup &
redirect.

4 — Identifying People to Enroll

Who controls
the resources
necessary for
success?

Who do you need
to help you?

Negotiate an
exchange with
those who will
enroll or...find
a way around
them!

Be specific!

3 — Grounding in the Now

The energy to
follow a path
comes from the
tension between
where you are
now & where you
want to be in the
future.

Describe where
you are now.

What is the
present like?

"Now" versus the
image of success
in the future.

Feeling Summaries

How are you
feeling now?

Use pictures
and words to
describe the
"Now".

Talk about the differences between how you
feel today and one year from now.

Feelings that describe your reactions when
you are in the future you are creating.

FIGURE 1.2 GUIDANCE FOR COMPLETING THE PATH TEMPLATE

Step 1: Form a Team

Consider assembling a team of individuals who can offer a diversity of perspectives and expertise. Your team may include family, friends of family, your child's peers with special needs, other parents, advisors, and people who may be involved in future support. You may want to include professionals who can advise on what needs to be done such as educators, psychologists, life skills coaches, job coaches, service providers, or care managers.

How many people should you involve? Some recommend a large group of 12 or more. Some recommend a smaller group of five or less. A large group will include more perspectives and generate more ideas. There are more people to take actions on the decisions made. However, a large group is cumbersome and may have difficulty reaching consensus. I suggest a group of five to eight, not counting you, your child, the facilitator, and the recorder.

Ideally, those who participate, including professionals, will know your child and genuinely care for his or her happiness. Nonetheless, you may include others who bring useful ideas or expertise.

Hopefully, at least some of the participants will continue their involvement by helping to implement current year goals and return for next year's session.

Step 2: Determine the Desired Outcome of the Session

You will be more likely to have a good session if you set clear objectives. I like to use questions. There are two kinds of questions. One type defines goals: "Would sending Aaron to a community college be the best thing we could do to help him with employment?" The other type defines actions to reach goals. These are "how" questions: "How can we make sure Aaron can manage himself independently when he attends Mountain Community College next fall?" If your objectives are not well defined, you start with questions to develop a set of goals. In a two-hour planning session you will likely have time for two to four questions. Consider them carefully. It sometimes happens that a planning session reaches the end of its scheduled time without answering all of the questions. Depending on the immediate importance of a question, a second session could be scheduled or the unanswered question deferred to the next annual meeting.

Step 3: Obtain a Facilitator

A facilitator is optional but recommended. A good facilitator can be so helpful with developing a solid, actionable plan that I believe you should consider paying a professional if necessary. A local agency or non-profit organization may be able to provide or recommend trained facilitators. A good facilitator will keep the group on task but will not be domineering or intrusive. The facilitator for our first planning session was so good that we sometimes forgot she was there until she had to remind us to get back on track.

I recommend you meet with the facilitator before the session. This provides an opportunity to review the process, the desired outcomes, the team members, what each brings to the party, and how to assure the participation of your child.

A good recorder can be a valuable resource as well. You should have a written record of outcomes. Enthusiastic brainstorming can result in ideas being thrown out helter-skelter. A good recorder will be able to keep up. Capturing a poorly expressed idea accurately and succinctly is a gift and may be valuable when someone in the group, like your child, has difficulty expressing themselves. A recorder with graphics skill is a wonderful find. The recorder for our first session had such skill. She used colored markers on an eight-foot strip of white butcher paper, two sheets doubled so the ink didn't bleed through onto the wall. The product was so striking it is hung in the hallway of our house. As we pass by, my wife, daughter, and I are reminded of the plan we made.

Step 4: Assure Participation of the Person Whose Future is Being Planned

It is important that a person with a cognitive impairment or serious speech impediment be helped to speak for themselves. If the person in the center of the planning circle is not verbal or may be overwhelmed in a large group, a pre-meeting with someone with skill and sensitivity may help him to think at his own pace and communicate in a way that works for him. This person may help him develop a presentation for the team. A pre-meeting can also help him to prepare to participate with more confidence and assertiveness. If the child is non-verbal, someone should be designated to be his spokesperson. If you ask one of your child's peers to be in the group, help them to contribute too. My daughter wanted her best friend, a young woman with Down syndrome, to be in her circle. Her friend made a meaningful contribution.

Step 5: Hold the Session

Planning sessions typically are scheduled for two or two-and-a-half hours, although there are overachievers among us who are tempted into three- or four-hour meetings. I suggest two hours for the formal session with time before and after for socializing, team-building and celebration. A two-hour time limit focuses the discussion. There is an old saying about meetings: "The time it takes to do something expands to the time allotted." I think the efficiency of the group drops after a couple of hours; people get tired. Set a cutoff time and stick to it. If you are facing a particularly complex set of issues, such as your child moving to an apartment on his own, you may need more than one PATH session. Multiple sessions can break a complex problem into manageable pieces to develop action plans.

The day of the week and time of day are important considerations. You want a time convenient for people, especially people who are busy or have obligations to others. I prefer a Sunday afternoon. Of the days in the week, Sunday is the one we tend to set aside for social and spiritual activities. Person-centered planning should be a social activity. For some of us, helping a person with special needs toward a good life touches on the spiritual.

Consider starting with a half hour of social time if team members do not know each other well. You may want to allow some time for team-building. Team-building is important. If the session feels like a staff meeting at the office, people aren't likely to feel enthusiasm and will be less likely to continue. It sounds corny, but give the team a name like "Bobby's Buddies." I suggest inviting team members to lunch or dinner following the session. Breaking bread together, for some of us, has significance in terms of committing to a group or community.

Schedule the meeting well in advance, six weeks or so. Busy people have busy calendars and, to put it bluntly, you want to beat other people to a date. If you are scheduling several weeks in advance, send a reminder a week or two before.

Have your child prepare the invitations if she can. One of the most touching requests I've seen on an invitation was: "Please come and help me make my dreams come true." I went.

Remember to send "thank you" notes, and perhaps a small gift. These should come from your child if she is able to create the note or choose the gift. Otherwise, be honest that the note or gift comes from you.

Step 6: Follow-up

Follow-up sessions are recommended to monitor progress. Typical intervals are three or six months after the session. If a major event or transition will take place during the year, you may need more frequent meetings.

Parents I have talked to, dissatisfied with the outcome of their meeting, mentioned one or more of the following reasons the process hadn't gone as well as hoped:

- They had not given adequate thought to what they wanted to accomplish.

- There was inadequate follow-up with actions.

- The plan was impractical. (You can get carried away with enthusiasm in a group.)

- The goal was too challenging to be met in the immediate year.

- The goal was too vague to translate into practical action.

The most egregious error is not doing annual planning and consequently making little or no progress toward a desired quality of life. A planning session that did not work as hoped or an action plan that proved ineffective can be discouraging and tempt you to give up or procrastinate in planning for the next meeting.

When to Plan

Hopefully, life planning started shortly after your child was born, at least at a basic level. Most parents don't start this soon. Whenever you start, the first life plan you develop will be the one you build on—expanding, revising, refining, accomplishing, and hopefully never having to start over. You must realize that the longer you wait to begin, the more catching up you have to do. You may find that you have forfeited some of the options you passed along the way. Those may have been the best options you will ever have.

Many parents fail to address life planning for their school-aged child. They may be overwhelmed by the problems of the moment. They may not understand the importance. But the pernicious error is to say, "I don't know what my child will be like when he grows up." This excuse is not acceptable. It's true that the development of a child with special needs is harder to predict than that of a typical child. Some parents use this as an excuse to procrastinate, rationalizing they will plan for the future when the future is better known. But the future will never be truly known so this becomes an exercise in waiting for the mirage on the horizon to come to you. By waiting for the future, one takes no control of that future. We want a future not merely known but made to happen. For example, autism is a condition with a very wide range of outcomes. Nonetheless, by consulting with the local Autism Society chapter, parents can establish reasonable assumptions for planning.

Parents of a very young child should take care of the following:

1. Prepare legal wills for both parents and designate a successor guardian for minor children or a child unable to care for himself.

2. Develop a family financial plan including an assessment of insurance needs and a plan to save for a better future for all family members.

3. Protect eligibility for government benefits and services; establish a special needs trust so that if something happens to a parent the child doesn't receive a bequest causing her to lose eligibility for government disability services.

4. Have a plan for the child's continued support and protection in the event of the death, serious injury to, or illness of either or both parents.

Planning for adulthood starts when your child is in middle school. The IEPs in high school and the ITPs in the Bridges or Transitions Program should be guided by goals for employment and possible independence.

An important transition comes when the child ages out of school. To a parent, it can feel like stepping out of a home into the cold. The advice and involvement of special education teachers, psychologists, occupational and speech therapists, life skills coaches, and other professionals come to an end. Suddenly, it's all on your shoulders. You should be prepared to take over.

Another critical transition comes when the child transitions from her parents' home to an independent residential environment, either state-provided or private pay. There is risk to your child in this transition. If you do not adequately plan and manage the transition, there is more likely to be a problem or failure.

Unless you have family or friends you can count on to take over care for your child, the most important and difficult life transition will be your death or incapacity unless you plan to leave your child to the mercy of the state, which you should never do unless you have no choice. The difficulty is the uncertainty as to when this will happen and the circumstances to plan for. You should have an on-going support network. Plan to pay professionals for roles you cannot find someone to fill if you can afford to do so. Document your final arrangements in a letter of intent and finalize the legal documents that will execute your estate plan.

When to Update

There are milestones and events when you should review your plan to see if the vision, the long-range plan, and annual goals need to be revised. Table 1.2 lists some of the changes in circumstances, some in the life of the child and some in the life of the parents or family members, which may require changes in your plan.

Table 1.2 Changes in circumstances that may require updates to a life plan

Changes in the life or circumstances of your child
Transiting out of school at age 21 or 22
Finding or losing a job
Transition from the parents' home into an external residential situation
Change in medical condition or cognitive faculties, perhaps with aging
Change in the inner circles of support
Receiving or losing government benefits
Change in financial support from others
An unplanned direct inheritance or gift
Special needs trust projected to run out of money during the child's lifetime
Tragedy
Victim of sexual abuse

Changes in the lives of the parents or family member
Birth or adoption of another child
Sibling enters or leaves college
Sibling becomes independent or an independent sibling requires support
Parents divorce
A parent remarries
Relocation to another city, especially another state
A risk event such as a family member being sued
Changes in family financial circumstances or unexpected expenses
A parent returns to the workforce
Parent loses a job
Job change significantly affects income
Changes in employment security
Success or failure of a family business
Bankruptcy
Retirement
Significant medical expenses
Disability or a long-term care need
Paying for a wedding
Need to care for someone else such as a parent's parent
An inheritance
A significant investment loss
Buying or selling a major asset
Adverse judgment from litigation
Tragedy
Death of one or both parents

Contingency Planning for the Death or Disability of a Parent

Parents should consider what should happen if tragedy were to strike—for example, premature death or serious injury to or illness of one or both. How would a surviving spouse cope with the death of a partner? Who would take care of the child if both parents died at the same time? What if both spouses were so badly injured, perhaps in an automobile accident, that neither could work or care for their child? What would happen if a spouse required extended hospitalization? Are there other family members the parents can turn to for help? How would the family's immediate circumstances be affected? How would their future be affected? Does the family have sufficient wealth to cushion the blow? Does the family have adequate insurance to replace lost income or meet increased expenses? These are questions that must be asked by a family that has a child with special needs, especially if there is no family or friends to take over from a parent.

Tragedy could strike an income provider or a primary care giver. Both possibilities should be considered but it is the death or disability of the primary care giver that is often overlooked. By primary care giver I mean a stay-at-home spouse or one employed part-time whose role is to care for a child while the other spouse works. When a primary care giver dies, the working spouse may need to hire childcare to continue working. Is there sufficient life insurance on the life of the primary care giver to cover this expense? The disability of a non-working care giver is hard to cover with insurance because disability insurance is designed to replace lost income, not create income.

With no insurance and little or inadequate income, a surviving spouse may feel the best option is to relocate to another state to be near family members who can help. However, an often overlooked problem with interstate relocation is continued access to disability services. In all states you must establish residency to receive state benefits. If that state has a wait list for services, one's place on the list is determined by the date of the application, which will necessarily be no earlier than when residency is established. Consequently, there may be a service gap following relocation. How will the surviving parent cope with a lack of services for their child for what, in states like Colorado, could be a very, very long time?

It is impossible to develop a complete and detailed contingency plan: the actions that will need to be taken in an emergency will depend on the circumstances at the time. Nonetheless I recommend that the parents spend an evening or two away from all distractions to talk about how each spouse would cope if something were to happen to the other. Discuss the adequacy of the safety net if something happened to you both. There may be some obvious actions that should be taken, like buying more life insurance. In some instances the best you may be able to do is find options to consider later, like the possibility of a spouse who is employed part-time stepping up to full-time employment or an unemployed spouse taking a job. Your conversation may uncover gaps that will require further discussion or action—for example, that no one has agreed to be the successor guardian of your children if both of you were to die together.

The intended outcome of contingency planning is to minimize as much as possible an adverse impact on the family and to leave them in the best possible situation. The effects of a tragedy can be mitigated to the extent a family has wealth, insurance, or family or friends to help. Otherwise, the survivors have to decide how to cope with a diminished quality of life and diminished hopes for the future. A special needs child is especially vulnerable. In the Preface I said that the worst nightmare of a parent is that their child will someday be left alone. This nightmare can become tragic reality if you have not planned adequately and something goes terribly wrong.

Wendy's PATH

Pat and Cathy have a 20-year-old daughter Wendy who has autism. In mid-2010, Wendy moved from her high school into her school's Bridges Program. The Bridges Program is a program to prepare special education students of 18 to 20 years old to prepare to enter the post-school adult world. It typically focuses on community participation and enhancing the potential for employment. (The Individuals with Disabilities Education Act requires that a person with a disability be provided an appropriate education through age 20. Some states allow continued education through age 21.)

In early 2011, Pat and Cathy became anxious about their daughter's future when she ages out of school. They attended a program, "Mobilizing Families," offered by the local Arc chapter. One of the program speakers was a parent mentor from the State Department of Education who spoke about PATH planning. The State DOE has a program offering PATH training to parents of children with disabilities in the 17 to 21 age range. The Department provides a facilitator to guide eligible families through the PATH process. The facilitator is assigned for an initial planning session and a second session one year later. The agency's thinking is that after parents have been through two sessions with assistance they should be able to continue on their own. Pat and Cathy applied and reached the top of the wait list some months later. Laura and Sarah were assigned to them, Laura as the facilitator and Sarah as the recorder.

Pat and Cathy met with Laura in their home in August 2011, two months before the day planned for the session. In the meeting with Laura, Pat and Cathy described their hopes for Wendy's future. Laura explained the PATH concept, gave Pat and Cathy materials describing the process in more detail, and made suggestions about how to arrange for the session. Laura spent some time with Wendy to get acquainted.

Pat and Cathy's first task was to assemble Wendy's PATH team. They obtained commitments from eight people, all of whom knew Wendy. These were:

- Wendy's older sister who lives out of state, her successor guardian

- two friends of Pat and Cathy from their church

- Wendy's best friend, Beth, who also has autism

- a mother who had completed a PATH plan for her son

- a psychologist who had participated in Wendy's ITP meetings

- an advocate from the local Arc chapter

- a case manager from the county adult disability services agency.

Pat and Cathy were pleased and grateful when Wendy's Bridges Program coordinator, Julie, asked if she could join the team when she heard about the session.

They scheduled the session for a Sunday afternoon in late October. Wendy prepared the invitations on her computer with directions to her home.

Wendy is high functioning and Pat and Cathy have hopes that she will be able to find employment and eventually live semi-independently. The near-term challenge is aging out of school and loss of the social structure and services. They also realize that, although they have an idea of what Wendy's future may hold, they haven't done practical planning to make anything happen.

Two weeks before the session, Pat and Cathy met with Laura and discussed the arrangements and objectives of the planning session. They had decided to raise three issues with the team:

1. We want Wendy to have friends, maybe even a boyfriend. We're worried about what will happen when she's out of school and no longer has all her schoolmates around her. She doesn't make friends easily.

2. Wendy wants a job but gets stressed when she's around a lot of people. She's good with computers. How can we find a job opportunity that fits what she can do, maybe something that uses her computer skills?

3. We don't have a plan for how Wendy would be taken care of if something unexpected were to happen to us. We get no state services because Wendy's needs aren't severe enough. Her IQ is 85 so the state doesn't consider her disabled. They say she's too high functioning. We need a safety net.

Pat and Cathy were concerned that Wendy would not participate in the planning meeting. They invited Wendy's friend Beth to make Wendy feel more comfortable. Wendy feels anxious in a large group of people, much preferring one-on-one social interaction. Although Wendy knows everyone in the group, she does not like being the center of attention even among people she knows. Wendy's Bridges coordinator Julie shared the concern and suggested that she and Wendy get together before the team met so she can help Wendy express her wishes and practice presenting to the group.

The group met in Pat and Cathy's home on a Sunday afternoon in October. They started about 2:30 in the afternoon. Pat and Cathy wanted the group to become a team so the first 40 minutes were spent with everyone getting to know each other. Each was asked to describe the beautiful qualities they saw in Wendy. The PATH session started around 3:15. The session was kept to two hours. Pat and Cathy had invited everyone to stay for dinner after the session ended, out of gratitude for their support and in hopes of their continued commitment.

At the beginning of the session, Laura explained the process and presented Pat and Cathy's issues. The group quickly decided that two hours was not enough time for the third one, but they could do good work on the first two.

As they were about to start with the first issue, Julie announced that Wendy wanted to make a presentation. Pat and Cathy held their breath, worried Wendy would suddenly flee to the safety of her room. To their surprise, Wendy stepped to the front of the semi-circle. She had two posters which Julie taped to the wall. One was labeled "Fun" and the other was labeled "Career." Wendy gave her presentation. She didn't make eye contact with anyone, shyly facing her charts, but she clearly explained what she hoped for. The posters were done with colored markers. They were beautiful. Pat and Cathy knew Wendy liked to draw and paint but the posters had obviously been done with unexpected care.

The team had a good session. Laura was an effective facilitator. Sarah had a talent for succinctly capturing ideas and keeping up with the discussion. The group found time to address a third matter, one triggered by something on Wendy's poster labeled "Career." Wendy wanted to be an artist. One of the actions taken for the coming year was for Cathy to enroll Wendy in an art program at the local community college. Pat planned to look for galleries or organizations that might show or sell her art.

A week after the PATH team meeting, Pat and Cathy and Laura met and talked about how the session went, what went well and what didn't. Pat and Cathy were embarrassed by one problem. Beth, Wendy's friend, had not participated. They had invited Beth into the group to make Wendy feel comfortable. Julie had volunteered to support Wendy's participation but no one had done anything to help Beth contribute too. Pat and Cathy realized they had let Beth down and felt badly about the oversight.

A year later, in September 2012, Pat and Cathy and Wendy sat around the kitchen table one evening to review the previous year's PATH. They pulled out the charts and Wendy's two posters. They had exceeded the goal to ensure that Wendy had friends and an active social life. Wendy had found a boyfriend, a funny, extroverted young man with Down syndrome whom Wendy met at an Arc picnic. (The relationship was nudged a little bit by the encouragement of both sets of parents.) They had made no progress toward the goal of finding a job that uses her computer skills. Pat and Cathy are now convinced that most employers won't hire someone with a disability. Wendy's artwork is thriving, though it is true that her family and friends are the only ones who buy her art. Pat can't understand why people pay six or seven figures for something stupid by Andy Warhol but no one buys Wendy's far more beautiful work, except the people who love her. Wendy has had three showings of her art, one at the community college, one at a local recreation center, and one at their church.

Pat and Cathy are starting to plan for the next PATH session, the second year for which the state agency will provide a facilitator. Laura and Sarah, the facilitator and recorder from 2011, will be back. Pat and Cathy are disappointed that three of the people in last year's group decided not to continue.

Pat turned 60 this year, and is not happy about reaching this milestone. Also, the third issue from last year, the one the group had agreed was too complicated to tackle, is beginning to haunt him: "We don't have a plan for how Wendy would be taken care of if something unexpected were to happen to us. We receive no state services because Wendy's needs are not considered to be severe enough. We need a safety net." This issue will be one of only two for this year's PATH session. The second is: how can we develop Wendy's artistic talent into a business?

Three people have been added to the group, replacing the three that have left. One is Wendy's art teacher. One is Beth's mother. One is the attorney who will help them update their estate plan.

Cathy doesn't want to discuss her death or Pat's with Wendy present. Pat is not comfortable either and thinks Wendy should be excluded from that part of the session. Julie, the special education teacher, has no hesitation. "I think she will surprise you. Wendy understands what's going on a lot more than you realize."

Where to Go for More Information

The two common life planning models are PATH (Planning Alternative Tomorrows with Hope), and PLAN-CA (Planned Lifetime Advocacy Network-Canada). PLAN affiliates in the US are known by state name—for example, PLAN-WA for PLAN-Washington.

PATH is the most common and there is an extensive line of books and materials one can order from the bookstore linked to its website, www.inclusion.com. The bookstore has materials on person-centered planning, circles of support, and another planning model called MAPS. A good introduction is *The PATH and MAPS Handbook* (O'Brien et al. 2010).

Plan Canada has resources on the web, at www.plan.ca, including one of the classic books on life planning: *A Good Life* (Etmanski 2000). *A Good Life* tells the stories of families and their life plans. You can order the book on the website or from PLAN-Canada at #260 – 3665 Kingsway, Vancouver BC, VSR SW2, phone 604.439.9566. PLAN materials are less extensive than PATH's but if there is a PLAN affiliate in your state, there may be local support including trained facilitators. PLAN should not be confused with the National PLAN Alliance (NPA). The latter is the Planned Lifetime Assistance Network. The NPA is an umbrella organization of charitable pooled-asset trusts with 26 affiliates in 21 states in partnership with the Arc, the National Alliance on Mental Illness, the Mental Health Association, and United Cerebral Palsy.

Ask a non-profit serving the special needs community in your area, such as a local Arc chapter, if they can refer you to a resource. Some local Arc chapters offer training and facilitators to plan and conduct a life planning session.

CHAPTER 2

CREATE THE CIRCLES OF SUPPORT

Almost all human beings need to be surrounded by other caring human beings. We look to others for love, friendship, respect, approval, encouragement, support, guidance, protection, and to take care of needs we cannot take care of ourselves. Obviously, people with disabilities have more critical and extensive needs for support than typical people. I described how to envision a good life and how to create a plan to get there in Chapter 1. How do you sustain a good life through all of the years to come? A network of caring people, forming circles of support around your child, is the most powerful means of supporting a quality of life. It is also a safety net to take care of your child if you are not able.

There are four key thoughts in this chapter:

1. Identify the key roles for your child's care and support.

2. Invite good people to take a role and join the circles.

3. Have successors for all key roles or a plan for finding someone when needed.

4. Intentional family groups can be a significant resource.

The Circles of Support

Hopefully your child will have a long and happy life. A possible consequence is that she may outlive you by a number of years, perhaps many years. It was not unusual in my professional practice to have a client family with parents in their late forties and a teenage child with autism. Autism is not necessarily life shortening. A teenager with autism can live for another six decades and could outlive her parents by one or two. This leads to a principle I will return to several times in this book:

When you develop a life plan, you must always have a time horizon that bounds your child's expected lifetime. Parents must consider the possibility that their child could outlive them for a number of years.

Circles of support manage aspects of a child's life that she is not able to manage herself. Many families with a special needs child get acculturated, almost without knowing it, to short time horizons and focusing on the challenges of the day. We must take a long view to assure a child's safety, care, and an appropriate level of independence. The circles of support will need to be robust and flexible, capable of adapting to changing circumstances, finding new members, and reorganizing as circumstances change. How can we do this? It is neither easy nor is there assurance of success, but there are ways to go about it.

Think for a minute of the organizations you belong to or are employed by, business or non-profit. They are organized to be on-going entities with the flexibility to operate and evolve with changing circumstances. They have characteristics that make this possible: leadership to manage the entity, staff to deliver products, programs, and services, and the capability to hire new workers or contractors as needed. Strong organizations are good at strategic planning and operations planning. Large organizations, particularly public corporations, are conscientious about having succession plans for key executives. They are diligent in recruiting highly qualified people for critical jobs. These characteristics of enduring organizations are principles to guide you in creating your child's circles of support.

The support team has four circles:

1. A leadership team to plan, manage and coordinate the team's resources and activities.

2. People who provide essential and on-going care and support.

3. People who fill occasional or non-essential roles.

4. Successors who take over for someone who leaves the first or second circle.

The parallels in a non-profit organization are its executive director and managers (the inner circle), the staff who run the programs (the second circle), and volunteers or part-time employees (the third circle). The circles are illustrated in Figure 2.1.

People in the leadership circle play the crucial role. This is the small group, perhaps four to eight people, who plan and coordinate the efforts of the team. They function like a board of directors or an executive committee. They are responsible for making decisions, managing projects, creating plans, recruiting replacements for people who leave, and reorganizing the team as needed. This inner circle will keep the team going when the parents are no longer there. They assure parents' wishes for their child and the child's wishes for himself are carried out. The inner circle may include close family members, the child's guardian, the primary care manager, one or two close friends, a life skills coach, a live-in companion, a personal assistant, or a care giver. It could include a medical professional for someone with significant medical needs. Logically some members of the leadership group should participate in the annual life planning sessions.

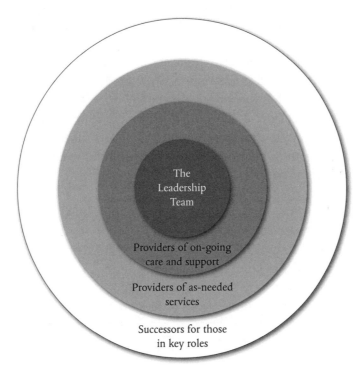

FIGURE 2.1 THE FOUR CIRCLES OF SUPPORT

Like an organization, the inner circle should include people who fill officer-like roles: a president or chairperson to preside over the team meetings and manage team efforts, and a vice-president or vice-chair to assist. Parents will probably serve as co-presidents as long as they can. The secretary has the responsibility to keep minutes of meetings and record decisions and actions with assignments and due dates. The secretary should keep the letter of intent current and distributed to key team members. One person should be a treasurer to monitor or manage financial arrangements. This individual could be the trustee of a special needs trust, a trust protector, a family member or friend with financial competency, or a financial advisor. It's frequently a challenge to balance a child's immediate needs for financial support against the necessity to conserve the assets for lifetime assistance. The inner circle collectively bears this responsibility. Members of the core team usually take the role of advocating for the child's immediate well-being and happiness because our natural tendency is to care. However, someone must have the un-thanked and sometimes resented role of being the prudent financial steward, protecting assets so they are not prematurely exhausted leaving the child in dire poverty or at the mercy of a government bureaucracy.

Any organization should have a succession plan to replace key individuals when needed. It's the same with a support team. There should be potential successors for all individuals in the inner circle or an understanding of how to obtain replacements.

On-going organizations have policies and procedures that define the organization's mission and guide how it operates. The equivalent to a policy and procedures manual in the circles of support concept is the letter of intent (LOI) described in Chapter 4. The LOI contains the team's mission statement, its strategic plan, and its current operating plan. It describes how members of the team work together and what must be taken care of if something happens to one or both of the parents.

The Key Roles

What are the key roles? How do you identify them? They emerge from life planning. Typical roles to consider are listed in Table 2.1.

Table 2.1 Roles to consider in the circles of support

The leadership team	*Special needs*
Team lead or co-leads	Care manager
Secretary or record keeper	Life skills coach
Financial steward	Live-in care provider or companion
	Job coach
Social	Advocates with privacy waivers
Friends	
	Government services
Medical	Case manager
Physician	
Dentist	*Finance and legal*
Optometrist	Guardian
Psychiatrist	Representative payee
	Bookkeeper or bank account manager
Therapy	Conservator
Psychologist	Trustee or trust officer
Speech therapist	Trust protector or trust advisor
Physical therapist	Investment manager
Occupational therapist	Residential property manager
	Agent with power of attorney

Not all of the roles shown will be part of your plan. You may identify a role in your circumstances not in the table. A role may appear only in the contingency planning for your death or disability—for example, a successor guardian. Many of the roles in Table 2.1 are easily recognized, but two merit comment: a care manager plans, manages, and coordinates all services a person needs, both government and private pay; a case manager is a government employee who manages the services provided or paid for by a government agency.

Inviting People to Join a Circle

How do you identify people to invite into your circles of support? Start with your social circles—family, friends, people you know, and people you work with. Start with core family members: parents, your other children, and closely involved relatives. Then consider the extended family, aunts and uncles, nephews and nieces, cousins, etc. The distinction between core and extended family is not that of blood or in-law relationship but rather reflects the strength of emotional ties and involvement in the life of your child. Next consider recruiting friends and volunteers. Volunteers are people willing to help because they care that our society is welcoming and inclusive for people with disabilities. Last, consider professionals, people who are compensated for their services. There are two types: government employees and professionals you hire to fill roles not otherwise taken. Consistent with the principle of person-centered planning, your child should have input regarding key people, especially guardians, live-in companions, and primary care givers. The outward progression from family to professionals is illustrated in Figure 2.2.

The relative sizes of the circles vary according to family circumstances. Highly social families are more likely to have a wide circle of friends. The core family may not be there at all. There may be a non-existent, narrow, or wide circle of extended family. Some families can't afford professionals. Some families are not eligible for or don't receive government services. Sometimes there is only one circle: government employees doing a job because there is no one who cares.

To develop a list of candidates, start with the set of roles that need to be filled, arranged in priority order, and think of people who would be good in those roles. As a name pops up, write it down and go for the next. If you can't think of a family member or good friend, move outward from obvious names. Think about casual friends and acquaintances—neighbors, co-workers, and people someone can introduce you to. Make a list of the organizations you belong to and the activities your family enjoys. For each, think of candidates in that group. I have read somewhere that most people know 200–300 people well enough to start a conversation. A list of names numbering a fraction of this is a good start.

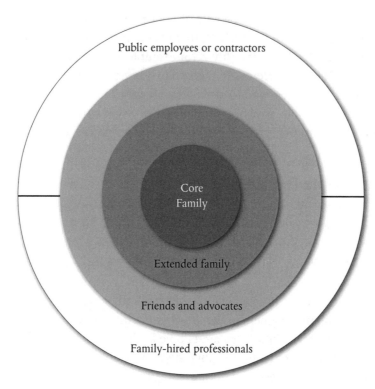

FIGURE 2.2 PEOPLE TO INVITE INTO THE CIRCLE OF SUPPORT

With a list of possible candidates, develop a contact plan, prioritize your efforts, and start recruiting. Start with core family, then extended family, then friends, and move out to acquaintances and people to whom you can be introduced. People in the circle of government employees, such as a case manager or a significant care provider, should not be taken for granted. You should consider whether they should be asked to join the team. Even if their job requires them to render a service, by asking you may create a personal commitment that would not otherwise be there. Inviting them also gives you an opportunity to describe the team and how you envision everyone working together.

You can expand your list by networking—asking other people to suggest names. Consider approaching the staff of non-profit organizations that serve your family and families like you. Ask professionals such as your child's special education teacher. Ask the priest, rabbi, pastor, or imam of your religious community. Approach organizations that match volunteers with people in need. When you're asking someone to suggest a name, explain the role and necessary qualifications. I suggest addressing only one role in a conversation. If a suggested person is someone you don't know, ask the person making the suggestion if he would be willing to make an introduction. If you're doing annual life planning, ask the planning team to identify roles and candidates.

I don't mean to make this sound easy. It may not be. Some people are naturally gregarious and building a support network is easier for them. Some people are shy or introverted and don't have a large group of friends and acquaintances. It can be uncomfortable asking for help. One may be afraid to ask because of fears about how someone will respond. A common fear is that he or she will say "no." There may be a fear they will say "yes" but resent being asked. There is the fear that by asking you will alter a relationship, perhaps risking a friendship. There is the fear someone will say "yes" but won't be there when needed. How do you keep from being blocked by these anxieties? Put yourself in the other person's shoes. What concerns might they feel that you should be prepared to address?

Some people will respond positively to being asked. Some will be interested but may have reservations or concerns. "Am I sure I know how to do this?" "How much time is it going to take?" "Is there a financial commitment?" "Can I take this on with all of the other things in my life?" "What if something happens and I can't continue?" "Where can I get help if I run into a problem?" These are the ghosts that may hang in the background of a conversation. Be prepared to bring these ghosts out in the open so they can be sent away. Ask the person what concerns she may have. Our instincts are wrong here; ignoring concerns does not raise the chances of someone saying "yes" unless she is one of those people who go through life unable to say "no."

Never pressure someone to say "yes." You risk getting a false commitment, a commitment that will not be there when needed. Don't rush a person to answer if they want to think it over. Ask them if they need any more information to make a decision and when you can resume the conversation. If a person says "no," ask if he or she can suggest someone else to ask. Some people will try to make up for saying "no" by going out of their way to help.

Let's take the concern about not being qualified. When you ask someone to join a circle, show them what the team looks like. Show them they are not alone. Show them that there are others they can turn to for help.

What about time? You should have planned in sufficient detail so you can describe the time commitment. Do not understate the nature and extent of the commitment and let someone be surprised later. He may withdraw when he realizes the real situation, perhaps with resentment for being misled. Your honesty helps people make a true commitment.

What about a financial burden? Family members are more likely to be willing to make a financial commitment, but some may not be able. They may have other commitments, like their own children. Taking care of the needed financial support yourself can make it possible for someone to say "yes" who would otherwise not be able to. Sharing some information about your financial arrangements can allay the fear of a hidden burden showing up in the future. Professionals will usually not serve without compensation unless there is an emotional bond or sense of duty eliciting their loyalty. However, contrary to a vicious social stereotype I know attorneys who help people out of the goodness of their hearts. You find good people everywhere if you take time to look.

What about changing circumstances? This is a valid concern. One client of mine had committed to being the guardian for her brother when her parents pass away. This was an unwavering commitment until the woman entered her early forties and was diagnosed with multiple sclerosis. Unexpected problems are a part of life. This illustrates the importance of taking the time to identify potential successors, especially for roles in legal documents such as a successor guardian. Let the person you are asking to take a role know there is someone who can take over if needed.

It should be obvious that no one can say "yes" until they have been asked. You must be willing to overcome your fear to ask for help for the sake of your child.

When people agree to join your circles, give them all of the help and encouragement you can. Bring them together periodically so they feel like part of a team. Throw an annual party or celebrate a significant event. Involve key team members socially if appropriate. Share your life plan, current arrangements, final arrangements, and letter of intent. Diligently seek to make sure everyone knows their contribution is appreciated.

Intentional Family Groups

Circles of support can take many forms. There is no ideal structure, only some that work and some that don't as judged by outcomes. Here is one of the more powerful possibilities: an intentional family group.

This is a group of families who share common values and goals in creating better lives for their children who have special needs. They come together socially and for celebrations. They work to create a stable social group for their children, help each other with life planning, investigate living arrangements, share financial burdens, and solve problems. Two projects commonly undertaken are exploring employment possibilities and residential options.

Intentional family groups should consist of 6–15 families. Small groups may lack the mass to tackle major projects or the critical mass to be self-sustaining. As a group exceeds 15 or so families, the feeling of being part of a close, cohesive group begins to weaken. It begins to feel more like an organization than people who care for each other. To put it another way, friendships become diluted into acquaintanceships.

Probably the most common activity of a group is to build a social circle for the young adults by creating opportunities for them to be together. There may be organized community outings—movies, concerts, theater, sports events, dining out, or travel. Social opportunities can be as simple as "hanging out." There may be celebrations, birthday parties or—how wonderful this could be!—a wedding for a couple in the group of children with special needs. Sometimes, coming together can be for more poignant reasons—to give support on the occasion of the death of a parent. I shouldn't have to cite many examples. If our children are more alike than different then we should facilitate their coming together in the same manner and for the same reasons as their typical peers do. The intentional family group my spouse and I belong to organizes a dozen community outings annually and encourages as many "hang outs" as members are willing to host.

The group may have a parent program for socializing, educational activities, or working together on a project. For example, the group might invite an attorney to give a presentation on estate planning. They might visit a local co-housing community. They might go out together for a night on the town. There are endless possibilities. The group might have bi-monthly project meetings and social gatherings in alternate months.

If all families have considered and agreed, the group could be a safety net for a child if his only parent passes away unexpectedly and there is no other family to step in.

Intentional family groups can be formed by parents who become acquainted in high school or a school's Bridges Program. Or the formation may be facilitated by a non-profit organization serving special needs families. Or a few families might start a group and recruit other families.

The cohesiveness of the group will be determined by common interests and mutual contributions. The more common are the interests of each family, the stronger will be their mutual commitment. Common interests will change over time. Just as annual life planning is important to the child with special needs, annual planning is important to the intentional family group. In an annual planning meeting, the group sets its goals for the coming year, plans its activities, and fairly allocates assignments to things that need to get done. Having everyone share in the tasks of the group is very important. A group can become an unpleasant entity to belong to when pervaded by resentments that some families are "free-riding." Consequently, an intentional family group should have a written policy describing member expectations. Joining the group should be understood as a promise to meet those expectations. Members who fail to do so without extenuating circumstances should be asked to leave.

One dilemma that a family group may face is the issue of exclusivity. For those who have spent years trying to create a welcoming and inclusive community for people with special needs, it may be personally difficult to exclude anyone from a group who wants to join. Yet there can be problems when a group gets too big. How does a group resolve this dilemma? A possibility is to help newer members and interested families form their own group and help the new group become self-sustaining. A well-established family group can help a fledgling by providing advice, connections, "lessons learned," and operational guidance. Remember the remark in the Preface about baby clothes? You don't give them back to the family who gave them to you; you pass them on to families who can use them. So it is with helping families in the special needs community form an intentional family group of their own.

CHAPTER 3

LIFE SKILLS ARE THE FOUNDATION FOR INDEPENDENCE

Teaching life skills was considered a waste of time in the era of institutional care and incarceration of people who were "mentally retarded" or mentally ill. Those so labeled were treated as having little intellectual capacity or human dignity. The "inmates" were managed by complete supervision. Tasks were done by staff or accomplished using direct commands to those under their care, sometimes by physically manipulating them. A person was told what to do and everything to do. Little personal autonomy was given nor considered imaginable. This belief paradigm was self-fulfilling and self-justifying. Such direct and continuous supervision resulted in a population of individuals accustomed to compliance and total dependence. The result was a population of human beings given no opportunity to develop their innate abilities. It was a population extremely vulnerable to abuse and neglect. (Have you ever wondered where the term "ward of the state," a term in guardianship law, came from? It came from a ward in an institution.) Societal values have changed greatly in two generations. It is now accepted that people with disabilities have rights to an enjoyable and meaningful life and an appropriate place in society.

Life skills open doors to the community. They are the foundation for a quality of life. There are two types of life skills. The first type are the empowerment skills for managing one's self, one's environment, and one's interaction with others. The second are task skills for daily living or a job. Preparing for independence begins early in a child's life teaching self-confidence and self-esteem. Setting higher expectations and meeting them is a process that starts at birth and continues to maturity. Parents should begin to assess the potential for independence in early adolescence and establish a program to reinforce capabilities and overcome limitations. Things to consider in assessing capabilities and limitations are listed in Table 3.1. The outcome of your assessment and the resulting action plan should be part of your life plan.

Table 3.1 Capabilities and limitations to assess for potential independence and employment

Cognitive
- Memory
- Attention
- Processing speed
- Predictive reasoning
- Abstract reasoning
- Adaptive reasoning
- Problem-solving

Physical
- Visual acuity
- Hearing sensitivity
- Strength
- Stamina
- Gross motor
- Fine motor
- Overall health and fitness

Communication
- Receptive
- Expressive
- Articulation
- Vocabulary, syntax and grammar
- Reading
- Writing

Social
- Self-advocacy
- Social interaction
- Relationships
- Emotional control
- Sexual awareness and behavior
- Ability to function in the general community
- Interaction with strangers
- Handling aggression
- Vulnerability to exploitation

Life skills
- Personal hygiene, bathing
- Toileting, continence
- Dressing
- Feeding
- Mobility
- Self-medication
- Manage physical fitness
- Coping when sick
- Meal preparation
- Laundry
- House cleaning
- Public transportation
- Safety and security
- Moral discrimination
- Money management
- Time management
- Ability to use appliances, technology
- Shopping
- Coping with emergencies

Job skills
- Ability to master tasks and routines
- Need for structure versus ability to handle unpredictability
- Appropriate interaction with co-workers, customers and public
- Schedule management
- Acceptable speed
- Completeness and quality of work
- Ability to follow directions
- Seeking information or help

The thoughts I hope you will remember after reading this chapter are:

1. Teaching the skills for independence should start at an early age and, for someone with a cognitive impairment, continue throughout life.

2. The most important skills are empowerment skills, taking care of oneself, and managing one's life and relationships with others.

3. There are nine challenges to be met for living on one's own. Once met, they become the nine supports for independence.

Empowerment Skills

Empowerment skills are the skills for managing personal care, one's interaction with others, self-help, and self-protection. High-level empowerment skills are listed in Table 3.2. Teaching these skills starts at an early age; they are the steps in a child's growing up. It takes longer if the child is cognitively impaired or has to struggle with other obstacles like a physical disability or behavioral problems.

Table 3.2 Empowerment skills to enable a place in the community

Self-esteem	Self-advocacy
Social relationships	Decision making
Communications	Personal care
Assertiveness	Healthy eating habits
Safety awareness	Hygiene
Healthy sexuality	Physical fitness

How do we teach empowerment skills? How did some of us teach our children to read? My three children were read to from the time they were babies, through the pre-school and elementary school years (mostly by their mother). They were read to after supper and before going to bed, every day of the week. My two typical children were not taught to read by their school teachers. They entered school knowing how to read and enjoying reading. Meg, delayed, didn't enter school knowing how to read but reading came for her too. Her teachers did a wonderful job teaching her to read phonetically. Reading was part of our children's environment. They absorbed reading like the developing human child absorbs language and social skills. So how do we teach empowerment skills? The same way we teach reading. They are taught continuously. They are taught from an early age. They are taught by example. They are taught in context. They are taught in the home. If you haven't been doing this, or if you have been relying on the school teachers or special education staff, start now.

It occurred to me, somewhat belatedly, that I needed to be empowered too. Rather than relying on special education teachers or social workers to teach my child, the better approach was for them to teach me how to teach. I want to bring whatever is taught in school or my daughter's life skills program home for practice, encouragement, and reinforcement. One does not learn life skills in a school classroom or in a weekly session with a counselor. One learns continuously. My wife and I can be our daughter's best teachers because we spend the most time with her.

When my daughter aged out of school, I became concerned—late to the party as usual—about how to teach Meg healthy sexuality. I found a book, *Sexuality: Your Sons and Daughters with Intellectual Disabilities* (Schweier and Hingsburger 2000). It is a terrific book. The title is misleading. It's about much more than sexuality. It is about life skills. On page 46, I discovered the concept of "parallel talk."

It was so natural; it was something I could do. Too often, busy parents, rushing to get things done, do things themselves rather than helping their child do them, or they try to speed things up with a burst of commands. The idea of parallel talk is doing things alongside your child, naturally describing what you're doing and why and what comes next as you move from task to task in the flow of things. For example, you and your child might be doing laundry. Parallel talk would sound like: "We start by separating the white clothes from the colored ones. We have to wash the white clothes separately so they don't get stained. Can you help me put the white clothes in one pile and the other clothes in another?" Done once, this has little effect. Done over weeks and months it becomes part of the routine of daily living. People with a cognitive impairment or intellectual disability have difficulty generalizing skills across different situations. Parallel talk brings things together, teaching empowerment skills and task skills and embedding them in the life that surrounds.

Empowerment skills are critical for employability. One must have the personal skills for dealing with the public, co-workers, and supervisors. The ability to communicate and be understood is another essential skill. We take courtesy for granted in our own lives but we can't with a child who has an intellectual disability or mental condition. When an employee interfaces with the public, sexually acceptable behavior is essential. An employer will not tolerate inappropriate touch, inappropriate language (such as commenting on a woman's physical attributes), or immodesty.

Task Skills

Developing a program to teach task skills is harder than it looks. I learned this helping my daughter cook supper one evening. We were fixing macaroni and cheese from a mix. Many of you know how it's done. You fill a pot with water, add the macaroni, boil the water, turn off the heat after so many minutes, drain the water, add milk, butter and cheese, and stir. The instructions are on the box with helpful pictures. No problem, right?

Yes, there was a problem, more than one. If the water is starting to boil and the time is now 5:38, what time will it be in 12 minutes when we're supposed to turn off the heat? Meg can't read a clock with hour and minute hands but she can read a digital clock. I show her using a hand-held calculator that 12 minutes from now is 5:50 on the clock. I'm glad we didn't wait until 5:52 to get the water boiling because there's no 5:64 on a digital clock. Next, Meg looks on the box and reads: "add 4 tbsp. butter." This is a problem. Meg reads phonetically but we hadn't taught her abbreviations. (You should have heard her trying to pronounce "tbsp.") After I explained it meant tablespoons, she did exactly what it said, taking four generous scoops with a tablespoon. A little too much but close enough given our cooking skills. Next, the box said: "Add ¼ cup milk." Another problem. The measuring cup is marked with ¼ cup markings, but only the ½, 1, 1½, and 2 marks are labeled. Meg doesn't know that ¼ is ½ of ½, or the next mark down.

Well, we fixed the macaroni but after we finished eating I thought to myself, "This is harder than I expected." Meg was happy though; she loves cooking. Later, I thought about how to design a set of aids so she could cook the meal herself. I made a list of pictures to take with a digital camera to put in a three-ring notebook. I listed assistive devices like a timer for minutes, a labeled measuring cup, and a list of abbreviations. I was stumped to design a device to help her pour a heavy pot of water through a colander. (This is an occupational therapist's area of expertise.) After a while I thought, "Maybe the answer is TV dinners. She can use a microwave."

Now multiply this by all the tasks in a day or week and the magnitude of the challenge comes into view. Later when I read about parallel talk in the Schweier–Hingsberger book, my mind leapt back to the evening when Meg and I cooked macaroni and cheese.

Some of the task skills to support independent or semi-independent living are shown in Table 3.3. The teaching challenge is more complicated than it appears. All tasks are a set of multiple steps. Consider the task of preparing supper. Not only are there multiple steps in preparing each dish, but it takes two or three dishes to complete a meal. One doesn't have just one entrée recipe to get through the week, but six or eight for variety and nutrition.

Individuals with a cognitive impairment learn visually. Digital cameras, video cameras, and tablet computers with audio and video capability can be used to create visual instructions and illustrations for many of the tasks of daily living.

Table 3.3 Task skills that support independence

Time management	Appropriate dress
Cooking	Money management
Laundry	Self-medication
Housekeeping	Home security
Shopping	Telephone
Calendar and schedule management	Transportation

Planning for Independence

Independent living or semi-independent living is possible for many people with disabilities given adequate planning, support, and resources. When I use the term "independence," I mean living on one's own. Semi-independent living means living on one's own supported *but not managed* by others. It is outside of the parental home and not in a state-managed residence. Independent living is a possibility for those with physical disabilities or mental illness. For those with a mild to moderate cognitive impairment, semi-independent living is conceivable. For those severely or profoundly challenged, needing intensive or constant care, semi-independence may be impractical and attempts ill-advised. Regardless of the nature or severity of the disability, the needs and capabilities of each individual should be considered to determine if some level of independence is possible or safe. Certainly the potential for independence for those with a moderate cognitive impairment is widely underestimated.

There are nine challenges that must be faced and resolved to make independent or semi-independent living possible. These challenges, once met, become the nine supports for independent living. The nine challenges are listed in Table 3.4.

Table 3.4 The nine supports for independent living

1. Life skills	6. Money management
2. Healthy sexuality	7. Transportation
3. Human supports	8. Safety management
4. Assistive technologies	9. Protection from sexual abuse
5. Residence	

There is not space in this book to discuss options to meet each challenge or how to integrate them into a system of supports. I will leave you with a few observations. The most significant of the nine challenges, the *sine qua non* for any degree of independence, is having the necessary life skills. This is especially true for those with a cognitive impairment. Teaching them life skills for independence will take time, care, patience, and persistence. It can take three to five years to implement a program of independence, longer if you have not already been working on the empowerment skills. The two most critical challenges, the two that absolutely must be resolved, are safety management and protection from sexual abuse. Failures in these two areas can be tragic. Any situation that the person cannot cope with or cannot manage with well-structured routines, aids, and assistive technologies will require human help. Carefully consider the nature and frequency of the support needed. You will need to decide whether the necessary assistance must be provided by someone with professional training or can be someone with reasonable diligence and common sense. The frequency will define whether support requires a live-in companion or care giver, someone to check in at an appropriate frequency, or someone the individual can call or go to for help. I call the human support options "live-in," "look-in," and "neighbor."

Planning for independent living is a big project. Start by laying out a week in the life of your child, every task or event that must be managed and completed. Break down each task into its component steps to identify the skills and tools needed. Color code each task. Blue might indicate a task your child can do. Something he can be taught may be colored green. Green tasks then define the structure of a task skills mentoring program. Tasks requiring human support may be colored red. Red tasks indicate the nature and frequency of support that will be necessary. Tasks that require an assistive technology or device could be colored brown. Brown tasks provide the basis for listing the appliances, household items, devices and tools, and software applications needed. Since many of the tasks involve sub-tasks you may need to break a task into its lower-level tasks for analysis. Color the top-level task in the order of red, green, and brown to indicate the most important element of assistance.

Personal safety must be carefully analyzed. Consider what can go wrong. Make a list of possible abnormal situations that could occur. There are two types of abnormal situation. The first are emergencies and safety-related problems such as an intruder or a house fire. I call these Type 1 problems. The second or Type 2 problems are the non-urgent problems like a toilet overflow. Whether a problem is Type 1 or Type 2 will depend on the individual and the nature of his limitations and his ability to cope with abnormal or unexpected situations. Once you identify the potential threats, evaluate whether the person has the skills to cope with them or can be taught what to do. This may depend on the degree to which you can predict the exact circumstances to determine an appropriate response. Consider hardware and software systems that can prevent a problem, help manage it, or alert an outside party to intervene. Such systems include environmental sensors, alarms, surveillance cameras, or software programs to prompt an action or summon help. An emergency may require immediate alert and response of an outside party, a fire for example. Concurrently, the threatened individual must be able to protect herself or reach safety until help arrives. Live-in support may be the only reliable solution.

Deciding whether an individual can handle a situation is not simply a matter of "yes" or "no." When safety or critical physical needs are involved, reliability or probability of success must be considered. Ninety percent reliability in attending to personal hygiene may be acceptable. Ninety-seven percent reliability finding the way home at night is not.

Because learning can be more unpredictable for someone with an intellectual impairment, take incremental steps to implement a program of independence. Take the first step in your home. Declare an area of the home to be the child's space to enjoy and manage properly, a trial apartment if you will. Teach and implement the routine of self-sufficiency in that space. After the adult child demonstrates the capability to manage his responsibilities and the daily routine, the next step is a trial period in someone else's home but still under supervision. This may be a host home, friends' home, the home of a family in an intentional family group, or a reciprocal arrangement with another family. The benefit of this step is breaking the parent–child dependency. If successful, the next step may be moving the child into his or her own home. This may require two steps. The first step would involve live-in support initially which is withdrawn when confidence is gained in the child's ability to take care of himself. Before the move-in, develop a comprehensive checklist and walk through all of the arrangements. This is a live test to uncover and fix unforeseen problems. Those contemplating buying a property—condominium, house, or multi-unit residence—should consider a trial period in an apartment before making a major financial commitment.

If independent living is your goal, consider making the transition when your child is in his or her twenties. She is more adaptable (and perhaps eager) when younger and you are there to ensure success and make necessary modifications. I also think it's cruel beyond words to allow a situation where someone who is cognitively impaired or mentally ill must experience the stress of moving out of the home they have known all of their life, without warning, concurrent with the trauma of losing a parent.

Nothing is permanent. Stability in life is not achieved; it is managed. Circumstances change over time. Things may change for the individual— changes in medical or cognitive condition, loneliness, a traumatic event, the desire to come home, or a wish to get married. If you have a child with a moderate cognitive impairment or mental illness you must have a support system that can continue, adjust, and renew if you or your spouse are not there to oversee his well-being and safety.

Where to Go for More Information

I haven't found a comprehensive book on life skills. Most books on the subject focus on specialized areas such as language and speech pathology, or on particular age groups, usually pre-school or elementary school children. I do, however, recommend the following books.

The book mentioned earlier, *Sexuality: Your Sons and Daughters with Intellectual Disabilities* (Schweier and Hingsberger 2000), is an excellent book on empowering adults. Healthy sexuality is a sub-set of life skills, and in discussing sexuality the authors bring in so much more. Also, the passionate advocacy of David Hingsberger for the civil rights of people with disabilities may open your eyes, as it has opened mine, as to how people with disabilities should be seen as human beings and how they should be treated. If you have never encountered Mr. Hingsberger in person or on DVD, you should.

The principles in Terry Couwenhoven's book on the topic of sexuality, *Teaching Children with Down Syndrome about their Bodies, Boundaries, and Sexuality* (Couwenhoven 2007), although written for parents of children with Down syndrome, are broadly applicable. I like practical books and Ms. Couwenhoven's is quite practical. It has an excellent Resources appendix.

I also note two books by Darlene Mannix: *Social Skills Activities for Secondary Students with Special Needs* (Mannix 2009a) and *Life Skills Activities for Secondary Students with Special Needs* (Mannix 2009b).

CHAPTER 4

WRITE A LETTER OF INTENT

So you developed a life plan, established a network of support, and are teaching and reinforcing life skills. What's next? You should prepare a letter of intent (LOI) to document your instructions, the arrangements made for your child's quality of life, and what needs to be done in the event of your death or incapacity. The purpose of an LOI is to provide information and guidance to those who will settle your estate and take over from you in your child's care.

The key points that you should remember after reading this chapter are:

1. Document your life plan with a letter of intent.

2. A letter of intent consists of three things and, for some families, a fourth:

    (a) a family narrative

    (b) a letter of intent summary

    (c) organized files with important information, documents, and records

    (d) an "In Case of Emergency" instruction if your child requires continuous or daily care.

3. Share your letter of intent with the personal representative of your estate, close family, your successor guardian, your agent with power of attorney, your healthcare proxy, and key members of your child's circles of support.

4. Keep your letter of intent current because you never know when it will be needed.

The Purpose of a Letter of Intent

A letter of intent describes your wishes for your child, his hopes for the future, the arrangements you've made, and what must be done if something happens to you. An LOI is what your representatives and successors will need to know to take over with little or no notice. It documents your life, resource, financial, and legal plans and your child's Individual Life Plan. If you fail to document your arrangements and something unexpected happens, what you have in place can fall apart faster than others can figure out what needs to be done. The result will be a disruption to your child's physical care or quality of life. Your letter of intent is as important as your legal directives.

An LOI is a personal record. No one knows your child better than you, knows the precious and lovable person she is, knows her fears and joys, the basis for her self-esteem, and better knows her needs. An LOI holds the wisdom and knowledge you have accumulated as a parent. The LOI is critically important if your child is severely challenged and cannot speak for herself. You are her voice. When you are no longer there to speak for your child, your voice speaks through your letter of intent.

An LOI is intended for non-spousal successors but may be needed by a spouse as well. It's common for spouses to take different roles and divide responsibilities for their child's care, for example: "You handle the business matters and I'll manage the care." Spouses should keep each other informed of how each is managing in his or her area of responsibility. The LOI should be drafted by both spouses together. Preparing it together will be helpful when one spouse has to take over for the other.

A letter of intent is not legally enforceable. However, I have found that personal representatives, guardians, and fiduciaries will follow your wishes unless circumstances and their judgment dictate otherwise. They will likely be grateful for your advice and instructions. It is possible to make an LOI binding through your legal documents but I urge you not to do so. You can't anticipate how life unfolds. Your successors should have flexibility and discretion to manage circumstances as they happen. You selected them because you trusted them and respected their judgment. Don't tie their hands.

What it Looks Like

A letter of intent has three common components: a family narrative, a letter of intent summary, and the documents and records of your plans and arrangements. Parents whose child needs constant or daily supervision should prepare an "In Case of Emergency" instruction.

People usually think of a letter of intent as a "fill in the blanks" form. There is a more important document, though. You should start by writing a family narrative. I discovered the power of such a narrative from one of my clients. In my years helping families with special needs planning, clients almost never come to my office with a letter of intent or a comprehensive life plan. However one day I met with a couple and asked, "Do you have a life plan?" The mother handed me a 28-page personal narrative about her family and her daughter with severe needs. The narrative described the members of the family, the daughter with cerebral palsy, the parents' roles in the daughter's care, and the relationship of the brother and twin sister to their sister. It described her daughter's personality, the qualities that made her special to those who loved her, her needs and capabilities, what she liked and didn't, and the important people in her life. The document went on to narrate a week in the life of her daughter and the daily care that she and her husband provided. After reading the narrative, I felt that if I had to step in for those parents, I had a good idea of what needed to be done and to whom I could turn for help. I felt empathy for this non-verbal and needful person. I had a sense of her as a human being. I am grateful to that mother for teaching me what the most important element of a letter of intent is.

What should you include in a family narrative? Table 4.1 has an outline. However, the document is your personal narrative. It should reflect what you want your representatives and successors to know about your family, your child, what you want for him or her, and what he or she wants for themselves.

Table 4.1 A suggested outline for a family narrative

- About our family
  - Mom
  - Dad
  - Our child with special needs
  - Brothers, sisters, and their spouses
  - Other close family
- What we want you to know about _____
  - Beautiful qualities
  - Personality
  - Abilities
  - Likes and dislikes
  - Care needs
  - What he/she wants for himself or herself
  - Friends and other important people in his or her life
- What we want for _____'s future
  - Level of independence
  - Social life
  - Spiritual life
  - Job or vocation
  - A good home
- A week in the life of _____
  - Daily routine
  - Personal care
  - Activities
- If something happens to us
  - Notifications
  - Immediate care or intervention

The second document is a summary of your plans and arrangements. Its purpose is to concisely describe what you have in place and what needs to be done in the event of your death or incapacity. It summarizes the information in your child's life plan including key people, their roles, and contact information. It explains medical, psychological, and physical needs. It describes the government assistance received, the assistance your child will be eligible for after your death, and how to apply for planned services. It describes the final arrangements for your child's death if you have made them. The summary tells your personal representative, family members, the successor guardian, and leaders of the circles of support who to contact and where to find the documents, records, and needed information. The summary allows someone to take over with little notice managing your child's needs and supports, quickly identifying what needs to be done, and more importantly, what needs to be done immediately. A suggested outline of an LOI summary is provided in Table 4.2.

Table 4.2 Outline of a letter of intent summary

1. Key people, their relationship or roles with contact information
   1. Immediate and close family
   2. Extended family
   3. Friends
   4. Description of the circles of support, key people, and roles
   5. Guardian and successor
   6. Personal representative
   7. Trustee or conservator
   8. Trust protector and successor
   9. Faith community with contact information for pastor, priest, rabbi, or imam

2. Personal information
   1. Date of birth
   2. Social Security number
   3. Marital status, information about spouse and children

3. Medical information
   1. Diagnosis of disabling condition
   2. Medical professionals including doctor, psychiatrist, dentist, ophthalmologist
   3. Psychologists, therapists, and behavioral analayst
   4. Personal care needs
   5. Dietary needs and restrictions
   6. Prescription drugs and pharmacist
   7. Health insurance
   8. Record of examinations, doctor visits, and hospitalizations (past 3 years)

Table continues

Table 4.2 Outline of a letter of intent summary *cont.*

4. Federal benefits and services (Social Security, Medicare, SSI, and Medicaid)
   (Description, Agency, Next required action, and Date due)
   1. Services currently receiving
   2. Services applied for or to be applied for

5. Disability services (state and private)
   (Description, Agency, Next required action and Date due)
   1. Behavioral specialist, skills coach, or therapist
   2. Residential services
   3. Professional guardian and professional care planner or manager
   4. Employment services
   5. In-residence care providers
   6. Transportation
   7. Day programs
   8. Respite care

6. Employment, business, or volunteer activity
   1. Employer with contact information for supervisor or personnel office
   2. Scheduled hours
   3. Transportation
   4. Job coach
   5. Earnings and employee benefits

7. Private Residence
   1. Lease for rental or deed for property owned
   2. Mortgage
   3. Property manager
   4. Service contractors
   5. Insurance

8. Automobile
   1. Description and title
   2. Tax and license
   3. Loan information
   4. Insurance

9. Parents' legal arrangements
   1. Estate attorney with contact information
   2. Personal representative
   3. Estate documents
   4. Agent with power of attorney
   5. Agent with medical power of attorney

10. Parents' financial information (share only on need-to-know basis)
    1. Bank accounts and institutions
    2. Investment accounts with broker/dealer or advisor
    3. Tax preparer or CPA
    4. Liabilities
    5. Health, life, disability, and long-term care insurance policies
    6. Real estate with title and mortgage
    7. Business ownership interests
    8. High value personal property such as collectibles

11. Financial information for person with special needs
    1. Representative payee
    2. Bank accounts
    3. Unearned income

12. Final arrangements in the event of your death

13. Final arrangements in the event of your child's death

Note: Identify the location and labels of relevant files and documents

You may have seen published versions of a letter of intent form or a last wishes document. They are typically "fill-in-the-blanks" forms distributed by funeral homes, memorial societies, life insurance companies, law firms, churches, elder care institutions, family service agencies, etc. One of the most widely known is the "Five Wishes" form published by Aging with Dignity. If you've seen a "fill-in-the-blanks" form, you know what most people mean by a letter of intent. When I started preparing an LOI summary for my daughter, I used a form in MS Word on a CD-RW that came with a book. It is comprehensive and well organized, but as I was filling it out I found myself trying to fit my daughter's life plan into someone else's structure. There were sections that didn't apply, topics not addressed, and things I wanted to emphasize. Some of the information was better placed in a family narrative. I decided to create my own summary. An LOI should contain everything you want your personal representative to know in a couple of hours of perusal so she can get to work quickly. If you are computer literate, I encourage you to build your own with word processing software in outline format. The disadvantage of creating your own summary is that you will spend more time developing an outline and setting up the format. The advantage is that it will reflect your situation, the plans for your child's future, and the essential information others will need in order to take over.

Whether you use a published form or create your own, expect to spend some time drafting the first version. There is information to collect, files and folders to organize and label, and decisions to be made about what to include or not. Although the document is called a summary, don't expect it to be short. My LOI summary is about 45 pages in length. However, it doesn't need to contain much detailed information. It should be a summary that directs your representative to the files with the more complete information. For example, suppose you have a life insurance policy. The summary should identify the insurance company, policy number, death benefit, the agent with contact information, and the location and label of the file with the policy. You don't need the summary to include the beneficiaries, premiums, cash value, riders, etc. If your personal representative knows that the policy exists and where to find it, she can pull the file when she's ready to contact the agent or insurance company.

A hard copy is cumbersome to revise. A paper form can become cluttered with cross-outs and inserts, eventually becoming confusing and almost unreadable. Major life changes may require discarding the current version and starting over. An electronic document can be more easily edited once prepared. The header of a document should show the revision number and date. You should always discard older versions to avoid confusion or error. The footer should contain page numbers so missing or misplaced pages can be identified. Your personal representative should always have the latest copy.

The third component of a letter of intent is your documents organized in file folders or ring binders in a file cabinet or on a bookshelf. My family files are kept in folders in four-drawer cabinets with a fire-proof safe for more important documents. One of the folders is labeled "SSI" (Supplemental Security Income). The folder contains the benefit determination letter from the Social Security Administration, the financial accounting for the latest disability review, correspondence with the Social Security Administration, and a log of phone calls. The fire-proof safe contains the letter from the geneticist who performed the chromosomal evaluation at our daughter's birth, a letter stating that she has Trisomy 21. This letter is the only document my wife and I or our successors will ever need to prove to Social Security, Medicaid, and state authorities that our daughter is "totally and permanently disabled" in accordance with the presumptive disability provisions of the Social Security regulations. You should keep documentation of your child's disability including the date or year of diagnosis. Keep a record of communications and meetings with government agencies and representatives. Good documentation will be important if you must appeal a denial of eligibility or services.

A concern for hardcopy files is their possible destruction. It is daunting to imagine the time and energy required to reconstruct them after a fire, flood, tornado, or other disaster. Keep important and hard-to-replace records in an environment where they will likely be preserved, such as in a fire-proof or water-proof safe or cabinet. Copies of your wills, trust agreements, powers of attorney, and healthcare directives should be kept on file in the office of your estate attorney. *Copies* of legal documents including property deeds, guardianship orders, contracts, etc. can be kept in a bank safe deposit box. However, do not put the originals in the safety deposit box—the box may be sealed after your death as part of the probate process until the court issues an order authorizing the box to be opened. This can significantly delay your personal representative in taking estate-related actions. Obviously, duplicate files pose the problem of keeping them contemporaneously updated. In this technology age, one can keep backup files in electronic form on a data storage device. Label electronic documents with version numbers and dates to avoid confusion.

You should periodically purge out-of-date documents. New papers should be filed promptly. When you open a file to insert a new document, check for papers that should be shredded or thrown away. Always shred documents with sensitive personal information. If you fall behind in this discipline, you will find it discouraging to even think of spending the hours to update a woefully neglected set of files. There is a problem caused by not removing obsolete material, a lesson I learned as the personal representative of my mother's estate. She saved everything. After she died, I spent days going through her papers, trying to figure out what was current and what to throw away. I found seven insurance policies. After contacting the companies, I found that only two were still in force. Only one had a current beneficiary designation. The other named my father. He had died 23 years earlier. Don't put your representative through this frustrating exercise. In addition to the aggravation (and cost if he or she is being compensated), necessary actions may be delayed until your representative identifies them. Property and money can vanish from an estate if no one knows of their existence and finds the records. If you have a bank safe deposit box, it is important that your personal representative knows that you do and where to find the key.

There is a fourth document that may be necessary for some families, an "In Case of Emergency" letter. Let's take a circumstance when this document can be very important. Suppose the parents of a child who requires constant supervision have an out-of-home appointment. They have arranged a sitter while they are out. The parents are in an automobile accident coming home and both are killed. What does the sitter do when the hours pass by and the parents haven't returned? How does someone in the family, a friend, or a neighbor know of the need for intervention in the child's care? Would they know what to do if they learn of the emergency? The "In Case of Emergency" letter should be short, listing key people to notify with contact information, and care needs that must be attended to immediately (insulin, for example). You need to think your way through who must be notified, how they can be contacted, what needs to be done to stabilize a situation, and where someone can get help. The "In Case of

Emergency" letter will probably be only a page or two. I suggest you laminate a copy and keep it by a phone or other prominent place in your home where it can be found quickly. Consider who should be given copies. A neighbor might be the first person to notice the unexplained absence of parents. Those listed as emergency contacts should have a copy. Your child's sitters, temporary custodians, or care givers should know where the instructions are. I recommend you carry a brief summary in your wallet or purse to alert emergency personnel that there is a special needs child at home who needs supervision.

If your child is sometimes left alone, does he know what to do if his parents don't come home? Teach him, if he possesses the cognitive skills for self-care, what to do when he starts to worry about Mom and Dad.

Sharing it with Those Who Will Come After You

You should review your family narrative and LOI summary with the personal representative of your estate and your successor guardian. They also should be shared with immediate family including adult brothers and sisters and their spouses unless you have reasons for not doing so. Others who may be appropriate include key people in your inner circle of support, the primary care manager, and the trustee and trust protector of the special needs trust.

A good way of sharing your plans and arrangements is an annual meeting with those who will be involved in managing your child's care. Distant relatives can be included by conference call. Describe the important elements of your LOI, changes since the last meeting and the in-case-of-emergency instructions. A meeting allows you to convey the same message to everyone at the same time. People get to hear the questions asked by others and the answers. Issues can be discussed and resolved. Some of those in your circle of support may be involved in your annual life planning, but don't combine the two meetings. The meeting to review the LOI has its own purpose and agenda.

How do you know that you have a good letter of intent—family narrative, summary of plans and arrangements, and data files? Ask your personal representative, your successor guardian, family members, and key members of your primary support team: "If something were to happen to us, do you know what to do?" If the answer is "yes," you probably have a good letter. "No" or "I'm not sure" indicates you have more work to do. Identify the area of confusion and get things clarified and documented.

CHECKLIST
CREATING A LIFE PLAN

		Yes/ Done	Action Req'd	Not Needed
	A Vision for Your Child's Life as an Adult			
1	Have you involved your child and considered his or her wishes?			
2	Have you assessed his or her personal skills and limitations for adult living?			
	(a) Physical condition, cognitive capability, and behavior control			
	(b) Communications, both receptive and expressive			
	(c) Social relationships			
	(d) Personal care management			
	(e) Safety awareness and self-protection			
	(f) The type and continuity of care and supervision needed			
	(g) Potential for independence with appropriate supports			
3	Is he or she eligible for SSI, Medicaid, state services, or housing assistance?			
4	Can you create a better quality of life by providing private financial support?			
5	Have you created a vision for the best possible quality of life as an adult?			
	(a) Social, community, and spiritual life			
	(b) Vocation—employment, personal business, or volunteer work			
	(c) Residential environment			
	(d) Care and support for special needs			
6	Is your child likely to outlive you and your spouse? For how long?			
	(a) Does your life plan extend for the years after your death?			

		Yes/ Done	Action Req'd	Not Needed
	A Written Long-Range Plan to Achieve the Life Vision			
1	Have you identified key events and dates in the lives of parents and family?			
	(a) Each parent's year of retirement			
	(b) Each parent's age for receiving Social Security or other pension			
	(c) Children's college or becoming self-sufficient			
	(d) Grandparents' care needs and their life expectancies			
	(e) Other significant events—job change, home purchase, starting a business, etc.			
2	Have you identified key milestones in your child's life?			
	(a) The year of aging out of school			
	(b) Receiving SSI, Medicaid, and state disability services			
	(c) Receiving Social Security Disability Insurance benefit, or dependent or survivor benefit			
	(d) College degree or certificate, vocational training, or job skills coaching			
	(e) Moving out of the parents' home into a state or private residence			
3	Have you identified the enablers or accomplishments to reach your hopes?			
	(a) An active social life and access to community activities			
	(b) Finding a vocation—job, business, or volunteer work			
	(c) Eventually moving into a long-term and stable residential situation			
	(d) Lifelong learning, skills development and retention			
	(e) Services for the care and support for special needs			
4	Do you have a plan for the next major transition in your child's life?			
5	Do you have a contingency plan for the death or disability of either parent?			
6	What are the uncertainties in the plan; when and how will you address them?			

		Yes/ Done	Action Req'd	Not Needed
A Written Long-Range Plan to Achieve the Life Vision (continued)				
7	Does your plan include the major life transitions in adulthood?			
	(a) Leaving the school system but still living with parents or family			
	(b) Moving out of the family home into a public or private residence			
	(c) The death of the first parent			
	(d) The death of the second parent			
The Annual Individual Life Plan (ILP)				
1	Have you developed your first annual Individual Life Plan?			
	(a) Decided on a process or model, e.g. PATH, PLAN, LifeSPAN, ELP			
	(b) Formed a team			
	(c) Obtained a facilitator			
	(d) Taken steps to ensure the child's participation to the extent able			
	(e) Determined desired outcomes for the planning meeting			
	(f) Made all of the arrangements			
2	Have you documented the goals and actions decided in the ILP meeting?			
3	Do you have a plan for following up and completing all of the actions?			
4	Do you have commitments from team members for continued support?			
5	Have you held an ILP meeting in the current year or within the past two years?			
6	Have you set a date for the next ILP meeting?			

		Yes/ Done	Action Req'd	Not Needed
	The Circles of Support			
1	Have you identified the critical roles in the circles of support?			
	(a) Guardian or advocate			
	(b) Primary care planner and care manager			
	(c) Psychologist, life skills coach, or behavior analyst			
	(d) Physical, speech, or occupational therapist			
	(e) Live-in care giver or companion			
	(f) Trustee, conservator, or financial manager			
2	Have you identified roles in each of the four circles?			
	(a) The core or leadership team circle			
	(b) The providers of on-going care and support circle			
	(c) Providers of occasional or as-needed services circle			
	(d) The circle of successors for key roles (leadership and primary care providers)			
3	Have you developed a list of individuals to invite to join a circle?			
4	Can you describe the expectations and time commitment to those you invite?			
5	Have you obtained commitments for key roles and possible successors?			
6	Do the key people in the inner two circles know all aspects of the life plan?			
7	Have the key people accepted responsibility to sustain and update the life plan?			
8	Is the team capable of adapting and renewing itself over the lifetime of the child?			
9	Does the team involve the child in the process of updating the plan?			
10	Does the leadership team hold regular meetings, involving others as needed?			
11	Have you considered joining or forming an intentional family group?			

		Yes/ Done	Action Req'd	Not Needed
A Plan for Mentoring Life Skills and Achieving Independence				
1	Are you teaching the life skills that empower a place in the community?			
	(a) Had a consultation with a life skills coach to develop an in-home program			
	(b) Working actively with your child to teach and reinforce, e.g. parallel talk			
	(c) Arranged for direct coaching in areas requiring professional expertise			
2	Prepared a "week in the life" of your child to determine needed task skills?			
3	Developed a set of visual aids showing how to accomplish each task?			
4	Consulted with an occupational therapist to design assistive devices and utensils?			
5	If independent living is the goal, do you have a plan to meet the nine challenges?			
	(a) Life skills			
	(b) Healthy sexuality			
	(c) Human supports			
	(d) Assistive technologies			
	(e) Residence			
	(f) Money management			
	(g) Transportation			
	(h) Safety management			
	(i) Protection from sexual abuse			
6	Have you considered incremental steps in moving toward independence?			
	(a) Implement a daily living routine in your home with planned independence			
	(b) Temporary living arrangement with a host home or another family			
	(c) Transition to an apartment with supports in place and stability verified			
	(d) Eventual move into the planned, long-term living environment			
7	Are the circles of support in place to sustain independence?			

		Yes/ Done	Action Req'd	Not Needed
	The Letter of Intent			
1	Have you prepared a personal narrative?			
	(a) About your family			
	(b) What you want others to know about your child			
	(c) Vision for your child's quality of life			
	(d) Summary of child's life plan with steps to reach the vision			
	(e) A week in the life of your child			
	(f) What needs to be done immediately if something happens to you and your spouse			
2	Have you prepared a summary document of current and future arrangements?			
	(a) Key people in child's life			
	(b) Personal information			
	(c) Medical information			
	(d) Government assistance and services			
	(e) Employment			
	(f) Residential environment			
	(g) Parents' estate plan and legal documents			
	(h) Parents' financial information			
	(i) Child's financial information			
	(j) Arrangements that need to be made in case of your death			
	(k) Final arrangements for the child when he or she dies			
3	Are files organized with backup copies or protection from destruction?			
4	Have you reviewed your letter of intent with those who will come after you?			
	(a) Family			
	(b) Personal representative of estate			
	(c) Leadership team in the circles of support			
5	Do you review your letter annually and keep files current?			

CASE STUDIES
LIFE PLANS

Let's check in with our four friends and take a look at their life plans.

Angel Herrera

In the Herrera household, Michelle is the one who takes responsibility for Angel's needs—making sure she has an active social life, managing her medical care, interfacing with the school's special education staff, etc. John takes the role of the family business manager—managing the finances and working with the family's investment advisor and tax accountant. John works long hours and travels frequently in his corporate management position. He is a regional marketing director for an advertising firm. As they talk about Angel's future, Michelle strongly feels that planning for it isn't just her job; it is John's job too. After a discussion, sometimes animated, John agrees that this is the family's highest priority in the coming months and he needs to be actively involved.

The largest school district in the metropolitan area holds a Transitions Day in the spring of each year for its special education families. John and Michelle, who live in an affluent suburb in a different school district, must pay a fee if they wish to attend. Since this program is the best offered by any of the metropolitan school districts, they register and pay the out-of-district fee. The purpose of the Transitions Day program is to help parents plan for their children after they age out of school. It is an all-day program with speakers, workshops, and a resource fair with tables of providers of adult services. One of the workshops they attend is on financial and legal planning presented by a financial planner, Sue Sundstrand, and a trust and estates attorney, Gene Taylor. At the resource fair they gather information on adult disability services from the state department of human services, non-profit organizations, and private providers. Four tables particularly interest them. At one they find a non-profit organization that provides training in a facilitated life planning process called PATH. At another table they talk to a representative of a non-profit corporation that operates a community living facility for adults with special needs. At a third table they meet a case manager with the state's Department of Vocational Rehabilitation who explains its job placement services. A fourth table is really intriguing. It is manned by people from the admissions office of Eastern New

Mexico University in Roswell. ENMU-R has a Special Services Department that offers an Occupational Training Program for adults who are cognitively impaired. It is a one-year (fall-spring-summer) program. Two courses of study seem to be interesting possibilities for Angel. One is a set of classes leading to a Veterinary Technician Assistant Certificate because Angel likes dogs. The other is a Certificate in Food Services because Angel likes her job at the senior center cafeteria.

John and Michelle know that the local Down syndrome association has educational programs for parents and for adults with Down syndrome. One of the programs for adults with DS is a life skills class. It is a 32-week program that covers self-advocacy, community participation, independent living, personal health, and safety awareness. There is a class taught by a Certified Public Accountant (CPA) on "budgets and managing your money" designed for adults who are cognitively impaired. Another class is presented by a regional representative of Apple, Inc. in the use of iPhones and iPads and useful applications for people with an intellectual disability. There are also classes in cooking, dating, and art.

John and Michelle decide to attend the National Down Syndrome Congress in the summer. This annual convention offers dozens of workshops for parents of pre-school children, school-age children, teens, and adults. It has a large resource fair with companies and organizations offering a wide range of products and services. It is generally held on the third Friday-Saturday-Sunday in July. They register Angel for the Youth and Adults Conference. While she is attending the Y&A Conference, John and Michelle will attend as many of the workshops as they can and peruse the displays and demonstrations at the resource fair.

John and Michelle belong to an intentional family group of 15 families. It formed when a group of parents of high-school children came together as a social club. There are diverse disabilities among the young adults including autism, cerebral palsy, Down syndrome, Williams syndrome, and Smith-Magenis. The group holds a parent meeting in the summer to plan activities for the coming year. At the meeting, John asks if there are any other families interested in Eastern New Mexico University-Roswell (one is), and if anyone is interested in exploring residential options (six are). John, Michelle, and the parents interested in private residential living (all of them indefinitely waitlisted for state residences) will meet to plan how they will investigate possibilities. They will keep the other families in the group informed of what they're finding.

Over a six-month period into the summer of 2012 John and Michelle have gathered a lot of information and identified many potentially valuable resources. A life plan is beginning to take shape. The most important thing they have concluded is that semi-independent living may be a possibility for Angel.

If it is, they want to make it happen. They plan to take four near-term actions. The first is to attend the National Down Syndrome Congress. The second is to gather a group of friends in the early fall to develop a PATH plan for their daughter. The third is to visit the ENMU-R campus. The fourth, which was prompted by the financial and legal planning workshop at Transitions Day, is to identify someone to be Angel's successor guardian should something happen to them.

John and Michelle schedule a PATH session for their daughter. The participants will be themselves, Angel's brother and sister, Angel's special education teacher, one of the Down syndrome association's life skills program teachers, the parents interested in their daughter attending ENMU-R, the parents of Angel's best friends Sarah and Tracy who are also interested in the three friends living together, and—of course—Angel. (A group of 13 participants for a PATH session is unusually large.) They plan on attending the training class offered by the non-profit organization discovered at Transitions Day and hiring one of its facilitators.

They identify a tentative sequence of steps for Angel's path to independence:

1. Sign up her up for the life skills class and for some of the other courses offered by the Down syndrome association starting in September 2012.

2. In January of 2013, after Angel ages out of school, hire one of the licensed clinical social workers who teaches the life skills class for one-on-one mentoring to prepare Angel to attend ENMU-R.

3. Enroll Angel in the ENMU-R program for the period of September 2013 through the summer of 2014.

4. After she receives her certificate of completion, help her find a job in the fall of 2014.

5. In early 2015 begin planning for an eventual move to an apartment, condominium, or community living facility.

John and Michelle are already court-appointed guardians for their daughter. They have applied for state disability services but Angel is waitlisted with no prospect of receiving any in the foreseeable future. John and Michelle also have wills, a special needs trust, and healthcare directives which should be reviewed because they were prepared a long time ago. The Herreras plan on completing a PATH plan, starting a life skills mentoring program, and coming to a decision on whether to enroll Angel in ENMU-R. With that done, they intend to visit the lawyer and financial planner they met at the Transitions Day workshop to develop financial and legal plans to support their goal that Angel will someday live independently with appropriate support.

Mike Olmstead

Sharon Olmstead's hopes for her son's future are simple—independence, a good job, a home, friends, and maybe marriage. The problem is making these hopes possible. She has a conversation with Mike to find out what he wants. To her surprise, he wants to go to college. Mike knows that going to college is what adults do when they graduate from high school, and he knows that he can study computers and maybe get a job working with them. She fears he does not know what college is like and may not be able to cope with the unstructured environment and pressure for academic performance. She asks Mike how he feels about his job at the computer shop. He wants to continue working there. He likes the work and his co-workers are his friends.

With this start, Sharon begins to explore the possibility of enrollment at a local community college to study computer science. She meets with an intake counselor in the admissions office and learns that the student services office has staff to help students with challenges adjust to campus life. However, Special Student Services is limited to helping with individual accommodations—one-on-one academic mentoring is not offered. The college has a student computer club (which calls itself the Iota Tau Geek Fraternity) which could be a social group for Mike. The college awards a two-year associate degree. If one's academic record is satisfactory, one can transfer to the four-year state university which has a campus in the city. Sharon thinks a four-year baccalaureate degree may be beyond Mike's capability but she likes the option. It is possible to get a job in information technology with a two-year associate degree, but a bachelor of science opens many more doors.

Sometimes in special needs planning, parents get a real break, an unexpected gift that falls out of the sky. Every special needs parent has probably felt that, after all the burdens they have had to shoulder, they deserve to have at least one thing go right. In Sharon's case, a gift from the sky falls when the special services counselor, Ms. Valdez, says, "One of our computer science instructors has Asperger's syndrome. I think Mr. Wyatt would be willing to help Mike develop a plan for his studies and a routine for campus life." (This would be the second sky gift after Mr. Carmody, Mike's high school math teacher.)

Sharon needs to have a support system for Mike to successfully attend college. She decides she wants to bring together some of the people who know Mike to discuss what this might look like. She decides to invite Mr. Carmody, Ms. Valdez, and Ms. Petraglia, the high school psychologist that has participated in Mike's IEPs for the past three years, to dinner. Sharon plans for Mike to participate in the discussion too.

The next problem is affordability. The in-state student cost for tuition, fees, and books is about $4500 per semester. Sharon wants to avoid borrowing money for college in case Mike is unsuccessful earning his associate degree from the community college. She may consider this option if he graduates and continues by enrolling at the state university for a baccalaureate. She plans on Mike living at home, at least initially, and does not need to budget for room and board. She makes this decision not because of cost but so Mike can live in a familiar environment with her support while becoming acclimated to college life. She cannot afford the cost of the community college with her take-home income but she identifies two possibilities for help. One, after consulting with a divorce attorney, she decides to approach her ex-husband about the two of them sharing the cost. He may feel enough loyalty to his son to agree. Or, from a selfish standpoint, he may agree knowing that child support will be terminated if Mike finds gainful employment. The second possibility is a part-time job in Mr. Allen's computer shop if Mike's college schedule can be integrated with a work schedule.

She looks at the possibility of applying for Social Security's Supplemental Security Income (SSI). However, SSI is a program for the poor and Mike's child support exceeds the unearned income allowance for SSI. There are ways around this obstacle, but at this stage in Sharon's investigation, she is not aware of them.

Sharon meets with Mr. Allen, the owner of the shop that employs Mike. She hopes he will be willing to accommodate Mike's college schedule. She believes Mike will be more enthusiastic and committed to college if he does not have to sacrifice his job to attend. Mr. Allen agrees to continue employing Mike in his part-time position, $112 a week for 14 hours for 50 weeks. Mike's work schedule will be integrated with his college schedule.

Sharon and her advisors have decided that a realistic employment goal for Mike is a computer systems administrator position with a medium or large company. The 2010 median salary for these positions, according to the Bureau of Labor Statistics *Occupational Outlook Handbook*, is $46,260, with 80 percent of the jobs paying between $28,300 and $76,970. A systems administrator is responsible for configuring and installing PCs, interoperability with mobile devices, intranet and Wifi operations, computer and network troubleshooting, technology upgrades, system security, and software applications such as office desktop suite, e-mail, file sharing, virtual meetings, PC security configuration, etc. After some social networking, she connects with Mr. Saunders, the IT Director of the state's department of human services. Sharon knows from her library position and from Mr. Carmody that government information technology infrastructures are typically less capable and state-of-the-art than the systems of medium and large corporations. Government employers have difficulty attracting and retaining talent because of lower salary scales than those in private businesses. She approaches Mr. Saunders not with the objective that he would eventually hire her son, but to get his perspective on the types of position that exist in the computer and information technology job markets and the education needed for various types of position. She asks Mr. Saunders to advise her in planning Mike's curriculum.

Sharon now turns to the biggest uncertainty in Mike's future. What will happen to him if something happens to her? She needs two contingency plans. The first is a plan to help Mike achieve and maintain independence. The second is Plan B if the plan for education and employment fails and he needs lifelong disability support. Even with Plan A, she can't be complacent if Mike gets his degree and a good job. Permanent stability for someone with Asperger's syndrome is never certain and it would be unwise to terminate all of his supports. Her initial thought is that if something happens to her, her home can be sold to buy a condominium for Mike with money left over for his support. She owns her home debt-free from the property settlement from her divorce. (For this, she gave up spousal support.) The local Autism Society has a list of attorneys who practice in disability planning. A mother she knows recommends one who set up a special needs trust for her. From advertising, Sharon knows of a national life insurance company that trains some of its agents in financial planning for special needs parents. She plans to meet with one of its representatives about a financial plan for herself and a plan to take care of Mike. She also has learned she needs to consider guardianship for Mike. She will discuss this with the disability attorney.

Sharon now has a preliminary plan of action. The next step is putting the resources in place for Mike's education. She also needs a financial and legal plan for her future and Mike's.

Noelle Williams

It is the spring of Noelle's sophomore year in high school. Robert and Dorothy have agonized over whether their daughter should finish at the local high school or transfer to the state school for the blind. So one day when both are off work they visit the state school, an hour from home. They tour the school, meet staff and students, and gather curriculum materials. Both are very interested in the guidance counseling offered by the school for colleges and careers.

On Sunday evening at the end of the week, they sit down to talk to Noelle. Robert and Dorothy have always been strict and demanding parents but both sense this is their daughter's life and future and that she should have a say in the decision. Like a typical high school student, Noelle does not want to give up her friends, social life, and activities.

Noelle's specialized education plan is coming up in late April. In preparation, Dorothy meets with Noelle's home room teacher at the high school. Ms.

Parks is a conscientious teacher and likes Noelle (who doesn't?), but she lacks specialized training in teaching blind students. An essential skill for the totally blind is Braille. Although the school has obtained a Braille reader and materials, Noelle is not highly proficient because none of her teachers understand the importance of Braille or how to teach the skill. Noelle records classroom sessions and has learned to physically navigate the high school but she has not been given specialized instruction in home management, independent travel in community settings, money management, assistive technology, or skills in independent function such as grocery shopping. Dorothy tries to teach what she can with what she knows, but her knowledge of how to teach her daughter is based on common sense and what she learns from self-study; she has not been shown proven best practices, life management skills, helpful technologies, or teaching strategies for the blind. The meeting for Noelle's education plan is coming up and the parents want a greater focus on their child's preparation for college including independent living on campus.

A few days later, Dorothy has an idea. She drives back to the state school to meet with the director and pleads with him to send a staff member to the school meeting and have someone work with Ms. Parks to design a program for her child. The director is reluctant. The specialty school does not have the resources to offer this assistance to all of the students and schools in the state. A mother's determination wins and he agrees to send one of his staff to meet with the high school staff. Two weeks later, Dorothy drives back to the state school to pick up the assigned staff person and drive him to the meeting. Mr. Vandenbark, a Braille instructor, meets Noelle for the first time and is quickly befriended. He attends the meeting with Ms. Parks and other teachers. One of the outcomes is that he agrees to serve as an advisor to Ms. Parks, albeit by long-distance phone and e-mail. It's the best solution Dorothy and Robert can come up with to keep their daughter in the local school and have expert help for Ms. Parks, Noelle, and Dorothy.

Robert and Dorothy fashion another compromise. The state school has a summer program for students. It offers a residential option for any student who lives more than 30 miles away. The curriculum includes Braille, use of a white cane, home management, assistive technology training, and a class in problem-solving skills. The Williams' are especially taken with the class in problem-solving skills. It dawns on Dorothy that one is not taught the routine of independence but how to be independent. This could be a truly empowering course, teaching someone how to solve for themselves the problems and obstacles they will face in day-to-day living. Although Noelle is not enthusiastic about living away from home for two summers, she accepts that it is the sacrifice that might help make possible her dream of graduating from college.

Higher education is increasingly a prerequisite in this country for professional employment. Dorothy begins to research careers and college programs in music. The high school guidance counselor has typical materials for students but admits he knows nothing about college for blind students. That night, a furious mother, describing the meeting to her husband, says emphatically, "I don't want her to go to blind school. I want her to go to college!" The counselor does make a useful suggestion. He informs Dorothy that the state's Department of Vocational Rehabilitation offers programs for the blind and visually impaired to help them achieve independence and employment.

The meetings and discussions are sobering for the Williams'. How will they ever pay for college? It's not one child's college education but two. Whatever door they can open for their daughter, they want Robert, Jr. to have the same opportunity.

Henry Lowenstein

Craig, Lucy, Jose, and Adam are Henry's small circle of friends. None of them knows much about mental illness or bipolar disorder. Henry naturally feels embarrassed and invaded when they press him on the subject and at Adam's suggestion they invite a family counselor from a family support organization to meet with them so they can learn how to help their friend. Martha Bishop, the counselor, is willing to be an advisory resource and gives them an orientation and literature on bipolar disorder. She is careful not to give medical, psychological, or pharmaceutical advice. She offers practical suggestions from her experience counseling families. The friends learn that bipolar disorder cannot be cured but it can be managed. The four pillars of support are medication, psychotherapy, self-management of one's moods and stressors, and social support. The four can't do anything about the first two, but they can help with the third and can provide the fourth.

Mental health counselors recommend that people with bipolar disorder take five practical actions to manage their mood cycles:

1. Track your mood and stressors on a daily mood chart.

2. Maintain a regular routine, especially a regular sleep cycle.

3. Avoid alcohol and other mind-altering substances.

4. Faithfully take your medications.

5. If you feel a mood cycle starting, contact your psychiatrist or counselor immediately.

Recognizing the signs and stopping a cycle before it starts is critical. Henry's psychiatrist and mental health counselor have gone over these recommendations with him. He has a mood chart and for the most part keeps the entries current. He has a medicinal tray to help him remember his daily medications. Henry generally avoids alcohol consumption. (This can be harder for a person with mental illness than most people realize.) Controlling sleep cycles can be difficult even with the best of intentions. Craig is the one person Henry allows to check how he is doing and the one person who can nag Henry without a lot of pushback. Craig drops in to visit frequently and can do this without creating a sense of intrusion. Craig also has been around Henry enough to sense when his mood is markedly changing.

Henry has Medicare coverage supplemented by Medicaid. Medicaid is crucial because without it Henry could not afford his medications, which cost almost $20,000 per year. Through Medicare and Medicaid he has a physician and a psychiatrist. Henry also receives help from his state's Home and Community Based Services Program for Persons with Mental Illness. Through the HCBS-MI program, which is administered and funded as a Medicaid-waiver program, Henry can get help to stay in his apartment in lieu of the much more expensive institutional care. The program provides in-home services, non-medical transportation, mental health counseling, and an emergency response system. The state's department of human services has partnership agreements with the courts, district attorney offices, and police departments in most of the state's cities and counties to keep mentally ill individuals from being swallowed up in the criminal justice system. Henry has a foundational level of support.

Henry's career aspiration is to become a counselor in mental health. The local community college offers an Associate of Applied Sciences degree in Human Services. The curriculum does not include courses in counseling; counseling is part of a study in psychology which requires a four-year degree. However, credits for the AAS degree are accepted as part of the psychology curriculum if Henry is able to continue his education. The 61 credit-hour Associate of Applied Sciences degree will likely take five semesters of study and cost about $11,000 for tuition, fees, and textbooks. A benefit of an associate degree is that it may open doors to jobs with other employers beyond his current part-time job.

Longer term, Henry wants the stability of owning his own residence. Lucy receives rent assistance from the US Department of Housing and Urban Development (HUD), as does Henry. Their rental assistance comes through HUD's Housing Choice Voucher Program (HCVP), also called Section 8 housing. Housing vouchers can be used for apartment rent or a mortgage subsidy, a possibility Lucy has been considering for herself. As a single mom, she is part of a targeted population for assistance. Henry may have the same option assuming he qualifies for a mortgage.

At this point, Henry has social support, a foundational level of government assistance, and a part-time job. What he wants is a meaningful job helping people, a job that will provide income and a source for self-esteem. The challenge is affordability. The irony in the willingness of these four friends to help him with his college goal is that none of them attended college themselves. We will pick up what happens next when we look at Henry's resource plan.

PART 2

RESOURCE PLANNING

MAKING IT POSSIBLE

CHAPTER 5

IDENTIFY THE SERVICES TO MEET SPECIAL NEEDS

Resource planning includes the care and supports needed to mitigate the effects of a disability, help a person overcome its limitations, and be part of the community. It covers the basic requirements for health, safety, personal care, and assistance to enjoy an appropriate level of autonomy and independence. This chapter addresses taking care of needs related to the disability. Developing a care plan requires an understanding of the needs of the person with the disability, how those needs can be met, and how to obtain services. Once needs are met, higher level goals for an active social life, employment, and independence can be addressed. The plan should identify all of the services required, whether paid for by the state or by the parents. Many of the services are listed in Table 5.1. Because the subject of this book is about creating the best possible life for an adult, I have not addressed pre-school services or services provided in accordance under the Individuals with Disabilities Education Act (IDEA).

There are three thoughts I wish to leave with you in this chapter:

1. A resource plan identifies the enablers for a social life, a safe and comfortable home, a job if employable, and the products and services to mitigate the disability. The first priority is to take care of needs related to the disability.

2. The resources may be government-provided to the extent the person is eligible, or privately obtained and managed to the extent the individual, parents, or family can afford.

3. The needs and capabilities of each individual are unique. Consequently, resource planning must be *person-centered. It should focus on the potential of an individual and not his or her limitations, and it should allow for the highest level of self-determination possible.*

Table 5.1 Disability services that may be required by an individual with special needs

Healthcare
    Medical
    Psychiatric
    Dental
    Vision
    Audiology
    Drugs and self-medication
    Substance abuse

Therapy
    Physical
    Occupational
    Speech
    Respiratory

Psychology

Service planning and management
    Care planning and management
    Case management

Skilled nursing

Personal assistance and supervision
    In-residence care
    Personal hygiene
    Meal preparation and feeding
    Transfer to and from bed, wheelchair, etc.
    Housekeeping and laundry
    Shopping
    Transportation to appointments
    Cognitive impairment supervision

Community access programs
    Adult day care
    Recreation
    Transportation

Training
    Life skills
    Employability skills
    Skills for the visually impaired
    Skills for the hearing impaired

Employment assistance
    Skills and job suitability analysis
    Job training
    Job placement
    On-the-job training
    Post-placement support

Residential services

Assistive technologies and devices
    Hardware/software systems
    Transfer devices
    Surveillance and security
    Motorized wheelchairs
    Devices for the visually impaired
    Devices for the hearing impaired

Home modifications and environmental controls
    Stairmasters
    Wide doors and ramps
    Accessible features and fixtures
    Air quality control
    Sterile environment

Vehicle modifications
    Drivability
    Wheelchair loading

Family respite care

General Considerations

Resource plans will be very different for someone who has a physical disability, a cognitive impairment, or mental illness. It will be different for those mildly, moderately, or seriously impaired.

Those who have mobility or sensory impairment but normal cognitive function may require care for their medical needs and assistive devices and technologies to hold a job, live on their own, and access the community.

Someone with a moderate to severe mental illness will need psychiatric care or personal counseling, probably supplemented by medication, to allow him to live independently and function in the community. The cost of care and medication is a serious problem.

Those who are cognitively impaired have a broad range of needs, including the need to be taught life skills and the need for human assistance to participate safely and fully in the community. This population is also more vulnerable to abuse because the person lacks the self-defense awareness of persons with full mental capacity.

Obtaining services can be a significant problem regardless of the disability. Services may be available from a state or local government but problems are encountered with adequacy, control, quality, and reliability. Alternatively, services may be arranged and paid for by the individual or family but the cost for those moderately or severely challenged make affordability a potential constraint. Typically some level of government assistance will be required by all but the most affluent of families to care for a child with a moderate or severe disability, whether physical, mental, or cognitive.

Care givers, assistants, and companions may be family and friends of family or paid. If professional, they may or may not require specialized training or higher education. When working with service providers who must be professionally trained because of the nature of their service, one should understand how to evaluate the qualifications of people you or your child will work with.

Licenses and professional designations establish minimum qualifications for those who practice in a profession. Licenses are legal permissions to engage in a profession. Licenses are required by law and administered by state regulatory agencies or legally empowered independent bodies like a state bar association. Medicine and law universally require licenses to practice.

Some professions, not regulated by law, are self-regulated by those within the profession. Self-regulatory agencies are independent boards that set standards for ethical behavior, professionalism, and education including continuing education. They administer competency exams to test the professional knowledge of applicants. They award designations and sanction those who violate standards of competency or conduct. For example, the self-regulating body for Certified Financial Planners (CFPs) is the Board of Standards for Certified Financial Planners. It cannot prevent someone from offering financial planning because it lacks the legal authority to do so, but it can stop someone from using the CFP designation.

One can obtain information regarding professional designations by searching Wikipedia on the internet. Meaningful designations have independent boards that set professional standards, establish minimum education requirements, and administer competency exams to practice. If you are a parent of a special needs child, you should do the best you can to evaluate the competency of service providers. Be very aware that "all that glisters is not gold" (Shakespeare, *The Merchant of Venice*, II.vii.65).

Healthcare

Healthcare includes medical, psychiatric, dental, vision, and hearing care and medication. These services are provided or supervised by professionals holding medical degrees licensed through state medical boards. Treating substance abuse comes under healthcare. Substance abuse is not widely recognized as a disability due to societal attitudes but physical addiction can be caused or aggravated by a disability. For example, dependency may develop from the extended use of pain medication. Healthcare services are expensive and affordability and insurance is a major consideration in special needs planning. Those not wealthy enough to pay for services must rely on private health insurance, Medicare, Medicaid, or do without. Not all of the healthcare needs for those with mental illness are covered by private insurers. The policies that do provide some level of coverage often cap reimbursements.

Therapy

Therapy is the physical treatment of a condition or teaching someone how to cope with its effects. Common types of therapy are physical, speech, occupational, and respiratory. Specialists may hold a Certificate of Clinical Competency (CCC) in Physical Therapy (PT), Occupational Therapy (OT), Audiology, or Speech and Language Pathology (SLP). Other designations include the Registered Respiratory Therapist (RRT) and the Certified Rehabilitation Counselor (CRC).

Psychology

This category includes counseling in mental health, behavior, and trauma recovery. Psychological counseling is an important component of a care plan for someone with Asperger's syndrome, autism, or mental illness. Psychologists typically hold professional certifications such as Doctor of Psychology (PsyD), Licensed Mental Health Counselor (LMHC), or Board Certified Behavioral Analyst (BCBA). Some are Licensed Clinical Social Workers (LCSW) or Licensed Master Social Workers (LMSW). In the past a bachelor's degree was sufficient to practice but increasingly a masters or doctoral degree in a specialty is a necessary credential, hence the PsyD and LMSW.

Service Planning and Management

A care manager, as I use the term, plans and manages all aspects of a care plan. He or she may be a parent, family member, or a professional. A care manager manages private pay services and integrates private services with those provided by a state agency or school system. A primary care manager is arguably one of the two most important roles supporting an individual with a disability. (The other is the guardian or advocate.) A case manager is a government employee who administers services provided by a state agency under a Medicaid Home and Community Based Services (HCBS) program or a state human services program. A case manager identifies needs and arranges for services and providers. He or she works with the individual, his parents, or his guardian to develop an Individualized Service Plan. Case managers also oversee the quality and adequacy of services delivered.

An extensive elder care support system has developed to keep frail seniors in their homes. In-home care is less expensive than facility care and most long-term care insurance policies cover in-home nursing and assistance with daily living. The elder care planner is a key part of this system, creating a plan and arranging the services to keep the elder in her home. A frail senior has special needs by definition. Many elder care planners can help parents develop a plan for their child with special needs. Elder care service providers also serve people with disabilities. Professional designations for care managers are the Licensed Clinical Social Worker (LCSW), a Certificate in Clinical Competency (CCC) in a therapeutic specialty, and the Certified Care Manager (CCM) designation. Some care planners hold professional designations in nursing (see below).

Skilled Nursing

This is in-home nursing care, full-time or for designated periods or tasks during the day. Skilled nursing care must be prescribed by a physician for insurance or state service coverage. Among the recognized professional credentials, in descending order of prestige and pay, are the Nurse Practitioner (NP), Registered Nurse (RN), Licensed Practicing Nurse (LPN), and Certified Nurse Assistant (CNA).

Personal Assistance and Supervision

This is in-resident care by someone other than a skilled medical, psychological, or therapeutic professional. Personal assistance is for the routine of daily living—dressing, bathing, toileting, transferring, eating, shopping, meal preparation, housekeeping, transportation, etc. Supervision is custodial care, typically for someone with dementia or a cognitive incapacity who cannot care for themselves. In state comprehensive service residences, personal assistance and supervision is usually staffed full time. With privately arranged care or non-residential services, personal assistance may be full or part time. Professional degrees and designations are not required but may be desirable. State agencies screen service providers and maintain approved provider lists. They do this to protect their clients and prevent waste of public funds. Agencies will share a list of their approved providers with care givers. Most state-approved providers accept private contracts, allowing parents to take advantage of state screening and qualification if private paying.

Another type of personal support is companionship. The duties of a companion may include personal assistance but the primary purpose is social. Companionship is not reimbursed by private insurance, Medicare, Medicaid, or state disability programs. It is a service that parents will have to pay for themselves if deemed desirable or necessary.

Community Access Programs

Community access programs supplement home care by offering social programs and activities in the community. They generally operate during normal work hours. They offer companionship, group activities, meals, and recreation with an emphasis on teaching and enhancing skills for active community participation.

Training

This category includes teaching life and employment skills, and training for the visually or hearing impaired in how to lead as normal a life as possible. Recognized professional designations are the Licensed Clinical Social Worker (LCSW) or a Certificate in Clinical Competency (CCC).

Employment Assistance

Services include an assessment of personal skills, identifying suitable jobs, job search and placement, job training (pre-employment and on-the-job), and post-placement support. Typically, state services are offered through a Department of

Vocational Rehabilitation (DVR). DVRs may limit services in units of time (hours) or duration (days) provided so families may want to consider supplementing its services. There are private employment services and job coaches in most towns and cities. Opening doors to employment is discussed in Chapter 6.

Residential Services

This covers a residence and supports related to the disability. State residential options are typically group homes, host homes, and what are termed "Personal Care Alternatives" in some states. There is a trend in state services away from group homes except to serve those with severe or profound needs or mental illness. The state may offer assistance for those living in private residences such as the parents' home or a home of the adult with a disability. State services are discussed in Chapter 10. Private options are covered in Chapter 7.

Assistive Technologies and Devices

This category includes hardware/software systems, physical aids, and personal computer and smart phone applications. Software systems can be quite sophisticated and expensive. There are PC-based systems with touch screen monitors connected to a home intercom system, capable of providing alerts, voice prompts, and visual instructions. Some offer query capability. Security and surveillance systems are used for personal safety and monitoring. The continued development of assistive technologies may someday open doors to independence for those with moderate cognitive impairment for whom it is not now feasible or safe.

There is a wide range of tools, devices, control systems, and computer technologies to assist those who are mobility or sensory impaired. An obvious example of an assistive device is a motorized wheelchair. There are devices for transferring from a bed to a wheelchair and devices for moving objects. Assistance devices for the visually impaired include devices that can convert text to speech, scanning devices, and digital readers. For the hearing impaired there are amplified phones, voice-to-text converters, alert devices, closed caption televisions, etc. For the physically impaired there are prosthetic devices, controls for quadriplegics, alternative input devices, and remote controls. There are also aids for the speech impaired.

Home Modifications and Environmental Controls

Home modifications are commonly required by the mobility impaired. Modifications include passive features such as ramps, wide doorways, accessibly placed appliances and storage areas, and roll-in showers. There are active systems such as elevators or stair masters to transfer an individual who uses a wheelchair from one level of the home to another. Home modifications include electronic and mechanical actuators and remote controls to open doors and access storage.

Environmental control systems are not commonly encountered but may be necessary for someone with unusual medical conditions such as an immune system deficiency. Those with respiratory problems in areas with persistent smog or air pollution may require an air quality system. Temperature and humidity controls are needed in areas of the country where heat stroke is a danger to the elderly and people with medical problems.

Vehicle Modifications

Vehicle modifications allow one with a physical disability to drive a vehicle and transport a wheelchair. Modified vehicles enable community access and employment. The cost of vehicle modifications can be substantial, well over $10,000.

Family Respite Care

It can be physically and emotionally exhausting to care for someone with a disability, especially if the need is intensive. Respite care is arranging for someone to take over temporarily so parents can get a break. It may be for a few hours to allow the care giver time for personal business or activities. It may be overnight or for a number of days. Government respite care programs provide short-term respite. Parents may privately pay for longer periods if they can afford it. Respite care providers should be adequately trained to meet the needs of the individual.

CHAPTER 6

A JOB ONE CAN BE PROUD OF

A job is a significant part of our lives. It is where we spend most of our waking hours. It is a place where we meet people and form cooperative relationships. It is a place where we can be part of a team, working with others for a common purpose. It is a place where we form friendships and social networks. It is an opportunity, hopefully, to identify with a respected organization and its contribution to the community. Many of us define ourselves by our careers. A job or career is a source of self-esteem, extrinsic and intrinsic reward, and independence. A job is the most visible and definitive way one takes his or her rightful place in the community.

It is no different for those with a disability. Most who are capable of holding a job are eager to do so, take pride in their work, and are conscientious about their responsibilities. It is not uncommon to find that a person with special needs has a higher attendance record than "typical" employees, remarkable since a disability can increase the likelihood of sick days.

We have come a long way since the days when a sheltered workshop was the best that a person with a disability could hope for. We still search for the Holy Grail, a society where people with noticeable impediments can thrive in a competitive employment market. We may never find it. Unemployment levels are distressingly high, especially for those with an intellectual disability. They are the most vulnerable to losing their jobs when the economy contracts. People with disabilities are employed on the margins. There's no denying they often need accommodations. Employment is the least controllable aspect of life planning. You cannot force someone to hire your adult child. You may need more than diligence in finding a suitable job for your son or daughter. You may need a fair amount of luck. Opening the door to a meaningful job is one of the more challenging aspects of special needs planning. And potentially, one of the more rewarding.

There are three things I hope you will remember when you finish this chapter:

1. Don't overlook the importance of empowerment skills for employability.

2. Start planning for employment when your child is in the early teens.

3. College programs structured for students with an intellectual disability can raise the chance of employment and may open doors to more meaningful employment.

Preparing for Employment

The physically disabled, intellectually disabled, and those with mental illness face different employment challenges. People with cognitive impairment face the greatest hurdle because employers doubt that they can function or be productive. Often overlooked are the obstacles those with mental illness face overcoming the stigma and fear of their condition. Opportunities for those with moderate mobility impairment were much enhanced by the Americans with Disabilities Act of 1990, especially the mandated architectural accommodations in public and commercial buildings. Nonetheless, employment is still a challenge for the physically impaired, especially the sensory impaired (deaf, blind, or both). A strategy to open doors for employment must consider not only the obstacles created by the disability, but also the perception of employers and suitability of the job and work environment.

Life skills are the foundation for employability, especially the empowerment skills for communication, appropriate behavior, personal hygiene, people skills, time management, and the ability to function independently. Teaching empowerment skills to a child with an intellectual disability should start early in life. Things don't happen quickly with our children. Early diagnosis, psychological counseling, and behavior intervention increase the chance for long-term employment for those with mental illness, Asperger's syndrome, or autism.

By late middle school or early high school, the special education Individualized Education Plan (IEP) should be preparing the student for employability. Don't fall into the trap of small, easy-to-meet IEP goals that lack long-term purpose or coherence. If you want your child to have a job someday, the IEP should have goals related to employment. Do your homework. Talk to agencies or non-profit organizations that provide employment assistance for people with disabilities. Identify jobs that may be suitable for your child. Talk to employers about expectations of employees and the requisites for success. Some of the necessary skills for employment are:

- appropriate dress
- schedule management and being on time
- ability to master tasks and routines and perform them reliably
- the ability to match clock time to a work schedule

- ability to follow verbal directions

- knowing when and how to seek help

- ability to meet quality expectations

- ability to adapt to variations in routine or circumstances.

How do typical children learn to be adults? They learn by playing. You can see this watching your daughter playing doctor with her dolls, watching your sons organizing a construction project to build a clubhouse, watching your children run a lemonade stand, and so on through myriad activities to try out on a small scale what it's like in a bigger world. Take this concept and think how one can give a special needs child a sense of what it's like to have a job. Create one in your home. Pay the child for the work they do. Open a bank account and accompany your child to the bank to deposit her weekly paycheck in *her* account. Help the child learn responsibility. From my experience, two internal attitudes that parents of a special needs child must fight are passivity and low expectations, especially when it comes to planning for employment.

You have a decision to make when your child is approaching the end of high school at age 18. One option is to continue high school until your child ages out. A second is to enter the Bridges or Transitions program administered by the school's special education department designed to prepare a child for the world after school. Preparation for employment is given major emphasis. The school may have arrangements with local businesses to place special education students in volunteer jobs. These programs are sometimes called SWAP for "The School to Work Alliance Program." A third option is to leave school early for higher education. If the child leaves the school system unemployed, the possibility of employment drops the longer he or she remains so unless positive action is taken. An investment in post-school job training or higher education can markedly increase the chance of long-term employment success, particularly for those with intellectual disabilities.

Public Agencies and Private Employment Assistance

There are state and local government agencies to help people with disabilities find gainful employment. The have names like "Department of Vocational Rehabilitation" (DVR) because most were created to help people with physical injuries. Typical DVR services are:

- individual testing and analysis of employment suitability

- rehabilitation or training to help a person overcome an occupational impediment

- job training

- job placement

- limited cash assistance to buy the tools or equipment

- licensing assistance with regulatory agencies

- limited post-placement support.

There are private employment firms that provide services similar to those of a DVR. Parents turn to them because the school or DVR was unsuccessful placing their child or the parents hope to find more meaningful employment. Private agencies charge a flat fee, ranging from $1000 to $2000, for evaluating an individual's potential for employment and suitable jobs. Some partner with employers to identify skills for potential openings and develop training programs to teach those skills. Training may be delivered in group classes or individualized instruction. The staff time for job search, placement, on-the-job training and post-employment support is billed at rates ranging from $50 to $75 per hour. Total cost for comprehensive job assistance can run from $4000 to $8000.

Parents should meet with the firm's staff after the initial testing and suitability analysis to understand how the company plans to conduct a job search, whether it knows of current openings, the companies it works with, how long the search is expected to take, and how confident the firm is in suitable placement. There are good agencies in this field and some to avoid. Try to check the firm's history of successful placement. Ask for a list of employers who hire its clients. Contact some of the employers and ask about their experiences with the firm and employees it placed. Check the firm's reputation with non-profit advocacy organizations and its record with the Better Business Bureau. Before hiring a firm, have an explicit understanding of the estimated cost or number of hours to be billed. Recognize that fixed fees and firm estimates are impractical in this arena, and success cannot be guaranteed. Avoid financial commitments lacking checkpoints to assess progress with an option to end the engagement.

Job Training and Higher Education

In our society it is widely accepted that education beyond high school is critical to meaningful employment. If this is true for typical children, should it also not be true for people with disabilities who face skepticism about their employability? Those seeking employment in the white-collar world know the importance of a résumé. Two important sections describe the candidate's relevant education and experience. Parents seeking employment opportunities for their child should think about how to help build a résumé. Continuing education after high school adds a credential that can help find a job.

There are four higher education possibilities for people with disabilities depending on the individual's academic ability, employment aspirations, and needs for personal assistance:

- a baccalaureate, four-year degree at a college or university

- an associate, two-year degree at a community college

- a certificate of completion from a vocational, technical, or trade school

- a college certificate program for people with a developmental disability.

Two- and four-year academic programs are for those who are higher functioning. They have academic coursework in addition to independent living courses and employment programs. These programs may not be open to or suitable for those with serious medical or behavioral needs or needs for personal mentoring and education support. However, there are private firms that provide academic mentoring and personal support to enable a student with special needs to attend college. They offer academic and independent living assistance with one-on-one mentoring or mentoring with a low student-to-mentor ratio. The cost of private, individualized support can exceed $25,000. In my community, a company partnered with a local community college offers an all-inclusive educational program which costs about $50,000 per year, one-third of which is the college's tuition, fees, and room and board; with the remainder to cover services provided by the company, including academic mentoring and personal assistance to participate in campus life.

Vocational schools offer training for skilled blue-collar jobs and lower-level white-collar positions. Examples of blue-collar trades are auto mechanic, truck driver, welder, electrician, cook, barber. Lower-level white-collar positions include bookkeeper, clerk, office manager, and administrative assistant. Some vocational schools specialize in training for IT technician positions in computer configuration and repair, phone or television system operations and service, communication network and data center operations, and software configuration and installation. Technology training may be a suitable option for individuals with Asperger's syndrome.

There are over two hundred two-year community colleges and four-year colleges and universities offering certificates of completion in career programs for students with intellectual or developmental disabilities (IDD). Certificates may be offered in:

- plant nursery and grounds keeping

- building janitorial and maintenance

- food services

- senior centers and facilities

- childcare or pre-school programs

- animal care or veterinarian offices

- office management and clerical including necessary computer skills

- copy center and printing.

Certificate programs are typically one-year or two-year. The cost of such college programs including campus room and board is typically $12,000 to $20,000 per academic year (fall-spring) largely depending on whether in-state or out-of-state tuition is charged. Some four-year colleges and universities offer similar programs, but will be more expensive. Many schools offer campus residential options with some limited supervision of students with an intellectual disability. Programs for IDD students carefully pre-screen candidates, the reason many schools claim high success rates in job placement. Pre-screening is part of the application process and includes an evaluation of whether the individual has the skills for living semi-independently in a college environment. The applicant must be capable of self-medication, behavior control, schedule management, and managing personal care and safety. The resource box at the end of the chapter will point you to internet resources to investigate certificate programs for students with intellectual disabilities. The cost of these programs may sound expensive but the pay-off can be quite high. Beyond the benefits of enhanced employability, there are intangible benefits—the independent living experience and the pride of completing a college level program.

The Hardest Challenge—Finding and Keeping a Job

Some parents rely on the school district's transition team to find a job match. Some rely on a state agency. Some hire a private employment assistance firm. A surprising number of parents find the job themselves, networking with friends, talking to firms they do business with, entering stores with "Help Wanted" signs, looking for job postings, cold-calling on potential employers, etc. The active approach takes persistence and luck but it works.

If your child doesn't have an immediate job opportunity, a volunteer position can be a good step in building a résumé for employment. This will probably be with a non-profit organization (perhaps a church) because commercial businesses must comply with fair labor laws. Success in a volunteer position can look as good on a résumé as a paid position. The individual will also acquire a reference for a paid-job opportunity.

Business owners have an advantage. They can hire their son or daughter. The job should have meaningful responsibilities and performance expectations. If a child becomes accustomed to make-work and lax rules, he or she may have difficulty later adjusting to an employer with firm job expectations. Persons with a cognitive impairment may not understand the significant difference between the two circumstances.

If one is looking at a job possibility, pay close attention to suitability. Look beyond the tasks involved and the child's ability to do them. Consider whether there is a good match between his or her limitations and the company and workplace. Much depends on the culture and values of the employer. How committed is the employer to diversity and inclusion? Is the company strongly profit-driven? Does it have a reputation as a good place to work? Is the company willing to make reasonable accommodations for people with disabilities? Co-workers can be an important factor in success. One of the surprises in our daughter's work experience was how her co-workers went out of their way to help her. It doesn't always happen but it's wonderful when it does.

A job's physical or mental demands can tax individual stamina. This is one reason many people with disabilities are limited to part-time employment. My daughter has no obvious physical limitations preventing her from holding a full-time job but experience has shown that four hours is her shift limit. Perhaps the need for continuous concentration and trying so hard to do well is too tiring for her. Maybe four hours for her is like eight or ten hours for me.

There are workplace considerations of pace, structure, supervision, environmental intensity, personal space, and interaction with the general public. Pace refers to the busy-ness of the job place, the need for speed. Can your child keep up? Structure refers to whether duties are predictable and routine or require adaptability and versatility. Many people who are cognitively impaired have difficulty in a dynamic environment. They need routine. It creates a world they can cope with. The child's need for close supervision versus an expectation to perform independently is another suitability factor. The intensity of the workplace refers to sensory stimulation—noise, light, bustle, people density, traffic, distractions, etc. It also refers to whether the workplace is a quiet office, retail store, or outdoors. Does the individual require a closed work space or does he function well as part of a team. Environmental suitability for someone with autism is much different than suitability for someone with Down syndrome. And of course, there's the issue of dealing with the general public and the unpredictable situations they can create.

I once talked to a franchise owner of a well-known hamburger chain. He employed two young men with Down syndrome. Both were conscientious, hard workers. They performed well in the food preparation area but had problems at the front counter. The counter environment was fast-paced and unpredictable.

One problem was the impatience of people in line if the young men were slow. A misplaced order could cause a problem since neither could quickly adapt to the unexpected. There were rude customers and complainers. There were a few who tried to take advantage of them. I felt respect and sympathy for this businessman. Apparently no one had helped him see how the talents of the two young men could best be used and the possible problems. He made a few mistakes, learned, adjusted, and found two good workers.

The point of all this is not to discourage you but to point out the need to assess the fit between the capabilities of the aspiring worker and the demands of the employer and workplace. You have to ask the question, will my child be happy working there?

If your child is starting a new job, especially a first job, take positive steps to enhance the chance of success. The employer is taking a chance too and you want them to have confidence that it will work. If possible, arrange for a job coach to provide initial on-the-job support and monitoring, perhaps hour-for-hour for the first week or two. Talk to the manager and assure them you want to partner with them. Tell them you want to know if they have concerns or problems. A parent should maintain on-going awareness of the job situation and the employer's satisfaction. Retail establishments, especially big box chains, pay low wages and have high manager and employee turnover. Floor and shift supervisors and co-workers come and go. Store general managers and personnel managers change. What may have started out as a promising situation with a supportive store team may not remain so with subsequent managers or supervisors who don't want to bother with an employee that requires attention and support.

If it looks like the job and the individual are a poor match and long-term success is unlikely, consider taking the initiative to terminate. Prolonging a bad situation can adversely affect the next opportunity by destroying the child's self-confidence or desire to have a job. One faces a difficult decision when an employer isn't a good fit but has the only job available.

I leave you with a last thought. There are employers who intentionally hire people with disabilities and conscientiously strive to make it successful. I urge you to do business with the companies that hire our children. Let the owner or manager know why you do business with them. Recommend the company to your friends and neighbors if you can do so honestly. Make sure non-profit advocacy and support organizations are aware of your experience and suggest they make their client families aware. Help the company build a reputation for making a positive contribution to the community. Hiring people with disabilities should be good business and not charity.

Where to Go for More Information

Think College is an initiative of the Institute for Community Inclusion at the University of Massachusetts-Boston. It is an excellent resource for information regarding college certificate and degree programs for aspiring students with intellectual and developmental disabilities. Its website www.thinkcollege. net has information about the college programs, how to prepare, fees and expenses, and financial aid. The website lists 200 community colleges and institutions of higher learning offering programs for those with a developmental disability. Think College's database allows you to search for schools in your area. It is disappointing to note that eight states have no such institutions.

To give you an idea of the range of possibilities, take the links to two colleges. The first is to one of the pioneers: ELSA, for Elmhurst Learning and Success Academy, Elmhurst College, Elmhurst Illinois. ELSA is a four-year program with academic, personal independence, and employment preparation courses. ELSA's website is http://public.elmhurst.edu/elsa. The second example is the Occupational Training Program at Eastern New Mexico University-Roswell, www.roswell.enmu.edu/student-affairs/special-services/occupational-training-program. This is a one-year, fall-spring-summer program that focuses on skills in specific areas of employment.

CHAPTER 7

A HOME OF ONE'S OWN

A home of one's own is a worthy goal for those who have the personal skills, supports, and financial capability to make it possible. It is a home where one has autonomy to manage one's personal and social life and not be under the continuous supervision of parents or the staff of a government agency. A home of one's own is a visible manifestation of independence.

I hope you will remember these things after you finish this chapter:

1. The home may be an apartment; or a house, condominium, or multi-family unit owned by an adult child, her parents, or a special needs trust.

2. If living semi-independently is a possibility, consider the move into a home of one's own when the child is in her mid to late twenties.

3. There are Federal and state or local housing assistance programs for people with disabilities, including help purchasing a suitable property.

4. There must be adequate, on-going support to sustain a stable situation.

Considerations

Living independently or semi-independently is more likely to be a feasible option for someone who is physically disabled or who has a mild or manageable mental illness. Those who have a cognitive impairment or brain injury face a greater challenge. They need more support and probably have lower incomes. Nevertheless, the possibility of a home of one's own should be considered for anyone with a mild to moderate cognitive impairment.

The home may be a rental unit, or a property owned by the child, his parents, or a trust. The individual, parents, or trust bears primary responsibility for rent, purchase, or financing although government housing assistance may be available. The individual may live alone, with a co-resident, or with a live-in care giver.

When our PATH team first met to develop a life plan for our daughter, Meg was asked where she wanted to live. My wife and I were surprised when she said, "I want to live in an apartment with my friends." Meg's best friends are two young women her age with Down syndrome. After the initial surprise I thought, "Well, why not. What child wants to live with her parents all of her life?" Meg has seen her older brother and sister go off to college, get jobs, and strike out on their own. Why not her? Our children's desire for independence is often stronger than we realize if they have limited expressive skills and assertiveness.

Nevertheless, a home of one's own is not for everyone. The lack of necessary life skills or need for significant medical, physical, or personal care may preclude the possibility. Some families cannot afford a private, independent option. Or parents may fear that something will go wrong and they want to personally assure their child's safety and well-being. Sometimes, it is the child with a cognitive impairment who prefers the comfort of the home she has lived in all of her life. She prefers living with those she loves and that she knows love her. People with an intellectual disability are instinctively aware of their vulnerability and prefer the familiar to the unknown. They know the stress of coping with situations at the edge of their abilities and naturally avoid stressful situations. In my experience, about half of the adults with intellectual disabilities prefer the routine and comfort of living with parents. Others want some independence. Each family will need to decide in its own circumstances, with appropriate consideration to the child's wishes, whether the family home, a state residence, or a private residence is the most appropriate situation for their child.

One may ask if there is a difference between parental supervision versus the supervision of a live-in companion or care giver. There is a big difference. Through all of the years of raising a child, parents get accustomed to doing things for him, and the child gets used to having things done for him too. It is not uncommon to see a child blossom into an unexpected level of independence when the parent–child dependency is broken. State residential care is not empowering either. State residential staff impose a high level of supervision to protect their wards. The blossoming into independence is more likely to happen in a thoughtfully planned, private residential setting than in the parents' home or a state residence.

Economics force many families into relying on state residential services. However, families that can afford to take control of their options often want to do so because of concerns for access, quality, control, and reliability of state services. Parents aware of the statistics of sexual molestation and assault may be concerned about the risk in state residences. The risk is certainly not unique to state facilities, though. It happens in the home, in the workplace, in public places, even in churches. However, the risk may be mitigated if parents can control the staffing and monitor the residential situation.

The move out of a lifelong home will happen eventually if the child outlives his or her parents. The only question is when and under what circumstances. If your child may outlive you, consider making the move sooner than later, and with careful planning and not in crisis. The child is more adaptable at a younger age. Physical or cognitive decline can make the transition more difficult in late middle age or old age. Success is more likely if the parents are there to manage the transition, an option they forfeit if they die first. The transition out of a lifelong home will be stressful to a person with a cognitive impairment even if she wants to live independently. Parents should avoid burdening the child with the stress of an unexpected, major change in living arrangements at the same time she is experiencing the trauma of losing a parent. The best time to target a move into a home of one's own is when the child is in her mid to late twenties as a natural transition into independence.

Private Residential Options

The nature of one's disability is a consideration in choosing a setting. For example, people with Down syndrome often prefer roommates or living in facilities with common areas for socializing. People with autism are more likely to prefer personal space. The need for trained staff will be a consideration for those with mental illness, as with those with serious medical challenges.

The most common, most flexible, and financially feasible option is an apartment. Buying a house, a condominium, or a unit in a multi-family dwelling is a possibility for those who can afford to do so. For those with an intellectual disability, there are community living facilities and clustered apartments serving larger numbers of residents. These are facilities with a number of adults living in close proximity with common staff support. It is ironic that as states are increasingly moving away from group homes, more families are turning to units of 6–12 adults, or a campus with multiple buildings or clustered apartments. There are reasons for this trend:

- In many states, the long wait lists for residential services causes parents to take over control of their child's placement.

- Community living offers natural social opportunities for residents.

- There is control over facilities and staffing (although there will be regulations and housing codes to comply with).

- The cost of staffing and other supports can be spread over more families.

Community living entities are almost always set up as corporations to protect individual families from personal liability. Typically the facility is a single building or co-located buildings with four to eight personal units in each. Buildings have common areas for recreation, socializing, meals, and entertainment. Some of the larger communities offer employment in affiliated small businesses such as a plant nursery or print shop. Many have organized community access programs. Units that can be rented or leased allow families more flexibility than individually owned units. There is around-the-clock support staff. However, facilities usually will not take residents with extensive care needs to keep the cost of staff affordable and uniform for all residents. The resident-to-staff ratio is the dominant factor in the economics of these facilities. The cost for an individual unit varies widely, but is likely to be in the $30,000 to $50,000 per year range.

I have found that parents can be very creative in developing residential options for their children:

- One client, a real estate developer who has a daughter with autism, bought a quadriplex (four units). His daughter lives in a ground floor unit with her care giver next door. The two upstairs units are rented to pay the care giver's wages.

- Four families, each having a child with autism, bought a quadriplex for their children and built a mother-in-law apartment for the care giver. The families formed a limited liability company to buy the property and hire the care giver.

- One family bought a boarding house and advertised in local non-profit newsletters for renters with disabilities. The hope was to attract residents with complementary disabilities to minimize the cost of staff. The plan was not achieved because there wasn't the hoped-for diversity among applicants, but the concept was sound.

Home Ownership

This is the ultimate home of one's own. Home ownership is more likely for someone physically disabled or with mental illness capable of full-time employment than for someone with an intellectual disability with greater need for support and more constrained finances. The property can be owned by parents, by a third party special needs trust, by the individual with a disability, or by a first party trust. (See Chapters 13 and 19 for special needs trusts.)

Trust ownership is the most common form of ownership, particularly if the house is purchased with parents' money. The house may be bought by parents and transferred to the trust or the trust can purchase the property. If the parents finance the purchase with a mortgage, the mortgage holder must approve the property transfer to the trust and the trust will have to qualify for and assume the mortgage. Alternatively, a trust can purchase a property or finance the purchase. If the child is cognitively impaired and vulnerable to financial exploitation, trust ownership provides more protection. A trust should charge a reasonable rent to the beneficiary to prevent a reduction in SSI. (See Chapter 9 for an explanation of SSI and the In-Kind Support and Maintenance rule.) Make sure the insurance company knows the house will be trust-owned as a different type of property insurance policy is required. If the wrong policy type is purchased, the property is not insured and the error may not be discovered until the trustee has a claim denied.

An adult with a disability may own the property. Certainly, this option has the advantage of pride and self-esteem. A home can be purchased by an individual with adequate income or assets, with or without assistance from others. She may have income from a full-time job, or assets from an inheritance, lawsuit damages, or prior employment. If a person individually owns a mortgaged home, a special needs trust can make mortgage payments on her behalf. This can be an important consideration in qualifying for a mortgage. If a person has a court-appointed guardian, individual purchase is precluded because the individual is legally incompetent to contract. If the person wishes to maintain Medicaid eligibility, there are legal considerations (reviewed in Chapters 9, 13, and 19). You should consult with an attorney if you are considering individual ownership and wish your adult child to be eligible for Medicaid or state disability services.

Government Rental and Home Ownership Assistance

The US Department of Housing and Urban Development (HUD) assists the elderly, people with low incomes, and people with disabilities to afford housing in the private housing market. This is the Housing Choice Voucher Program (HCVP), more commonly known as the HUD Section 8 Voucher Program. Vouchers are funded by HUD and the program is administered by state and local public housing authorities (PHAs). To be eligible for a voucher, individual or family income cannot exceed 50 percent of the median for the metropolitan area, with 75 percent of the assistance targeted to people with incomes less than 30 percent of median. There is no asset limit for eligibility, but HUD counts the return on assets as income in determining eligibility and the amount of assistance. Local PHAs have wide discretion in administering the program to reflect local housing needs.

The dollar amount of the voucher is the difference between a local housing payment standard and the individual's or family's required payment. The payment standard is the cost of a suitable, moderately priced rental in the local market. The individual or family required payment is 30 percent of total income. To illustrate, suppose a three-bedroom apartment in the community for a family of four typically rents for $900 per month. This is the payment standard. Suppose the family income is $18,000, or $1500 per month. The required family contribution is 30 percent of $1500 or $450 per month. The voucher will be $450 (the $900 payment standard less the $450 required family contribution). The rental unit must meet HUD standards for adequate housing and the landlord must agree to participate in the program. HUD pays the landlord directly and thus the voucher is not counted as income for purposes of SSI or Medicaid eligibility. There will be restrictions on who can live with the person receiving assistance but a live-in care giver is permitted a person with a disability.

In the 1990s HUD broadened the HCVP rental assistance program to allow vouchers to be used for mortgage payments. The home ownership program is for first-time home buyers. The voucher is computed in the same way as for rentals, equaling the difference between the local payment standard and the required family contribution. If an individual or family has received rental assistance for one year, the voucher can be used for mortgage payments. Mortgage payments can be greater than the local payment standard and greater than 30 percent of income depending on the amount borrowed. The purchase price of the home or the mortgage payment is irrelevant to the value of the voucher. HUD sets an upper limit on mortgage payments for program participants. The reason is obvious: to protect the individual or family from a mortgage they can't afford. As with rentals, the property must meet Federal housing standards. An inspection will be required and substandard units must be repaired or improved prior to occupancy. One problem with HUD assistance is the limited availability of vouchers. Not all PHAs participate in the home ownership program.

Some states and local housing authorities offer mortgage assistance for eligible individuals and families. The mortgages are usually 30-year fixed with below market interest rates. One can obtain a supplemental loan for renovation to bring the property up to HUD standards or make it suitable for a person with a disability—for example, a stair master for someone using a wheelchair. A supplemental loan can also be made for down payment assistance. The total amount one can borrow will be limited by the income required to qualify. The borrower needs to have an acceptable credit score, typically a FICO score of 620 or above. It is also common to require the borrower to make some of the down payment, usually in the range of $750 to $1000. The low interest loans are financed by bonds issued by the housing agency and are bought by investors who get tax breaks on the interest income. The tax breaks make it possible for the bonds to carry lower interest rates and still attract investors. The lower interest paid to bondholders allows the housing authority to offer its clients a lower mortgage interest.

There will be an upper income limit to be eligible for assistance. The limit will depend on family size and the economics of the area housing market. The upper limit will be greater for large cities than for rural communities. The agency that administers the program sets the limits for its area. For an individual with a disability, the upper income limit will likely be $30,000 to $60,000 depending on the housing market. In some expensive areas with less generous assistance programs, people with low incomes or disabilities will be priced out of the market. There is no fixed lower income limit but qualifying for a loan sets a floor around $20,000. All sources of income are considered, including distributions from a special needs trust.

Orchestrating all of the elements of buying a home with government assistance is a complicated undertaking. Many people will not be able to navigate the system alone and almost certainly people with a cognitive impairment will need help. One must understand the eligibility requirements, assistance available, how to apply, how to qualify for a mortgage, and compliance with property standards. One must find a suitable home to purchase, arrange for an inspection, and make improvements or repairs required by the inspector. If the person is disabled, the home may require modifications such as those necessary for full accessibility for a person in a wheelchair. It is best if one works with a real estate broker and a mortgage broker who understands both HUD's Section 8 Voucher Program and local mortgage assistance programs. The system is so complicated that many states have a non-profit organization to help people with a disability buy a first home. These non-profits offer education, budget counseling, referrals to qualified and ethical mortgage and real estate brokers, help with the applications, and help obtaining approvals.

Maintaining a Stable Situation

It is cause for celebration when an adult with special needs makes a successful transitioning to an independent residence. However, success may not be sustainable without adequate support. People, property, and circumstances change with time. Sometimes these changes go unnoticed except over long periods of time, and what began with promise deteriorates into an unsafe or substandard situation. The circles of support described in Chapter 2—family, friends, and professionals—can provide a safety net to keep the individual in a comfortable apartment or home.

There are on-going costs in a private residence. These costs must be estimated and budgeted, and there must be adequate income or support to pay for them. In a rental residence, the on-going costs will be the rent, utilities, and renters insurance. The budget should also include repairs and periodic replacement of furniture, appliances, and household items. With a purchased property, you need to budget for:

- principal and interest on the mortgage

- home owners insurance and property taxes

- home owners association (HOA) fees

- utilities

- maintenance and repairs, including major renovations such as a roof replacement, painting, or carpeting

- replacement of household items, dry goods, electronics, and furniture

- contract services, including lawn care and snow removal

- monthly fees for a home security system or property management.

The support team should monitor socioeconomic changes in the neighborhood such as increasing crime rates and a proliferation of abandoned properties. People with disabilities are particularly vulnerable in unsafe neighborhoods. The team should watch for deterioration in the individual's medical, mental, or cognitive condition. The level of support may need to be increased to offset the loss of skills or function or the situation may need to be terminated for safety.

Legal Considerations

Difficult issues arise in special needs planning when different domains of law intersect. Social Security, Medicaid, Federal Housing, and the Internal Revenue Code are not harmonized. Who owns the home and the form of title are important considerations. Having a third party special needs trust own the property works well under Social Security and Medicaid regulations but public housing assistance is only available to individuals and families. HUD defines income differently than Social Security or Medicaid. HUD counts regular payments to third parties made by a special needs trust (a mortgage payment, for example) as income to the housing assistance recipient. This rule can eliminate eligibility by increasing countable income, and it increases the required individual contribution, reducing the voucher's value.

If the individual has a large sum of money, using the money to purchase a residence and spending down to less than $2000 cash can enable the person to qualify for SSI and Medicaid. One is converting cash, which is countable for eligibility determination, into a personal residence which is not. There will be a Medicaid lien on the property, but a home purchase usually makes sense in this instance especially if the individual is young and likely to live in the home for a long time.

If the property is owned by a first party special needs trust, there will likely be a Medicaid lien payable upon sale or transfer of the property. There are, however, exceptions to this rule. (There are always exceptions in complex regulations.) One must obtain legal advice regarding how (or if) one may qualify for an exception. In some states (California, for example), the home with a Medicaid lien can be transferred to another individual who is disabled without triggering Medicaid repayment. However, the lien stays attached to the home, following it to the new owner.

If the home is owned by the individual, he should have a will to transfer the property to an heir at his death unless the property is owned with a spouse as joint tenants with right of survivorship. If the home is owned by a special needs trust, the trust should have a remainder beneficiary to whom the property transfers or who receives the sale proceeds. However, a Medicaid lien will have to be discharged before the property can transfer or sales proceeds are distributed.

Federal and state laws seem to begrudge the public assistance provided to the elderly, blind, and disabled. There are malicious traps for the unwary. If you are considering the purchase of a residential property for your child with special needs, you should consult with local housing authorities and obtain competent legal counsel regarding home ownership and its effect on government assistance. Nonetheless, one should not underestimate the pride and self-esteem felt by an adult with special needs living in his or her own home. If affordable and with adequate support, it is a practical goal.

Where to Go for More Information

The website of the US Department of Housing and Urban Development is http://portal.hud.gov/hudportal/HUD. Under "Topic Areas" at the top of the home page, choose "Housing Choice Voucher Program (Section 8)." You can search the internet to find the public housing authority which administers housing assistance in your area.

Non-profit organizations that serve the special needs community may be able to refer you to community living facilities in your state. Many families across the US are trying to create options in their areas. If a community living option appeals to you and you are working with others to establish a facility, consider the model created by Specialized Housing, Inc. in Brookline, MA, one of the oldest of the community living entities in the nation. SHI's website is http://specializedhousing.org. You can purchase a handbook that describes its history, business model, and operation by clicking on the "Buy Our Books" link. The book is *Passport to Independence: A Manual for Families* (Specialized Housing 2010).

CHAPTER 8

UNDERSTAND THE BASICS OF SOCIAL SECURITY AND MEDICARE

There are three types of public program important to the elderly, blind, and disabled. These programs are established, funded, and administered by either the Federal government or a state. (Some county and municipal governments have limited programs.) The architecture of government programs for people with disabilities is shown in Figure 8.1.

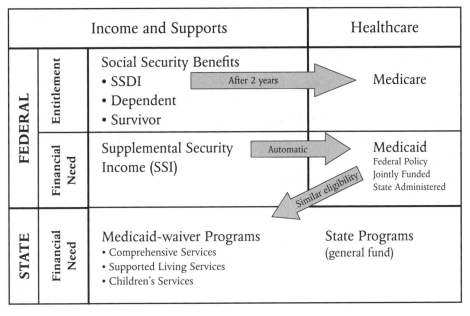

FIGURE 8.1 FEDERAL AND STATE PROGRAMS FOR PEOPLE WITH DISABILITIES

There are two types of program: entitlement and needs-based, also called means-tested. An entitlement program is an insurance program. Means-tested programs exist to care for the poor. There are two Federal entitlement programs: Social Security for income and Medicare for healthcare. There are two Federal means-tested programs: Supplemental Security Income (SSI) for income and Medicaid for healthcare. SSI is administered by the Social Security Administration. Medicare is managed by the Centers for Medicare and Medicaid Services under the US Department of Health and Human Services. Medicaid and state "Medicaid-waiver" programs adhere to Federal policies, are jointly funded by the Federal government and the states, and are state-administered. Some states establish and fund their own disability programs, usually services for children or assistance to parents so they can continue to work while their child receives care. The two Federal entitlement programs, Social Security and Medicare, are the subject of this chapter. SSI and the Federal Medicaid are described in Chapter 9. Medicaid-waiver programs are covered in Chapter 10.

There are three thoughts you should take away from this chapter:

1. Social Security and Medicare are entitlement programs; your child is entitled to benefits because you or your child paid Social Security and Medicare taxes.

2. Social Security's definition of a disability is very narrow and includes an earnings test.

3. A person who has received Social Security Disability Insurance payments for 24 consecutive months is eligible for Medicare.

"Entitlement" to a Social Security benefit means one is entitled to benefits because one paid taxes, or is a dependent or survivor of a retired, disabled, or deceased parent who paid Social Security taxes. (There are other eligibility criteria.) Needs-based or means-tested programs are for those who essentially live in poverty: poor families with children, the poor elderly, and the disabled. There are limits on the income or money one can have and be eligible for means-tested program assistance.

The debate over entitlement programs and programs for the poor is becoming intense because of the national deficit. It is colored by misconceptions and misrepresentations. The stakes are high for people with disabilities. To become informed in the debate, one should know the numbers that make up Federal government expenditures, also called outlays, in the Federal budget. The budget enacted by the United States Congress for fiscal year 2012 (ending October 31, 2012) appropriated expenditures summarized in Table 8.1. There are two program categories: discretionary and mandatory. Discretionary programs are subject to annual Congressional authorization and fiscal appropriation. The budgets for executive branch cabinet agencies such as the Department of Commerce are discretionary budgets. Mandatory programs are established by law and the resulting outlays are mandatory in accordance with the law. Social Security and Medicare are examples of mandatory programs. One thing often not mentioned in the debate is that Social Security, Medicare, SSI, and Medicaid are not the only mandatory programs. Federal employee retirement and healthcare benefits, military veterans' benefits, farm subsidies, and some smaller programs are also classified as mandatory. Bold font in the table indicates mandatory programs or groupings of programs.

Table 8.1 Federal government expenditures as enacted, FY 2012

	Outlays ($ billions)	(Notes)
Discretionary National Security	868	Department of Defense, Homeland Security, Nuclear Weapons (DOE), National Intelligence Programs, Overseas Contingency Operations (Afghanistan, Pakistan, Iraq, other)
Mandatory programs other than Social Security and Medicare	**746**	Federal employee retirement and retiree healthcare, veterans benefits, farm subsidies, other
Social Security	**725**	OASDI—Old Age (Retirement), Survivors, and Disability Insurance benefits
Medicare	**478**	
Discretionary other than National Security	451	All other Federal departments, agencies and administrations discretionary expenses
Medicaid	**255**	Federal only, excludes state expenditures (State expenditures were $126bn in FY2010. *Source:* Kaiser Family Foundation)
Interest on the National Debt	225	
Supplemental Security Income (SSI)	**48**	
Total outlays	$3796bn	Total deficit: $1327bn (35% of expenditures)

Source: Office of Management and Budget, www.whitehouse.gov/omb/budget, see Table S-5 et al.

Some ideologically driven parties to the national debate have managed to redefine the word "entitlement" as a welfare program. This is false. Entitlement programs are social insurance programs. The insurance benefits were "bought" by citizens by paying taxes, similar to the way people buy private insurance with their premiums. One can argue that the benefits were mispriced but this is irrelevant in the same way that an insurance company that misprices its policies cannot avoid paying valid claims. Moreover, specific benefits were promised when the taxes were paid. This is often overlooked in the debate. Reducing benefits for which one has already paid is breaking a contract. Private employers are forbidden by law to reduce the pension benefits already earned by employees. They can reduce benefits for future contributions or years of service, but they may not reduce the benefits earned for past contributions and years of service.

Another factor often ignored in the debate is that Social Security still collects more in taxes than it pays in benefits. The money in the "bank" (i.e. past surpluses in the Social Security trust funds) that should have been available for future benefits was systematically looted by politicians to pay for tax cuts and discretionary programs, including a series of wars. One could argue that the money expropriated from the trust funds for other political purposes should be repaid first before we restructure entitlement programs for the future.

Social Security Disability, Dependent and Survivor Benefits

Social Security provides retirement, disability, dependent, and survivor benefits to those who pay Social Security taxes, also called FICA (Federal Insurance Contributions Act) taxes. The benefits are non-linearly proportional to the amount of taxes paid, meaning that lower wage-earners will receive a higher percentage benefit. Social Security benefits are also called OASDI benefits for Old Age, Survivors and Disability Insurance. It covers most individuals employed by private employers and self-employed persons. Federal, state, and local government employees are usually covered by a government retirement plan such as the Federal Employee Retirement System (FERS). Eighty-eight percent of individuals who pay FICA taxes have earned enough work credits for full coverage, though not necessarily maximum benefits. As of September 2012, over 56 million people were receiving a Social Security benefit. There is no question that this number will increase dramatically as the baby-boomers retire. (This is what the accumulated money in the Social Security and Medicare trust funds would have covered had it not been diverted for other purposes.)

Table 8.2 shows the make-up of Social Security beneficiaries and the average monthly payment for various categories. Social Security outlays are not large because of generous payments; they are large because of the large number of beneficiaries. It's useful to compare monthly average Social Security payments with the National Poverty Guidelines published by the United State Department of Health and Human Services, shown in Table 8.3. The National Poverty Guideline for an individual in the contiguous 48 states was $931 per month in 2012, and will be $947 in 2013 if the cost of living adjustment is 1.7 percent. A look at the average payments for disabled workers and their families shows how painful the national fiscal dilemma is. There is not a lot of margin to cut the Social Security Disability Insurance benefit without inflicting economic hardship on many. The numbers shown are averages—half of the payees receive smaller payments.

Table 8.2 Social Security benefits by class of recipient (September 2012)

	Recipients (thousands)	Average monthly benefit
Retirement		
Retired workers	36,506	$1237
Spouses	2286	613
Dependent children	600	605
Survivors of deceased workers		
Widow(er) and parents	4215	$1163
Children	1874	784
Widowed mothers and fathers with child in their care	153	888
Disabled workers and families		
Workers	8786	$1111
Spouses	164	299
Children	1863	330
Supplemental security income recipients	8247	$518

Source: Social Security Program Factsheet, www.ssa.gov

Table 8.3 Estimated 2013 National Poverty Guidelines (annual $)

No. in household	48 states and DC	Alaska	Hawaii
1	11,360	14,207	13,079
2	15,387	19,242	17,706
3	19,415	24,276	22,333
4	23,442	29,310	26,961
5	27,469	34,344	31,588
6	31,496	434,362	36,215

Source: Federal Register Notice (Document Number 2012-1603) January 26, 2012
CY 2012 numbers with 1.7 percent adjustment for 2013
US Department of Health and Human Services

I will focus on Social Security Disability Insurance (SSDI) and dependent and survivor benefits here. It is disability income and dependent and survivor benefits that are relevant to individuals with special needs and their families. One must understand Social Security's definition of a "disability" because it is very restrictive. One must satisfy both medical and income criteria. The disease, disorder, or injury must be expected to last for more than 12 months or result in death. If one is likely to recover or be successfully rehabilitated within one year, Social Security does not consider one to be disabled. This is a major reason so many applicants are denied benefits. A medical or physical condition must be so debilitating that one is not able to work in a gainful job. The Social Security definition of a gainful job is called a Substantial Gainful Activity (SGA), which is employment with earnings of $1040 per month in 2013 or $1740 if blind. It doesn't matter whether you worked or not—you cannot have been *able to work* because of the medical condition. The SGA is roughly equivalent to earnings in a 33 hour per week job at the Federal minimum wage ($7.25 per hour). The SGA is indexed to inflation measured by the National Average Wage Index.

To be eligible for an SSDI benefit, one must have paid Social Security taxes for a minimum number of work credits. In 2013, one earns one work credit for taxes paid on $1160 in earnings, up to a maximum of four credits in a year. This figure is indexed to inflation. The required minimum number of credits varies according to one's age when becoming disabled. If disabled before age 24, one only needs six work credits. Because the wage required to buy a credit is quite low, equivalent to 160 hours per quarter at minimum wage, a child with a disability, working part-time, may be able to earn enough credits to qualify for an SSDI benefit on her own work record.

How do you find out if you are eligible for a benefit and how much the benefit might be? The Social Security Administration mails a Personal Earnings and Benefits Estimate Statement (PEBES) to eligible individuals annually. The statement shows the earnings on which you paid FICA taxes by year and an estimate of your retirement, disability, and family benefits. It also shows if you are eligible for Medicare. If you have a dependent child, your PEBES will show your child's benefit if you retire, die, or become disabled. If you are entitled to a government pension in addition to Social Security, some of your benefit will be reduced by the Windfall Elimination Provision which is too complicated to address here.

A child disabled before age 22 and unmarried is eligible for a dependent payment if a parent is receiving either Social Security retirement or disability payments. The child is entitled to a survivor benefit if a Social Security eligible parent dies. If the disabled child marries a non-disabled person, he or she loses the dependent or survivor benefit. The child's survivor benefit is proportional to the parents' full retirement benefit they could have earned had they not died. There is an important implication to the requirement that a parent must be receiving a Social Security benefit or was eligible for a benefit at death: a disabled child will not be eligible for a Social Security dependent or survivor benefit as long as both parents are alive and neither receives a Social Security check. However, the child may be eligible for SSI (see Chapter 9).

The child with a disability receives dependent and survivor benefits only until age 18, or 19 if continuing as a full-time student in high school. If the child remains disabled, he or she can continue to receive benefits on a parent's work record as an SSDI payment for an "adult disabled since childhood." The significance of the distinction between an SSDI benefit versus a dependent or survivor benefit is Medicare. Once the adult disabled child receives SSDI for 24 consecutive months, he or she is eligible for Medicare. Dependent and survivor benefits do not establish Medicare eligibility.

Social Security has programs and incentives to help a disabled person return to work. Many of these incentives were created under the Ticket to Work and Work Incentives Improvement Act, or TTW for short. Social Security allows a trial work period (TWP) of up to nine months for people returning to work. During this period, the person continues to receive disability payments while working. If the person is unsuccessful returning to work, his or her benefits continue. If successful, the disability payments made during the trial work period do not have to be repaid. Another Social Security support allows earnings to be offset by Impairment Related Work Expenses (IRWE). This can mean the difference between one's income being above or below the SGA level to qualify as disabled. A PASS (Plan for Achieving Self-Support) allows an individual to set aside some of their wages to allow him or her to obtain vocational training, education, or a business start-up allowance. The income set aside under a PASS plan does not reduce SSI payments nor count toward the SGA. These programs have complex provisions. To obtain information on how they work, get the publication, *The Red Book*, from the SSA website. The 2012 version is publication 64–030.

Medicare

There are four Medicare benefits, called Part A, B, C, and D coverage. Part A covers care in hospitals, skilled nursing facilities, hospices, and home healthcare for those receiving occupational therapy. Part B covers doctors, outpatient care, home healthcare assistance, and a variety of other services. Part C is Medicare's equivalent of a Health Maintenance Organization (HMO) or Preferred Provider Organizations (PPO) plan. Part D covers prescription drugs.

If one has paid Medicare taxes and earned the necessary work credits, Part A coverage is free. One may buy Part A coverage if one has not paid Medicare taxes. One must pay a premium for Part B coverage with higher income earners paying higher premiums. One pays for Part C coverage based on a complex set of rules. One also pays for Part D coverage with higher income enrollees paying higher premiums.

There are only three exceptions to the Medicare "eligibility at age 65" rule. One can enroll at any age if one has amyotrophic lateral sclerosis (Lou Gehrig's disease) or end-stage renal disease (kidney failure). The third exception is significant for people with disabilities: if one has been eligible for SSDI for 24 consecutive months, one is eligible for Medicare. The term "has been eligible for" is significant. One does not need to have actually received benefits. If one was denied disability by Social Security and wins an appeal, the 24-month count started when the person should have received the first payment. Since a child cannot get SSDI until he or she is 18, the earliest age of Medicare eligibility is age 20.

One can be eligible for both Medicare and Medicaid. For dual-eligibles, Medicare is the primary insurer with Medicaid supplementing coverage. Private insurers offer Medigap insurance for things Medicare does not cover. People with disabilities who receive Medicaid have little need for Medigap insurance because Medicaid covers such a broad range of services. If one is eligible for Medicaid, Medicaid will generally pay for out-of-pocket medical expenses and Medicare deductibles, and co-insurance. Part B and D premiums may also be paid. Because Medicaid is state-administered within broad Federal guidelines, the rules are different from state to state. You should obtain the rules for your state.

Where to Go for More Information

The Social Security Administration has an excellent website at www.ssa. gov. There are numerous publications one can download, and most have a Spanish language version. Most of the publications are clearly written, no small feat for such a complicated system. Hardcopy publications are available in Braille, audio CD, or large type in most cases. The site's search engine works reasonably well. The Center for Medicare and Medicaid Services has information on Medicare at www.cms.gov but recent site redesigns have made it harder to find information, and the search engine does not work nearly as well as the SSA's. The Medicare publication that you will find helpful is *Medicare & You* (current year's version). The book is mailed to Medicare recipients annually.

The best book on Social Security I have found is *Social Security: The Inside Story, an Expert Explains Your Rights and Benefits* (Landis 2012). It explains the program comprehensively, logically, and in easy to understand language. It has a chapter on Medicare. It includes numerous examples to illustrate how individual and family benefits are determined. It also has a helpful guidance to help individuals decide on when to file if wishing to maximize lifetime family benefits.

Nolo is a major publisher of law books for the general public. Its more popular books are usually updated at roughly two-year intervals. Two Nolo books describe Social Security's eligibility requirements, application procedures, documentation requirements for applications, and appeals procedures. The two books I recommend are:

- *Social Security, Medicare & Government Pensions* (Berman and Matthews 2012)

- *Nolo's Guide to Social Security Disability: Getting and Keeping Your Benefits* (Morton 2012).

The second book is especially helpful with guidance for completing applications, with illustrations of completed forms. The book has a chapter for each of the 14 categories of diseases and disorders contained in the regulations, the listed conditions within each category, and the regulatory language for assessing the severity and residual functional capacity for each listing. This book may be very helpful to parents whose child has an uncommon condition with uncertain eligibility. Knowing how the condition will be assessed for eligibility can help a parent identify and assemble the documentation for an application or decide whether to hire an attorney.

CHAPTER 9

UNDERSTAND THE BASICS OF SUPPLEMENTAL SECURITY INCOME AND MEDICAID

More than eight million people who are 65 or older, blind, or disabled with low income and few assets receive Supplemental Security Income (SSI) monthly payments. SSI is administered by the Social Security Administration and is a program for the poor. Medicaid pays for the healthcare and long-term care of nearly 60 million Americans in defined at-risk populations with low income and assets. Medicaid is state-administered and there is variation in its operation from state to state. Because they are means-tested programs, both have financial asset limits to qualify for benefits. Medicaid has an income limit set by the states. SSI does not have an income limit *per se*, but instead sources of income reduce the payment based on a formula shown later.

Income for eligibility purposes is defined very broadly. Almost all money that passes into a person's wallet or bank account is considered income, including gifts from family. Income also includes anything that can be easily converted to cash such as a pre-paid gift card. Items of monetary value not considered income include tax refunds, low-income energy assistance, low-income housing assistance, food stamps, and payments made by others to third parties on behalf of the individual. There are over 50 items not counted as income or given designated treatment but most affect few people. (An example is Agent Orange settlement payments.) A Social Security publication lists the exceptions to the broad definition of income.

Assets are also defined broadly. Basically an asset is the cash in one's wallet or assets in a financial account at the end of the month. Countable assets do not include household items, personal possessions, one automobile, the home one lives in, a burial plot, and other items listed in the regulations. Collectibles that can be sold and converted to cash, such as jewelry, are counted. The home one lives in is subject to important restrictions covered in Chapter 7. *An individual cannot have more than $2000 in countable assets to qualify for SSI or Medicaid. The couple limit is $3000. These numbers are not indexed for inflation.* To put it starkly, one has to live in poverty to receive SSI. Medicaid's rules for couples, if one spouse requires institutional care, are complex but the general policy is that Medicaid covers only people who cannot afford healthcare.

Key points to take away from this chapter are:

1. SSI and Medicaid are means-tested programs for the poor. There are limits to the income and assets one can have and qualify.

2. Parents should consider applying for SSI for their child when he or she turns 18.

3. The $2000 asset limit for SSI and Medicaid eligibility dominates special needs planning.

Supplemental Security Income (SSI)

The maximum Federal SSI monthly payment, called the Federal Benefit Rate (FBR), is $710 per month for an individual and $1066 for a couple (2013). The FBR is indexed to inflation. Some states, typically those with a high cost of living, supplement the Federal payment. There is no income limit *per se* to be eligible for SSI. Instead, payments are reduced according to the following formula:

SSI Monthly Payment =
FBR−(Unearned Income less $20)−50% of (Earned Income less $65)

SSI is reduced by one dollar for every dollar of unearned income less a personal allowance of $20, and by 50 percent of one's wages after an allowance of $65. Unearned income includes most income except wages or self-employment earnings. A person can receive SSDI and SSI in the same month but the SSDI is considered unearned income and reduces SSI dollar for dollar. The income one can receive and be eligible for SSI depends on the mix of earned and unearned income.

There is a basic government policy at work here. It is government policy to support a person with a disability at the poverty line. Needs-based programs are designed to meet an individual's basic needs for healthcare, food, and shelter. Consider the numbers. The National Poverty Guideline for an individual is $947 per month (Table 8.3). The 2013 maximum Federal SSI payment is 75 percent of this number. What makes up the difference? For some it may be food stamps, low-income housing, or low-income energy assistance.

Table 9.1 shows an example of an SSI calculation for a hypothetical situation. John is hypothetical but the numbers are typical. Note that John's total income is $951 in the example, $4 above poverty level. The government has done what it set out to do. The combination of John's Social Security Disability and his SSI supports him at the poverty line. Public assistance is not generous. John has little to celebrate, and little to celebrate with.

Table 9.1 Example of an SSI payment calculation

John is receiving an SSDI benefit of $361 per month (unearned income) and holds a 12 hour per week job that pays the Federal minimum wage of $7.25 per hour. He worked 52 hours and was paid $377. What was his SSI payment and total income? John's state is one of the 32 that does not supplement the Federal SSI payment.

SSI benefit calculation		Total income	
Federal Benefit Rate	$710	Job	$377
Reduction for SSDI $361–$20	-341	SSDI	361
		SSI	213
Reduction for earnings ($377–$65) × 50%	-156	Total	$951
SSI payment	$213	*Note:* Poverty level for individual = $947	

There are two important SSI rules that one must understand: the "Deeming" rule and the "In-Kind Support and Maintenance" rule.

Let's start with the "deeming" rule. Parents have a legal responsibility to support a biological or adopted minor child. Federal regulations define a minor as someone under the age of 18. Consequently, parents' income and assets are "deemed" (counted) as the child's if he or she is 17 years old or younger. A minor disabled child will not be eligible for SSI unless he or she has no parents or the parents are themselves within the eligibility limits for means-tested government assistance. When the child reaches his or her eighteenth birthday, Federal policy considers him or her to be an adult. The parents' obligation for child support ends. At that point only the adult child's income and assets can be counted by Social Security. This is true even if the parents or someone else has been appointed the child's legal guardian(s). Parents usually apply for SSI when their child turns 18. This is the "deeming rule" in practice.

Now for the IKSM rule. SSI pays for food and shelter. When an individual lives in someone's residence rent-free, it is defined as receiving "In-Kind Support and Maintenance." SSI will be reduced by one-third of the Federal Benefit Rate. Essentially, someone has assumed part of the government's obligation. The IKSM rule applies when the child lives rent-free with parents. The SSI reduction can be avoided by charging a reasonable rent—Social Security will not question rent equal to the one-third reduction. Parents can charge a higher, market-based rent with proper substantiation. If parents charge market rent, I advise preparing a written rental agreement and keeping the data that substantiates the reasonableness of the rent charged.

The SSI recipient, or someone acting for them, is required to report countable income to the SSA monthly. Typically this means mailing copies of pay stubs. If there is unearned income, it must also be reported. The government may treat failure to report income as a fraudulent act. It is unwise, not to mention immoral, to intentionally not report income. (It is quite logical for the SSA and the IRS to cross-index SSI payments to W-2 wages using Social Security numbers.) When the SSA receives the income report, it responds by sending a letter notifying the recipient of the adjusted payment for a subsequent month. Wages for one month typically affect the SSI payment in the third following month because of system processing delays.

Social Security conducts Continuing Disability Reviews (CDRs) on all SSI recipients. If the SSA considers an SSI recipient to be totally and permanently disabled or unlikely to medically improve, it will typically examine only the financial records. If the SSA believes there is a possibility of improvement, current medical records will be reviewed. CDRs are nominally done at three-year intervals. In practice, limited manpower requires the SSA to prioritize its reviews to those whose condition may have improved. It's not unusual for those permanently disabled to go many years without a CDR.

Medicaid

Medicaid is three programs. One, it is healthcare and health insurance for the poor, elderly, and disabled. Medicaid is the second largest health insurer in America, second only to Medicare. Two, Medicaid is the largest insurer for institutional long-term care in the nation, underwriting almost half of the total expenditures for care in skilled nursing, assisted living, and cognitive impairment facilities. Contrary to a widespread misconception, HCBS does not pay for long-term care except in narrow circumstances. Third, Medicaid is the umbrella and major funding source for the Home and Community Based Services (HCBS) programs administered by the states. In 2010, The Federal government accounted for 68 percent of total Medicaid expenditures with the balance paid by the states.

Medicaid covers more services than any other form of health insurance. It covers many goods and services limited or excluded by private insurance policies. It covers a more broad range of services than Medicare. In most states it covers prescription drugs, a very important benefit for people with mental illness or severe medical needs. Some states provide coverage for vision care, dental services, physical therapy, and prosthetic devices.

If a Medicaid-eligible person has private insurance (perhaps as a dependent under a parent's policy), Medicaid supplements the private insurance. Medicaid can also supplement Medicare by paying for deductibles, co-insurance amounts, Medicare premiums, and items that Medicare does not cover.

Federal guidelines require mandatory coverage for some groups and allow the states the option of covering additional groups or expanding coverage for mandated groups. Examples of optional coverage groups are pregnant women, persons with AIDS, pre-school and school-age children. The Patient Protection and Affordable Care Act of 2010 added mandatory coverage groups to reduce the nation's uninsured population. The United States Supreme Court struck down these requirements in its July 2012 ruling.

The $2000 Medicaid financial asset limit is universal in all states, with some variation in the definition of countable assets. The income limits vary in approach and specifics. States take one of two approaches in setting income limits. One approach is to set absolute dollar limits on income. States that use this approach are called "categorically needy" states. There are 33 of them. Other states apply a "medically needy" approach, sometimes called the "spend down" approach. If projected healthcare expenses are likely to cause a person to spend their assets down to below the eligibility limit, one becomes immediately eligible rather than waiting to apply after the assets are exhausted. Whether a state is "categorically" or "medically" needy, it determines income eligibility using one of two approaches. In the first approach it may define the income limit as a percentage of the National Poverty Guideline (NPG). For example, the limit might be 200 percent of the guideline for those with disabilities and 133 percent for pregnant women. The rationale behind numbers greater than 100 percent is that the National Poverty Guideline assumes one has health insurance, and therefore the NPG includes only an allowance for out-of-pocket medical expenses. The second approach applies a multiplier to the SSI maximum payment. For example, if the multiplier is three times, the 2013 individual income limit would be $2130 per month in a state that does not supplement the Federal payment. The Affordable Care Act sought to require the states to cover mandatory groups with incomes less than 133 percent of poverty level. These provisions were also struck down by the Supreme Court.

In 32 states and the District of Columbia, a person automatically qualifies for Medicaid if the SSA determines that he or she is eligible for SSI. Other states require an individual to separately apply to the state's Medicaid administrator. Social Security's disability determination is not automatic in these states.

Parents often have difficulty finding doctors, dentists, ophthalmologists, and psychiatrists who will take Medicaid patients because of reimbursement rates that are well below market. One can see noticeable differences in the quality of care in assisted living and cognitive impairment facilities depending on whether one is paying privately or has long-term care insurance, versus the facility being reimbursed by Medicaid. Nonetheless, for all of its shortcomings and restrictions, Medicaid is the insurer of last resort for people with disabilities.

It is essential that one understands the Medicaid policies of one's state, especially the eligibility criteria, the application procedures, and the appeal procedures if one is denied. These policies should be obtained from the state's Medicaid administrator, from an attorney, or from knowledgeable staff of a non-profit organization serving the special needs community.

Where to Go for More Information

There are excellent publications on Social Security's website (www.ssa.gov) explaining the rules for SSI. A good publication to begin with is No. 05–11015, *A Guide to Supplemental Security Income (SSI) for Groups and Organizations*.

The website for the Centers for Medicare and Medicaid Services (www. cms.gov) has web pages organized by topic, population group, and state. It is still wise to obtain policies and procedures from the state's Medicaid authorities. The Federal government and the states aren't always in communication.

CHAPTER 10

UNDERSTAND STATE-PROVIDED SERVICES FOR ADULTS WITH DISABILITIES

State disability services are more extensive for people with developmental disabilities than for those with mental illness or physical disabilities. There is also a greater emphasis on the needs of pre-school and school-age children than for adults. Supports for the physically impaired are primarily for rehabilitation and job assistance although there are specialized services for the sensory impaired (visual and hearing).

Non-institutional disability services are delivered by different government entities as children move from pre-school through school and into adulthood. Children from birth until entering the school system are usually served by a child services division within a state agency providing disability services, for example a department of human services or social services. Children from age 5 to 21 are served by the school system under the Individuals with Disabilities Educational Act of 2004 (IDEA). Children who finish the school system at age 18, 21, or 22 (depending on parent decision and state policy) are served by an adult services division of the state human services agency.

Disability services are delivered in either institutional or community-based settings. Social values and government policies strongly encourage community care. The values that moved our society from institutional care to a community support model acknowledge the rights of people with disabilities to participate in the community. There is also a monetary incentive. Community care is cost-effective and lessens the burden on national and state budgets. Institutions, that is, facilities with large client populations such as hospitals, nursing homes, or custodial facilities, primarily serve those requiring intensive supervision due to disruptive behavior, the risk of self-injury or injury to others, or the need for intensive medical intervention or custodial care.

Disability service programs are run by the states. There are two program types: programs administered under the Federal Medicaid system and programs established by a state with its own legislative enactments. Medicaid programs are the more common and serve many more clients. The Federal government funds 50–70 percent of the cost of Medicaid services (depending on the state) with the states funding almost all of the balance. I describe here the Medicaid

Home and Community Based Service (HCBS) programs because of their extent and importance. State-established programs typically serve a smaller population, generally pre-school and school-age children.

You should remember:

1. Most state disability services are funded and delivered through Medicaid-waiver programs, also called Home and Community Based Service programs.

2. HCBS programs use Medicaid eligibility criteria.

3. Threatened cutbacks in Medicaid and state appropriations will force many families to assume a greater burden of care for their loved one and for a longer period of time.

Medicaid-Waiver Programs: Home and Community Based Services (HCBS)

Medicaid was established in 1965 to provide healthcare for the poor and long-term care for the elderly and disabled. In its early years, long-term care was provided in institutions like hospitals, skilled nursing facilities, or custodial care facilities. Medicaid Home and Community Based Service programs, also called Medicaid-waiver programs, were conceived to offer more flexibility in the delivery of services and to lower cost. States were authorized and encouraged to submit proposals to the Centers for Medicare and Medicaid Services (CMS) for community care programs, identifying target populations and the services needed by those populations. The elderly, blind, and disabled are target populations. There are sub-populations, targeting people with developmental disabilities, physical disabilities, mental illness, and even specific conditions such as autism or AIDS. Once approved, the programs are administered by the state under Federal regulations and are eligible for Federal matching funds. States must meet six "assurances" to receive Federal funds:

1. The community level of care criteria must be consistent with the criteria for residents in institutions.

2. Each client must have an individual service plan.

3. The providers of services must be qualified to deliver them.

4. Clients must be protected from neglect and abuse.

5. Financial controls are required to assure that expenditures can be traced to individual clients and their service plans, and expenditures for community services cannot exceed the cost of equivalent institutional care.

6. Each state must have a designated agency to administer Medicaid and HCBS programs.

HCBS programs are the primary vehicle for disability services in all states. Recipients of services must meet the Medicaid eligibility criteria, including those that define a disability and the financial criteria for "means tested" public assistance. A disability is defined by the medical condition, severity, loss of function, and residual functioning capacity. A means test limits the amount of income and assets a person can have to be eligible for services.

States are given considerable flexibility to design an HCBS program within the requirements of Federal regulations. Some restrict disability services to those deemed medically necessary or directly related to mitigating the effects of a disability. A narrow definition can exclude services for quality of life such as life skills coaching or community access.

Programs for Those Who Have a Developmental Disability

The largest population of people with special needs in any state is the population with an intellectual or developmental disability (IDD or DD). DD services take the greatest share of state expenditures for people with disabilities. There are generally two types of HCBS program for adults: comprehensive services and supported living services. There are not many state-funded, non-Medicaid programs for adults. Most state-established programs focus on children under 17, particularly pre-school children.

Comprehensive services programs provide for the needs of those in state-operated or state-funded residences. Residences include group homes, adult foster care, host homes, clustered apartments, and small group residences (sometimes called Personal Care Alternatives or PCAs). Group homes typically have 4–8 clients. Host homes serve one or two. The number of clients in clustered apartments may be ten or more, depending on how many units can be supervised by a "look-in" staff person. Small group residences have one to three clients. The common configuration is a four-bedroom house with three client bedrooms and one bedroom for full-time staff.

All reimbursable services identified in an Individualized Service Plan (ISP) are delivered by a comprehensive services program. The cost per client in a comprehensive program is quite high and beyond the reach of most families. The cost of the residence and full-time staff alone can exceed $50,000 a year, 20 percent of which is the facility cost, the remainder being the cost of staff. Another major cost element, which can double the cost, is skilled professional services such as healthcare, therapy, behavioral intervention, and skilled nursing.

The cost of day programs and employment assistance may add an additional several thousand dollars. There is a movement to make comprehensive services available to those in private residences such as the home of parents, individual residences, or other private settings. This will save money for the Federal and state governments. It also provides flexibility for families. However, private residential care must comply with Medicaid financial controls, notably the requirement that all reimbursements be traceable to a client and his or her service plan.

Supported living services are provided to those who live in a non-state residence such as the parents' home, one's own residence, or someone else's home or apartment. The services offered are the same as those offered under comprehensive services except for the residence, but there is a cap on the amount of money that can be spent on a client. The individual or family can select from a range of service options to include in an ISP up to the dollar limit. If the parents wish additional services or units of care, they must pay for them. The level of care and the cost cap is determined by a numerically scored assessment such as the Support Intensity Scale used by many states. The numerical score reflects the severity of need. The state either provides or pays contractors directly; payments are not made to the individual or his parent or guardian.

Programs for Those Who Have a Mental Illness

Many people with mental illness are capable of functioning in the community, managing their affairs, and productively holding a job, provided they have the necessary social supports, psychotherapy, behavioral counseling, healthcare, self-help skills, and medication. With early diagnosis and adequate intervention, there can be successful outcomes in the MI system. Mental illness is too often not diagnosed until one's teen years. This is unfortunate: a child who receives early diagnosis and help will have much better prospects for later in life.

The difficulties faced in helping individuals can be daunting. One of the most difficult challenges is the cost of healthcare and medication. Another problem is stability; this can never be taken for granted. Sometimes the individual has achieved independence, employment, and socialization, only to experience a relapse in their condition. Because most individuals are intelligent and physically able, there are reasons for optimism that a good life is possible. And yet, creating such a life is often as hard for someone with a mental illness as it is for someone who is developmentally disabled. The emphasis in special needs planning is on creating opportunities for gainful employment, access to adequate healthcare, and establishing circles of support. It is not as easy as it sounds.

Care in institutional settings, such as psychiatric hospitals or intermediate care facilities, is more common in the MI system than in the DD system because of the need for full-time staff trained to work with people with mental illness. Compared with the DD system, the MI system is more likely to be underfunded. Nonetheless, a broad range of services may be offered, some of which have no DD system counterpart. For example, one may be able to get help with substance abuse, gambling problems, eating disorders, domestic violence, and criminal system intervention.

Four problems in the MI world deserve mention. These issues are rarely understood by those outside the MI system but are acutely recognized by those within it.

The first is the cost of medications. People unaware of how depression, bipolar disorder, schizophrenia, and other mental conditions are treated are often astounded by the high cost of drugs. Frequently this cost can only be met by Medicaid coverage which consigns those affected (and often their families) to poverty.

Second is the stigmatization of a person with behavioral problems, a poignant problem for school-age children. The child may be expelled from school because the teachers can't cope with his behavior. In a segregated setting he or she never develops social skills or friends. The societal price will be paid later in life. Early diagnosis, intervention, and psychotherapy can keep the child in school and enhance chances that he or she can lead a productive life as an adult.

The third problem is criminalization of behavior. A person with aggressive tendencies, abnormal sexual behavior, or substance abuse can easily get caught up in the criminal justice system. The prevalent attitude in America equates justice with vengeance. The criminal justice system operates as a system of punishment rather than correction or rehabilitation. It is unremitting and unforgiving. This system falls with exceptional cruelty on the mentally ill. People fear and will not forgive one's failure to control his behavior, especially aggression, violence, or sexual assault. They particularly will not forgive the middle-aged male. Because of the problem of criminalization of the mentally ill, state and local MI service agencies typically work cooperatively with law enforcement agencies and district attorneys to extricate an individual from the criminal system so they can keep their place in the community. This is quite appropriate when the behavioral problem is temporary, caused by a failure of the drug regimen to control a condition perhaps due to changing chemical balances in the body.

The fourth area is help for families. Families often experience a high level of stress and physical strain coping with a mentally ill loved one. It can be exhausting and overwhelming. The problem is exacerbated by a phenomenon observed with mental illness—it clusters in families. It can affect more than one individual in an immediate family and repeat from generation to generation. Crisis intervention and family supports are necessary elements in the MI services system.

I have found that the most difficult problem in special needs planning is the middle-aged male with mental illness. If government supports are inadequate and the individual or family is not wealthy, it is not likely that a plan can be developed with a reasonable hope of success in keeping the individual employed and in community living.

Programs for Those Who Have a Physical Disability

Many people with physical disabilities have little need for special needs planning. A person who has normal intelligence, a good education, and can manage his own affairs can live independently, hold a well-paying job, or successfully run a business. The necessity for special needs planning arises when the physical limitation seriously limits a normal life without adequate and effective intervention. Physical disabilities sometimes can come with serious medical problems which can only be met through Medicare and Medicaid because the person cannot obtain private health insurance.

Most state programs for the physically disabled are focused on vocational rehabilitation. Services include job training, job placement, and temporary on-the-job support. Education can range from vocational training to assistance with higher education. Generally the focus for someone who is mobility impaired is employment, assistive devices, and mobility aids including motorized wheelchairs, modified vehicles, and home modifications.

Blindness and deafness are conditions that need not prevent a person from independence and employment if the individual has effective schooling early in life. The school system must be able to implement appropriate educational strategies, have properly trained teachers, and have a complete academic and community living curriculum, supported by assistive technologies. The co-occurrence of deafness and blindness is a seriously limiting condition requiring a more intensive and extensive planning solution. Most states have special schools for the deaf and blind. There is a difference between true blindness and visual impairment, with the former obviously being a more limiting condition. Most people thought by the "sighted" to be blind are actually visually impaired. Generally the focus on planning for a person who is deaf or blind will focus on enabling full employment through education, assistive devices, and self-management skills.

Brain injury is technically a physical disability but often the needs for supports are more closely akin to the services in the DD system. Vocational rehabilitation can be helpful to an individual who recovers enough function for re-employment.

There is a population of people who are not now physically disabled but who predictably will become so. These people are affected by degenerative conditions such as multiple sclerosis. The planning for this group will focus on personal financial planning to help them accumulate wealth so that a person has resources to support themselves when no longer employable or capable of living independently. There can be significant costs for care givers and assistants. Access to Medicare and Medicaid will be needed for healthcare needs. There are few state services available to this class of people.

Applying for Services

HCBS programs follow Medicaid eligibility criteria and state programs use them as well. There are two dates, or ages, that parents should be aware of. One is the age of eligibility to receive services. The other is the age when one is allowed to apply for them. Although one may be eligible for services, that does not mean that the individual will receive them on the eligibility date because of the wait lists. Usually, the date when one applies for services determines where one stands in the line. States allow emergency placements for those with no one to care for them, and these go to the head of the line, jumping ahead of others. (One can't argue with this.) This situation occurs when parents who have been taking care of their child can no longer do so because of death or infirmity. As our population ages, this will become a serious problem. More and more aging parents are caring for children waiting for services and they are entering the life stage when they eventually will not be able to continue.

Many parents are not aware that they can apply for services at an age earlier than one can receive them. For example, the eligibility date for residential services for an adult may be age 18 but the state may permit a parent to apply for the child at the age of 14. This is historically associated with the wait list problem. By applying for services early, one took one's place in line and hopefully would reach the front of the line about the time services were needed. Today's increasingly long wait lists due to funding constraints defeat this. *It is very important that parents know the age one may apply for services and always apply as soon as regulations permit so your child can take his or her place in line.* Generally one can apply for more than one HCBS program at the same time but can only receive services from one. Parents in the DD system usually apply for both comprehensive and supported living services. The child will usually receive supported living services first because the comprehensive program has the longer line. Once comprehensive services become available, the family drops supported services. Apply for services even if you are not sure of the future need. You can remain in line in most states if you turn down a slot when offered.

One must know the documentation requirements to support an application for state services. This is usually not an issue if one has already qualified for Social Security Disability, SSI, or Medicaid. However, HCBS and state programs may have more restrictive criteria. (This sometimes trips people in the autism spectrum.) The staff of an advocacy or family support non-profit organization can explain what you need to know. Research your state's website. Obtain copies of forms and procedures. By far the most important documentation will be the records of the medical condition—diagnosis, severity, and functional limitations. Respond quickly to any request for additional documentation and pay attention to deadlines. Some human services agencies do not simply put aside an application until questions are answered or records are produced. Instead, they reject the application if the parents miss a narrow window to respond.

One must be a resident of a state to receive its services. This can cause a problem when a family relocates to another state. When the parents or guardian apply for services in the new state, the child starts over on that state's wait list. The result may be a delay or an interruption in receiving services. Medicaid is a Federal program but it is state-administered. Medicaid-waiver services are not portable across state lines.

Problems of Access, Control, Quality, Reliability, and Adequacy

Most people who have a loved one with a disability, or serve those that do, are aware of the problem of waiting to get the services. Once in the door, however, problems persist. A prevalent problem in the disability system is the poor compensation paid to employees and service providers. An increasingly common problem is the growing scarcity of doctors who accept Medicaid patients because of low reimbursement rates and payment problems. Another problem is hiring and retaining qualified people, particularly those holding a respected professional designation. High staff turnover can cause system errors and service discontinuities. The coming and going of care providers can be distressing for those with cognitive impairment or mental illness who have a psychological need for a predictable environment.

One must recognize the most serious potential problem—the abuse and neglect of people with disabilities in care facilities. The problem tends to be more serious in institutions but can be encountered in community settings as well. It happens in group homes, host homes, foster care homes, and small group residential settings. All states have quality control agencies and procedures to investigate and respond to concerns about abuse and neglect. However, for a state agency to take corrective action, someone must see and report the problem.

Parents should be aware of the protections established by the state department of human services. Who receives complaints or concerns of a possible violation of a person's rights? What are the procedures for reporting a suspicion of abuse or neglect? How are investigations conducted and closed? What corrective actions or alternative placements are available if incidences are confirmed? When interviewing potential contract service providers, ask about their policies and procedures, their safeguards to prevent abuse, how to report suspicions, how they investigate complaints, and what actions they will take if abuse or neglect is found. Put the provider on their guard that you are vigilant in protecting your child.

Parents must be particularly vigilant about sexual abuse if their child is non-verbal, or has limited verbal skills or cognitive function. Be concerned about unexpected or unexplainable changes in behavior. Take note of an injury and inquire what caused it. Ask your child if she is happy and if she likes her care givers. A person who receives constant care may accept abuse because she doesn't know how to cope with the situation. She may be afraid to tell someone that her care giver did something to her when she relies on that person and doesn't want him to go away. Perpetrators often threaten victims with harm if they tell someone. (Incidentally, 30% of the people with intellectual disabilities who are sexually abused are male. Sexual abuse is not an issue of gender; it is an issue of vulnerability.)

Protection from abuse and neglect must be given serious consideration by parents whose child may outlive them. Consider appointing a successor guardian or advocate with explicit instructions to ensure that your child receives adequate care. If you rely on an advocate rather than a guardian, the advocate must have signed privacy waivers. The problem of neglect and abuse of the disabled, especially those with a developmental disability, is not recognized to be as serious as it is because most incidences go undetected and unreported. As more parents become aware of the problem and take meaningful precautions, the frequency of abuse and neglect will decrease as potential perpetrators are deterred by the risks of being caught, and actual perpetrators are removed from the system by prosecution, conviction, and imprisonment.

CHECKLIST
CREATING A RESOURCE PLAN

		Yes/ Done	Action Req'd	Not Needed
	**Identify Services to Meet Special Needs**			
1	Have you assessed your child's needs, related to his disability, for adult services?			
	(a) Healthcare			
	(b) Psychological counseling or behavior intervention			
	(c) Therapy			
	(d) Personal assistance and supervision			
	(e) Employability			
	(f) Personal management and daily living capability			
2	Have you reviewed your child's last IEP or tri-annual evaluation?			
3	Are you prepared to take over the supports previously provided by the school?			
4	Are all components of the care needs evaluation no more than three years old?			
5	Do you keep records of past evaluations and watch for changes?			
6	Have you considered consulting with an elder care planner for a plan of care?			
7	Does the life plan reflect the latest assessment of your child's care needs?			
8	Do you watch for changes in your child's needs over time, as with aging?			
9	Is your care plan described and documented in your letter of intent?			

	Yes/ Done	Action Req'd	Not Needed
Employment			
1 Have you made employability a major focus of high school IEPs and ITPs?			
2 Have you identified resources for employment preparation and placement?			
(a) The School to Work Alliance Program (SWAP) or similar program			
(b) State employment agency and the department of vocational rehabilitation			
(c) Private employment services			
(d) Business owners you know or do significant business with			
3 Have you evaluated the kinds of jobs that might be suitable?			
(a) With consideration to pace, structure, supervision, and environmental factors			
(b) Social skills and ability to appropriately interact with the general public			
(c) Child's preferences for a job and comfort level in an employment setting			
4 Have you considered education and training after aging out of school?			
(a) Colleges including 4-year and 2-year degree and 1-year certificate programs			
(b) Vocational training			
(c) Job coaching			
5 Have you helped your child develop a résumé and complete job applications?			
6 Would volunteer work help prove the child's employability and commitment?			
7 If your child gets a job, will he need some on-the-job support, at least initially?			
8 Do you watch how your child is doing on the job, talk to supervisors, etc.?			
9 Do you partner with the employer to make it a success for both parties?			
10 Do you support employers committed to hiring people with disabilities?			

		Yes/ Done	Action Req'd	Not Needed
Home				
1	Have you investigated the availability and adequacy of state residential services?			
	(a) Is your child eligible?			
	(b) Is there a wait list? If so, when can you expect an opening?			
	(c) Have you visited facilities to check standards of cleanliness, upkeep, etc.?			
	(d) Have you observed the staff and their interaction with clients?			
	(e) Are their problems with staff coverage, training, or high turnover?			
	(f) Risk of abuse and neglect? Can you monitor personal safety and intervene?			
2	Is a personal residence an option—an apartment, condominium, or house?			
	(a) Will your child require human supports, live-in, look-in, or neighbor?			
	(b) Does your child have the skills for daily living and personal care?			
	(c) Can you get a HUD Section 8 voucher for rental or mortgage assistance?			
3	Is individual or trust purchase of a residential property possible?			
	(a) Have you investigated government financing assistance for home ownership?			
	(b) Can you afford a condominium or house and qualify for a mortgage?			
	(c) Who will own the property—the child, the parents, or a special needs trust?			
	(d) Who will monitor safety and comfort in the residence and long-term stability?			
	(e) Will you hire a property manager or contract for other services?			
	(f) What will happen to the property if your child can no longer live there?			
	(g) Have you planned for taxes, insurance, maintenance, utilities, HOA fees, etc.?			

		Yes/ Done	Action Req'd	Not Needed
Home (continued)				
4	Have you considered community living options for people with disabilities?			
5	Have you explored a clustered apartment arrangement with other families?			
6	Could you form or join an intentional family group to create residential options?			
7	Have you integrated home ownership with other elements of your estate plan?			
Social Security and Medicare				
1	Do you understand Social Security Disability eligibility rules and benefits?			
	(a) Social Security Disability Insurance (SSDI) benefit, dependent and survivor benefits			
	(b) The Substantial Gainful Employment (SGA) limit			
	(c) The documentation needed to apply for a Social Security disability benefit			
2	Do you know that if you retire, your child may be eligible for a benefit too?			
3	Can your child qualify for SSDI from part-time employment and paying FICA?			
4	If the child is employed, do you know about the TWP, PASS, and IRWE rules?			
5	Are you aware that your child can be eligible for Medicare after 24 months of SSDI?			
6	If in another government pension plan, has it dependent and survivor benefits?			
SSI and Medicaid				
1	Do you understand the $2000 asset limit for SSI and Medicaid?			
	(a) Will you or someone manage your child's finances to not exceed the limit?			
2	Do you understand the eligibility rules for Supplemental Security Income?			
	(a) Do you know how SSI payments are calculated?			
	(b) If your child is 17 or under, do you plan to apply for SSI at her eighteenth birthday?			

		Yes/ Done	Action Req'd	Not Needed
SSI and Medicaid (continued)				
	(c) Do you understand SSI's In-Kind Support and Maintenance (IKSM) rule?			
	(d) If your child lives with you, do you charge rent to avoid the IKSM reduction?			
3	Have you gathered the documentation for the SSI or Medicaid application?			
	(a) Do you know where and how to apply for SSI with a Social Security office?			
	(b) In your state, if a child qualifies for SSI, is Medicaid eligibility automatic?			
	(c) Do you know where and how to separately apply for Medicaid at state level?			
4	If applying for Medicaid without SSI, are you planning to do so on your child's eighteenth birthday?			
5	Have you found doctors and dentists who accept Medicaid patients?			
6	Do you understand the income limits for Medicaid and how to comply?			
7	If you cover your child on private insurance, can Medicaid supplement it?			
8	Are you aware that Medicaid can supplement Medicare and pay for premiums?			
State Disability Services				
1	Do you know the services available in your state for people with disabilities?			
	(a) Home and Community Based Services (Medicaid-waiver) programs			
	(b) Programs separately established and funded by the state			
2	Have you met with the intake coordinator of your state human services agency?			
3	Are you prepared for the ISP meeting?			
4	Are you prepared for the state's Support Intensity Scale (SIS) evaluation?			
	(a) Understand how to answer the questions or risk an understatement of needs			

	Yes/ Done	Action Req'd	Not Needed
State Disability Services (continued)			
5 If the Medicaid evaluation understates your child's needs, do you have options?			
(a) Request reassessment or appeal			
(b) Private evaluation by psychologists, therapists, or clinical social workers			
6 Are state services adequate and adequately funded?			
7 If you can't get adequate state services, can you afford to obtain them privately?			
(a) Will your private health insurance pay for some services?			
(b) Have you considered the cost of private services and your ability to pay?			
8 Are you prepared to fight the system for your child's rights to receive help?			
9 If considering moving to another state, have you investigated its services?			
(a) How do services compare with what your child now receives, if any?			
(b) Does the other state have a wait list and how long is it?			
(c) Will services be interrupted with the move and how will you bridge the gap?			

CASE STUDIES
RESOURCE PLANS

It's time to revisit Angel, Mike, Noelle, Henry, and their parents and friends to see how their resource plans are coming together.

Angel Herrera

John and Michelle Herrera established a special needs trust shortly after Angel was born. It was set up by opening a bank account and depositing $1000. They have not added to it since. When Angel turned 18, the parents were court-approved to be Angel's guardians. John and Michelle applied for SSI not because they needed it but to establish Angel's Medicaid eligibility and access to state disability services. However, with Angel indefinitely waitlisted, John and Michelle have begun to doubt that they can rely on the state for any help and decide to go forward on their own. They decide to hire a life skills coach with their own money, pay for their daughter to attend an occupational training program at an out-of-state college, and pursue private residential options. (The reason that the Herreras looked out of state is that Colorado has no program at any of its community colleges or universities designed for people with an intellectual disability.)

To enroll in the Occupational Training Program at Eastern New Mexico University-Roswell, an applicant must take a test for intellectual aptitude and capability for independent living. The purpose is to assure that the applicant has a reasonable chance to succeed in the program. The results of the test reveal that Angel is an acceptable applicant. ENMU-R does not offer one-on-one mentoring for special needs students but there is residence hall supervision. Another family in the Herrera's intentional family group intends to send their daughter Lilly, who has autism and who is a friend of Angel's, to ENMU too. To some extent, Lilly's and Angel's abilities and limitations are complementary and it's comforting to know that the two young adults can room on campus with someone they know. The cost for the one-year program, including tuition, fees, books, room, board, personal, and travel expenses is expected to be $20,000, which the Herreras can easily afford. They decide that Angel will take the food assistant curriculum. When they talk this over with Angel, they find that she is thrilled and very proud to be going to college like her older siblings Jo and Paul.

In conversations with the managers of the senior center where Angel has her Transitions Program job, the Herreras detect reluctance on their part to hire their daughter after aging out of school. They are not sure why but attribute it to the fact that the managers are concerned that there be no mistake or accident in serving their elderly residents. The managers are not willing to take a chance on someone who is "mentally retarded." (In the current volunteer job, Angel has some on-the-job support.) John and Michelle believe, however, that the food assistant certificate could lead to other job possibilities with company or school cafeterias or public eating establishments.

John and Michelle talk to the staff at Eastern New Mexico University about the campus routine to understand the activities and transitions that Angel must be able to manage independently. With this information, John and Michelle meet with the social worker who teaches Angel's life skills classes to develop a one-on-one mentoring program to prepare their daughter for college. In the period from January (after Angel ages out of school) through July (before starting at ENMU-R), Angel will have 12 bi-monthly sessions for a payment of $150 per session. The parents know that once Angel becomes familiar with a routine, she will reliably follow it. They decide that Michelle will accompany her daughter on campus for the first week or until confident that Angel can manage her schedule. Software applications for a smart phone or tablet computer, such as a schedule manager with voice prompts, can also help Angel with her routine.

After Angel leaves for college, John and Michelle turn their attention to residential options. One option that interests them is a community living facility, the New Horizons Community. It has two buildings, one for females and one for males. In each building there are eight private bedrooms, seven for clients and one for staff. There is a community social area, kitchen, and dining area. The cost for a personal unit is about $35,000 annually. The main drawback with New Horizons is that it is 45 miles from the Herreras' house and they are not sure how they can manage Angel's transportation to and from a job.

A second option is a clustered apartment arrangement with six other families who are similarly interested. The families would establish a corporation (for limited liability purposes) by filing articles of incorporation and by-laws with the Secretary of State. The parents would serve as the corporate board of directors, setting the schedule of fees to be paid by participating families. The corporation will hire the person who will monitor the well-being of the young adults. The cost of the support person will be shared by the families. The cost, including the apartments for the young adults and the employee, would be about $15,000 per year if shared by seven families. The potential problems with this option are the commitment of enough families to make it economically viable and long-term stability if based on a rent model.

A third option is a privately owned residence, either a condominium purchased by Angel's parents or a mother-in-law apartment built in the rear of the Herreras' house. A house purchase would also be a possibility if there were others interested in living there. The mother-in-law apartment allows for closer oversight of Angel and a friend or friends living with her, but it has less of a sense of independence from parents. A condominium or house presents the challenge of assuring Angel's safety. With parental conservatism, John and Michelle are hesitant about a house or condo. A live-in companion may be required to have high confidence in their daughter's safety.

The final decision will depend primarily on whether there are enough families willing to join in a clustered apartment cooperative. If this doesn't happen, then the choice between New Horizons Community and a condominium will likely be decided by which better coordinates with Angel's employment.

Last, John and Michelle consider the question of a successor guardian. They conclude that, if something were to happen to them, a professional guardian will succeed them. Neither wants this burden to fall on the other two children. A second decision in this discussion is made regarding how their estate legacy will be shared among the children. They believe that Jo and Paul have good career prospects and will likely be successful on their own. So John and Michelle decide that their priority is to take care of Angel's needs first. After Angel's access to a good life is assured, their remaining wealth will go to Jo and Paul equally when they pass away.

As these plans have come together, John is starting to feel uneasy about affordability, thinking about the accumulated cost of a residence, a companion or care giver, a successor guardian, and other supports for independent living and employment. At this point the Herreras need a financial plan, and more specifically an estimate of the money they will need to set aside for Angel. They could face a difficult decision. Must they compromise their standard of living so Angel's future isn't diminished? Both John and Michelle grew up in poverty. Both have come to enjoy the comfort of affluence and neither wants to return to a life of want. Nor will they accept that for Angel. Finally John says, "My parents worked really hard so me and my sister and my brothers could have a better life than they had. Papá held two jobs most times I can remember. Mamá worked as a night janitor and raised us during the day, and made sure we stayed in school. I just can't see not sacrificing for my children so they can have a good life too, not being willing to sacrifice like Mamá and Papá did for me." Michelle, an only child, understands and couldn't agree more.

Mike Olmstead

With help from his mom, Mike applied for and was admitted to the local community college to study computer sciences. Upon enrollment at the college, Mike was assigned a counselor from the Student Special Services office and an academic counselor, Mr. Wyatt, from the computer sciences department. Mr. Wyatt, who has Asperger's syndrome himself, understands most of Mike's needs including the need for a structured environment, strong expectations for academic performance, help organizing his studies, accommodations for his noise sensitivity, and help managing a campus routine.

Sharon knows that Mike will need a psychologist or social worker to help him cope with academic demands, the campus environment, and social relationships with other students. Ms. Petraglia, the school psychologist who has known Mike for several years, recommends that Mike and his mom work with Ms. Coberley, a licensed clinical social worker, for counseling. Sharon and Ms. Coberley agree to weekly meetings with Mike during the first semester until everyone has confidence Mike is coping with college. Ms. Coberley's fee will be $150 per week, or about $2500 for the fall semester. Hopefully, the frequency of the counseling sessions can be reduced by half in the second semester. Sharon is not sure if her health insurance caps the coverage for behavioral counseling, something she must investigate. Regardless, she considers the counseling necessary and will pay for it if the insurance company won't by reallocating some of Mike's current expenses. If she can get insurance reimbursement, she will set aside the money as a fund for Mike's continued education after community college if possible.

Mr. Allen hired Mike for a part-time job. Sharon sees an important side-benefit to Mike's job, relevant employment experience on a résumé and a reference for future job applications. Mike's dad agrees to contribute $4000 for the spring and fall semesters for two years in addition to his current child support. Sharon's divorce attorney recommends she not seek a modification of the court order. Mike's dad has faithfully met his child support obligation and there is no reason to believe he won't meet his commitment to his son's education. Getting attorneys involved in a court proceeding would serve little purpose and could create adversarial feelings between Sharon and Frank. It might be better to postpone renegotiating the court order until a decision is made whether Mike should transfer to the state university to obtain a baccalaureate degree.

Sharon's estimate for Mike's first year at college is $10,000 including tuition, fees, books, labs, and a laptop computer conforming to the specifications of the computer science department. Frank's additional support and Mike's wages from his part-time job total about $11,500. Sharon can set aside $1500 to cover a summer school class if needed. She also has a cushion if his hours at the computer shop must be reduced so he can keep up with his studies.

Regarding whether to apply for Supplemental Security Income, Sharon decides that since she has the financial means to pay for Mike's college, she doesn't need to pursue this at this time. The answer here is tricky because child support is considered unearned income for determining SSI eligibility. Qualifying for SSI would require a restructure of the child support or establishing a first party special needs trust and Sharon doesn't want to risk the agreement with Frank unraveling.

And how is it from Mike's perspective? He has a job he likes, and for the first time in his life, he wants to go to school.

Noelle Williams

The focus on the Williams' planning for Noelle's future is a college degree in the field of music. The summer before high school junior year is early for most families to begin preparing for a college admissions application but the Williams' are concerned about affordability and improving Noelle's academic performance. They, and Noelle, identify two possibilities. The preferred school is the University of Evansville in Indiana. The cost of attendance is over $40,000 annually including tuition, fees, books, room and board, and personal expenses, a daunting sum for the Williams'. The fallback position is Western Illinois University, the closest state institution to their home. The cost to attend WIU is about $20,000, less than half of UE.

Robert and Dorothy decide to take a three-day trip to visit Evansville and the admissions office. UE is a respected regional university with a well-regarded music department. The admissions counselor explains the curriculum, the application procedures, applying for financial aid, how the amount of aid is determined, and campus life—residential living, student activities, etc. There is a lot to learn since neither parent attended college. One can major in general music, music performance, music education, music therapy, or music management which includes both business and technology study. It is not unusual for a student to begin in the general curriculum in freshman year and decide on a major area in sophomore year after exploring one's options. One of the most fascinating things they learn is that Evansville has a sister college in England, Harlaxton College in Grantham, Lincolnshire. For the Williams', who have lived all of their lives in the rural United States and had never been out of it, the thought of their daughter studying in England was almost beyond belief.

Of greatest importance to them is how financial aid is determined. The counselor explains the process of completing the FAFSA (Free Application for Federal Student Aid) and how the Expected Family Contribution is calculated. Theoretically the financial aid will be the difference between the cost to attend the college and the EFC but colleges often deviate from the theoretical aid when allocating funding to individual students in an admissions class. The counselor probes a little into their financial circumstances and believes the college might offer a Federal Pell Grant, a Stafford Loan, and a scholarship from the University endowment to cover the cost of tuition, fees, books, and perhaps a portion of the room and board if Noelle's high school record meets the university's academic standards and she receives an adequate score on the SAT-I college admissions test. The Williams' also spend a day visiting Western Illinois University in Macomb. Its curriculum is similar to UE's as is its admissions and financial aid processes.

There are scholarships available through foundations and non-profits for blind students and Noelle should apply to as many of them as she can find. Some colleges, with heavy demands on financial aid, may offer a student less than the Expected Family Contribution. One must list other scholarships the student is receiving on the FAFSA form, and it's quite possible a college will reduce its aid offer accordingly.

The Williams' know that Noelle will need assistive technologies to perform well in college. Mr. Vandenbark, the Braille teacher at the state school, provides them a list of recommendations. He suggests Noelle should have a Braille Notetaker (about $6300 with case and battery), scan and read software hosted on a laptop computer ($1300 each for software and laptop), and scan and read software on a smart phone to read paper currency, labels in grocery stores, restaurant menus, etc. An Apple iPhone and a 13 inch Macbook Pro would be ideal for Noelle's needs. The total cost of the items on the list is dismaying to the Williams, almost $10,000. The school guidance counselor at Noelle's school urges them to visit an office of the state Department of Vocational Rehabilitation. The US Department of Education's Rehabilitation Services Administration gives matching grants to states to provide rehabilitation services to people with disabilities including training the blind in the use of assistive technology. Using grant money, a DVR can provide a blind person with hardware devices and software to enable employment or higher education.

The Williams' follow the counselor's suggestion and visit the DVR office. It has a program for which Noelle is eligible. If she participates, DVR will pay for the Braille Notebook and most of the blind-specific items on Mr. Vandenbark's list. The iPhone and Macbook are not covered. It is a relief to the parents that DVR will pay for 85 percent of the assistive technology devices for their daughter's college.

By now the possibility of college for Noelle is becoming exciting to all members of the family, including Robert, Jr. The emphasis during Noelle's junior year in high school will be on her raising her academic performance and preparing for the college admissions test. Robert and Dorothy have always set high standards for their children, and for the most part their children have tried to meet them. Noelle, wanting so badly to go to the University of Evansville, is determined to exceed them.

Henry Lowenstein

Henry is aware that his mother left him a small inheritance in a trust with his brother Alan appointed trustee. The relationship between the two brothers is distant and Henry doesn't know the specifics. The question of contacting Alan is discussed among the group and they decide Craig will call. When he reaches Henry's brother, he explains who he is and why he is calling—he is helping his friend figure out how to pay for college. Alan and Craig agree to meet. Alan is somewhat guarded in the conversation due to his trustee duty of confidentiality but once he has a sense that Craig is truly interested in helping his brother, he shares some information.

Henry's mother established a third party special needs trust with about $50,000 in it when she died. Some of the money has already been spent for legal fees when Henry was arrested, paying off debts he ran up during a manic mood swing, the purchase of an automobile, and payments for major repairs over the years. Alan won't say how much money is left but notes that financing an associate degree in a community college is possible. Alan states that for a couple of reasons he won't give the money directly to Henry. Alan explains the eligibility rules for SSI and Medicaid and that giving his brother several thousand dollars could cause him to lose the government assistance he receives. Alan further states that, given his brother's problems with impulse control and money management, he is afraid Henry will foolishly spend any substantial sum given him. Alan tells Craig he will make payments as trustee directly to the college for tuition, fees, etc. without creating an eligibility problem for means-tested government benefits. Craig asks about funding a four-year degree and Alan replies he wants to see how Henry does in the first college year before getting into this.

While Craig is gathering this information, Lucy has been doing an internet search using the terms "bipolar disorder" and "college scholarships." She finds there are several scholarships, typically $750 to $1000, available through foundations and non-profit organizations serving people with mental illness. She also finds by searching on "jobs" and "mental illness" that a number of institutions and organizations serving the MI community affirmatively hire people with mental illness. (This is also true of many organizations that serve people with sensory or mobility impairments. It is less true of organizations serving the developmentally disabled. It's hard to accept justifications for this. Entities that serve people with cognitive impairments simply have to be more conscientious about practicing what they preach.) Finding that many institutions, government agencies, and non-profits have affirmative hiring practices, Henry is encouraged to share his plans with his employer. He will need accommodations for his college schedule and it may be to Henry's benefit that his employer knows of his aspirations for a full-time, meaningful position with fair compensation.

Henry also very much wants to have a residence of his own some day. This dream is unlikely to be within reach unless Henry can get a full-time job. Thus enrolling in the community college becomes the immediate goal. One thing that Lucy knows from participating in the Housing Choice Voucher Program and investigating buying a condominium is that one must attend classes in budgeting, money management, and credit management to receive mortgage assistance. Sometimes the counseling is paid for by the agency administering low-income housing assistance or non-profit organizations that receive grant funding for this purpose. Lucy obtains a list of credit counselors from a non-profit organization that assists people with low incomes to purchase a home. Henry needs help anyway setting up a budget and tracking his expenses so he can go to college, so the next step is for him to meet with a budget counselor. (Budget counselors for people with low incomes charge lower fees than financial planners and they have more experience helping this population than CFPs or ChFCs do.)

So the plan of action now is for Henry to: (1) get counseling in preparing a budget and managing money, (2) apply for admission to the community college, and (3) apply for as many scholarships for people with mental illness or bipolar disorder as can be identified.

PART 3

FINANCIAL PLANNING
PAYING FOR THE RESOURCES

CHAPTER 11

DEVELOP A SPECIAL NEEDS FINANCIAL PLAN

Financial planning is grounded in one's values and directed toward the achievement of important goals. Money is only a tool to help you realize what's most important to you. What's important, except for the spiritual or philosophical, can be reflected in one or more of life's five great financial goals:

1. To have a meaningful and enjoyable life—security, independence, dignity, and the capability to do what you want to do.

2. To provide for your children and be assured they will be taken care of if something happens to you.

3. To care for others you love.

4. To help your children provide for their children.

5. To leave a legacy to loved ones, or a cause, church, charity, or institution.

I have three thoughts I want to leave you with in this chapter:

1. Financial planning and sound financial management can create a better quality of life for you, your child with special needs, and your other children.

2. There are usually two financial plans: a plan for the child with special needs, embedded in a plan for the family to verify affordability and to best allocate family income and savings to meet the needs of all family members.

3. Financial planners who focus on special needs planning are rare; if you cannot find one, your best option is likely to be a Certified Financial Planner (CFP) practicing in retirement planning, taxation, and estate planning.

Financial Planning for the Family

Financial management starts with a budget, a personal discipline for spending money wisely, and controlling debt. This is taking care of today. Financial planning looks to the future. A financial plan is a plan for managing cash flow, debt, insurance, and wealth to enjoy a better quality of life, either now or at some point in the future. A plan provides a family with a picture of its financial future based on what it is doing today and improvements that can be made. A good financial plan recommends how to allocate money across multiple goals in a prioritized sequence of actions, addressing higher priorities first and lower priorities as cash flow improves.

There are seven steps to a sound financial future:

1. Balance the budget.

2. Establish a prudent level of reserves to meet unexpected needs.

3. Reduce and eventually eliminate debt.

4. Have an insurance safety net in case something goes wrong.

5. Save and invest for the future.

6. Harvest one's investments prudently, especially in retirement.

7. Create an estate plan to pass one's wealth to those you love or causes that are important to you.

In the case of special needs financial planning, the focus is on creating the best possible life for an individual with a disability while taking care of the needs and goals of all family members. Affordability is a concern for most families. Consequently there are usually two financial plans, one for the child and one for the family. If the child's life and resource plans are unaffordable, they must be scaled back until within the family's financial means.

Typically parents will provide for the child's support from current income for as long as they can. However, they must anticipate their eventual retirement and the drop in income that comes with it. Planning for retirement is an essential element of special needs planning.

Financial planning should include an examination of the adequacy of health, life, disability, and long-term care insurance to assure support for a special needs child and other family members. If the family's wealth and insurance is inadequate, it is important to address Medicaid and Social Security planning.

Often a difficult, and sometimes poignant, issue in family planning is how to treat all of the children fairly. Can the aspirations of other children be met while providing for the special needs child? Fairness is a difficult question. Does it mean equal shares in the parents' support? Does it mean the special needs child receives needed support and the other children receive what's left? Does it mean abandoning the special needs child to the mercy of the state so that the other children can go to college? Only the parents can define "fairness" to their children based on their personal values. As a financial planner who cared very much for his client families and their special needs children, I have found this often to be a touching problem. When I ask parents who will take over their roles as guardians, a common answer is one of the other children. This is often a good choice. It may be the only choice. However, I sometimes feel uneasiness. What if the parents do not have the financial means to take care of son Mark who has cerebral palsy and also send daughter Mary to a respected university so she can pursue her aspiration to be a physician? What if they must choose between the children? I call this a "Sophie's Choice" from the novel by William Styron. There could be a subtle concern here. What if Mary's life aspirations had to be sacrificed to provide for Mark's needs? If she is expected to serve as Mark's guardian at some point in the future, could her bond of love and loyalty be tinged by resentment over the loss of her dreams? I cannot answer this question. I can't judge the bonds that unite a family but this dilemma requires careful thought.

There are two uncommon but challenging situations in special needs planning. One is blended families when one or both spouses have children from a previous marriage and the current one and one of the children is a special needs child. Posing the question of fairness across different sets of children can provoke a difficult discussion. The other issue is same-gender unions or marriages. I do not treat the subject in this book, but I will point out that estate planning for same-gender couples is more challenging than for traditional married couples. State laws vary widely with regard to the treatment of such unions. If you are a same-gender couple, you should consult with a family law or estate attorney to make sure you have a plan that protects a child with special needs.

Financial Planning for the Child with Special Needs

The financial plan for the child will address how to pay for private resources while maintaining eligibility for government assistance. In most plans, there are five tasks:

1. Estimate the child's lifetime financial support.

2. Structure the family's financial arrangements to meet the income and asset limits of SSI, Medicaid, and state disability services.

3. Develop a plan to fund and manage a special needs trust.

4. Ensure proper title is used in all financial and legal documents so that assets, gifts, bequests, and insurance benefits go to the child's trust and not the child.

5. Trace the flow of estate and insurance benefits at the death of either or both parents to verify that the estate plan executes as intended.

A most important and difficult problem is estimating the child's lifetime financial support to pay for the life and resource plans. How to do this is described in Chapter 12.

The child's income and assets must be managed to comply with SSI and Medicaid eligibility limits described in Chapter 9. Assets and insurance that parents earmark for the child's needs should be directed to a third party trust established by the parents. In narrow circumstances, a first party special needs trust must be set up to accept the child's assets so he can be eligible for government support. Special needs trusts are treated in Chapters 13 and 19. A special needs trust is not needed if parents are wealthy enough to take care of their child and are not planning on government assistance.

Prior to engaging an attorney to create a trust, parents should consider the family decisions—who will serve as trustee, whether to appoint a trust protector and whom to appoint, and who to designate as remainder beneficiaries. Once the trust document is executed, the attorney's work is done. Decisions remain regarding when and how to fund the trust, investments, distributions, whether the trust should own residential or income-producing property, how to conserve assets over the child's lifetime, managing trust taxes, etc. It's like buying a car. The salesman sells the car but doesn't give driving lessons nor does he drive the car. It is the same with a special needs trust. The attorney creates the trust but the trustee manages it. The parents may choose to serve as trustees but may need professional financial and accounting advice when the trust is funded and operating. Or they may choose to appoint a professional trustee. An experienced financial planner can advise parents what to do with a trust once they have it. This will be treated in more detail in Chapter 13. (Having the family financial planner serve as trustee creates a conflict of interest since the trustee's undivided loyalty must be to the beneficiary.)

After the trust is established, the beneficiary designations for all bank and financial accounts, individual retirement accounts, employer-sponsored retirement plans, life insurance policies, and annuities must be reviewed and updated to designate the child's trust as beneficiary.

A competent financial advisor or accountant should trace the flow of all asset transfers, bequests, financial distributions, and insurance benefits at the death of either or both parents. The primary purpose is to verify the special needs trust funds as planned. An important second purpose is to uncover "back door" transfers to a special needs child that could cause her to lose government assistance eligibility. The financial and legal aspects of estate planning are treated in Chapters 16 and 17.

Selecting a Financial Planner

There are not many financial planners with expertise and experience in special needs planning. One reason is a lack of societal experience. People with moderate to more severe disabilities born prior to 1970 rarely lived in the community. They were institutionalized, uncared for, unseen, and forgotten. They were wards of the state and died early from neglect of their basic human needs. We are only now seeing the large population of people who were socially mainstreamed since the late 1970s moving into adulthood and middle age. The life spans of this generation will be greater than for any previous, and as a society we don't have a full picture of what this will look like. Another reason is that few financial advisors practice extensively in this field. Experience is important: it is a challenging domain. (Technically, it is a sub-domain of estate planning.) There are no educational programs or professional materials to teach this specialty. It is not surprising that most planners who practice in this field have been touched by someone with special needs—a child, sibling, spouse, other family member, or a friend.

When you examine the situation closely, you see two flaws in special needs financial planning as it is generally done today. Let's identify the problem with a crude metaphor. You start out from home on a road toward a destination. The road has to cross two ravines. There must be bridges across the two ravines if you are to reach your destination. If either bridge isn't there, you're blocked unless you can jump the gaps. In special needs planning, you are driving a road to a destination—a good life for your child. There are two ravines to cross, two knowledge gaps. One is an estimate of lifetime support. The second is how much money to contribute to a special needs trust based on the estimate—in financial terminology, the funding. Someone must build these two bridges, an estimate of need and a trust funding strategy. Without these two bridges, getting from where you are today to where you want your child to be in the future will be a leap across two gaps in your planning, two leaps of faith or two wild guesses, however you wish to describe it.

Today's state of the art in special needs financial planning lacks the tools and knowledge base to bridge from the child's life and resource plans to the parents' estate plan that ties everything together in a comprehensive and integrated strategy to take care of the child. In Chapter 12 I describe how to build the first bridge, the lifetime support estimate. In Chapter 13 I will take up trust funding. One of my purposes in writing this book is to provide parents and financial advisors with the materials and blueprints to build these two bridges. However, I faced a problem writing Chapters 12 and 13. Given the space available in this book and the enormity of the subject, I feel I have only described the broad outlines of what must be done—Chapters 12 and 13 merit a book of their own. If I ever write that book, the word "bridges" will probably be somewhere in the title.

There are three types of financial professional: financial planners or advisors, investment advisors or managers, and insurance agents or brokers. The term "insurance producer" is used in some states. Many financial planners practice in all three roles so they can help clients implement their recommendations. Financial and investment advisors are regulated by the Federal government, either directly or by delegation to the states. Insurance producers, brokers, or agents are state regulated.

One usually reliable approach to finding an advisor is a referral from an individual or agency whose judgment you trust. A special needs family may recommend an advisor to you who served them well. A non-profit organization serving the special needs community may be able to suggest financial planners who serve their client families. Elder law attorneys and trust officers work with advisors and they may suggest one or more to you. (Attorneys are forbidden to do so on a *quid pro quo* basis.)

Without a referral, you must do your own due diligence. The characteristics you look for in an advisor are ethics and competence. These are hard to objectively evaluate. As a surrogate for ethics, focus on the advisor's ethical duty to clients and his compensation. The indicators of competence are the areas of specialty in which he practices, his experience, and his professional designations.

Advisors commit to either of two ethical duties to clients. The higher standard is to advise clients in their best interest. Those who hold themselves out as investment advisors or financial planners must adhere to the higher standard. The lower standard is one of suitability of advice. Bank and securities broker/dealers and their representatives typically operate to the lower standard. Investment advisors are regulated under the Investment Advisors Act (IAA) of 1940. Financial planners are considered investment advisors because investment advice is necessarily a part of financial planning. The IAA imposes the ethical standard of a "fiduciary" on investment and financial advisors. The *Merriam Webster Dictionary of Law* defines a fiduciary duty as "…a duty to act in good faith and with care, candor and loyalty in fulfilling the obligation…" Loyalty is generally interpreted as advising "in the client's best interest." However, much confusion was caused by the United States Congress when banks and broker/dealers were allowed to escape to the lower standard of "suitability." Under the less protective suitability standard, the broker/dealer representative or bank is obligated to recommend investments suitable for purchase, not necessarily in the client's best interest. Insurance agents and brokers are held to the suitability standard in most states. Suitability is a loose standard that provides less protection to the general public largely unaware of the substantial difference. As an advisor that has subscribed to the higher standard of professionalism, I view the standard of suitability as poorly serving financially unsophisticated families.

A significant clue to the advisor's duty to his clients is his compensation. When an advisor charges a fee to a client, he must advise the client in the client's best interest. When the advisor receives a commission for selling an investment security or an insurance policy, the standard is one of suitability. The key is who pays the advisor. If the client pays for advice, the fiduciary standard applies. If an investment or insurance company pays the advisor a commission for selling its product, the advisor's duty is to the company whose product he sells. Certified Financial Planners voluntarily subscribe to the higher fiduciary standard when selling commissioned products. Causing some confusion, some financial planners do not charge a fee if the client buys the products recommended from them to avoid the perception of double-charging. Regardless, two of the most important questions to ask the advisor are: "What is your ethical duty to me?" and "How are you compensated?" Regulatory titles such as "advisor" and "broker/dealer" are not reliable measures of the inner man or woman. Many broker/dealers and insurance professionals are highly competent and ethical. Nonetheless, by understanding an advisor's standard of conduct and compensation you have a basis for evaluating the likelihood of being well served.

With regard to licensing, the fact that an advisor or broker/dealer holds a securities license tells you nothing about his fiduciary responsibility. Securities licensing is an unreliable indicator of expertise. A license simply means he passed a basic competency test allowing him to practice under relevant government regulations. I won't go into the complexities of licensing here, but I will note that Bernie Madoff had all of the required licenses to conduct his business.

One indicator of an advisor's competency is to understand the three levels of knowledge to practice in the field shown in Table 11.1. The three levels (my terminology) are basic competency, special needs financial planner, and expert practitioner. Companies that train representatives to work with special needs families typically train at the basic competency level. Advisors reach the second level with a base of client experience, self-study, continuing education, and familiarity with legal principles in important areas of law. Experts have significant experience in complex cases.

Table 11.1 Levels of special needs financial planning competence

Basic competency	Special needs financial planner	Expert practitioner
Personal life plan	*Family financial plan*	*High net worth estate plan*
Government programs Social Security SSI Medicare Medicaid	*Life plan for the child* *Resource plan* State disability services "Private pay" supports Residential options Employment preparation	*Supported independence plan* *Resource plan* 100% private pay resources Professional services Home ownership Supported college
Guardianship		
Legal documents Wills Special needs trust Power of attorney Medical directives	*Lifetime financial support estimate* *Special needs trust management* Funding plan	*Detailed support estimate* *Divorce* Spousal maintenance Child support estimate
Insurance Life Disability Long-term care	Amount of contributions Cash and property transfers When to fully fund Incremental funding strategy	Assure lifetime child support Special needs trust funding with property division Guardianship
Death benefits Use of proper title Update forms	Real estate ownership Investment asset allocation Trust administration Trust taxation Schedule of distributions	Coordinate two estate plans Child support with both parents' retirement Pre-nuptial agreements
	Estate plan verification Trace distributions of money and asset transfers at death	*Tort litigation* Estimate of damages Structured settlements

Good advisors tend to specialize because financial planning is a sophisticated field covering a broad range of domains. A generalist rarely has the competence of a specialist in a given area. Ask the advisor you interview their primary areas of specialty and years of experience in them. A special needs financial planner should have solid experience in retirement planning, taxation, and estate planning. The advisor who says, "I do everything" probably lacks depth in these more challenging domains.

You should understand the significance of the professional designations held by the advisor. There are many professional designations in financial services, some prestigious, some requiring minimum qualifications, and some bordering on the fraudulent. You should be able to recognize which is which. There are five factors that indicate a professional designation is awarded with rigorous standards and is prestigious enough to attract the best professionals:

1. The designation is offered by an independent board of standards, not a company selling products.

2. The board administering the designation establishes the standards of ethics and professionalism to which those holding the designation must adhere. Violators are sanctioned or forbidden to use the designation.

3. The board sets minimum education requirements to be completed at an accredited institution.

4. The applicant must pass a rigorous exam to test competency.

5. There is a requirement for continuing education after certification.

Table 11.2 lists the commonly encountered designations. The most prestigious is the Certified Financial Planner (CFP). The designation is administered by the Certified Financial Planner Board of Standards, an independent body. The Board publishes a comprehensive set of standards covering ethics, advisor practices, and product standards for financial plans. An applicant must complete courses at institutions such as the College of Financial Planning in financial planning, insurance, investments, retirement planning, estate planning, and taxation. Applicants must pass a difficult two-day test which has a pass rate less than 60 percent. Holders of the CFP must complete 32 hours of continuing education each two years, including a course in professional ethics. Less than 15 percent of financial professionals hold the CFP designation. You can benchmark the relative value of a designation by comparing its requirements to those of the CFP. A few professional designations are unreliable indicators of competence. Some are awarded by companies to their representatives as marketing ploys. Some border on the fraudulent, issued to anyone who pays a fee for an impressive piece of paper. Do not be impressed by a designation unless you know who awards it and the requirements to earn it.

Table 11.2 Common professional designations held by financial professionals

Certified Financial Planner (CFP)

One of the prestigious professional designations and the most respected in the area of financial planning. The educational requirements cover almost all important domains in financial planning. Applicants must pass a rigorous exam to test competency.

Chartered Financial Analyst (CFA)

This is a prestigious designation, usually held by portfolio managers and analysts with investment management firms. It is a difficult designation to obtain. Awarded by the CFA Institute.

Chartered Life Underwriter (CLU)

The CLU is typically held by life insurance professionals. It requires meaningful course work and testing in a range of insurance subjects not limited to life insurance. It is issued by the American College.

Chartered Financial Consultant (ChFC)

A financial planning designation issued by the American College to insurance professionals along with the CLU. The combination CLU and ChFC is a solid certification.

Personal Financial Specialist (PFS)

This is a designation awarded by the American Institute of Certified Public Accountants to CPA holders who have received training in financial planning. The PFS is a significant designation often held by CPAs who advise small business owners.

Certified Investment Management Analyst (CIMA)

A respected designation held by investment managers who manage large client accounts. The study and examination does not include financial planning.

Chartered Mutual Fund Counselor (CMFC)

A meaningful designation but focused in a narrow area of specialty.

Accredited Wealth Management Advisor (AWMA)

A meaningful designation but not in financial planning. It is somewhat broader than the CMFC.

Accredited Asset Management Specialist (AAMS)

Similar to the AWMA, it is not a financial planning designation.

Note: There are no *independent* professional designations in the domain of special need planning as of July 2012

Certified Financial Planners adhere to seven practice principles: integrity, objectivity, competence, fairness, confidentiality, professionalism, and diligence. Table 11.3 is the personal statement of principles that I subscribed to before I retired from active practice. The seven principles were established by the CFP

Board of Standards but the statements describe what each principle meant to me and how I applied them in my practice.

Table 11.3 A CFP's seven principles of conduct as practiced by the author

Integrity—My advice will be what I sincerely believe to be in your best interest.

Objectivity—When making a recommendation, I will explain the benefits of a course of action, its risks, cost, and options so you have the information to make a good decision.

Competence—I maintain competence and current knowledge in my profession through membership in professional societies and continuing education. I acknowledge a duty to "confer" or "refer." If I lack adequate expertise in an area of an engagement, I will consult with a professional having such expertise or refer you to a qualified professional.

Fairness—I will disclose any conflict of interest that could influence my recommendations, including compensation from other sources if my recommendations are accepted. I will not accept a financial planning engagement with a party who has interests that may conflict with yours.

Confidentiality—I do not share a client's personal or financial information with anyone except as necessary to complete the financial planning engagement. I do not disclose the names of clients unless given permission. I do not disclose client information to other family members without permission. I treat as confidential matters discussed with prospective clients who subsequently choose not to engage my services.

Professionalism—I believe that financial planning is an honorable profession. Those who practice with competence and integrity can make a meaningful improvement in people's lives. I will do nothing to dishonor my profession.

Diligence—I take care that my advice is appropriate for a person's personal circumstances, risk tolerance, financial sophistication, and personal goals.

Unless you know of an experienced advisor who practices in this specialty, I suggest you consider a Certified Financial Planner. However, there is another possibility if you cannot find a CFP in this specialty. Two national life insurance companies—MetLife and Mass Mutual—have made a corporate commitment to serve special needs families. They train their agents who wish to practice in this specialty. Consider their agents who have completed the training program and hold a CLU/ChFC designation.

You should interview an advisor before committing to a contract. The advisor should be willing to have a no-obligation, no fee, 30-minute preliminary consultation to allow you to explore their qualifications, fiduciary duty to clients, how he proposes to help you, and the scope and fee of an agreement. The initial meeting should be a relaxed conversation. If you are pressured to sign a contract, end the meeting and leave. This is a clear signal you have not found the right advisor. Ask the basic questions in Table 11.4. I suggest you also ask the advisor if he contributes to the special needs community in some way—for example as a volunteer or board member, accepting *pro bono* work, educating the public, or donating to non-profit organizations. It is wise to interview two or three advisors unless you have a high-confidence referral.

Table 11.4 Interview questions for a financial advisor

1. How long have you been practicing?
2. What is your educational background?
3. What duty do you owe your clients? A fiduciary duty to advise them in their best interests? Are your recommendations for investments and insurance company-specific? If so, are they products you sell?
4. What professional designations do you hold? What company or institution issues the designation? What are the requirements for education and experience?
5. What areas of financial planning do you practice in? Retirement planning? Estate planning? Taxation? Which estate attorneys do you generally work with?
6. How are you compensated? Will you disclose any compensation from other parties?
7. How much experience do you have in special needs planning? How did you become educated in the field?
   (a) Can you estimate the lifetime support our child will need? How do you do that?
   (b) Can you recommend a strategy to fund a special needs trust? How do you develop a funding strategy?
   (c) Do you work with banks or trust companies and can you refer me to corporate trustees?
   (d) Can you review our estate planning documents and financial records to make sure we have everything set up properly?
8. Do you contribute in some way to the special needs community by volunteering, *pro bono* work, educating people, or donating to one of the organizations? Which organizations?
9. Are there people in the special needs community who recommend your services?

Structuring a Financial Planning Agreement

Once you decide which advisor to work with, how do you structure a financial planning agreement? There are two types of agreement: fixed fee and hourly billing. With fixed fee arrangements, you pay the advisor to deliver a written financial plan with recommended actions for a fee agreed to prior to signing the contract. You have some control over the fee by defining the scope of the financial plan—that is, the number of elements or goals you want addressed. Advisors may offer three levels of financial planning, illustrated in Table 11.5. Basic plans are suitable for younger families with uncomplicated financial situations and with a pre-teen, special needs child. People with more complicated financial situations and older children should consider comprehensive planning. Affluent families, business owners, and those with exposure to estate and gift taxes require the most sophisticated level of planning.

Table 11.5 The levels of financial planning and the elements included

Plan elements	Foundation plan	Comprehensive plan	Premier plan
Budgeting, managing expenses and debt	X	–	–
Financial reserves	X	X	X
Asset and liability projections	X	X	X
Detailed cash flow analysis	–	X	X
Tax projections	–	X**	X
Investment planning	X	X	X
Retirement planning	X	X	X
Life insurance needs	X	X	X
Disability insurance needs	X	X	X
Long-term care insurance needs	X	X	X
Estate planning	–	x (basic)***	X
Business planning	–	–	X
Major purchases such as a home	–	X	X
Major investments	–	–	X
Funding for higher education	–	X	X
Providing for a child with special needs	x (basic)*	X	X
Pre- and post-divorce planning	–	X	X
Charitable giving	–	–	X

X—a typical plan element
X—an optional element

* Excludes modeling lifetime financial support with time-phased trust funding and distributions
** Excludes AMT and business tax projections
*** Excludes advanced estate planning to minimize gift, estate, and generation-skipping transfer taxes

What can you expect to pay for a financial plan? You should view financial planning as an investment in your future and not a cost, but it's a fair question. Many CFPs bill their services in the range of $100–$200 per hour. Hourly fees are higher in large metropolitan areas than in small or rural communities. The advisor's fee will reflect his billing rate and the hours he expects to spend on the engagement. A comprehensive plan can cost from $1000 to $3000. A detailed estimate of lifetime financial support can require several hours to prepare, increasing the cost of a plan to the high end of the range. The cost of a detailed estimate may not be justified until you have good life and resource plans and need to verify their affordability. If a level of independence is your goal, you should have a detailed estimate of the required supports before you proceed.

Hourly contracts are necessary when the advisor cannot reliably predict the hours necessary to complete the engagement. This will be the case when multiple parties are involved, when research and complex analyses are required, and with litigation (divorce for example), especially if the advisor may be called as a trial witness.

Where to Go for More Information

The Certified Financial Planner Board of Standards has established the professional standards required to be awarded a CFP designation, *The Standards of Professional Conduct for Certified Financial Planners*. It includes the *Code of Ethics and Professional Conduct*. It may be downloaded from the Board's website, www.cfp.net. You may find two other CFP-BOS publications useful: *What You Should Know about Financial Planning* and *Your Rights as a Financial Planning Client*.

Most Certified Financial Planners belong to the Financial Planning Association. The website of the FPA, www.fpanet.org, has a search capability to help you locate an advisor. Look for "Find a Planner" on the menu bar.

Check the Federal and state regulatory websites to see if the advisor has a record of regulatory violations or client complaints. (Such a blemish on one's professional record is aptly called a "dirty U-4" in the trade.) The regulatory organization at the national level is the Financial Industry Regulatory Authority (FINRA). The FINRA website, www.finra.org, has a broker check tool. Look under "Investors," then "Tools & Calculators," then "BrokerCheck." It will be helpful if you have the advisor's CRD (Central Registration Depository) number. The BrokerCheck tool may yield poor results if you do not enter the advisor's full name with middle initial and suffix (e.g. Senior, Junior, II, etc.). If you use an advisor's nickname, you may not find him in the database.

Insurance professionals are state regulated. Check the website of the state commissioner of insurance to see if an advisor has a mark on his record. Some states have a securities commissioner that keeps a regulatory database on broker/dealers.

CHAPTER 12

ESTIMATE LIFETIME FINANCIAL SUPPORT

One of the most difficult challenges in special needs planning is estimating the lifetime financial support for an individual with special needs. The task is to estimate what you or other members of your family must provide for a desired quality of life. This will equal the costs of "private pay" goods and services less the child's income and government assistance. If the amount of income, assistance, and support does not meet all of the "private pay" expenses, then the life and resource plans must be scaled back.

The takeaways from this chapter are:

1. The estimate should be explicitly linked to the life and resource plans.

2. There is no such thing as absolute accuracy when estimating over a period of many years. We want a reasonable estimate that addresses the things for which costs will be incurred, with consideration to milestones when line items of income and expenses start or stop or change significantly.

3. The period in the child's life after the parents' death is too often ignored or poorly addressed.

Estimating Financial Support

How do you estimate lifetime income and expenses? Start with the life and resource plans. The resource plan identifies the products and services that must be paid for. The life plan identifies two things. One, it identifies the assumptions for employment, residence, and the degree of independence. Two, it identifies milestones in the lives of the individual and her parents when income or expenses start or stop, or increase or decrease significantly. Some milestones are predictable, like the age of emancipation (legal adulthood). Some are controllable, such as when a parent chooses to retire. Some are uncontrollable and uncertain, for example when death comes. Regardless of whether predictable, controllable, or uncertain, major milestones should be identified and associated changes in income and expenses estimated. Examples of key milestones were listed in Table 1.2 in Chapter 1.

One should estimate the flow of cash in and out of the family's wallet and financial accounts, whether taxable or not. Don't get confused by the difference between cash income and taxable income. For example, child support must be included in the estimate although not taxable to the child or the parent receiving the payments. Ignore non-cash tax deductions and tax credits. They are irrelevant except as they affect taxes paid.

There are two approaches to dealing with taxes. One approach is to estimate take-home pay after payroll tax deductions. The other approach is to estimate gross income and estimate taxes as a line item of expense. The first approach is simpler and should be adequate if income is largely from employment and tax withholdings approximately equal the taxes owed. When there are complications such as income for which no withholdings have been taken or the Alternative Minimum Tax (AMT), you should use the second approach. Families facing gift, estate, and generation-skipping transfer taxes will need these estimated too. Transfer taxes should be estimated by a tax accountant, tax attorney, or a financial advisor with estate planning and tax expertise.

Income

Typical items of income and support are shown in Table 12.1. It notes which items are taxable and which affect SSI payments. There are four categories of income: government cash assistance, income per court order or contract, the child's personal income, and support provided by others who do not have a legal obligation to do so. There are different levels of risk with each, risks that a source of income may not be available when planned or in the amount estimated. I am mindful of the uncertainties when preparing an estimate. Overestimating income can cause a disruption in the child's quality of life when expenses must be reduced to balance a budget.

Significant items of income should be verified with documentation from the income source. When estimating Social Security future retirement benefits, use the Personal Earnings and Benefits Estimate Statement (PEBES) issued by the Social Security Administration. Check the PEBES for both parents and use the higher benefit. Social Security does not pay benefits on both records; it pays the higher. Obtain an employer pension benefit estimate from the plan administrator or the employer's human resources department. For employee group benefits such as short- and long-term disability, consult with the personnel department or read the employee benefit handbook or summary plan description. For income from insurance policies or annuities, check the policy declarations page or illustration. For court-ordered child support, read the decree and note provisions for future adjustments and expiry dates or events.

Table 12.1 Possible sources of income or support for an individual with special needs

	Taxable	Affects SSI
Social Security or government income assistance		
Supplemental Security Income (SSI) payments	No	*
SSDI or Social Security dependent or survivor payments	Yes	Yes
HUD Section 8 vouchers	No	No
Food stamps	No	No
Earned Income Credit (personal income tax credit)	*	No
Court ordered or contractual payments directly made to the individual		
Child support	No	Note 1
Alimony or spousal maintenance for personal divorce	Yes	Yes
Damage awards or settlements from lawsuit	Note 2	Yes
Pensions and annuity payments	Yes	Yes
Insurance death benefits	No	Yes
Inherited traditional IRA	Yes	Yes
Personal income		
Wage or salary from employment	Yes	Yes
Profit from personal business	Yes	Yes
Interest, dividends	Yes	Yes
Income from rental property	Yes	Yes
Retirement plan distributions or withdrawals	Yes	Yes
Sale of assets	Note 3	Yes
Support from others		
Cash received from parents or family	No	Yes
Third party payments by parents, family or trust	No	Note 4
Free room and board provided by parents	No	Yes
Gifts and bequests	No	Yes
Personal distributions received from a trust	Yes	Yes

Note 1: A percentage of child support is considered income for computing SSI; see SSA policy
Note 2: Generally, non-economic or punitive damages are taxable; compensatory damages are not
Note 3: Capital gains are taxable; sale proceeds are considered income for computing SSI
Note 4: Room and board paid to third parties reduces SSI

You should not include gifts and bequests from other family members, your parents for example, unless included in their legal documents and you have reasonable certainty they will not change their estate plans. Unplanned adversity, like significant medical expenses, can cause someone to revise an estate plan that was originally drafted with the best of intentions.

Some sources of income are adjusted for inflation, Social Security benefits being the most common. The basis for Social Security cost of living adjustments (COLAs) is the National Average Wage Index. COLAs for other income sources are often calculated using the Consumer Price Index (CPI). COLAs may be capped or may be calculated as a percentage of the CPI. This is becoming increasingly common with state and municipal pension plans.

Investments returns will determine how much income can be provided over long periods of time. Most people do not know how to project reasonable returns or how to determine an investment harvesting strategy. Unless you are knowledgeable in investments and retirement planning, consult with an investment advisor for a realistic projection of investment returns and a financial planner for a prudent harvesting strategy.

Expenses

You must understand that it is government policy to provide for only the most basic of human needs, supporting a person with a disability at roughly the poverty line. We are talking food and shelter, essential healthcare, job assistance if they can work, and someone to manage their care. It gets no better than this. It is what is called derisively in the advocacy community as "eats and sheets." Parents, if they can afford it, will want their child to have a good home, community activities, to be with family including those in distant cities, to have fun, and most important of all, to be surrounded by those who truly care for her. This challenge lies at the heart of special needs planning.

I estimate expenses in the three categories shown in Table 12.2: personal, special needs, and professional services. Personal expenses are for the things most people need or enjoy—housing, food, transportation, entertainment, etc. Special needs expenses are for "private pay" goods and services related to the disability—care management, medical needs, therapy, parental respite care, skills coaching, environmental adaptation, etc. You don't need to estimate the value of state services, but if you plan on paying for additional services or units, you should include your out-of-pocket payments in the estimate. Professional expenses are fees for services provided by professionals which the parents do not provide. The first category—personal expenses—is the easiest to estimate. The second—special needs—can be the most uncertain given the risk of cutbacks in government social service programs. The third—professional services—can be the largest lifetime expense if the child outlives his parents for many, many years.

Table 12.2 Typical expenses for individuals with special needs

Personal

Housing

Rent and renters insurance

Mortgage payments, taxes, insurance, HOA fees, maintenance, repair, and contract services

Utilities

Automobile payments, taxes, licenses, maintenance, repair, insurance, and gasoline

Insurance premiums for health, life, disability, long-term care, or liability coverage

Out-of-pocket medical, dental, vision, drugs

Food and beverage

Clothing

Furnishings and household items

Personal and miscellaneous expenses

Travel

Gifts

Pets

Pleasure, entertainment, recreation, or hobbies

Health and personal fitness

Professional continuing education and skills maintenance

Employment or business expenses

Charitable contributions

Personal debt payments

Associated with the disability or medical condition

Case management (government services)

Medical, dental, vision, and psychiatric care

Prescription drugs

Drugs for mental illness

Skilled nursing or skilled personal care and supervision

Personal assistance and supervision

Psychological counseling and behavior modification

Life skills coaching

Occupational, speech, and physical therapy

Job suitability assessment, coaching, placement, and post-placement support

Community access or day programs

Residential services

Assistive technologies and security systems

Home modifications and environmental control systems

Automobile modifications

Transportation services

Respite care

Table continues

Table 12.2 Typical expenses for individuals with special needs *cont.*

Professional services
> Guardian and/or conservator
> Care planner and care manager
> Trustee, trust tax accountant, and trust protector (or trust advisor)
> Investment and financial asset managers
> Financial planners
> Property managers
> Bookkeepers, representative payees, tax preparers, and bank account managers
> Legal, including agents with powers of attorney

There is a major fallacy in all of the published estimating guidance I have found in special needs planning. There is an unstated assumption that expenses will be constant over time adjusted only for inflation. This is an incorrect assumption. It is an absurd assumption. It is probable that *the expenses of the individual with special needs will increase over his lifetime at a rate greater than inflation with step increases at major life transitions.*

You want a bottom line estimate that is somewhat conservative, likely to be a little high and certainly not low. There are two causes of a low estimate: high-cost items have been left out, or some estimates are too low. Both are possibilities but leaving out major cost items will cause the greater error. When preparing an estimate, concentrate on the high-cost items; don't waste time on the minor. (Unfortunately, the minor are usually the easiest to estimate.) Get quotes for high-cost items or estimates from providers and knowledgeable professionals.

A technique to cover the possibility of a low estimate is to apply contingency factors to an estimate (a multiplier like 1.1). It makes sense to apply a higher factor to items with the greater uncertainty or to estimates farther in the future. I cannot give you generalized guidance; it depends too much on specific instances. I am judicious in applying contingency factors because you don't want a grossly inflated estimate either. There is an adverse consequence to an overly conservative estimate: aggressive conservatism will cause an estimate to balloon dramatically over long time horizons, appearing unaffordable. The life plan is then scaled back, perhaps more than it needed to be. Striking a balance between the risk of being too low and the possibility of being way too high requires care. A human being's quality of life will be affected by a poor estimate, either high or low.

The significant impact of inflation over many years on the cost of living is not appreciated by most people. Figure 12.1 shows that 4 percent inflation over a period of 30 years reduces one's standard of living to less than one-third of today's. This is how a couple can go from steak dinners to meatloaf as they age. The rate of inflation is impossible to predict but you can't ignore it. Figure 12.2 shows annual inflation from 1945 through 2006. Note the difference in values as you look back 10, 20, 40, and 60 years (2.5%, 3.1%, 4.6%, and 3.8% respectively). The standard of living over a 30-year period with a 2.5 percent rate of inflation is 30 percent higher than with 4.6 percent inflation. Which should you choose? I use 4 percent but I worry that current government monetary and fiscal policies will eventually cause a return of the abnormally high inflation of the late 1970s. We don't predict the future; we guess at it.

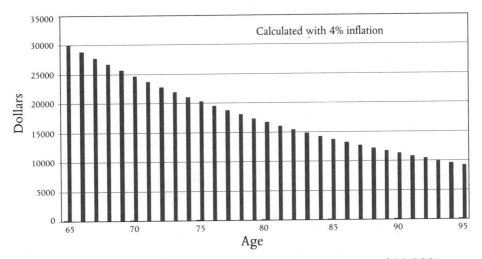

FIGURE 12.1 IMPACT OF 4 PERCENT INFLATION ON STANDARD OF LIVING—$30,000 TODAY ERODES TO $9250 IN 30 YEARS

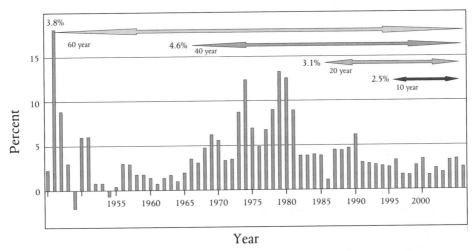

FIGURE 12.2 HISTORIC INFLATION FROM 1945 THROUGH 2006
Source: US Dept of Labor, Bureau of Labor Statistics News, December 2006

Personal Expenses

If you don't know how to prepare a budget, you certainly won't be able to estimate your child's lifetime expenses. Seek help from a money management counselor or a financial planner to learn how to prepare a budget.

It is useful to have some idea of the minimum support needed by an individual. The National Poverty Guideline, published by the US Department of Health and Human Services, is approximately $11,360 for 2013. The guideline includes expenses for a minimum-standard apartment, utilities, food, clothing, transportation, a small personal expense allowance, and a small allowance for out-of-pocket medical expenses. Expenses for quality of life and enjoyment are not included in the poverty guideline. Our national ethos is that poverty should be punishing to encourage people to get out of it (except that people with disabilities often have little choice in the matter). Many families attempt to assure an additional $500–$1000 per month above the poverty level to raise their adult child out of poverty. However, this modest amount will not cover a property purchase, education for employment, or independent living. The more affluent are the parents, the more income they will feel is necessary for an acceptable quality of life.

The purchase of a house or condominium is a major financial commitment and you should consult with real estate and mortgage brokers. Hiring someone for live-in care, supervision, or companionship is a significant expense which must be included in the estimate. Home modifications, security systems, and assistive technologies are also major expenses. The cost of moving into and furnishing an apartment, condominium, or home is easy to underestimate. Don't overlook repairs, maintenance, taxes, insurance, and replacement of household and personal items.

Often families seek to enhance employment possibilities by paying for higher education, vocational training, job coaching, job search, and post-placement support. You should view this as an investment in your child's future but the investment is usually not small.

Special Needs Expenses

To create a list of special needs products and services, I reviewed policies for Colorado's Medicaid HCBS programs and the list of services covered. You can obtain the policies for your state and develop your own list. If your state has non-Medicaid programs funded by state general appropriations, obtain policies for them as well. The resource coordinators of your state or county human services agency may be willing to provide you cost information for the services they manage. Be aware that if you are private paying, you will likely pay higher rates than the state agency because of caps placed by the government on services and provider reimbursements.

There are two problems with the adequacy of state services. One is the restrictive eligibility criteria and the wait lists for those who are eligible. A second, more subtle and more difficult to assess, is that those who do receive services often find them inadequately funded. This is particularly true for people with mental illness. A disability advocacy organization may have a sense of state's underfunding. This could give you an idea of the burden the state is shifting to you. Don't naïvely assume your child will get what she needs.

The value of state comprehensive services for someone moderately or severely impaired can run to $75,000–$125,000 per year. The major cost component is "24 by 7" supervision. Intensive skilled professional care can drive expenses beyond the upper end of the range. Many states have assisted living programs, with names like supported living services, for those who are not in a state-provided residence. Such assistance can include community access programs, job assistance, respite care, home care, or therapy. The dollar value of these services is often capped. Also there is a trend to tighten access to services by imposing "medically necessary" criteria, refusing coverage items like life skills coaching. The level of need is often determined by a scored evaluation. The maximum dollar amount for services is determined by the score. Your state agency intake coordinator should be able to provide cost bands for different levels of assisted living services.

If you plan for your child to live semi-independently, an elder care planner can be helpful in preparing a care plan and an estimate of care services. The needs of the frail elderly and people with disabilities have surprising commonality.

Professional Services

Professional expenses are not a big issue for families with extended family to help or for families with strong circles of support. However, professional services can be a major expense for other families. My family's situation illustrates a common circumstance when these expenses can become significant. We have no other family here in Colorado. If something were to happen to my wife and me, perhaps a fatal car accident, would we want our adult daughter to move to Seattle to be in her brother's care? Would we want her to lose all that we have worked so hard to establish—a circle of friends, a job, participation in a dance company, the life skills program at a local university, being a much-loved member of our faith community—and have her start all over in a different city, perhaps never having her quality of life fully restored? The answer is "no." Keeping Meg in *her* community may require that a professional guardian, a care manager, and a corporate trustee take over our duties when we're not here for her. These will be major expenses in our special needs plan absent a strong network of supports from friends and volunteers.

Professional services are often billed for hours spent multiplied by a billing rate. Billing rates for attorneys in the Denver area typically run to $250–$350 per hour. Rates for CPAs and CFPs run to $150–$200 per hour. Professional guardians and conservators are $75–$125 per hour. Paid companions and personal assistants not required to have professional skills are in the $15–$25 per hour range. Nurses and those professionally trained are in the $25–$40 per hour range. Consult with appropriate professionals for billing rates in your area.

Let's take an example of how professional services may be estimated. Frank is an adult with a moderate cognitive impairment living in a state-provided, four-bedroom house with 24 × 7 staffing. His mother Marion personally assures that he receives the services he needs and is not neglected or abused by his care providers. His brother Ed, who lives in another city, is Frank's only other immediate family member. Ed is concerned about Frank's welfare but cannot personally oversee it.

Marion has a comprehensive estate plan. Ed is the personal representative for her estate. She funded a special needs trust for Frank's support. She prepared a letter of intent and reviewed it with Ed and the trustee of the trust. Her letter instructs Ed to hire a professional guardian to look after Frank's well-being when she dies. The professional guardian's fees will be paid from the special needs trust.

After Marion died, Ed settled her estate. Following her letter of intent, he interviewed three professional guardians from a list provided by a non-profit guardian referral service. Ed selected Sean from the candidates. Ed and Sean negotiated a contract with the following duties and estimated hours:

- Sean is to visit Frank's residence once per week to check on his well-being, at varying times and with short or no notice. If denied access by the staff, he is to contact the family attorney. (1.5 hours per week)

- Sean will take Frank to lunch or dinner once each month to talk about how things are going. (3 hours, 12 times a year)

- Sean will communicate monthly with Frank's government case manager and will respond to all document requests for Frank's annual service eligibility review. (1 hour per month plus 6 hours for the annual eligibility review)

- Sean will meet with the trustee of Frank's trust once per month and recommend disbursements for goods and services. Sean will meet with him once per year to review Frank's care plan. (1 hour per month plus 2 hours for the annual meeting)

- Sean will send Ed monthly reports and they will meet once per year. The contract will be renegotiated annually. (1 hour per month for reports and four hours for the annual review)

Based on the above, it is expected that Sean will invoice 162 hours for services in a 12-month period. Ed and Sean agreed to a $90 per hour billing rate. Sean's annual billings are estimated at $14,580 (rounded to $15,000) plus documented expenses. Monthly invoices are to be submitted to the trustee for payment. The contract provides that should Sean need to urgently intervene for Frank's safety or care, he is authorized to do so immediately with notice as soon as possible to Ed and the trustee. The hours for unplanned interventions will be reimbursed at the negotiated billing rate. Ed and the trustee have the prerogative to direct an additional four hours of duties in a month. Additional hours are limited because Sean has other clients to serve. The guardian's fees over a 20-year period, adjusted for inflation, require a trust funding of approximately $250,000.

The Problem of Accuracy—What is a "Good" Estimate?

Realistically, you cannot estimate expenses accurately over a number of years, much less for decades. Nevertheless, you must do the best you can. You or your financial advisor will use the estimate to determine if you are making enough, saving enough, and investing enough to provide for your child's needs. The estimate will be used to assess whether you have adequate insurance and personal wealth to assure continued support in case of your death or disability.

Estimating lifetime financial support with confidence requires three things:

1. Adequate life and resource plans.

2. Information regarding government disability services and when they will be available.

3. Medical certainty, personal experience, or knowledge of those with similar needs to confirm the realism of the life plan.

You may not be able to develop a reliable estimate until your child is in his or her twenties. The estimate will be "ballpark" for a young child. It will gain in accuracy as the child gets older, as their needs and capabilities are better understood, and with experience as they move into adulthood.

A financial support estimate can require hours of work identifying the things for which costs will be incurred, time-phasing the resources, and performing calculations. I spend 2 to 12 hours depending on the adequacy of the life and resource plans, the complexity of the estimate, and the circumstances of the family. The number of hours depends on the number of line items in the estimate, the milestones, and the number of years in the plan. Litigation—for divorce or personal injury lawsuits—requires many hours developing detailed substantiation because the estimate will either be negotiated or cross-examined in court. If it is planned to incrementally fund a special needs trust, a by-year estimate is required. I avoid spending more time preparing an estimate than circumstances call for to spare the family needless fees. A "ballpark" estimate is appropriate for a very young child. There is too much uncertainty in his future to justify a detailed estimate. For this, I develop order-of-magnitude estimates for the following life phases:

1. The pre-school and school years until the child leaves the school system.

2. As an adult living with parents or relatives.

3. After leaving the parents' home, living in an external, public or private residence.

4. After the death of the first parent.

5. After the death of the second.

The factors that cause the most significant estimating uncertainty are the things over which you have least control. Table 12.3 lists several factors that can significantly affect the reliability of an estimate.

The greatest threat to your child's well-being and the most difficult to assess are future cutbacks in government benefits and services. There are funding pressures at both the Federal and state levels. Changes in eligibility requirements, program benefits, or fiscal appropriations cannot be predicted. Significant cutbacks can be readily absorbed only by the affluent families. Most other families simply cannot carry a much greater burden if the government abandons them. Major cutbacks in services will mean a lessening of hopes for their child's future. Despite the risks and uncertainties, it is necessary to prepare the best possible estimate and update it as laws are passed and budgets adopted.

What is a good estimate? I never use the word "accurate." "Accurate" is measured by a future outcome that is impossible to control or predict. I use the word "reasonable." A reasonable estimate is based on the life and resource plans, uses sound estimating techniques, incorporates the best information available, and is updated as things change or better information becomes available. It includes all items of income and expense and planned life transitions. We strive not for absolute accuracy but relative accuracy. We want to get in the ballpark. Once in the ballpark and by continuing to refine, you will eventually have an estimate that will reasonably reflect the support needed for the rest of your child's life.

Table 12.3 Significant estimating cost drivers and estimating uncertainties

Life plan
Medical condition and cognitive faculties, especially significant changes over time
Supports for independent living
Employment
Life span
Premature death or disability of parents
Family or friends not available or able to provide support or oversight of care needs

Resource plan
Availability of or access to government disability services
Changes in government program services and funding
Unplanned relocation to another state causing disability service interruption

Financial plan
Investment performance
Loss or lapse of insurance, especially medical
Changes in parents' or family's economic circumstances

Estimating errors and uncertainties
Significant items left out of the estimate
Inaccurate estimates for high-cost items
Incurred hours for personal services
Long-term inflation

Estimating lifetime support is like playing a par 60 hole of golf. The green in this analogy is the stable adult situation envisioned in the life plan. The ball in the cup is assuring the support for your child's lifelong well-being and happiness. The tee is when you get serious about planning and take the first club out of the bag. You are not trying to reach the green with your tee shot on this par 60 hole. It will be some time before you see the green hidden by trees, doglegs, and ground contours. Until the green comes into view, all you want to do is to keep the ball in the fairway, hit a reasonable distance, and have a good lie for the next shot. Things will go wrong on this hole—a shot in the rough, a bunker, a water hazard, or out-of-bounds. If you hit a shot in the trees, you will need to play the ball back to the fairway as efficiently as possible. Hopefully, you will incur few penalty strokes. This par 60, 12,000-yard hole can be tiring to play.

But you know, golf can be an enjoyable game. A golf course is a beautiful place with its trees, rolling contours, shades of color, the grass of its greens and fairways, the blue-gray of its ponds and creeks, and the white of its sand. If this hole is played well, the green will be reached in a reasonable number of strokes. Once on the green, all that's left is getting the ball in the cup. But remember as you play this par 60 hole of life, you may not be the one who putts out.

CHAPTER 13

PLAN FOR FUNDING AND MANAGING A SPECIAL NEEDS TRUST

This chapter should be read along with Chapter 19, which describes the legal aspects of special needs trusts. Typically, special needs trusts are created in two simple steps: an attorney drafts a trust agreement naming the parents as trustees; and the parents open a bank account registered to the trust and make a small initial deposit. This creates a shell trust. The trust is like an empty bowl sitting on a shelf waiting for something to happen later. Many parents give little thought to what happens later, except the thought that a life insurance will pay to the trust when someone dies. This chapter is about what happens later.

The takeaways from this chapter are:

1. The non-legal decisions related to managing a special needs trust are:

    (a) how to fund the trust—how much, with what, and when

    (b) what to invest in and how to manage the investments

    (c) whether to hold residential or income-producing property

    (d) distributions and payments for the beneficiary's needs

    (e) administrative matters such as tax returns and record-keeping.

2. Consider funding a trust before you die, perhaps with periodic contributions.

3. Managing investments requires skill to balance risk with return, immediate income with capital growth, and distributions with asset longevity. Parents should consider a corporate trustee or hire an investment advisor unless they are knowledgeable and experienced investors themselves.

The concepts described in this chapter apply to third party special needs trusts— trusts commonly funded by parents and grandparents. Most principles apply to first party special needs trusts as well except that a first party trust is funded by the assets of a person with a disability. Purchase of a residential property by a first party trust, or transfer of an existing property to one, has legal implications and you are advised to consult with an elder law or trust attorney.

Funding—How Much, With What, and When

How Much Money Should I Put in the Trust?

My clients always ask me: "How much money should I put in the trust?" They want a single number, hopefully not too big. One can't pull a number out of the air. One of the most serious flaws in special needs planning is fixing a value to fund a trust that has little or nothing to do with the beneficiary's quality of life or his or her life plan. You have to start with a life plan. Then you estimate what the desired lifestyle will cost. Then you have some basis for deciding how to fund a trust.

Even if you follow this sequence of steps, there still isn't a single funding number for two reasons. First, it depends on when and how (one time or incrementally) you fund the trust. Second, the mathematical equation to calculate a value has five input variables in the simplest of scenarios, seven in more realistic scenarios, five of which can vary by year. You need to set values for each variable to solve the equation. Quite simply, there are a number of moving parts.

When a financial advisor states a value to fund a trust, she usually means the "net present value" or NPV. NPV is a notional dollar amount adjusted for the time value of money. What is time value of money? It is a concept that adjusts the value of a dollar spent or earned at different points in time and expresses it in today's dollars. For example, if you are buying a dollar's worth of gas today, you won't pay a dollar for the same amount ten years from now because of the rising cost of fuel. If the cost of gasoline increases by 5 percent per year, you will pay $1.63 ten years from now. Take another example. If you invest one dollar today and withdraw it ten years from now, you will not necessarily receive one dollar back because the investment will have gained or lost value. If the investment yields a 7 percent return, you will get back $1.97 ten years from now. When a financial professional calculates NPV, she is expressing a value to fund the trust in today's dollars considering the impact of inflation on expenses and assuming a return on investments. She is also assigning values, perhaps not explicitly stated, to the other input variables, either by guessing or by estimating them on some basis.

There are five input variables in the simplified equation to calculate NPV. The calculation can be done easily on a hand-held financial calculator. For example, if the child needs $1000 per month, is expected to live for 50 years, and the rate of inflation is assumed to be 4 percent, and investment returns are projected to be 6 percent, and the trust will run out of money at the child's death (remainder value = 0), you have specified the five variables to solve the equation. If you punch these values into the calculator, it figures the NPV. The displayed result is $385,258. This is generally the state of the art in special needs financial planning with regard to how trust funding is calculated. We must do better. There is a human being's quality of life at stake here.

The advisor is making two important and unrealistic assumptions to solve the equation. These two assumptions underlie all of the trust funding models I have found on the internet or in literature. These models are deeply flawed.

The first unrealistic assumption is that the values of each variable in the equation will not change from year to year except that income and expenses increase at a constant rate of inflation. *In real life, expenses will probably increase over time at a rate greater than inflation and will take step increases at major life transitions.* Other factors in the equation will vary from year to year. For example, projections of investment returns should be adjusted for changes in the investment asset allocation, which is a fundamental tool used to manage a portfolio. *You can't disconnect trust funding calculations from real life just to make the calculation easy!*

The second assumption is that the trust is funded *now* with one contribution, what I call "big bang" funding. Trusts are rarely funded up-front unless someone has already died or unless done so for asset protection purposes. Trusts may be funded with a single contribution at the death of a parent, or two contributions for two parents. However, contributions are sometimes not made at a single point in time but in irregular amounts over a lifetime.

Mathematically one assumes constant variables and one-time funding to solve the simple equation, but these simplifying assumptions are almost certainly unrealistic. We need more sophisticated funding models that explicitly link the required funding to the child's lifetime financial support, with a realistic and thoughtful strategy for the amount and timing of trust contributions. Parents usually support their child out of current income for many years, normally during the years they are working and earning a living. The trust takes over when parents will no longer support their child from the family budget. (One needs to separately assess the contingent scenarios of a parent dying or becoming disabled today or both parents dying or being seriously injured together.) For a time-phased strategy, one should calculate the NPV for each year using the seven variables listed in Table 13.1.

When I am working with a family to develop a funding strategy without the life and resource plans to work with (which unfortunately is usually the case), I start with an estimate of the child's annual expenses for the first year after aging out of school, or the current year if he or she already has. I identify milestones or transitions when expenses significantly change, like when the child moves out of the parents' home into an apartment. I estimate financial support in blocks of time corresponding to life phases or the intervals between major milestones. I use an Excel workbook with two linked spreadsheets, one for the child's support by year and one for trust funding. I enter the child's expenses less her earned and unearned income to calculate the support from parents or other sources, for example a special needs trust. For the trust funding purposes, I separate the years when the parents provide direct support, focusing only on the years when the support will come from the trust. (In the contingency scenario of an income-providing parent dying today, trust distributions obviously start right away unless the other parent can continue to provide all of the support.) The required trust distributions from the first spreadsheet automatically transfer to the second spreadsheet to develop a trust funding plan. Screen shots of the spreadsheets for lifetime financial support and trust funding are shown in Figures 13.1 and 13.2. For each year I calculate the net present value for trust income less distributions for all future years. The result in any given year is the dollar amount required to complete funding of the trust. A negative number in a year indicates how much must be contributed in that year to complete the funding. A zero or positive NPV means the trust has been adequately funded; no further contributions are needed.

Table 13.1 The seven variables to calculate the net present value of a trust

1. Amount and timing of future contributions
   Gifts, bequests, and property transfers from estate planning
   Income assigned to the trust

2. Trust distributions by year
   Based on the estimate of lifetime financial support in accordance with a life plan, plan of care, or letter of intent

3. The number of years until the beneficiary's death
   Depends on the child's assumed age of mortality

4. Investment returns
   Investment returns (net of investment management fees)
   Income from property owned by the trust

5. Trust expenses   TRUST TAXES
   Administrative expenses
   Fees for special services

6. Remainder value at beneficiary's death

7. Present value of trust assets

Note: Italicized text denotes factors in estimating the variables

Estimate of Lifetime Financial Support

Estimated For:

Date:

Year	2012	2013	2014	2015	2016	2017	2018	2019	2020
Father's age		1	2	3	4	5	6	7	8
Mother's age		1	2	3	4	5	6	7	8
Child's age		1	2	3	4	5	6	7	8

Income less Expense

	0	0	0	0	0	0	0	0	0

Deesc'n Factor	1.000	1.00000	1.00000	1.00000	1.00000	1.00000	1.00000	1.00000	1.00000	1.00000
In Today's $	0	0	0	0	0	0	0	0	0	

Income — Inflation CY $ 0.00%

SSDI	1.000	0	0	0	0	0	0	0	0	0
SSI	1.000	0	0	0	0	0	0	0	0	0
Earned Income	1.000	0	0	0	0	0	0	0	0	0
Parents Support	1.000	0	0	0	0	0	0	0	0	0
Other Income	1.000	0	0	0	0	0	0	0	0	0

Total Income

	0	0	0	0	0	0	0	0	0

Expense — Inflation 0.00%

Special Needs		0	0	0	0	0	0	0	0	0
Personal Expenses		0	0	0	0	0	0	0	0	0
Guardians and Other		0	0	0	0	0	0	0	0	0

Total Expense

	0	0	0	0	0	0	0	0	0

FIGURE 13.1 SPREADSHEET—ESTIMATE OF LIFETIME FINANCIAL SUPPORT

Special Needs Trust Funding Plan

Name:

Date:

Total Contributions

Remainder Value

Remainder in Add'l Years

For Years
Gross Return
Asset Mgmt Fees
Net Return

# of Years

Begin in Year

End in Year

Return on Assets

0-2	3-5	6-10	10+

	Trust Assets at BOY	Capital Contribut'n	Trust Distribut'ns	Asset Appreciat'n	Trust Assets at EOY	Future Funding (NPV)
2012	0		0	0	0	0
2013	0		0	0	0	0
2014	0		0	0	0	0
2015	0		0	0	0	0
2016	0		0	0	0	0
2017	0		0	0	0	0
2018	0		0	0	0	0
2019	0		0	0	0	0
2020	0		0	0	0	0
2021	0		0	0	0	0
2022	0		0	0	0	0
2023	0		0	0	0	0
2024	0		0	0	0	0
2025	0		0	0	0	0
2026	0		0	0	0	0
2027	0		0	0	0	0
2028	0		0	0	0	0
2029	0		0	0	0	0
2030	0		0	0	0	0
2031	0		0	0	0	0
2032	0		0	0	0	0
2033	0		0	0	0	0
2034	0		0	0	0	0

FIGURE 13.2 SPREADSHEET—SPECIAL NEEDS TRUST FUNDING PLAN

I want a trust to have a remainder value in the year of the beneficiary's death, equal to some number of years of additional distributions. This provides a margin of safety should the child live longer than expected. I choose the number of years considering the child's disability. I use a remainder value of an additional five to ten years of support because the life expectancies of people with disabilities continue to increase.

Both spreadsheets allow variables to be changed from year to year in accordance with the life and resource plans and the parents' plans for their future, retirement for example. Variables can be changed as life happens. Special needs planning is a process not an event, and if you treat it as an on-going process and update as you go along you will be steadily moving toward your goals. A model doesn't need to be an accurate prediction of the future. It needs to be a reasonable basis for the decisions of the day.

There is no general answer to the question, "How much money should I put in the trust?" because each family has unique life and resource plans and financial circumstances. The obvious next question is, "Is there a typical range of values?" There is a wide range of values. The Net Present Value of a third party trust, unconstrained by affordability, can range from less than a hundred thousand dollars to well over a million. The largest I have encountered was $3.4 million. Table 13.2 lists factors that substantially increase or decrease the calculated NPV of a trust. The range is rising as Medicaid and state service cutbacks force parents to take a greater burden for their child's care.

There is not enough space here to illustrate how a funding plan is developed. But I wrote this book not only for parents and families, I also wrote it for my colleagues, the Certified Financial Planners and the CLU/ChFCs who practice in special needs planning. Many have a thorough understanding of the principles of financial planning with expertise in investment management, retirement planning, and estate planning. Many possess sound analytical skills and sophisticated tools. I hope that they will quickly grasp how to apply the arts and sciences of our profession to solve what has been, in the past, a poorly structured problem.

Table 13.2 Factors that significantly affect the required trust funding

Factors that increase the required funding

Future cutbacks to Social Security, Medicaid, and state disability services

Not eligible for government assistance or wealthy family chooses not to use it

Government services are inadequate or significantly delayed

Life plan sets semi-independent living as the goal

Purchase of a home or condominium

Higher education to enhance employment possibilities

Child outlives parents for a long time, professionals hired for parental roles

Privately paid companions and human supports

Alternative therapies

Mental illness and the cost of psychiatrists, psychologists, and medications

Factors that decrease the required funding

Child has shortened life expectancy

Parents will support child from current income for most of his life

Reliance on government assistance for supports and services

Family and friends make up a comprehensive circles of support team

Child has significant income (e.g. from a good job, child support)

Child has substantial assets (e.g. from an inheritance, damages award)

What Do You Fund the Trust With?

The most common approach is to fund the trust with life insurance when a parent dies. An alternative strategy is to routinely save and invest through one's working years to create sufficient wealth to allow the insurance to be partially or completely retired at some point in the future. A financial plan will identify the parents' bank and investment accounts, retirement plans, other assets, and how much each is worth. If one knows the NPV to complete the trust's funding, and the value of assets in the same year, one can earmark which assets, or a percentage of them, to fund the trust with. If assets are not sufficient to complete the funding, we look to life insurance to cover the shortfall. Financial assets can be transferred to a trust by changing the title or registration on an account, or assets can be sold and the cash deposited. Funding a trust with an Individual Retirement Account (IRA) can be tricky so I like to use other sources of funding first, unless it makes sense from a tax standpoint.

When Should You Fund the Trust?

A trust should be fully funded after the second parent dies. However, there are other points in life where it may be desirable or necessary to fund a trust.

Strategies to fund a trust with incremental or periodic contributions when the parents are alive can make more sense. Let's look at some examples.

Early in my career, I had an elderly woman come to me. She was in her eighties and had a middle-aged son with a cognitive impairment. During the preliminary consultation I asked the common question posed by financial planners, "Well Helen, what do you want to do?" And she said, "I just need to lay it all down." She had reached the point with diminished physical strength and stamina where she could no longer care for her son. I now believe, given the physical and mental deterioration with age, especially with the rising incidence of Alzheimer's as people enter their eighties, that planning to fund a trust when the parents are in their mid-seventies is a better strategy. Even if it is not necessary to do so when one reaches that age, the risk in not planning for this possibility is that the parent may not have made financial arrangements for someone to take over. If the only arrangement made is life insurance, what will be done between the time of entering a nursing home and the time one dies?

A parent's retirement could be the milestone when the trust could be funded. In retirement a parent's income drops, possibly to zero except for Social Security. One's wealth accumulation slows and absolute wealth may even decline. There should be enough wealth and life insurance to meet the child's future needs when the parents retire. Even if contributions and asset transfers are not made then, you should verify that there are sufficient financial resources to take care of the child before one retires.

The third example is my own. My daughter wants to live in an apartment with her two best friends. While planning to make this happen, it occurred to me, "Why not start funding her trust now?" Why? Frankly, I am an at-risk person for a cardiovascular incident. I want to make sure everything works to support my daughter's independence while I'm alive and can make any necessary or desirable adjustments. I want to experience working with a corporate trustee (a charitable, pooled-asset trust) to gain confidence that it will serve my daughter well. The advantage of funding a trust while living is that parents will gain experience working with a trustee and, hopefully, a long-term relationship will develop between the trust officer, the family, and the beneficiary.

Investments

An investment portfolio serves two purposes: to provide immediate income or asset growth for a greater level of income in the future. This is an either/or choice. One must choose or compromise between taking income today and sacrificing income in the future to some extent, or forgoing income now to have more income later.

One of the fundamental laws of investing is that you must accept a higher risk of loss to achieve a higher rate of return. Investors should pay close attention to their risk tolerance. An investor's financial or objective risk is determined by how much he can afford to lose without seriously affecting his financial security or ability to reach future goals. An investment manager looks at several factors in analyzing a person's objective risk: cash flow, net worth, future goals, and adequacy of risk protection—that is, insurance. Investors also have a psychological risk tolerance which reflects their feelings of anxiety or fear in falling markets. Good financial advisors use the more conservative of the two risk tolerances when designing an investment portfolio. Portfolios can be categorized for risk as conservative, moderate-conservative, moderate, moderate-aggressive, and aggressive. Income-oriented portfolios are more conservative; growth-oriented portfolios are more aggressive.

When an investment manager designs a portfolio to match a client's risk tolerance and objectives, she starts by allocating the value of a portfolio across five classes of investments: stocks, alternative assets such as commodities, real estate, bonds, and cash and cash equivalents. This process is called asset allocation. Stocks and alternative investments are typically higher risk; bonds and cash are lower risk. After determining an asset allocation, the manager selects specific investments within each class. In the long run, the asset allocation will contribute more to investment performance than the selection of securities, perhaps accounting for as much as 90 percent of the portfolio's performance. There are five typical portfolio models used by investment managers, the names of which express the balance sought between income and growth: income with capital preservation (most conservative), income with modest growth, growth with some income, growth, and aggressive growth (highest risk). A table of possible asset allocations for different portfolios is shown in Table 13.3.

Current investment income, also called investment yield, comes from the interest and dividends paid by securities held in the portfolio. Total investment return is the interest and dividends plus capital gains or minus capital losses. Yield and total return are expressed as a percentage of the value of investments. The performance of investments in a special needs trust can make a significant difference in the beneficiary's standard of living. For example, a $100,000 account with a 2 percent net annual return can generate an income stream of $303 per month that will last for 40 years. Increasing the return to 5 percent will generate $482 per month over the same period, 60 percent more. Sound investment management requires expertise and experience. The choice of an investment manager, yourself or a professional, is one of the most important decisions you will make in managing a trust.

Table 13.3 Asset allocation examples for five common portfolios

Portfolio objective:	Income w/ capital preservation	Income w/ modest growth	Growth w/ some income	Growth	Aggressive growth
Relative risk:	(Conservative)	(Moderate conservative)	(Moderate)	(Moderate aggressive)	(Aggressive)
Asset class					
US stocks	15	30	35	40	35
International stocks	10	10	15	20	25
Bonds	65	45	30	20	15
Real estate		5	6	7	8
Commodities			3	4	5
Alternatives	5	6	8	9	12
Cash	5	4	3		

Note: Numbers are percentages of the total portfolio

Trust investing is challenging even for professional investment managers. The objective is to provide a beneficiary with a decent standard of living. For a beneficiary who lives near the poverty line, which is usually the case for someone with special needs, there's not a lot of margin for error. At the same time, we can't stick the money in a checking account earning no interest, with the account continuously depleting over the child's lifetime and running out of money before he dies. With special needs trusts, especially those with modest assets, an investment manager will likely construct a portfolio to protect current income with low risk of loss—a conservative or moderately conservative portfolio, with an objective of income with capital preservation or income with modest growth. An improved strategy, which takes skill and sophistication to execute well, is to partition the portfolio into three or four parts for distributions in different future time horizons. These are not separate accounts but pots of money within an account. I use four pots with four horizons:

1. Cash or relatively safe investments (certificates of deposit, money market securities, or short-term bond funds) to provide income needed in the immediate two years. The asset allocation for this pot corresponds to an income-with-capital-preservation or conservative risk model.

2. A moderate-conservative, income-with-modest-growth objective for three to five years' needs, generating income to refill the first portfolio.

3. A growth-with-some-income, moderate-risk portfolio for income six to ten years in the future. This portfolio pours money into the second to replenish it.

4. A growth portfolio, moderately aggressive, for income more than ten years in the future. It is used to refill the third portfolio.

I rebalance the four portfolios annually. Again, prudent and effective investing is a sophisticated skill. When parents think their way down the long and winding road of their child's future, they may well realize that the best choice for managing trust investments is a corporate fiduciary.

What Can a Trust Own?

A trust can own anything—cash, securities, real estate, insurance polices, annuities, collectibles, mortgages, business interests, timberland, etc. However, the purpose of a special needs trust is to support the beneficiary's standard of living by making routine and regular disbursements. Consequently, a trust should hold investments that either generate income or can be readily sold. Investments must be liquid and marketable. Mutual funds, exchange-traded funds (ETFs), and publicly traded securities are assets commonly held in trusts. Although somewhat unusual, a special needs trust can hold life insurance policies and annuities. Annuities provide monthly income and a life insurance policy provides a legacy. Exotic or illiquid assets such as raw land or a gun collection have no reason to be owned by a special needs trust.

A special needs trust may hold real estate such as the residence of the beneficiary or rental-income property. If you plan for the trust to hold residential property, be aware of two things. One, trusts do not get the capital gains tax exemption on a personal residence that is available to individuals and married couples. Two, a standard home owner's insurance policy does not cover a home owned by a trust. A different policy form is required. Inform your insurance agent that the residential property is or will be trust-owned to assure proper coverage. Real estate purchased by parents should be owned by a third party special needs trust. If owned by a first party trust, it will be subject to a Medicaid lien when the trust beneficiary dies.

If the individual owns or is purchasing a residence and wants to maintain Medicaid eligibility, personal ownership or trust ownership are options. If needing public housing assistance to finance the purchase, the property must be individually owned. Having the first party trust own the home may be the better option for property management and protection from financial exploitation. Trust ownership will better protect the individual from loss of the home. However, if individuall owned or held by a first party trust the property will be subject to a Medicaid lien at the death of the owner if over 55 at the time of death. If the owner can transfer the property to another family member with a disability, individual ownership may be the preferred option. When considering individual versus first party trust ownership, one should consult with an elder law or trust and estates attorney, the local HUD Housing Choice Voucher Program administrator, and the state or local housing authority that makes home ownership loans for people with low incomes and disabilities.

Distributions

Distributions must be made in accordance with language in the trust agreement that describes the goods and services that the trust can pay for. Normally this is not a problem because attorneys use broad language for allowable payments. Nevertheless, I would not treat the language as legal boilerplate. Read it in the context of your life plan, looking for things that should be mentioned in the list of allowed purposes for disbursements. For example, if the individual needs alternative medical treatments for pain relief or physical therapy, for example Chinese Qigong, the language should explicitly permit payment for alternative treatments.

Distributions from the trust must be made for the benefit of the beneficiary, although not necessarily for her sole benefit. With others living in the same residence, sole benefit can be unnecessarily restrictive. However, there must be a strong connection between the goods and services bought by the trust and the beneficiary's benefit. A trust protector, seeing the trustee has purchased a home theatre system, knowing the beneficiary is blind and lives with several family members, should ask him some very pointed questions about who requested the purchase and inquire as to who is enjoying the system.

Trustees prefer to have a plan of care for the beneficiary to guide distributions. If you have a life plan or a letter of intent, review it with the trustee. If annual or periodic PATH plans are prepared, the parents, guardian, advocate, or someone from the inner circle of the child's support team should meet with the trustee and review the most recent plan and discuss disbursements for the coming year. From personal experience and knowing many trust officers, I believe that most are genuinely interested in their beneficiary's welfare.

The trust should make payments directly to third party providers for goods and services, distributing only modest living allowances to the beneficiary. Distributions to the child are counted as income by Social Security and Medicaid. Payments to third parties are not. A trustee should be aware of the child's countable income and not exceed the income eligibility limits for means-tested government assistance. A trustee should avoid the error of allowing the beneficiary to accumulate money in his bank account exceeding the $2000 SSI/Medicaid asset limit.

The difficult dilemma a trustee faces is balancing two conflicting purposes: providing for an adequate quality of life today and conserving trust assets to last a lifetime. The trustee or parents' financial advisor should make periodic asset projections based on trust income and the plan of distributions to verify that assets will not be exhausted unexpectedly while the beneficiary is still alive. If there is a possibility that the trust will run out of money, tough decisions must be made. Sometimes there is simply not enough money, immediate needs are paramount, and there is no dodging the consequences. Decisions about how to provide the best possible quality of life, balancing immediate needs with long-term asset conservation, should reflect the values of the family and the wishes and needs of the child. Freedom from pain may be the most basic value of all.

Administration

A trust incurs expenses for investment management, trust administration, and special services. Investment management expenses are the internal expenses of an investment portfolio. They are incurred for investment research, security selection, security safekeeping, securities trading, market monitoring, performance measurement, and record keeping. These embedded expenses are charged directly to the investment account and reduce the portfolio's returns. One should be aware of high internal management fees because of the drag on investment returns. However, what the beneficiary ultimately cares about is the net returns since that is what he or she lives on. If one is projecting the value of trust assets over time, one projects capital appreciation using net returns.

Trustee administrative expenses are incurred for accepting deposits, making disbursements, investment performance reviews, instructions to the investment manager, managing cash accounts, meeting with clients, regulatory fees, etc. Administrative fees are often charged as a percentage of trust assets, typically on a sliding scale. There are services unrelated to the account value for which a flat fee is charged. Administrative fees should be estimated and treated as an expense because they are billed to the trust.

Special services are those required for the unique needs of the client. Preparation of trust income tax returns or Form 1099s are examples. If the trust holds property such as real estate, mineral rights, life insurance policies, business interests, etc., there will be fees charged to the trust for managing those assets. For example, the management fee for rental property might be 5 percent of gross rent receipts. Fees for special services should be estimated and treated as an expense.

How do you estimate trustee fees? When you interview the trust officer of a corporate trustee, obtain its schedule of services and charges. Fees are negotiable for high-value trusts, but most special needs trusts will not meet a bank's or trust company's threshold for negotiations. The best you can do is comparison shop. An example of a schedule of services for a bank or trust company is shown in Table 13.4.

Table 13.4 Example of a fee schedule for a special needs trust (sample of services)

Monthly administrative fee	$60 per month
Deposits and disbursements	
Accounting	
Client meetings	
Fiduciary reports	
Management fee	
On the first million dollars in assets	$10.00 per $1000
On the second million dollars	$9.00 per $1000
On the third million dollars	$8.00 per $1000
On the fourth million dollars	$7.00 per $1000
Over $5,000,000	negotiable
Special services	
Grantor trust Form 1099	$500
Form 1041 tax return for irrevocable trust	$750
Rental property management	5% of gross rental receipts
Residential property management	$250 annual fee plus third party contracts
Mortgage fee	$200
Other services (non-attorney)	$250 per hour

Where to Go for More Information

A practical book on special needs trusts was authored by a team of attorneys: *Managing a Special Needs Trust: A Guide for Trustees* (Jackins et al. 2012). Despite its focus on Massachusetts' system of services, it contains useful guidance for trustees and trust protectors in other states.

Financial and investment advisors may have recognized that the practice of partitioning a trust investment portfolio into separate pots for different time horizons with different asset allocations for each pot was taken from the retirement planning concepts developed by Raymond Lucia, CFP. I highly recommend his book, *Buckets of Money: How to Retire in Comfort and Safety* (Lucia 2004), to those who already are knowledgeable and experienced in managing investments.

CHAPTER 14

MAINTAIN AN INSURANCE SAFETY NET

The seven steps to a secure financial future were listed in Chapter 11. Having adequate insurance was one of the steps. An insurance safety net is more important than investing until you are wealthy enough not to need insurance. Families with little savings or families just starting out need insurance to protect their financial security, especially if one of the family members is a special needs child. The types of insurance below should be considered a necessary part of comprehensive risk management:

- health insurance to protect against sickness or injury

- life insurance to protect against the premature death of an income provider or a childcare giver, or to provide a survivor legacy

- disability insurance to protect against the loss of income if one is unable to work or manage a business

- long-term care insurance to pay for assisted living, skilled nursing, or custodial care for dementia

- annuities to guarantee a lifetime income

- property and casualty insurance to protect against the loss or damage to a home, automobile, personal possessions, and collectibles; and liability coverage in case someone is killed or injured on one's property or by a vehicle one owns

- general liability insurance for harm caused by personal acts or negligence

- property, casualty, and liability insurance for a business

- professional liability insurance for physicians, attorneys, accountants, consultants, engineers, financial advisors, and insurance professionals.

This chapter describes the roles that various types of insurance play in special needs planning. The chapter briefly covers how to obtain insurance. There is also a description of the process called underwriting that insurance companies use to decide whether to insure an individual and the premiums to charge for a policy.

One should not procrastinate in obtaining needed insurance coverage. Premiums for life, health, disability, and long-term care insurance increase with age. Health problems can develop unexpectedly, leaving one uninsurable or having to pay higher "table rated" premiums.

Health Insurance

Healthcare is for prevention and treatment. Preventive healthcare can extend life and allow one to enjoy the benefits of being healthy. It is impossible for anyone to go through a long life without needing treatment for sickness or injury. But more importantly, the cost of healthcare for a catastrophic medical condition can cause family impoverishment. High medical bills not covered by health insurance are the greatest cause of personal bankruptcy in this country. The inability to treat injury or illness because one cannot afford to do so can shorten life or take it away. Once parents have their heads above water financially—that is, they have adequate income to meet expenses and can repay their debts—quality health insurance is the most important financial asset they can have.

Most people under age 65 are covered by group plans sponsored by private and government employers. The self-employed typically purchase private, individual insurance. People over 65 typically have Medicare and Medigap, or retiree health insurance offered by private and government employers. Those with disabilities may have Medicaid. However, there is a large population missing from these categories; the percentage of Americans lacking any health insurance is among the highest of developed, western nations.

Many states have high-risk or catastrophic insurance pools for those who cannot obtain coverage. However, this insurance is often quite expensive and beyond the means of those with a disability who are unemployed or in low-wage or part-time jobs. The Patient Protection Act's healthcare exchanges are intended to replace these pools.

A disturbing trend in this country is the increasing numbers of employers dropping group health insurance altogether. The obvious motivation is to increase profits. The trend threatens millions of workers and their dependents with loss of coverage. With simultaneous cutbacks in government health insurance, the rise in the numbers of uninsured may become a serious national problem.

Special needs planning should address health insurance because people with a disability usually cannot afford it and insurance companies often refuse to cover them individually. Many people with a disability are covered as a dependent on a parent's employer group insurance. Typically, such coverage is offered by larger employers who employ skilled and educated workers. Small companies and employers who employ the unskilled often do not offer health insurance, or do not cover dependents. Many small companies cannot obtain affordable insurance if any employee or dependent has a serious medical condition or a disability. The Patient Protection and Affordable Care Act (PPACA) has two features that could benefit people with disabilities. The first is the formation of insurance exchanges to help small companies obtain affordable insurance. The second is the requirement that if an employer offers dependent coverage, it must cover a disabled dependent through age 26. People with disabilities who earn between $387 and $1040 per month or $1740 if blind (2013, indexed to inflation) can indirectly become eligible for Medicare by first becoming eligible for Social Security Disability Insurance (SSDI) benefit. The lower limit is the income necessary to earn a work credit to qualify for SSDI. The higher limit is the SGA. If one's income exceeds the SGA, one is not considered disabled under the Social Security regulations. Medicaid becomes the insurer of last resort for many people with a serious disability. Eighty-six percent of the people receiving Medicaid are children, the frail elderly, and people with disabilities. For them, the drastic cut in Medicaid demanded by political conservatives (40% in one prominent politician's plan) is a serious threat. For some, the cuts could be life-threatening.

Life Insurance

There are two basic types of life insurance: term and permanent. Term insurance provides a death benefit. It is the cheapest insurance, especially when purchased through a group plan. One can purchase a guaranteed renewable policy which guarantees the right to renew coverage if the annual premium is paid. Guaranteed level premium term insurance has a fixed, level premium for the number of years purchased. It can be purchased for from 5 to 30 years of coverage. Because the cost of term insurance increases with age, it is usually bought by people when younger and for needs that go away, for example to ensure that children can go to college or to repay a mortgage if a wage-earner dies. Since the cost of insurance increases with age, becoming increasingly expensive as one reaches the late 50s, it is rarely extended into one's retirement years. If a child is permanently disabled, term insurance on the parents' lives may not be the right type of insurance. Permanent insurance is likely to be more appropriate.

Permanent insurance (the word "permanent" is misleading because no insurance is permanent if you don't pay the premiums) is usually a better solution in special needs planning. Permanent insurance is intended to provide coverage for an insured's entire lifetime. Policies were designed in the past to mature or "endow" at the insured's age 100. With increasing life expectancies, most policies today are written to remain in force indefinitely. Permanent policies are designed for level premiums despite the increasing mortality cost with age. One pays a higher premium in the early years which exceeds the cost of insurance. The excess premium is invested, creating a fund which builds in value to pay the premiums in later years. Permanent insurance policies have a cash value created by the early excess premiums. If the annual premium and cash value is insufficient to pay the cost of insurance, an additional payment must be made or the policy will lapse. "Lapse" is an insurance term meaning the policy is no longer in force and the death benefit is no longer available. Insurance companies may allow the restoration of the policy in limited circumstances but some do not.

There are three common types of permanent insurance: whole life, universal life, and variable universal life (VUL). Whole life insurance is the most conservative and predictable. If one pays the specified premium, the death benefits and cash values are guaranteed. Universal life insurance offers some flexibility in premium payments. UL policies typically have a slightly lower premium than whole life. However, if one underpays the premiums and does not make them up later, the policy will eventually fail. Variable universal life policies are the most risky of the three but VULs have powerful advantages for a family who can accept the risk. The premiums paid into a VUL, after the insurance charges are deducted, are invested in a policy owner account allowing for growth in the cash value and death benefit if the investments perform well. A VUL has attractive tax advantages which I won't go into here. Theoretically, VUL premiums will be less than for whole or universal life policies. Practically, since investment performance is not guaranteed, it may or may not be the cheapest type of insurance. A VUL policy is a powerful and flexible financial instrument but it places risk on the owner which must be managed. A VUL is not a "buy and forget" policy. Investment performance must be reviewed periodically with attention to the level of premiums needed to keep the policy in force and the projected lapse year at the current premium level. If the lapse year is getting close, premiums must be stepped up to protect the policy. A financially unsophisticated individual who does not understand these policies or one who is not inclined to pay attention to financial matters should have a financial advisor monitor policy performance or avoid VULs altogether.

There is another type of permanent insurance, called survivorship or "second to die." Such policies play a useful role in special needs planning. Both spouses are named as insured parties but the policy only pays a benefit on the second death. A survivorship policy is used to provide a legacy for a child who outlives both parents. Survivorship policies cost less than the cost of two individual insurance policies with equal combined death benefits. Survivorship policies are usually of the universal life type.

There are decisions to make regarding the amount of insurance to buy, the type of insurance, and the policy features and riders. Table 14.1 lists decisions in selecting a policy. These decisions are best made in the context of financial planning so that the insurance fits a family's financial situation, its goals, and needs for managing risk. Financial planning provides the best basis for determining the amount of insurance needed. Absent a financial plan, life insurance agents often recommend an amount of insurance based on income replacement; the death benefit is a multiple of the insured's income. A death benefit determined in this way may have no correlation to the needs of the family or the special needs child.

Table 14.1 Decisions for purchasing individual life insurance

1. Death benefit

2. Policy type
   1. Term
        Annually renewable term
        Guaranteed level premium term, 5-year, 10-year, 15-year, 20-year, 25-year, or 30-year
        Convertible term (convertible to a permanent policy)
   2. Permanent
        Whole life
        Universal life
        Variable Universal Life (VUL)
            Death benefit Option A or Option B
            Risk tolerance, investment allocation, and investment selection
   3. Survivorship or second-to-die universal life

3. Beneficiary(s), primary and secondary

4. Premium payments
   1. Payment mode—annually, quarterly, monthly
   2. Premium payable until age 65 or for life (permanent insurance)

5. Term insurance riders
   1. Additional purchase option
   2. Waiver of premium
   3. Additional insured (for family, covers spouse and children as factor of primary insured)

6. Permanent insurance riders
   1. Waiver of premium rider
   2. Accelerated death benefit rider
   3. Long-term care rider

7. Company selection
    1. Financial soundness rating
    2. Customer service reputation
    3. Premium (primary consideration for term insurance with first and second factors)
    4. Permanent insurance
        Mutual insurance company versus investor-owned company
        Whole or universal life illustration
            Premium
            Guaranteed and current tables of cash values, charges, death benefit, dividends (by year)
            Policy loan interest
            Insured's age when policy lapses should be at least age 100 for illustrated premiums
        Variable Universal Life
            VUL premium—target, minimum and maximum non-MEC premium
            Cash value and death benefit at 0 rate of return and ROR for risk classification
            Policy loan interest
            Insured's age when policy lapses should be at least age 100 for illustrated premiums

I prefer whole life or universal life insurance unless I'm working with a financially secure and sophisticated family, in which case a VUL will be the preferred option. Each parent should have a policy on their own lives with a second-to-die policy to leave a final legacy. Term policies can be layered on top of the permanent policies for protection needs that eventually go away, such as the repayment of a mortgage.

Disability Insurance

Disability insurance (DI) is purchased to replace income if an insured is unable to work because of sickness or injury. It is an often overlooked type of insurance; it should not be. If someone is disabled at an early age, the lost earnings over the working years can far exceed the amount of life insurance one would likely need. One should always carry adequate disability insurance. Arguably, it is the most important insurance to have through the late middle-age. The chance of becoming disabled is higher than the chance of dying until one reaches the late fifties. The loss of lifetime income if an individual is disabled at an early age can destroy any long-term hope of a good life.

Disability threatens a family in three ways. The first threat is lost wages. The second is the cost of treating the injury or illness that caused the disability. The third is increased monthly expenses not directly related to the disability, such as the increased cost of childcare if a parent care giver is disabled. A common gap in special needs planning, one with no good insurance solution, is the disability of a stay-at-home, care-giving parent. With no income to replace, disability insurance is not an option.

There are two types of disability insurance: short-term and long-term. Short-term usually provides a benefit of 100 percent of income for a period of time, typically 10 to 90 days. Long-term disability pays a monthly benefit, typically 60 percent of income, after the short-term coverage ends. Most DI in this country is obtained through employer group plans. Those who are privately employed must purchase individual insurance. Those with inadequate employer coverage, not uncommon in the government sector, can purchase private insurance to supplement their group coverage. Professionals such as doctors, accountants, attorneys, etc. can obtain relatively inexpensive coverage through professional societies. However, professional group plans typically provide only basic coverage. Individual insurance will often better serve the high-income professional.

DI policies, group and private, are often integrated with Social Security Disability. If the insured qualifies for SSDI, the policy's monthly benefit will be offset. The logic here is the restrictive definition of a disability used by Social Security and the fact that many who apply for SSDI are denied. Alternatively, the policy may provide a basic benefit with a supplement that kicks in if Social Security is denied. Supplemental coverage will have a lower premium. Either way, the company can lower the aggregate premium charged over the entire population of insured, taking advantage of the fact at least some will receive Social Security Disability.

The definition of a disability used by an insurer, regarding whether the disabled person can work, is important. There are three definitions: "own occupation," "modified own occupation," and "any occupation." "Own occupation" means you are disabled if you cannot hold the type of job you held prior to being disabled. If you were a surgeon, you are disabled if you can't return to surgery. Professionals such as doctors usually can obtain own-occupation coverage. "Modified own occupation" means any job for which you are qualified by education and experience. White-collar employees are usually offered modified own-occupation policies. "Any occupation" means what it says—if you can do any job, you are not disabled. Usually blue-collar workers can only obtain any-occupation insurance. Get the best affordable coverage that you can.

Table 14.2 lists the decisions you will make in selecting a disability insurance policy.

Table 14.2 Decisions for purchasing disability insurance

1. Short-term disability (generally employer group)
   1. Monthly benefit
   2. Waiting period in days
   3. Benefit period in days
   4. Premium
   5. Benefits taxable or non-taxable (taxable if employer pays premiums)

2. Long-term disability
   1. Monthly benefit
   2. Waiting period in days
   3. Benefit period in years or until age X
   4. Premium (not taxable if premiums are paid by insured)
   5. Definition of disability—own occupation, modified own occupation, any occupation
   6. Premium payment mode—monthly, quarterly, annual
   7. Features
      Social Security integration
      Partial disability
      Residual disability benefit
      Rehabilitation and transition back to work benefits
      Recurring disability
   8. Riders
      Cost of living adjustment or additional purchase option
      Social Security replacement supplement if policy integrated with Social Security benefit

3. Company selection
   1. Financial soundness rating
   2. Customer service reputation

Long-Term Care Insurance

Families with a special needs child should consider obtaining long-term care insurance (LTCI). LTCI covers the cost of a stay in an assisted living facility, a custodial care facility (think Alzheimer's), or a skilled nursing facility. The cost of assisted living or custodial care in most areas of the country is of the order of $50,000 per year. Skilled nursing is $80,000 or higher. The cost varies widely from state to state. If a parent requires care for several years, the family assets that may have been used to support a special needs child can be dramatically drained or exhausted.

Most people think that Medicare pays for long-term care. This is a dangerous misconception. Medicare pays for assisted living or skilled nursing care only in narrow circumstances. Medicare covers about 17 percent of the cost of long-term care in this country. Medicaid covers almost half. About 10 percent is paid by insurance companies from claims against long-term care policies they have written. The remainder, almost 25 percent, is paid by individuals out-of-pocket, many of whom have to deplete their assets or sell their homes.

LTCI is fairly expensive but the cost of not having it can be ruinous. Premiums for a policy for a 50-year-old male in good health can exceed $2000, payable for life or as long as the coverage is desired. One reason for the relatively high cost is the cost-of-living rider. One is insuring a need that may be two or three decades in the future. One should elect the cost-of-living rider to cover inflation in the cost of care.

It is true that not everyone will need long-term care in their lifetime. About one-sixth of those over 65 require long-term care assistance in any given year. The probability of needing long-term care increases with age and passes 50 percent in one's mid-80s. Too many families take a chance that the odds will not catch up with them. The cost of long-term care can be catastrophic to a family. In special needs planning, the role of LTCI is to prevent the quality of life of a special needs child from being seriously diminished in order to pay for a parent's care. One should not roll the dice when the care of a special needs child is at stake.

Long-term care policies are complex products with many benefits and features and optional riders. Careful consideration should be given to policy design and affordability. Table 14.3 lists considerations in purchasing LTCI policies. I encourage you to consult with an advisor knowledgeable in this type of insurance to help you balance benefits with affordability.

One should consider purchasing long-term care insurance no later than in one's late forties. Policy premiums begin to increase dramatically in the late fifties. The underwriting standards for LTCI are tougher than for life insurance. As one ages, the chance of becoming medically uninsurable is not small. For those who cannot obtain LTCI, a less attractive possibility is annuity-based long-term care protection or a life insurance hybrid. However, annuity-based and life insurance hybrid coverage will have less coverage and fewer features and benefits than a good LTCI policy. If LTCI is obtainable and affordable, both parents of a special needs child should have LTCI coverage. If the couple obtains spousal policies the premiums will often be heavily discounted. Why? Because in the initial stage of a long-term care need, one spouse will usually try to take care of the other until the burden gets too great. The insurance companies know this.

Table 14.3 Considerations for purchasing long-term care insurance

1. Type of policy and benefit
   1. Expense reimbursement
   2. Monthly benefit
      Daily limit
      Monthly limit
   3. Spousal policy
      Shared benefit period
   4. Tax qualified versus non-tax qualified

2. Facility coverage
   1. Skilled nursing
   2. Assisted living or cognitive impairment
   3. Home healthcare

3. Additional benefits
   1. Adult day care
   2. Respite care
   3. Care planning
   4. Equipment and home modifications
   5. Bed reservations
   6. Care giver training
   7. Hospice care

4. Benefit triggers
   1. No. of Activities of Daily Living (ADLs) requiring assistance—bathing, dressing, toileting, transferring, continence, eating
   2. Cognitive impairment
   3. Doctor's decision (non-tax qualified)

5. Monthly benefit

6. Waiting period in days

7. Coverage period in years or total benefit dollars

8. Riders
   Inflation or cost of care adjustment—simple or compound
   Additional purchase option
   Waiver of premium
   Spousal discount if each spouse has policy
   Restoration of benefit
   Survivorship
   Non-forfeiture protection
   Return of premium

9. Company selection
   1. Financial soundness rating
   2. Customer service reputation
   3. Premium considering policy features

Annuities

Annuities are contracts offered by life insurance companies that in their simplest form pay a person, called an annuitant, a guaranteed income stream for life. Commonly, the annuitant is the person who purchased the contract, but it can be someone else. One company allows parents to buy an annuity that continues to pay a benefit to a special needs child who outlives them. Life insurance is priced assuming an age of mortality, the median age of death for a population. With life insurance, the company is at risk if policy holders die early before having paid their premiums. Annuities are not underwritten like life insurance policies. The annuity company is at less financial risk selling contracts to people in poor health. With annuities, the annuitant wins by living beyond the age of mortality, drawing more payments than the company figured when it priced its policies.

There are two types of annuity: immediate and deferred. With an immediate annuity, you pay a lump sum premium for an income stream that starts immediately. With a deferred policy, you pay premiums for a number of years and elect when you want the payments to start. This is called "annuitizing" the contract.

Annuities are characterized as fixed and variable. With a fixed annuity, the contract is credited with a specified interest rate and it pays a fixed monthly benefit based on the premiums and the interest earned. Fixed annuities are usually not indexed to inflation so the annuitant will experience a gradual erosion of purchasing power as the years go by. The cash account inside a variable annuity contract is invested as directed by the owner. If investment performance is above expectations, the annuitant receives higher monthly payments. If investment performance is poor, the annuitant receives less and the contract can run out of money before the annuitant dies. Because monthly payments vary with investment performance, the contract is called a variable annuity. Variable policies transfer risk from the annuity company to the annuitant. However, they indirectly offer inflation protection if the investment accounts perform well.

In recent years, companies have tried to boost sales of deferred variable annuities by offering guaranteed death benefits, guaranteed lifetime withdrawal benefits, and guaranteed lifetime income benefits. In effect, the companies are allowing you to transfer some of the risk back to them if you pay a fee. Variable annuity products have gone well beyond being simple products. They have become quite complex and potentially quite expensive if you buy multiple guarantees. With these products, you should carefully consider what you need and buy only the guarantees that fit your needs.

Consumer advocates criticize annuities for being unnecessary and too expensive. The criticism of being unnecessary is too simplistic. For some purposes annuities are an ideal solution. Variable annuities purchased with lifetime benefit guarantees prior to the Great American Recession have been great investments. Such annuities preserved value through a terrible financial meltdown (unless the company selling them went bankrupt). However, both fixed and variable annuities sold since the recession have struggled to offer good value in the distorted financial environment of interest rate suppression and sub-par investment returns. The financial planning lesson here is that one's best course of action is often obvious only in hindsight. The criticism of being expensive does have some basis, especially if the purchaser buys a lot of unneeded features or guarantees.

Annuity contracts pay lucrative commissions to the agents who sell them. It should be no surprise then that they are often oversold to the general public, especially to the elderly. When considering a purchase, you should work with an advisor who commits to advise you in your best interest. A commission salesman, operating to the standard of suitability, may sell you the most expensive product he can. Because of the complexity of deferred variable annuities, you are vulnerable to being taken advantage of by salesmen seeking primarily to maximize their commissions.

I have not mentioned one type of annuity: an equity-indexed annuity (EIA). I didn't because I do not like EIA products and have never recommended one to a client. They are so complex and have such subtle caps, triggers, and algorithms that one can't project on any reasonable basis a probable financial outcome.

Where do annuities fit in the priority scheme? There are a lot of exceptions to blanket statements but I place higher priority on having adequate health, life, disability, and long-term care insurance, and on diligent saving and investing in one's income earning years. I consider annuities primarily for retirement to provide a guaranteed level of income in one's retirement years. In some circumstances, layering a variable annuity on top of a fixed annuity, assuming one can afford it, makes a lot of sense.

Property and Liability Insurance

Most individuals and families have automobile insurance coverage because states mandate purchase. Most home owners have home owners insurance because mortgage companies require it. Most professionals in private practice (doctors, lawyers, accountants, engineers, etc.) have professional malpractice or errors and omissions insurance because they are targets for lawsuits. Owners of businesses with employees, assets, and inventories will carry liability insurance and coverage for loss, theft, damage, or liability because it's good business.

Renters should have coverage for their furnishings, household goods, and personal belongings. Families should have personal liability insurance, called "umbrella liability," for personal acts not covered by other forms of insurance. The upper-middle class and the wealthy typically have adequate property and liability insurance because they tend to be informed consumers. Many in the lower-middle or working class do not have adequate coverage, either for reasons of affordability, a desire to save money, or failure to understand the need.

The issue for families with a special needs child is that the loss of home or belongings, or a liability claim from a third party for injury or death, can reduce the family wealth that supports a special needs child. Parents of a child with a disability should thoroughly review the adequacy of property and liability coverage and obtain the coverage needed. Many financial advisors, including many excellent CFPs, give inadequate attention to this class of insurance. One reason is that many do not sell it. A competent advisor should do a complete property, casualty, and liability risk assessment. If the assessment uncovers a gap, the advisor should refer you to an agent licensed in the product line.

Obtaining Insurance

The Underwriting Process

The most significant factor that determines the premium for a given amount of life, disability, or long-term care insurance is one's age. The older you are, the higher your premium will be. You may have to pay an even higher premium if your health has begun to deteriorate beyond the population normal. Or you may become uninsurable. Many health indicators deteriorate in late middle age. Any deterioration can adversely affect the insurance company's underwriting decision.

Underwriting is the process an insurance company uses to evaluate the financial risk of insuring someone. The underwriting decision is two-fold: whether or not to offer a policy; and the premium to charge if it does. The information needed for underwriting is obtained from the insurance application, an interview with the applicant (usually by phone), laboratory tests (blood samples), and a review of a physician's medical records. Typically one must have had a physical exam within the past 12 or 24 months. There are three categories of factors that go into underwriting: health indicators, health history, and lifestyle. Health indicators are parameters such as weight versus height, cholesterol levels, blood pressure, blood sugar, etc. Health history is looking for prior health problems such as past surgeries, heart attacks, strokes, diagnoses of disease, and prescription drugs recommended by a doctor. Often considered is the occurrence and cause of the premature death of a parent. Lifestyle factors include smoking, alcohol use, recreation, and driving history. Life insurance companies think someone with a lot of speeding tickets is a poor risk. They don't like scuba divers either. They may offer a policy, but probably for a higher premium.

The most important lifestyle indicator for insurance purposes is *smoking*. Companies maintain one premium table for non-smokers and a higher premium table for smokers. Smokers pay a 30–50 percent higher premium on that factor alone. The increase may be compounded because smoking causes deterioration in other health factors like blood pressure.

There are certain events in one's health history that will eliminate any possibility of obtaining a policy—a diagnosis of a degenerative disease for example. These are "go/no-go" criteria. Other health indicators are numerically scored. The underwriting sheet has a list of factors with a score for each factor based on a range of values. For example, there may be four cholesterol ranges for one's age. A reading in the lowest band may be scored "0." The score in the highest band may be "5." The numbers are added and the total determines the premium category. Lower numbers place the applicant in a lower premium category. You may be considered a "preferred plus," a "preferred," or a "standard" insured. If you have a high underwriting score, you may be charged the standard premium times a multiplier like 1.15. Premiums higher than the standard table are called "table rated" in the trade.

Most financially strong life, disability, and long-term care insurance companies are quite selective in whom they insure. By setting high underwriting standards, they insure a more healthy class of policy holders which allows them to charge lower premiums. You may be turned down by one company and find another with lower underwriting standards willing to insure you, probably at a higher premium. However, if you are denied by one company, its decision goes into an industry database and other companies may discover it. Before you apply for a policy, discuss your health situation with your insurance agent. The good ones will have a good idea which company will likely offer a policy, and which may be reluctant.

The Insurance Application

Your financial advisor or insurance agent will assist you in completing an application. The application requests personal information, beneficiary names, physician's name, type of policy, and the desired features and riders. The application has a set of medical history questions to be answered "yes" or "no." These are considered "material representations" and an untrue answer can be treated as insurance fraud. If the company issues a policy and finds that a material answer was not true, it can refuse to pay a benefit and refund the premiums paid. It does not have to prove intent to commit fraud to void the policy.

The advisor or agent taking your application must give you a policy illustration or a premium quote. The advisor will usually illustrate a smoker or non-smoker standard premium. It is typical to collect a payment for two months of the quoted premium with the application. If the company offers a policy at a higher premium than quoted, you have a right of refusal and the pre-payment will be refunded. In most states, you have a 30 or 60 day "free look" period after the policy is delivered. If you decide you do not want the policy during the free look period, you may return it and any premiums paid will be refunded.

Selecting an Insurance Company

One of the most important factors in selecting an insurance company is its financial strength as scored by one of the insurance company rating services. There are five rating services—A.M. Best, Moody's, Fitch, Weiss, and Standard & Poor's. The most commonly recognized is A.M. Best. The scales used by the raters are shown in Table 14.4. As you can see from the table, a B+ rating by Fitch, for example, is not as good as it sounds.

I also encourage you to choose a mutual insurance company, not a stock company owned by investors. Mutual insurance companies are owned by policy holders and are obliged to serve them and not investors. A mutual insurance company pays dividends to policy holders if the company's claims history and investment performance are better than the assumptions underlying the premium tables. Dividends may reduce the premium you owe or you may choose, in the case of life insurance, to use the dividend to purchase an increased death benefit. Over time, the accumulation of dividends in a mutual company's life insurance policy can substantially and painlessly increase the death benefit.

It is striking how the best customer service companies tend to cluster in the top of the financial ratings given by the rating companies. However, there are a few companies with strong financial ratings that have a history of ethical lapses in the conduct of their business, typically questionable sales practices on the part of their agents. I suggest you check articles in consumer magazines that rate insurance companies for consumer service. The most notable is *Consumer Reports*. The magazine has an index of recent articles in its December and January issues. Also check the complaint records of the company and its agent with the state commissioner of insurance office. Often this information is available on its website.

Table 14.4 The categories used by the five insurance rating companies

A.M. Best	S&P	Moody's	Fitch	Weiss
A++	AAA	Aaa	AAA	A+
A+	AA+	Aa1	AA+	A
A	AA	Aa2	AA	A-
A-	A+	Aa3	AA-	
	A	A1	A+	
	A-	A2	A	
		A3	A-	

Acceptable for your consideration

Not acceptable

A.M. Best	S&P	Moody's	Fitch	Weiss
B++	BBB+	Baa1	BBB+	B+
B+	BBB	Baa2	BBB	B
B	BBB-	Baa3	BBB-	B-
B-	BB+	Ba1	BB+	C+
C++	BB	Ba2	BB	C
C+	BB-	Ba3	BB-	C-
C	B+	B1	B+	D+
C-	B	B2	B	D
D	B-	B3	B-	D-
E	CCC	Caa1	CC+	E+
F	CC	Caa2	CCC	E
	R	Caa3	CCC-	E-
		Ca	CC	F
		C	C	
			DD	
			D	

CHAPTER 15

EFFICIENTLY MANAGE INCOME, TRUST, AND ESTATE TAXES

Over a lifetime, taxes can be one of a family's largest expenses. Minimizing them can have a significant impact on lifetime wealth and standard of living. A family should take advantage of all of the deductions, credits, tax exemptions, and tax deferrals that may be available to them. A tax strategy addresses more than the parents' income tax. Taxes paid by a child with a disability, by her special needs trust, or by a wealthy family on its estate should also be managed and legally minimized. State taxes are also a part of the total tax obligation; rates vary widely from state to state but can add one-third or more. One should not focus on the percentage of income that goes to taxes but the after-tax money available to support a person with special needs. A middle-class family saving a few thousand dollars each year over a span of decades can noticeably improve their child's quality of life. This chapter does not treat general Federal tax provisions but addresses aspects of the tax code relevant to special needs planning.

There are three important things to remember about taxes in special needs planning:

1. Whether or not you can claim a dependent exemption for your adult child on your tax return will be determined by the qualifying child test if he or she lives with you and the qualifying relative test if he or she does not.

2. Contributions to an irrevocable special needs trust are taxable gifts if exceeding the lifetime gift tax exemption or annual gift tax exclusion. This can affect affluent families with a high-asset trust.

3. Distributions made directly to your child from a special needs trust are taxable income to him or her and can affect SSI and Medicaid eligibility.

The Parents' Income Taxes

Probably the most important and most common tax benefit for parents of a special needs child is the dependent exemption. Most parents have taken an exemption since their child's year of birth but may not be aware of the rules for claiming the exemption when the child turns 19 (24 if a full-time student). You may claim a dependent exemption in the year of the nineteenth birthday and in years following if the following conditions are met under *the qualifying child test*:

1. Your child lives with you for at least half of the year (residence test).

2. The child is totally and permanently disabled regardless of age (age test). Social Security's definition of a disability applies.

3. The following relatives can be claimed as a qualifying child: your child, step-child, grandchild, legally adopted child, and their descendants; and your siblings including step-brothers, step-sisters, and their descendants (relationship test).

4. No one else can have claimed the exemption, including the child, on his or her tax returns in the same year.

5. The child cannot have provided more than one-half of his or her support.

Note the eligibility of a grandchild or sibling under the relationship test. Sometimes the child with special needs is in the care of a grandparent. The grandparent can claim the dependent exemption if the other tests are met. The eligibility for a sibling is significant because sometimes people care for a disabled brother or sister.

The residence test is critical. A qualifying child must live with the parents for more than one-half of the year to claim the child as a dependent under the qualifying child rules. *The potential problem with parents claiming the exemption is the child who lives in a state residence, his own residence, or other residence and not his parents' home.* If the child does not live with his parents, the parents cannot claim him as a qualifying *child* dependent, but they may be able to claim him as a qualifying *relative* dependent. If the child moves out of the parents' home, parents should be aware of the potential loss of the dependent exemption. If a child lives with grandparents, they can take the exemption but the parents cannot. If the parents are divorced, it is possible with split custody that either could claim the exemption. The divorce decree will specify which spouse gets the exemption, often in alternating years.

If the child does not meet the qualifying child test, the parents may still claim the exemption if he meets the qualifying relative test. There are two additional tests for the qualifying relative exemption: the gross income limit and the support test. The child's income must be under $3800 and the relative claiming the exemption must provide over 50 percent of his support. It is possible that the support test can be passed if the child is living in his own residence, has minimum income, and the parents provide most of his support. If the child's support comes from an irrevocable special needs trust, distributions from the trust do not count as support provided by the parents to claim the exemption. If the child receives state comprehensive services, it will be difficult for the parents to pass the support test because of the amount of money the state spends on the child's needs.

The credit for "Child and Dependent Care Expenses" (line 48 on the 2011 Form 1040—US Individual Income Tax Return) can be claimed for an adult with a total and permanent disability if the other rules for the credit are met. Total and permanent disability is an exception to the requirement that the child must be under the age of 13. However, the "Child Tax Credit" (line 51 on the 2011 income tax form) does not have an exception for a disabled child. That credit is only available if the child is under 17.

If you or your spouse are blind or over the age of 65, you may claim a higher standard deduction. Blindness does not affect the total of itemized deductions. The fact that a dependent child is blind does not affect the standard deduction on the parents' return.

Two little-used tax-exempt strategies are available to parents and others who wish to contribute money for the education of a special needs child. They are Coverdell Education Savings Accounts (ESAs) and Section 529 Qualified Tuition Programs. In both cases, contributions are not tax deductible but investment earnings accumulate tax-free. Some states allow a state income tax deduction for contributions to that state's 529 Plan. If money from these accounts is withdrawn for qualified education expenses, there is no income or capital gains tax on the withdrawals. However, if money is withdrawn and not used for qualified expenses, the person receiving the withdrawal (either the owner or the beneficiary) must pay tax on the investment gains at ordinary income tax rates plus a 10 percent penalty tax. There are pros and cons to the two types of plan.

Section 529 plans are the most common and generally the most flexible. There are two types of 529 plan: pre-paid tuition and college savings plans. The latter is described here. Section 529 college savings plans can be used for higher education expenses at a college or university in any state, but cannot be used for kindergarten, elementary, middle, or high school expenses. All states have 529 plans and you can invest in any state's plan; you are not limited to your state's. Qualified expenses include tuition, fees, room, board, and textbooks, but not personal expenses. These plans can also be used for vocational school or certificate programs for people with disabilities (described in Chapter 6) as long as the school or program qualifies for Federal financial aid. There are no income limits that prevent high-income individuals from contributing to 529 plans. There are total contribution limits which vary from state to state, but the limits are generally higher than the cost for four years of enrollment at all but the most expensive of educational institutions.

Any individual can contribute up to $2000 per year to Coverdale ESA accounts. This is quite limiting, but two parents and four grandparents can contribute a total of $12,000 in one year. One advantage of Coverdell accounts is that tax-free withdrawals can be used to pay for kindergarten, primary, middle, and secondary school expenses at private schools, as well as for higher education. If the intended beneficiary cannot use the money for education, the account can be transferred to a qualifying relative but this must be done prior to the beneficiary's thirtieth birthday. Parents may contribute to both 529 plans and ESAs in the same year. However, there are income phase-out limits that prevent high-income individuals from contributing to an ESA.

These accounts must be parent-owned or owned by someone other than the beneficiary if the beneficiary receives or is to be eligible for SSI and Medicaid. If registered in the name of the child, assets in the account are countable as the child's assets. Parents who own 529 plan accounts must designate a successor owner in the event of their deaths to preclude the accounts from being inherited by the child. The parents of a special needs child must weigh the possibility that the child will not be able to use the accounts for his or her education, exposing them to a tax liability and the 10 percent penalty. Money can be withdrawn without penalty if the beneficiary dies. Both plans allow the money in the accounts to be used for another qualified relative. The tax risk is mitigated if there is at least one other child in the family who could use the money set aside. If the child with special needs is an only child, contributions to a 529 plan may be ill-advised.

The Child's Income Taxes

The Internal Revenue Code considers most money received by an individual to be taxable (see Table 12.1). Taxable income includes:

- Social Security Disability Insurance and dependent and survivor benefits
- distributions from an irrevocable special needs trust to the beneficiary
- punitive damages awarded as an outcome of a lawsuit.

Income that is not taxable includes:

- Supplemental Security Income (SSI)
- payments to third parties made by a special needs trust
- child support
- life insurance death benefits
- inheritances (except a tax-deferred retirement plan)

- HUD Housing Choice Voucher Program payments

- food stamps

- compensatory damages and damages for pain and suffering awarded as a result of a lawsuit.

Due to inconsistencies in the Social Security Act and the Internal Revenue Code, an income source that is not taxable may be countable as income in determining Medicaid and SSI eligibility and in computing SSI payments. Gifts, cash received from others, child support, life insurance death benefits, and damages awarded in a lawsuit fall in this category.

Although uncommonly used, the Earned Income Credit may benefit some people with disabilities. The Earned Income Credit (EIC) is primarily intended to benefit low-income families with children. However, a low-income, childless individual who is at least 25 years of age but under age 65 is eligible to take the EIC if adjusted gross income is under $13,660 ($19,190 if married and filing jointly). The EIC can generate a tax refund. Significantly, an EIC refund is not considered countable income for SSI or Medicaid purposes. The maximum EIC is $475. The child cannot claim the EIC if he is claimed as a dependent by another taxpayer. Most parents claim the dependent exemption because they are in a higher tax bracket.

Child support is not taxable income. However, two-thirds of child support is countable income for SSI and Medicaid purposes if the child is 18 or younger. All child support is countable if the child is 19 or older. Child support is fully countable for Federal housing assistance.

Trust Income Taxes

There are two types of trust: grantor trusts and taxable trusts. A revocable trust is a grantor trust. Trust income is taxable to the person who created the trust at her individual tax rates. An irrevocable trust is a taxable trust (ignoring one weird creature of the tax code, an intentionally defective grantor trust, a trust that benefits the wealthy). An irrevocable trust is a separate tax-paying entity, has its own tax number, and must file a Form 1041—"US Income Tax Return for Estates and Trusts" annually. Irrevocable trusts pay onerous tax rates in comparison with individual rates, as seen in Table 15.1. The problem is not higher tax rates but lower tax brackets. A trust reaches the 35 percent rate at $11,650. Married couples filing jointly do not reach the 35 percent rate until taxable income is $388,350 (2012). All disability trusts, including special needs trusts, are entitled to a tax deduction of $3700.

Table 15.1 Trust income tax brackets compared
to personal income brackets (2012)

Tax rate for each bracket in percent	Tax brackets	
	Married, joint return	Trust
10	Up to $17,400	
15	From $17,401 to $70,700	Up to $2300
25	From $70,701 to $142,700	From $2301 to $5450
28	From $142,701 to $217,450	From $5451 to $8300
33	From $217,451 to $388,350	From $8301 to $11,350
35	Above $388,501	Above $11,350

Trusts pay taxes in any given year on income accumulated in that year. If the trust makes distributions to the beneficiary or other parties for his or her benefit, it gets a tax deduction for the distribution. The rules are more complicated than this, but rather than go into the mechanics of what is called Distributed Net Income (DNI), for our purposes let us say the trust pays money on its income less distributions for the tax year. With this simplification, let's assume the Smiths have established an irrevocable special needs trust for their son John. The trust has assets of $500,000 generating $25,000 of income. It distributes $5000 to John. Its taxable income is $20,000 less the $3700 disability trust deduction, or $16,300. The tax is $4670 computed using the tax rates and brackets for trusts shown in Table 15.1. Note that this is an effective tax rate of 28.6 percent, much higher than the 10 percent rate for an individual with $16,300 in taxable income. One of the ways to minimize taxes on an irrevocable trust is to balance, to the extent practical, distributions for the beneficiary's support and the income generated inside the trust.

There are challenges to efficiently managing a trust. One is efficient investing. Another is managing taxes. Many parents do not have the knowledge and skills to do either well. They should get professional advice or appoint a corporate trustee when a trust is substantially funded. Trust tax computations are very complex and few individuals will be able to complete a Form 1041 correctly. Parent trustees of a funded, irrevocable trust should have a professional prepare the trust's tax return.

Estate, Gift, and Generation-skipping Transfer Taxes

The transfer tax system includes the estate tax, the gift tax, and the generation-skipping transfer tax (GSTT). The estate tax is called the "death tax" in certain ideological circles, a deliberate misrepresentation by those pushing for its repeal. Less than 0.4 percent of the people who died in the United States in 2011 had an estate that filed a gift, estate, or GSTT tax return (Commito 2012 and the 2011 IRS Data Book). These taxes are not death taxes because few people who die pay them. They are wealth transfer taxes. In 2012, the exemption for these taxes was $5,120,000 for an individual. A married couple may use twice this exemption, thus passing $10.24 million tax-free. It is possible for estates larger than this to escape taxation with sophisticated estate planning techniques due to the many tax loopholes such as the minority-share discount for family limited partnerships. In the period of 2000–2006, transfer tax revenues averaged about $26.7 billion per year. The tax exemption was increased in each of the next five years and by 2011 tax revenues had dropped to $2,506,991,000 ($2.5 billion), a 90 percent reduction (Commito 2012). The estate tax was repealed four times in the twentieth century. It was reinstated after each repeal to reduce the Federal budget deficit.

One can give unlimited money to a spouse or charity and the gift is removed from one's taxable wealth. Tax must be paid on gifts to anyone or anything else if the total of all gifts exceeds the exempted amount, $5.12 million. Money contributed by parents to an irrevocable special needs trust is potentially taxable as a gift. Practically, contributions will escape taxation because of the generous exemption unless other gifts have used it up. However, if the exemption is rolled back by future changes to the tax code, gift tax could become a consideration for highly funded trusts. Generation-skipping transfer taxes apply to grandparents creating a trust for a grandchild but, as with gift taxes, the GSTT is not likely to be of concern at current exemption levels.

Many parents with a special needs child carry large amounts of life insurance. What most don't know is that the death benefit of life insurance owned by a person is included in the valuation of his taxable estate. This provision was inserted in the tax code to prevent wealthy families from escaping estate taxes by buying large amounts of life insurance for no other purpose than to avoid taxes. The inclusion of life insurance in the taxable estate is not likely to be a consideration for middle-class families given the current estate tax exemption. However, if the exemption is rolled back, parents should estimate their taxable estate to see if the insurance they carry creates an unforeseen tax liability. If this happens, effectively they will find they have less life insurance than they thought they had. If life insurance causes or increases the estate tax liability, transferring policy ownership to an irrevocable trust will remove it from the taxable estate after three years.

Transfer tax returns and tax avoidance strategies are very complex. If you are exposed to estate or gift taxes or the GSTT, you should hire a tax attorney. Those wealthy enough to be exposed to the transfer tax system probably know this and already have estate-tax attorneys and CPAs to advise them, but some of the newly wealthy, or those drawn in by owning large amounts of life insurance, may not.

Where to Go for More Information

The IRS website is www.irs.gov. It is reasonably well organized but IRS publications are not as clearly written as those of the Social Security Administration. In fairness to the IRS, the Internal Revenue Code dwarfs the Social Security Act in complexity.

Arguably the best tax guide for individual income taxes is published annually by J.K. Lasser. Lasser publishes its guide at the end of the year for tax returns to be filed in the following year. Lasser guides are widely available in bookstores.

CHAPTER 16

UPDATE YOUR FINANCIAL RECORDS TO IMPLEMENT YOUR ESTATE PLAN

This chapter should be read with Chapter 17 which covers estate planning from a legal perspective. As described in that chapter, an estate plan for distributing property and cash after your death will be implemented in one of three ways, in accordance with your will, your living trust, or through prearrangements made while you are alive.

Prearrangements include title on real estate and other assets and beneficiary designations for insurance policies and financial accounts. Prearrangements can also include contracts for the future sale, liquidation, or transfer of a business, and legal documents such as self-canceling installments notes, private annuities, charitable trusts, etc. Prearrangements must cover everything not covered in your will or living trust. It is surprising but not rare for families to have their legal documents prepared by an attorney and then fail to complete the financial documents to implement their estate plan. I once had a client couple who established revocable living trusts (RLTs) so most of their assets would bypass probate. I was surprised to find they had not transferred their assets to the RLTs. Consequently, their estate plan would not execute when they died. Nor had they updated their insurance policy death beneficiary forms. Their wills made no mention of some high value assets (art and jewelry). The overall result was a potentially devastating failure of their estate plan, all the more dismaying because one of the three children was a child with Down syndrome. His special needs trust would not fund due to the incomplete arrangements. As a parent, I was shocked by the clients' failure to follow through with the actions to implement their estate plan, leaving their children at risk.

Remember these points after finishing this chapter:

1. You must take the actions to implement the estate plan as defined by your legal documents by completing or updating your financial documents.

2. Use proper title for your child's special needs trust.

3. Trace the flow of estate property transfers and monetary distributions at the death of either parent or the simultaneous deaths of both.

Proper Title for Assets, Bequests, and Beneficiaries

Title to property defines who owns it. It is the name on a bank account, an investment account, a title to real estate, a promissory note, or ownership documents. With real estate, the owner is named by the property deed. The name on a bank or financial account is the account registration. An account may have a single owner, for example John Smith. It may have co-owners, for example John and Mary Smith. There are two common legal forms of co-ownership: "Joint Tenants with Right of Survivorship" (abbreviated JTWROS or JTTEN) and "Tenants in Common" (TIC). With JTWROS the co-owners each have 50 percent ownership of the asset and the survivor automatically inherits the share of the owner who dies. With tenants-in-common there may be more than two owners, their shares may be unequal, and the inheritance of each owner's share is independently passed by his will. The other tenants-in-common owners do not automatically inherit a share at his death. There are also custodian accounts, Individual Retirement Accounts (IRAs) being the most common. The title or registration on an IRA reflects the type of IRA, the custodian, and the person for whose benefit the custodian manages the cash or investments. For example, the registration on an IRA might be "Traditional IRA FBO Michael Banks, the Fidelity Fiduciary Bank, Custodian." A "traditional" IRA is a type of IRA as distinguished from a Roth IRA. "FBO" is an abbreviation of "For the Benefit Of." The bank is the custodian managing the investments for Michael's benefit. UTMAs (after the Uniform Transfer to Minors Act) are also custodian accounts and are similarly designated—account type, benefitting person, and custodian.

Trusts have a title as well. In most states, a trust is named by designating the trustee, the legal name of the trust, and the date the trust was created. Thus, the title might be "Donald Martin, Trustee of the Alfred E. Newman Special Needs Trust dated April 1, 1954." In some states like Colorado the trust title and date are sufficient to name the trust, for example "The Alfred E. Newman Special Needs Trust dated April 1, 1954." The name of the trust is declared explicitly in the first or second paragraph of the trust document with language such as: "This trust shall be known as the Alfred E. Newman Special Needs Trust." It is important in wills, property titles, account registrations, and beneficiary designations to name a trust unambiguously. Ambiguity can arise when two special needs trusts, first party and third party, are created for the same beneficiary on the same day. An irrevocable trust may be unambiguously named by its tax identification number. A revocable trust's tax ID number is the Social Security number of the grantor.

The key thing to remember about title is that bequests, gifts, asset title, or beneficiary designations should not use the name of a person with a disability if that individual is receiving or is to receive government means-tested assistance. One must designate the person's special needs trust. The gift of a small amount can be made to the individual if one is careful about the $2000 asset eligibility limit. A check made out to Meg Wright for her weekly allowance can be deposited in her personal bank account. For larger amounts, I make the check payable to her trust. Parents will have this explained to them by an attorney or financial advisor. However, it is important to communicate the need for using proper title to other family members such as grandparents. An attorney will provide a letter for parents to send to other family members when a special needs trust is created that explains how to make gifts or bequests to the trust.

Beneficiary Designations

Life insurance policies, both individual and group, allow a policy owner or employee to name primary and contingent beneficiaries. "Secondary" is a synonym used for "contingent." One completes a beneficiary form which can usually be downloaded from the insurance company's website. The completed form is mailed to the insurance agent or company's customer service address. Annuities and other forms of insurance which have a death benefit also have beneficiary forms. There can be more than one primary or contingent beneficiary, in which case one should specify the percentage of the death benefit each is to receive. If there is more than one beneficiary and no percentage specified, the insurance company will pay equal shares. If there are no living primary beneficiaries and no *per stirpes* beneficiaries, then the contingent beneficiaries receive the death benefit. A special needs trust, or for that matter any type of trust, can be named a beneficiary.

If there is more than one primary beneficiary, one can designate whether payments are made *per capita* or *per stirpes*. *Per capita* means that if one of the beneficiaries dies before the insured, the remaining beneficiaries share the death benefit in proportion to the percentages specified for each. For example, if three beneficiaries are named to receive equal shares but A dies before the insured, B and C each receive 50 percent of the death benefit. If a beneficiary is a couple and one dies, the survivor receives the couple's share. *Per stirpes* means that if one of the beneficiaries dies, his or her children receive his or her share. Thus, if A (a person) dies and has three children, B and C receive 33.33 percent of the death benefit and A's three children each receive 11.1 percent. *Per stirpes* has a hidden danger for grandparents who have a special needs grandchild. If the parents die before the grandparent, the special needs child will inherit directly if a *per stirpes* beneficiary designation is specified.

Bank and financial accounts allow one to name beneficiaries. Bank accounts use a "Pay on Death" (POD) form. Investment accounts use a "Transfer on Death" (TOD) form. Basically, these two forms accomplish the same thing. One obtains the form for the account from the firm holding it. Most employer retirement plans and pensions allow non-spousal contingent beneficiaries or non-spousal primary beneficiaries if the spouse waives his or her right to a survivor benefit.

Traditional (non-Roth) IRAs have complex beneficiary distribution rules and one must be aware of them. These rules are mandated by the Internal Revenue Code. The purpose of the rules is to prevent tax deferrals from being indefinitely extended through multiple inheritors. However, payments can be stretched out over a beneficiary's lifetime if the rules are followed. The rules are quite complex. When you are naming IRA beneficiaries you should consult with an estate attorney or financial advisor who knows these rules. If the owner does not name a "designated beneficiary" (an IRC term) and he or she dies, the IRA must be fully distributed to someone within five years. If the IRA has substantial assets, this causes someone to inherit a large, annual tax bill with the IRA.

A devastating mistake can be made by naming a special needs trust as an IRA beneficiary. IRA distributions are mandatory after an owner's death. Many attorneys feel that if distributions are made to a special needs trust, the distribution must be passed on to the beneficiary by the trustee. This converts an otherwise acceptable discretionary special needs trust into a conduit trust. If the trust becomes a conduit trust, then Social Security and Medicaid *can count all of the assets in the trust for SSI and Medicaid eligibility determination.* The child could lose his means-tested government assistance. Some attorneys believe that an IRS Private Letter Ruling (PLR) allows one to avoid the conduit trust problem if the trust is structured as an "outright-to-now-living-persons" (O/R-2-NLP) accumulation trust (Choate 2011). The broad applicability of the PLR is questionable; the PLR was requested by a spouse and spouses often get preferential treatment in the tax code. The criteria that must be met for the trust to meet the definition of an O/R-2-NLP accumulation trust are esoteric provisions of the tax code. If you are planning to fund a special needs trust from an IRA, you must seek legal advice from a trust and estates attorney or risk a serious mistake. You should use other assets to fund the trust if possible by rearranging beneficiaries and their percentages. Creating an intermediary step between an IRA and a special needs trust may work but you should get advice to avoid being caught by the IRS practice of looking for collapsible transactions.

The Necessary Actions

To implement your estate plan, start by collecting all of the relevant legal and financial documents: your estate legal documents, the registrations and titles on your assets, and the beneficiary forms for insurance policies and accounts. Make a checklist of all assets that are not explicitly dispositioned in your will;

keep separate categories for insurance policies and annuities, financial accounts, property, and assets that will be sold for cash. List the insurance company, bank, investment firm, or trust associated with each asset. Don't forget that disability and long-term care insurance policies can have a death benefit. Check each policy's declarations page. Contact the insurance company or agent for each policy or annuity; obtain, complete, and submit to the company or agent its beneficiary form with the proper trust designation. Contact all banks, investment management firms, or broker/dealers and complete, sign, and file a TOD or POD form for all financial accounts. Visit the personnel department of your employer and complete beneficiary forms for employer group life insurance policies and for employer-sponsored retirement accounts and pensions. See an estate planning attorney or expert financial advisor if funding a special needs trust with an IRA.

Trace the Flow of all Transfers and Distributions

If you are uncertain of your skills in accurately tracing the distributions through an estate, see a financial planner who is experienced in estate planning. Most financial planners have software to perform this analysis. You or your advisor should trace the flow of all insurance payments, property transfers, and cash and securities distributions at the death of either spouse or the simultaneous death of both spouses. If a piece of property is to be sold and the cash distributed to a devisee or trust, use the cash value of the asset in the analysis. Pay particular attention to IRA and retirement accounts or pension distributions. Also pay attention to bequests in a will and look for accounts, property, or assets not named in the will for which prearrangement have not been made. These assets will flow through the will's residual property clause. Determine for each beneficiary, trust, or charity the monetary value or property that each receives. Assure that no cash or property is distributed to a special needs child in his or her name and that the intended contributions to fund a special needs trust actually reach it. One may find as I did with the couple mentioned at the beginning of the chapter that a lot less money reaches the trust than intended because of gaps in structuring or implementing the estate plan.

Figure 16.1 depicts a schematic of an estate plan. It is worth creating or having an advisor create a schematic so you can visualize the flow of money and property at death. A schematic gives you a picture of plan elements and their interaction. The plan depicted is not a complicated one. If you have a trust-based estate plan, it will look quite different. Business owners and high net worth couples will have more complex estate plans, probably much more complex plans, and a schematic can be helpful in grasping the execution and outcome of the plan.

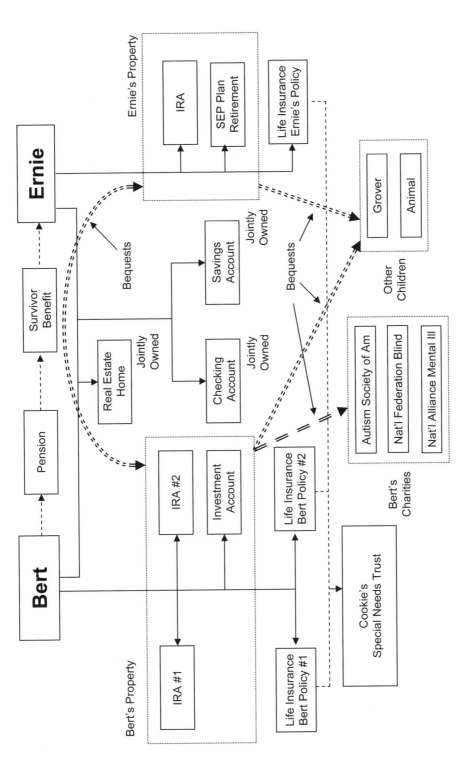

Figure 16.1 Bert and Ernestine Muppet's estate plan

Where to Go for More Information

For the rules regarding beneficiary designations for individual retirement plans including the problem of conduit trusts, I recommend financial planners consult the standard reference book for individual retirement plans: *Life and Death Planning for Retirement Benefits* (Choate 2011).

CHECKLIST
CREATING A FINANCIAL PLAN

		Yes/ Done	Action Req'd	Not Needed
	Family Financial Planning			
1	Have you identified goals and major life changes for each member of the family?			
2	Are you clear on your values and obligations?			
	(a) What gives life meaning, and the difference between meaning and enjoyment?			
	(b) What do you want for your children and how do you define fairness for each?			
	(c) Will you need to care for someone else you love, like one of your parents?			
	(d) Do you want to leave a legacy to someone you love, or a charity or institution?			
3	Are you taking the necessary steps to create a secure financial future?			
	(a) Balancing the budget and setting money aside			
	(b) Reducing or eliminating debt			
	(c) Creating an insurance safety net in case something goes wrong			
	(d) Maintaining liquid financial reserves for unexpected expenses			
	(e) Saving and investing for the future			
	(f) Following a strategy to accumulate, harvest, and transfer wealth at death			

		Yes/ Done	Action Req'd	Not Needed
Child's Special Needs Plan				
1	Have you developed life and resource plans for your child?			
2	Will your child need SSI, Medicaid, and state disability services?			
3	Can you provide financial support to create a better quality of life?			
	(a) Enhancing chances for employment			
	(b) Private residential options			
	(c) Disability services that aren't available from government programs			
4	Does the family plan verify that the child's life and resource plans are affordable?			
Selecting an Advisor				
1	Do you know of any special needs financial planners in your community?			
	(a) By reputation or from referrals from parents or non-profit organizations			
2	If not, can you find a CFP experienced in estate and retirement planning			
	(a) Alternatively, a CLU/ChFC insurance agent or advisor			
3	Does the advisor have adequate education and experience?			
	(a) Training or experience in special needs planning			
	(b) Professional designations that are reliable indicators of ethics and competence			
	(c) Regulatory record of complaints and sanctions			
	(d) Experience in other areas of your planning needs such as investments			
4	Does the financial planner offer insurance and investing advice or products?			
5	Does the advisor have a fiduciary obligation to advise you in your best interest?			
6	How is the advisor compensated and are there possible conflicts of interest?			

		Yes/ Done	Action Req'd	Not Needed
	Estimate Lifetime Financial Support			
1	Do you have a good life and resource plan to serve as a basis for the estimate?			
	(a) Identifying all major items for which costs will be incurred			
	(b) Milestones or events when income or expenses change significantly			
	(c) If not, can you describe what each transition or life phase will look like?			
2	Have you calculated financial support on the basis of cash income less expenses?			
3	Is level of estimating detail appropriate to the age of the child?			
4	Have you identified the child's potential income and payments received?			
	(a) Social Security payments, HUD housing, other government assistance			
	(b) Payments from a structured settlement, annuity, child support, other			
	(c) Wages or earnings from employment			
5	Have you estimated expenses annually or for each life phase?			
	(a) If the child will outlive you, have you estimated continued support after death?			
	(b) Have you identified the largest cost items and those with greatest uncertainty?			
	(c) Have you decided what to assume for availability of government assistance?			
6	Do you understand the problem of accuracy and how to get a best estimate?			
	(a) The completeness of the life and resource plans limits determines reliability			
	(b) Does the estimate incorporate the best current information?			
	(c) Do you update as circumstances change or after major transitions?			

		Yes/ Done	Action Req'd	Not Needed
	Plan to Fund and Manage a Special Needs Trust			
1	Have you decided when to fund the trust, while living, at death, or incrementally?			
2	Have you calculated how much will be needed for the child's lifetime support?			
3	Have you decided what assets will be used to fund the trust?			
4	Do you have successor trustees named to take over from you if needed?			
5	Once the trust is substantially funded, will new trustees be appointed?			
	(a) An institutional trustee or co-trustee			
	(b) A family member with the necessary investment skills			
	(c) A family member with business skills who hires an investment manager			
6	When will the trust start making payments and distributions?			
	(a) Are you aware of the potential problems with direct distributions to the child?			
7	Who will manage investments in the trust, you or a professional manager?			
8	Will the trust own real estate, either the child's residence or income property?			
9	Do you have a life plan and letter of intent to guide the trustee?			
	Insurance			
1	Have you had a financial plan or insurance review in the past three years?			
2	Have you assessed the adequacy of coverage for different insurable risks?			
	(a) Health insurance for the family			
	(b) Life insurance on both parents' lives			
	(c) Disability insurance for each working spouse			
	(d) Long-term care protection for both parents			
	(e) Property and casualty insurance on homes, automobiles, and valuables			
	(f) Personal liability insurance			

		Yes/ Done	Action Req'd	Not Needed
	Insurance (continued)			
	(g) Professional liability insurance			
	(h) Business insurance			
3	Do you understand how life, disability, and LTC insurance are underwritten?			
	(a) Do you have personal risk factors that could fail to pass underwriting?			
	(b) Medical conditions with aging that can preclude insurance			
	(c) Or conditions that result in a rated higher premium			
4	Did you check company financial ratings and consider only A-rated?			
	Taxes			
1	Have you taken advantage of deductions and credits on your income tax return?			
	(a) Do you know the rules for claiming your adult child as a dependent?			
	(b) Can you take advantage of education credits such as 529s and Coverdells?			
	(c) What about other credits for blindness, childcare expenses, medical, etc.			
2	Do you file a tax return for the child?			
	(a) No personal exemption for child's return if you claim dependent on your own			
	(b) Does child qualify for the Earned Income Credit?			
	(c) Does the child receive direct payments from a special needs trust?			
3	Do you understand the tax implications of revocable and irrevocable trusts?			
	(a) Do you avoid substantially overfunding or pre-funding an irrevocable trust?			
	(b) Do you have a tax accountant to prepare a Form 1041 trust income tax return?			
4	Are you potentially exposed to estate, gift, or generation-skipping transfer taxes?			
	(a) Considered possible tax implications of establishing and funding a trust?			

		Yes/ Done	Action Req'd	Not Needed
	Update Financial Records			
1	Have you listed and valued all property (also known as your estate)?			
	(a) Real estate including home and rental property			
	(b) Bank accounts, financial accounts and IRAs			
	(c) Insurance policies with death benefit or cash value, also annuity contracts			
	(d) ERISA-covered employer pension and retirement plans			
	(e) Valuable collectibles			
	(f) Rights to payments such as promissory notes			
	(g) Business interests including family limited partnerships			
	(h) Valuable intangible assets such as patent rights and licenses			
2	Have you made the arrangements while alive to transfer property at death?			
	(a) Primary and contingent beneficiary designations on insurance policies			
	(b) Pay on Death (POD) forms for all bank accounts			
	(c) Transfer on Death forms for financial accounts naming primary and contingent			
	(d) Title transfers for real estate			
	(e) Contractual arrangements for business interests			
	(f) Transfers of property to living trusts			
3	Is all property not covered by prearrangements disposed of in your will?			
4	Have you assured that all gifts, bequests, and transfers go to child's trust?			
5	Have you communicated to other family members about how to leave a legacy?			
6	Has someone traced the flow of assets at the death of either or both parents?			

CASE STUDIES
FINANCIAL PLANS

Let's check in with our four friends and take a look at their family's financial plans, or in Henry's case, his plan.

Angel Herrera

Sue Sundstrand, a Certified Financial Planner (CFP), is the financial advisor who co-presented the financial and legal planning workshop attended by John and Michelle at the school district's Transitions Day. The Herreras schedule a meeting with her shortly after meeting with the attorney who also presented, Gene Taylor. They plan to develop their financial and legal plans concurrently.

The parents have decided to enroll Angel in the Special Services Occupational Training Program at Eastern New Mexico University-Roswell for a Certificate in Food Services. They have three options for possible independent living. Instinctively they feel forming a parent cooperative to implement a clustered-apartment living plan is the least expensive option and the one they prefer, but they have the least control over it. They are not sure whether purchasing a property, either a condominium or small house, is more or less expensive than the New Horizons Community. Angel wants to live with her two best friends, Sarah and Tracy, who also have Down syndrome. The home purchase option supports this but the community living option is beyond the means of Sarah's and Tracy's parents. As John and Michelle discuss the problem of assuring the safety of these three young women living independently, particularly the concern for protecting them from sexual abuse, they decide they will need to hire a live-in companion under the property purchase option. They have an exploratory conversation with Sarah's and Tracy's parents. Both the Hatchers and the Kinseys are interested but hesitant. John and Michelle believe the reason is the worry about affordability. Both are middle-class families. The residential property would be purchased by the Herreras with the Hatchers and the Kinseys paying a fair rent for their daughters. This is not the problem. The problem is the cost of a live-in companion and a sophisticated home security system. John and Michelle decide to absorb the cost of the companion and security system if Sarah's and Tracy's parents pay rent for their daughters' rooms.

After the Herreras finish completing a PATH plan for Angel, they meet with Sue to develop a financial plan. They decide to have two alternatives studied, one with the purchase of a four-bedroom home for Angel and her friends and one for a community living facility. They have a life plan that includes other goals for Angel's employment, support for an active social life, and caring for her special needs. They want to see how the baseline plan would be affected if John were to die today (since he is the primary income provider) or if both parents die. This will be an uncommonly expensive financial planning engagement because of two fully developed options and the Herreras' need for detailed cost estimates for Angel's support. The contractual agreement requires payment for Sue Sundstrand's hours multiplied by her hourly billing rate. Sue's billings will likely total between $3500 and $4000.

If John dies, Angel's trust will be immediately funded and a corporate trustee appointed. Michelle wants to have the mortgage on their home paid if she and Angel continue to live there. She may choose to sell the home and downsize but the conservative case is to remain in the home. If John and Michelle were to die together, Angel would be placed with the New Horizons Community. A professional guardian and a care planner will be hired. Table FP.1 shows the significant aspects of the Herreras' finances. Other than the mortgage on their home, John and Michelle are debt-free.

After the cost estimates are prepared, the next step is to develop a funding strategy for Angel's special needs trust. Sue calculates the Net Present Value of Angel's lifetime support for the two baseline options plus the additive support in case of the premature deaths of John and Michelle. The results are shown in Table FP.2. Although the trust will not be immediately funded in either baseline scenario, the NPV can be compared to the Herreras' net worth and life insurance to verify they have the means to take care of their daughter in accordance with her life plan.

Table FP.1 Financial summary for John and Michelle Herrera

2012 Salary and incentive compensation	
John's salary	$215,410
John's incentive compensation	50,000
Michelle's salary	48,480
Total 2012 salary and incentive compensation	$313,890
Net worth summary	
Value of home (net of selling costs)	$651,000
Less outstanding mortgage balance	422,396
Realizable home equity	$228,604
John's 401(k) retirement plan	$542,494
Stock options	56,850
John's deferred compensation	72,660
Joint investment account	687,666
Total net worth	$1,588,274
Life insurance	
John's Variable Universal Life Policy—death benefit	$617,948
Cash value	162,536
Michelle's Variable Universal Life Policy—death benefit	$571,605
Cash value	146,282
John's 20-year, Guaranteed Level Premium Term Life—death benefit	$400,000
Michelle's 20-year, Guaranteed Level Premium Term Life—death benefit	400,000
Total death benefit	$1,989,553

Table FP.2 Funding analysis for Angel's special needs trust

Trust funding for baseline plan—purchase home for Angel	NPV = $801,675

Funding assumptions

Trust return on assets 6.5 percent less 1.1 percent fee for investment management

Angel is eligible for SSI and Medicaid

2013–2014 Eastern New Mexico University-Roswell

2015 Angel has part-time job, 4 hrs/day, 5 days/wk, $8.00/hr

2016 Angel moves into apartment with Sarah and Tracy, look-in supervisor

2018 Herreras purchase 4-bedroom home for Angel

$50,000 down payment, $10,000 furnishings, $4000 closing costs

$200,000 30-year mortgage, 4.00 percent fixed interest, $954.83 monthly payment

Live-in companion hired, roommates Sarah and Tracy pay rent

2020 Angel becomes eligible for SSDI on her Social Security record

2022 Angel becomes eligible for Medicare after 24 months receiving SSDI

2024 Michelle retires at 62

2026 John retires at 65

2036 Trust fully funded at John's age 75, corporate fiduciary

2042 Professional guardian and care manager hired at Michelle's age 80

2047 Angel moves to assisted living center at age 55, Medicaid funding

2051 John dies at age 90

2052 Michelle dies at age 90

2062 Angel dies at age 70, trust terminates, remainder value $9

Trust funding for baseline plan option—New Horizons Community Living	NPV = $944,564

Funding assumptions

2015 Move-in, $35,000 annual cost with meals and private bedroom

Additional funding if John were to die today	NPV = $45,064

2012–2035 Immediate trust funding, Trustee administrative fees

Additional funding if John and Michelle die together	NPV = $455,824

2012–2041 Hire professional guardian and care manager for Angel

2012–2017 Immediate move to New Horizons Community Living

Total trust funding requirement if parents die today, with placement in New Horizons Community Living	NPV = $1,445,452

The Herreras are relieved to see the results. If they both die together, the total death benefit of their four life insurance policies, almost $2 million, exceeds the amount required to fully fund Angel's trust and pay the outstanding balance on the mortgage. Both of the independent living options are affordable. The community living option is more expensive but its implementation is more straightforward and in the long run likely to be more stable.

If John dies, Angel's needs are about $1 million, less because Michelle will continue to be Angel's guardian and care giver. John barely has enough insurance to cover this. The mortgage repayment would be made from their investment account (and not the retirement account to continue tax deferrals). The analysis reveals a common mistake made by parents. Frequently, when they take out life insurance they purchase two policies with equal death benefits. The better strategy, if the insurance is purchased for income replacement, is to purchase life insurance in the ratio of each spouse's share of total earned income. If both John and Michelle live to their normal life expectancy, with Angel outliving her mother by ten years, the insurance becomes irrelevant because John and Michelle will accumulate significant wealth during their working years and in retirement. They purchased the term insurance policies when they bought their home, choosing a death benefit essentially to cover the mortgage and college for Jo and Paul. When the term policies reach the end of their guaranteed premium period, they can be dropped. Family wealth is more than sufficient for future needs.

The financial plan prepared by Ms. Sundstrand reveals two problems. The subtle one is with John's employer group disability coverage. The income replacement provided by the plan is based on John's salary, *but it does not cover his incentive compensation.* John should consider purchasing a private disability policy with a monthly benefit of $2500 to replace the loss of his IC if disabled. He can easily afford it. Michelle does not have long-term disability at all. She should apply for a policy with a similar monthly benefit. Both are in good health and likely to receive a favorable underwriting decision.

Michelle hopes that she can quit her position as the development director for a non-profit organization. The financial plan demonstrates she has this option. The long-term accumulation of family wealth will taper off from its current trajectory but this is acceptable since both consider their current standard of living adequate. Their concern is the investment in Angel's future and the plan indicates their financial resources are adequate. There is a significant advantage in Michelle's immediate retirement. Creating an independent living option for her daughter will take time and energy which she can devote to the task without the full-time job.

If John and Michelle live to their normal life expectancies, their two variable universal life insurance policies are a hidden financial asset. When the death benefit for a permanent insurance policy is required for a survivor's needs, the cash value should never be included in a family's net worth statement.

However, if the insured lives into old age, the cash value can be harvested by taken withdrawals up to the amount of the premiums paid with loans against the remainder in the investment accounts as long as the policy is not allowed to lapse (a tax nightmare), unless the policy was purchased to create a survivor legacy which would be reduced. VUL policies offer terrific tax advantages as investments. Under the tax code, withdrawals and loans from the sub-accounts are taken income tax free. When the insured dies, the loans are repaid from the death benefit and the remainder is paid to the beneficiaries, also income tax free. The potential problem with large amounts of permanent insurance is that the death benefit is part of an insured's taxable estate. The Herreras will likely see their wealth grow over the years to the point where they will have an estate tax liability. Families unaware of the problem with life insurance being counted as part of a taxable estate may find at someone's death that the value of the insurance owned is effectively less than expected. Some of the death benefit will be bled off by estate taxes. Gene Taylor, the estate attorney, will be addressing this concern as he prepares the Herreras' legal documents. The problem is avoidable by placing the policies in an irrevocable trust.

Unlike whole life insurance with the cash value and death benefit guaranteed by the insurance company as long as premiums are paid, variable universal life policies place the risk of lapse on the insured. Premiums and investment performance must be monitored. If the investments perform poorly, premium payments must be stepped up to protect the policies. Failure to do so can cause them to collapse when the cash value goes to zero. Despite the powerful tax advantages of these policies, they are inappropriate for financially unsophisticated people who are not properly advised and who do not have flexibility to increase premium payments if needed. The Herreras are financially sophisticated and they have competent financial and tax advisors. They can easily step up premium payments and have done so in the past. These policies are wonderful assets for them. However, Sue Sundstrand does have a recommendation. They need to significantly change the asset allocation for the investments held by the policies from a growth objective to capital preservation. Since the death benefits support Angel's needs, the allocation needs to be much more conservative. In the long run, the Herreras will give up appreciation in the cash value and death benefit, but one should view these policies as Angel's money (which she needs) and not her parents' (who don't need it).

The last step in the Herreras' financial planning will come after they execute the legal documents prepared by the estate attorney. The flow of assets and death benefits must be traced to verify the estate plan executes as intended. The Herreras may need to update their contingent beneficiary designations on their financial accounts, John's retirement account, and their insurance policies. The contingent beneficiary for the insurance policies will be Angel's special needs trust. Over time, the percentage marked for Angel can probably be reduced from 100 percent with Jo and Paul receiving the benefit not needed by Angel. John and Michelle have a decision to make regarding their legacy for Jo or Paul: should the legacy go to them directly or to a trust holding the assets for their benefit? The parents' decision will be made on their belief in their children's maturity and financial discipline and confidence in the long-term solidity of their marriages. The conservative approach is to leave Jo's and Paul's legacy in trust, possibly with discretionary provisions for the trustee to also make distributions for their children. A multi-generational support trust should be considered, a matter for the Herreras to take up with their attorney. However, they should be aware that a multi-generational trust could trigger the generation-skipping transfer tax if not well planned and administered.

Mike Olmstead

Sharon meets with Steve Christiansen, a financial advisor and insurance agent of a national life insurance company. He has the professional designations Chartered Life Underwriter and Chartered Financial Consultant commonly held by insurance producers who also give financial advice. Steve also has taken courses in special needs planning offered by the company to some of its agents. After a discussion of Sharon's goals and concerns, they reach agreement for a financial plan that will include an analysis of Sharon's net worth (assets less debt), cash flow (income less expenses), insurance needs, and retirement income. Steve's fee for delivering a written plan with recommendations will be $1500.

Sharon has a simple financial situation except for the complication of Mike's Asperger's syndrome. She has two sources of income—her salary as an associate librarian and Frank's child support. The money she receives in child support is spent for Mike's therapy, personal needs, social programs, and his hobby—computers. Otherwise she balances her budget and tries to put a little aside every month in savings. She carries no debt except an auto loan. She contributes 6 percent of her wages to the library's 401(k) retirement plan so that she captures her employer's 50 percent match. She has no investment accounts but maintains $5000 in a money market account and $1000 in checking. Sharon has health insurance through her employer and $50,000 of group term life insurance. She has 90 days of short-term disability insurance but no long-term disability.

Sharon has worked out a budget so Mike can go to college, shown in Table FP.3. The budget shows how little financial flexibility she has. Perhaps things will improve if Mike is successful in his pursuit of a degree.

Table FP.3 Sharon's budget

	Current	Mike in college
Income		
Sharon's salary	$27,905	$27,905
Child support	9000	9000
Mike's wages		7500
Frank's help with college		4000
Total	$36,905	$48,405
Expenses		
Income taxes	1455	2205
FICA and Medicare taxes	1981	2555
Health insurance	2000	2000
Retirement plan contribution	1675	1675
Home owners insurance	810	810
Property taxes	1315	1315
Utilities	2989	2989
Food	4278	4278
Clothes	942	942
Housekeeping	409	409
Auto loan, fuel, taxes, maintenance, insurance	4664	4662
Medical expenses	1022	1022
Entertainment	1636	1636
Weekly cash	1492	1492
Charity	500	500
Mike's expenses	9000	5400
College tuition, fees, etc.		9000
Laptop for class		1000
Therapist for college (fall, spring)		3600
Total expenses	$36,168	$47,490
Net cash flow	$737	$915

The significant deficiency in Sharon's financial picture is a lack of long-term disability insurance. Steve considers it a high priority that Sharon obtain a private insurance policy to replace 65 percent of her salary (probably the most a company will insure). He recommends she apply for a policy with a $1500 monthly benefit, a 90-day exclusion period (equaling the library's short-term disability policy benefit period), benefits to age 65, and a waiver of premium rider if disabled. The annual premium for a female her age with standard non-smoker underwriting is $838.50. This will be a stretch on Sharon's budget. If she can qualify for preferred underwriting on her medical record, this will help with the affordability concern. If Sharon cannot carve enough money out of her budget for the disability premium, she should apply for as high a monthly benefit as she can afford, perhaps paying for an additional purchase rider so she can add more insurance if her cash flow improves.

Sharon's health insurance is a high-deductible, high co-pay, high co-insurance insurance policy, primarily intended to cover significant medical bills. It is the type of policy normally used in conjunction with a tax-deferred Health Savings Account (HSA). Steve was alerted to this by her uncommonly low premium for her group health insurance. Sharon does not contribute to an HSA because of limited cash flow. The HSA contribution should be a priority to create a reserve for out-of-pocket medical bills.

Sharon obviously needs additional life insurance and long-term care insurance but neither is affordable in her circumstances. If she were to require long-term care, Medicaid will be her only option. The equity in her home will be eventually wiped out by a Medicaid pay-back lien, depriving Mike of a legacy.

Steve explains options to pay for Mike's third and fourth year in college. These include a Federal subsidized student loan or a home equity loan. Steve gives her literature which details the loan options, how to prepare a FAFSA form (the Free Application for Federal Student Aid form used by most colleges), and how need-based financial aid is determined based on parents' and child's income and assets.

If Sharon were to die today, Mike has $23,000 annually for his support (his job, $7500; his father's child support, $9000; and a survivor's benefit on Sharon's Social Security record, $6500). The combination of Mike's job and his father's child support render him ineligible for SSI but not stand-alone Medicaid in his state of residence. Sharon should apply for Medicaid even though he is covered by her employer group policy. Medicaid would be a valuable supplement, especially considering the gaps in her employer policy. If Sharon dies and Mike remains disabled and unemployed, her successor guardian should return to the court to petition for an increase in Frank's child support.

As long as Mike receives child support as an adult child, strategies to qualify him for SSI are ineffective. It's possible that Mike, if he keeps working and pays Social Security and Medicare taxes on his part-time wages, can earn Social Security Disability Insurance benefit and Medicare on his own Social Security record within a few years.

Steve understands the problem of Steve not being eligible for state disability services. Mike's IQ is too high to qualify as developmentally disabled under the state's restrictive definition of a disability (IQ less than 70). Sharon has learned a bitter lesson about a population of people known as the "tweeners," people in between those who don't need help and those who can get help because of the severity of their disability. Mike is a tweener.

If Frank were to retire, die, or become disabled, Mike would be entitled to a survivor benefit on his father's Social Security record as an adult disabled child. The benefit amount is highly uncertain. There is a family maximum Social Security benefit and since Frank has a wife and three other children, Mike will likely receive a reduced benefit depending on circumstances at the time of Frank's death.

Sharon's financial planning illustrates a painful fact. It is very hard for a single mom, on a modest salary, with a seriously challenged child, with inadequate support from the ex-spouse, to create options for a better life. This is one reason the social safety net is so important to so many households in our society that have a loved one with a moderate or serious disability.

Once Sharon's legal documents are executed (described in the Legal Plans case study), she will need to name her revocable living trust as the death beneficiary for any insurance benefits and her 401(k). Steve recommends that they should revisit her plan in two years when hopefully Mike is ready to graduate from community college.

Noelle Williams

Dorothy is the one that manages the family finances, watching every dollar so that the family can live comfortably on modest means. She and Robert almost always control expenses so that there is a little left over at the end of the month to put into savings. Over the years they have accumulated $34,000 invested in CDs (Certificates of Deposit) purchased from the town's only bank. They are conservative with their finances and have rebuffed efforts by the bank manager to get them to invest in more exotic securities. They instinctively avoid purchasing something they don't understand and are wary of "smart salesmen" taking advantage of them. They bought their home six years ago with a 30-year, fixed-interest mortgage. The only other debt they have is an auto loan. They own two cars, one purchased three years ago and one bought eight years ago when they moved to Illinois.

They sit at the kitchen table one evening to go over expenses to see how they can boost their savings to pay for their children's college. They find that almost two-thirds of their money goes to things they can't touch, such as the mortgage, or things that would be unwise to cut, such as medical care. They go through all items and come up with a plan to cut discretionary expenses by a total of 16 percent, raising their level of savings to almost $3500 per year. Their analysis is organized and summarized in Table FP.4. They face eight years of college in the next eight years. They probably need $80,000 to pay for two educations assuming Noelle and Robert receive financial aid similar to that discussed with the admissions counselor at the University of Evansville.

They have most of it between the extra monthly set-aside and drawing down their life savings. If they don't buy another car when the auto loan is paid off, they can reallocate the money to the college fund. Another possibility is taking out a loan against the equity in their home. At this point, they are seriously constrained by the loan-to-value ratio a lender would require, but this will ease by the time Robert is in college.

Table FP.4 The Williams' budget analysis

	Current	Revised	Reduction
Income			
Robert's wages	$56,000	$56,000	
Dorothy's wages	8400	8400	
Total	$64,400	$64,400	
Expenses			
Federal and state income taxes	4721	4721	
FICA and Medicare taxes	4435	4435	
Health insurance	6420	6420	
Required pension contribution	4480	4480	
Mortgage	7825	7825	
Taxes, insurance, maintenance on house	1768	1768	
Utilities	4000	4000	
Food	8180	7362	818
Clothes	1767	1414	353
Household expenses	626	563	63
Auto loan	3478	3478	
Transportation—fuel	2961	2813	148
Transportation—taxes, maintenance, insurance	2762	2762	
Medical expenses	1533	1533	
Entertainment	2830	2123	707
Personal	980	780	200
Credit card interest	300	0	300
Church	4434	3550	884
Total expenses	$63,500	$60,027	<$3473>
Net cash flow (annual savings)	$900	$4373	+ $3473
Net assets			
Home		$140,000	
Mortgage balance		<114,173>	
Savings		34,000	
Auto loan balance		<9882>	
Net assets		$49,945	

The painful cut in their budget is the church tithe. With some anxiety and embarrassment they visit the Reverend Cleveland to explain they need to reduce their contribution. Reverend Cleveland assures them they are doing the right thing and that everyone wants Noelle to go to college. (Two years later Reverend Cleveland and the church would make good on that statement. Upon hearing the news of Noelle's acceptance at the University of Evansville, the church comes together for a gospel thanksgiving. The little congregation of 37 families raises almost $1400 in contributions to see Noelle off. At the thanksgiving service, the greatest laughter and shots of jubilation will come when Reverend Cleveland launches into Washington Phillips' "Denomination Blues," recorded in 1927, with the lines, "*You can go to your college/You can go to your school/But if you ain't got religion youse an educated fool.*")

There are huge holes in the Williams' financial plan in the area of insurance. Robert, the major bread-winner, should have life insurance to cover the mortgage and the children's college. An option is $250,000 of 20-year, guaranteed-level-premium term life insurance with spousal coverage. Robert also should have disability insurance. Both should have long-term care insurance or anticipate Medicaid planning. A good financial planner could design a much more efficient plan for the Williams'. However, in their small town, there are no financial planners or trust and estates attorneys. The only financial professionals are either bank employees or insurance agents. There are only three attorneys in general practice to handle the basic legal business of the farm community. If the Williams' were advised to buy insurance, they would point out that the cost doesn't fit their budget and that their priority is their kids' college. There is a problem with the cost of insurance. Robert has hypertension and Dorothy is overweight with its attendant health risks. Neither would get policies with a standard underwriting rating even though neither smokes. If pressed on the risk of premature death or disability, they would simply say in their abiding faith that "The Good Lord will provide." As financial planners, we are only advisors who help families by pointing out risks, explaining options, helping with priorities, and suggesting a plan of action. Ultimately, the values that guide family decisions and decisions themselves belong to our clients.

Henry Lowenstein

Henry meets with a money management counselor, Betty Willis, to develop a budget and be taught how to use a tool for managing it. Ms. Willis obtains Henry's monthly bank statements, copies of his checks, and copies of his credit card statements for the previous 12 months. Henry doesn't manage his expenses. He simply spends whatever comes in each month. He sometimes overspends using his credit card. Ms. Willis constructs a record of Henry's income and expense for a 12-month period, shown in Table FP.5.

Table FP.5 Henry's budget analysis

	Monthly	Annual
Income		
Wages from part-time job	$832	$9984
SSDI	766	9192
Total	$1598	$19,176
Expenses		
Federal and state income taxes	6	72
FICA and Medicare taxes	52	624
Rent	480	5760
Utilities	166	1992
Renters insurance	25	300
Food	156	1872
Clothes	30	360
Housekeeping	38	456
Transportation—fuel	124	1488
Transportation—taxes, maintenance, insurance	91	1092
Medical expenses	168	2016
Entertainment	66	792
Weekly cash	25	300
Tobacco	27	324
Credit card interest	164	1968
Total expenses	$1618	$19,416
Net cash flow	<$20>	<$240>
College		
Tuition		$2706
Fees		516
Books		480
Total		$3702

Henry's expenses are neither unreasonable nor unexpected, except, of course, the money spent on cigarettes. Ms. Willis will mention this but she knows from experience that it's not likely to have an effect. To Henry's credit, there is no indication of alcohol consumption. The obvious area for improvement is the elimination of credit card interest. Credit cards can be very dangerous for someone with impulse control issues and Ms. Willis concentrates her powers of persuasion to try to get him to give up the card. She notes that by eliminating credit card interest Henry can pay for half of the cost of his college. Henry resists giving up his credit card; in his mind having a credit card is a sign of independence and self-sufficiency.

Since Henry chooses to keep his credit card, a budget control tool becomes even more important. Ms. Willis has a commercially available tool she teaches clients to use. During the month, a person enters each check and each credit card charge. Each transaction posts to a summary that shows actual expenses for the year by month and the budget for the remaining months. Each entry has an account number so the amount posts to the proper category of expense. The spreadsheet provides an on-going illustration of positive or negative variances to budget with visual warnings of significant variances. Ms. Willis knows that people can lose control of their budget by charging unbudgeted items to credit cards and by an accumulation of numerous, small charges. Ms. Willis wants Henry to avoid any charge less than $15 to break the habit of small, thoughtless purchases, only charge for unbudgeted expenses when they are necessary, and make sure the credit card balance is paid in full on time each month.

There is another significant issue to address: the Medicaid $2000 asset limit. It is important that Henry not allow his bank account to exceed this limit on the month-end closing date of his account. When Henry was spending everything that came in, the asset limit was not an issue. Now that he is trying to set aside some money he must be mindful of the limit. Henry understands the limit and is capable of managing his account accordingly *unless he enters into an unstable mood cycle.* Ms. Willis wants to meet with Henry ten days before the end of the month for the first four months to see how he is doing with his budget. He must bring in the on-line report of account transactions, his monthly bank and credit card statements, his check register, and all credit card receipts. Ms. Willis and he can decide on actions to manage his bank account balance to stay below the Medicaid limit. For example, he might take his automobile to the shop for maintenance. He can pay for purchases by check rather than his credit card so the debit is posted sooner to his account. If necessary, Henry can pay an expense early, like his college expenses. Craig, Lucy, Jose, and Adam will be observant and sensitive to detect signs that Henry might have an oncoming cycle of mania or depression which could cause him to lose control of his money management discipline.

Henry, with help from Lucy, applies for several scholarships and receives a $1000 award. It is not guaranteed renewable so Henry must go through the application process each year. Between annual scholarships and controlling his budget, Henry can possibly pay for a substantial part of his education. With Henry's natural intelligence and a system of supports, he has excellent prospects for earning his associate degree in applied science from Metropolitan Community College.

Something for the future—if Henry has an opportunity to take a job that pays a monthly salary or wage in excess of Social Security's Substantial Gainful Activity, Henry should meet with a Social Security benefits planner and apply for Social Security's incentive programs to help people return to work without immediately losing their disability status. Return-to-work incentives include a trial work period, temporary continuation of Medicare coverage, recognition of impairment-related work expenses, an approved Program for Achieving Self-Support (PASS), and a Ticket to Work for access to vocational rehabilitation services. The advantage in participating in these programs is that, should the attempt to return to work fail, one will not have one's SSDI, SSI, Medicare, or Medicaid benefits interrupted. The termination of disability benefits will only occur if the return to work is successful.

PART 4

LEGAL PLANNING

PROTECTING YOUR VISION AND YOUR CHILD

CHAPTER 17

ESTABLISH A COMPREHENSIVE ESTATE PLAN

One's personal estate is everything one owns—real estate, personal possessions, financial assets, businesses, insurance policies, contracts, and rights to payments from others. The purpose of estate planning is to control and protect one's wealth and transfer it to others as one wishes either during one's lifetime or after one's death. It is a set of decisions regarding who receives how much money, which property, and when and how. We may own property jointly with someone else, such as a home jointly owned with a spouse. But the principles of control and distribution are constants in estate planning. Estate planning is secondarily a set of legal documents to direct our decisions. Estate planning is not done by an attorney. The plan is yours. An attorney advises you on your options and prepares the legal documents to implement your plan.

Estate planning includes financial and property transactions made while we are alive, for example gifts to someone or trust contributions. Some actions will be taken after we die, either as directed by our will, a living trust, or as a result of prearrangements made while living. The legal process for distributing assets per the articles of a will is called "probate." A living trust, or *inter vivos* trust, is a trust established while we are alive to hold and manage cash and property in accordance with our directions. Prearrangements include survivorship title on assets and beneficiary designations for insurance policies and financial accounts. Beneficiary designations are contractual prearrangements. Someone is contractually obligated to do something after we die in accordance with the forms we have prepared. The purpose of this chapter is to identify some key estate planning decisions and options to direct what you want to happen.

There are some key things to remember about estate planning:

1. Estate planning is about family. It starts with a discussion between you and your spouse about how your wealth and insurance will be used to take care of each other, your children, and others you love. It may also include planning for lifetime gifts, and bequests to charities, churches, and institutions.

2. Many of the transfers of cash and property at death can be taken care of through arrangements made while living. This is often preferable to having your assets go through probate.

3. A necessary component of your estate plan will be the arrangements made to protect and provide for a special needs child. For many families, this will be the most difficult component of an estate plan.

Family Planning

Estate planning is fundamentally grounded in one's spiritual values, personal values, and family values. Special needs estate planning is family planning with the needs and hopes of a child embedded in the needs and hopes of a family. So it starts with my wife and I sitting down at the kitchen table talking about what we need to do while we are alive and what needs to happen when we're not. Here is where you may encounter a difficult discussion about what defines fairness to all of the children. An estate plan includes property we own individually, such as our IRAs and permanent life insurance policies, and property we own jointly, such as our home and joint bank and investment accounts. As the outlines of a plan take shape, we bring in our children, Meg's older brother and sister, and Meg herself to explain our plan, what it means to them, and what is expected of them. Don't be afraid to talk about death around an adult child with special needs. It will come someday and silence won't shield her from it. It can lessen her trauma knowing she is still surrounded by people who love her and will care for her.

There are practical aspects to estate planning. You must decide how much money will be set aside for your child with a disability and who will manage her needs. Knowing what we have and roughly the value of the legacy we wish to leave, we decide which bank accounts or assets to set aside or earmark to take care of her. This could be a percentage or the entirety of an account or an insurance payment. We decide what to do about lifetime gifts and trust contributions, beneficiary designations, and the distributions that will be made to those we love by provisions in our will. Once the outlines of a plan have been developed, perhaps with advice, the next step is to see an attorney, a financial advisor, and an insurance agent to prepare the legal documents, beneficiary forms, and deeds to real estate.

I described creating a child's circles of support in Chapter 2. Part of estate planning is involving those in the inner circle in developing a plan. Team members may help us with ideas and advice for parts of the plan. The conversations start with the hopes for those we love and how we intend to provide for those hopes. We walk through the arrangements we have made, what remains to be done, how our possessions will be distributed when we die, and what we have not yet decided. The most important document to review with our child's circles of support is our letter of intent. We also review our legal directives—wills, trust agreements, power of attorney documents, and medical directives for the end of life. Does it sound morbid? Maybe for some. It depends on your outlook in life. For me, it's touching the strings of love and caring that sustain me now.

Estate planning has two parts: what you want to happen and how to make it happen. To give a specific example, suppose I want to fund my daughter's special needs trust. How much money should the trust hold? Let's say I decide the amount is $500,000 (for illustration only). When do I want to deposit money in the trust? Let's say I want to do it when I die because I plan on supporting her from income and investments while I'm alive. Where will her remaining legacy come from—a life insurance policy, 50 percent of an investment account, or selling a piece of property? If the contribution comes from the investment account, how does the money get from the account to the trust? I file a "transfer on death" form with the investment company directing the percentage of the account I want to go to my daughter's special needs trust, and who is to receive the balance. If it's selling a piece of property, I direct that action in my will. These are the sequence of decisions that are part of my estate plan. I also have other goals. I want to leave money to my spouse since she may outlive me by two decades. I want to leave bequests to my other children and to various charities. Putting these pieces together is my estate plan.

An estate plan should be periodically reviewed and updated. The death of an important person in one's plan—a beneficiary, one's personal representative, a successor guardian, a care giver, or a family advisor—should trigger a review. A divorce will require a complete update to an estate plan. Acquisitions and disposal of property may require additions or deletions to a will or a living trust. Significant changes in the needs of beneficiaries may require reconsideration of fairness to children and others. And of course, significant changes in one's wealth, particularly a diminishment, should prompt an update to the plan. The actions to be taken to implement an estate plan are summarized in Table 17.1. An estate planning checklist concludes Part 4 of this book and lists many of the decisions you will need to address.

Table 17.1 Estate planning actions during life and after death

Estate distributions during one's lifetime
Gifts to individuals and charities
Cash contributions and property transfers to trusts
Prearranged alternatives while living to transfer assets at death without probate
Establish *inter vivos* or living trusts
Survivorship title on assets
Beneficiary designations
Life insurance policies
Annuities with a death benefit
Pay on Death (POD) forms for bank accounts
Transfer on Death (TOD) forms for investment accounts
Designated beneficiaries for IRAs
Beneficiaries for ERISA-governed retirement plans
Probate actions directed by a will
Pay creditors
Pay taxes
Sell assets
Transfer real estate, financial assets, and possessions to devisees (inheritors)
Cash bequests to devisees
Final cash contributions or property transfers to a trust
Charitable planned giving
Bequests
Charitable lead and remainder trusts
Charitable gift annuities
Business planning
Transfer ownership interest
Sell business or interest
Liquidate and distribute cash

Probate

Probate is a legal process where the will of someone who has died is submitted to a court for validation that it is legal and genuine. Once the will is admitted, the court authorizes the decedent's personal representative (called executor or executrix in some states) to carry out the will's directions. The word "probate" comes from the Latin verb *probare* meaning "to certify," "to give assent," or "to approve." Once the personal representative takes the actions directed in the will, pays creditors, settles tax issues, and distributes the money and property to the named beneficiaries, the probate court closes the decedent's estate.

When a person dies with a will, the decedent's personal representative (PR), a family member, or an attorney files it with a probate court. The opening of a probate proceeding is announced through a notice mailed by the personal representative to those named in the will and newspaper notices to potentially interested parties that cannot be located or are unknown. The notice specifies a deadline by which claims against the estate must be filed. The court "proves" the will by verifying that it was properly drafted, signed, and witnessed. If someone contests its validity, the court decides whether to admit the submitted will or accept an alternate as the decedent's last wishes made while mentally competent. Once the will is admitted by the court, the personal representative is given documents, called "letters testamentary," that authorize the PR to collect all money, sell assets, pay debts, pay taxes, and make distributions to those named in the will. The PR takes the letters testamentary to banks and financial firms as evidence of his or her power to take control of the assets. The letters also authorize the PR to transfer real estate. When the PR presents evidence to the court that all actions have been completed, the court closes the estate. After that, no creditor has a claim against the estate or against any of the devisees or family members. An advantage of probate is court supervision to ensure that a decedent's directives are carried out. Probate also provides legal and financial finality to the family.

There are disadvantages to probate. It can cost of from 1 percent to 5 percent of an estate depending on its size, complexity, and the state of domicile. The cost of a contested estate can be much higher. Court proceedings will take at least three months or as long as it takes to wind things up. A notable disadvantage of probate is a lack of privacy. Court filings and orders are public records. There are individuals and companies that troll court records, legal notices, and newspapers looking for estates with significant assets. They sell findings to attorneys and financial professionals who contact families to solicit business, or they search for interested parties who may have claims against the estate or a basis for contesting the will. Most states have expedited probate procedures for small estates. Some states have adopted the Uniform Probate Code that allows for an informal probate of the will and unsupervised administration of the estate. The amount of public information is limited.

A will makes bequests and transfers property, including real estate, to devisees (those named in the will). When there is a special needs child receiving means-tested government assistance, it is important that the child's bequest is to her special needs trust and not to the child by name. Watch for of "back door" distributions from property not mentioned in the will that flow through a residual property clause to a special needs child.

A potential problem with an improperly planned estate is the legal right of a spouse to an elective or spousal share. The spousal share can range up to

50 percent depending on the length of the marriage. If the estate is inadequate to satisfy the spouse's legal share and a bequest to a child's special needs trust, the spouse's right prevails over the child's bequest. You may ask, why would a spouse contest a child's inheritance? *The current spouse may not be the child's mother or father.* Care must be taken to ensure that estate divisions are made in conformance with the law. Or one must assign money or property to the trust while alive so they do not flow through probate or through non-probate assets that can be drawn into the estate by an elective share.

An estate can be attacked by claimants and creditors. Targeted estates are usually those of the wealthy and those who have incurred substantial liabilities. An estate plan may need to include legal protections for assets earmarked for the child. The assets that have been placed in an irrevocable special needs trust are shielded from creditors and lawsuit plaintiffs (unless a fraudulent conveyance was made), and are not subject to property division in a divorce. Assets in a revocable trust are not shielded. Assets that have not been transferred to an irrevocable trust are subject to claims by creditors, plaintiffs, and other claimants. Asset protection must be done when one is alive, in control, and free from known or imminent creditors. Probate is far too late to have a desired effect.

The most serious mistake one can make in estate planning is to *not do anything at all.* If there is no will or if a will is legally invalid, then a state's intestacy laws govern. Intestacy law operates rigidly to transfer a decedent's property and possessions to a succession of heirs. Typically, a spouse gets one-half of the estate and children share equally in the remainder. (This varies by state.) If the estate is not distributed to spouse and children, there is a line of other family members to receive distributions—parents, siblings, grandchildren, and others as the law edicts. A major risk of intestacy is that a special needs child directly inherits a sum of money causing loss of government assistance. Another is that her legal share may be far less than she needs or the legacy one intended to leave. In the case of a relative who dies intestate and wanted to provide for a grandchild, nephew, or niece, the child may not inherit at all.

Lifetime Transfers and Alternatives to Probate

Probate is something that happens after death. However, estate planning has a time horizon that begins today and continues through life. There are arrangements that can be taken during life to avoid probate. A transfer of real estate can be made by survivorship title on a deed. Most financial assets can be transferred with beneficiary forms. Cash, of course, can be freely moved from an account one owns to another account, including a trust account. Anyone can contribute money to a third party special needs trust except the beneficiary for whom it was created.

One common probate-avoidance tool is a revocable living trust (RLT). Suppose we have a family of five, a married couple with three children, one of whom is a special needs child. Each parent establishes a revocable living trust and transfers his or her property to their trust. When one spouse dies, the property in his or her trust passes to the other spouse's trust or to secondary beneficiaries if the spouse predeceases. A special needs trust receives the share of a child with a disability. If other children are minors, a minor's trust or custodian account (UTMA or UGMA) will receive their shares.

Private insurance policies are contracts and the owner has a right to designate primary and secondary death beneficiaries. Insurance policy death benefits do not pass through probate unless the policy owner has failed to send the insurance company a signed beneficiary form. Employer group life insurance also allows beneficiary designations under the employer's master policy.

Bank and investments accounts have death benefit designations, called "pay on death" (POD) forms for bank accounts, and "transfer on death" (TOD) forms for investment accounts. Individual retirement accounts use TOD designation forms. Beneficiary designations are contractual provisions of an insurance policy or a financial account that execute independent of probate. The provisions of a will do not invalidate or override a beneficiary form.

A spouse is legally entitled to a survivor benefit with employer-sponsored, ERISA-governed retirement plans—that is, 401(k), 403(b), and 457 plans, and pensions. Most of these plans allow designating a contingent beneficiary. (It is sponsor discretion whether to do so and some plans do not.) Contact your employer's employee benefits department to make a secondary beneficiary designation. A commonly overlooked step in implementing an otherwise complete estate plan is failure to make a contingent beneficiary designation for an employer-sponsored retirement plan. If the plan does not allow contingent beneficiaries, you will need language in your will to distribute the retirement plan should it pay into your probate estate. Your spouse must waive her right to a survivor benefit if you want to make a child's trust a primary beneficiary. The waiver must be signed by the spouse using the plan administrator's forms.

Real estate can be titled to transfer automatically to a surviving co-owner. This form of title is called "joint tenant with right of survivorship." It is a common form of ownership for real estate owned by a married couple but can be used by any two individuals or entities. A joint owner can be a trust. If the form of title does not transfer the property at death, it will transfer by will or intestacy. The property becomes part of the probate estate.

The common estate planning tool for special needs parents is an *inter vivos,* third party special needs trust. An *inter vivos* trust is a trust established in one's lifetime by executing a trust agreement and making an initial monetary contribution or asset transfer. The three key estate planning decisions are how much money to contribute to the trust, when to contribute, and what asset or insurance policy to earmark for funding (and percentage if not 100%). Death beneficiary forms for insurance policies, bank accounts, and investment accounts allow designating a trust to be named. In most states, one designates the trustee of the trust (who is legally the owner of trust assets) and the trust by name and date. If a trustee is replaced by succession or otherwise, then one needs to review all beneficiary forms for update. A few states like Colorado allow designating a trust without naming the trustee, a convenience if there is a change of trustees.

Gifting is straightforward but to a special needs child it must be done considering the asset and income limits of SSI and Medicaid. Usually, this means transferring significant amounts of money to a third party special needs trust. In uncommon instances usually involving the wealthy, consideration must also be given to the possibility that the aggregate of all gifts could be exposed to gift taxes. At the present time, the generous gift tax exemption likely will exceed the funding of a special needs trust unless other gifts use up the exemption. Wealthy families need to watch for future reductions in transfer tax exemptions as the nation struggles to control its debt.

A little-used estate planning tool is a "life estate." A life estate is the right to the lifetime use of a property or its income without outright ownership. In Louisiana it's called a "usufruct." The owner of the property retains the right to the property and the right to name a final beneficiary when the life beneficiary dies. Life estates are usually created as a type of trust. It can serve in certain circumstances. For example, I once worked with a couple and the husband had an adult special needs child from a prior relationship. His current spouse was much younger. He owned a small apartment building. He wanted his adult son to live with his care giver in one unit with rent from the remaining units to provide for his son's support. His plan was initially to transfer the building to his son's special needs trust. In conversations with the couple, it seemed that his wife was unhappy about the transfer. What removed her reluctance was a life estate for the son to live in his unit with a care giver for as long as he lived. This accomplished the same thing from the son's perspective. The wife's hesitation seemed to be the trustee, a bank wealth management office, and the fact the trustee would own the property to manage at its discretion solely for the son's benefit. The life estate protected her potential future interest in the property. The life estate did not count as an asset for SSI and Medicaid purposes but it was "in-kind support and maintenance" for purposes of computing SSI payments.

Estate Planning Mistakes with a Special Needs Child

There are planning errors one can make in special needs planning. Such errors include registering an account or titling an asset in the name of the child and not to a Social Security and Medicaid conforming trust. A somewhat similar mistake, often made by grandparents, is opening a Uniform Transfer to Minors Act (UTMA) account in the name of the child. Two states, South Carolina and Vermont, continue to use the older Uniform Gift to Minors Act (UGMA). People set up UTMA accounts because it's easy and inexpensive. UTMA and UGMA accounts have the same serious disadvantage: the money in the account belongs to the child and must be released to him when he turns 18. He may not be competent to manage a large sum of money and this can cause him to exceed the $2000 limit for government assistance. The UTMA/UGMA money must then be spent down to restore SSI and Medicaid eligibility. If the account holds a lot of money, setting up a first party, Medicaid payback trust is a less painful alternative but it may take court approval for the custodian to make the transfer. The custodian of a UTMA or UGMA account cannot transfer the money to a third party special needs trust. Nor do parents or guardians have any control over the situation. The money is the property of the child and no one, except a court, has legal power to take it away from him.

A sophisticated trust and estates attorney unfamiliar with Social Security and Medicaid may create a trust that fails to protect government benefit eligibility. Examples are minor's trusts under IRC §2503(a) for income and IRC §2503(b) for assets. Minor's trusts do not work in special needs planning. The income or assets in these trusts are legally the child's and are countable for government assistance eligibility. Disability trusts which require distributions to the beneficiary are countable assets and can cause loss of SSI and Medicaid.

Joint bank accounts with the child as one of the owners will not work unless the account is kept under the $2000 asset limit. US Savings bonds have two forms of ownership: "A and B" (joint ownership) and "A payable to B" (transfer on death). Joint ownership creates a countable asset for means-tested government benefits. The "payable to" type is not countable when owned by "A" but when the bonds are received by "B" at "A's" death, they can cause "B" to exceed the $2000 asset limit.

For some reason, a few parents decide to leave money to an individual to manage for a special needs child's support, effectively disinheriting their child. *I cannot envision a set of circumstances where this is a wise option.* Avoiding attorney fees for setting up a trust is no excuse. Too many unforeseen things can happen to deprive the child of her support. The person given the money may die without making a provision for the child's future needs. The person may have his or her own children and their needs may get priority. The person may become entangled in a divorce with the ex-spouse claiming a share of the money. The individual given the money may spend it on themselves. The proper way to leave money for a special needs child is to a trust for her benefit.

Where to Go for More Information

A comprehensive overview of estate planning is *Plan Your Estate* (Clifford 2012).

A good introduction to special needs estate planning is by two Illinois attorneys: *Planning for the Future: Providing a Meaningful Life for a Child with a Disability after your Death* (Russell and Grant 2005).

Estate planning should involve the family. However, it is uncommon to do so except in the case of high net worth families dealing with dynastic wealth. This is unfortunate. For those who are unfamiliar with family estate planning, whether wealthy or not, I recommend two books that will help you see the power of this approach. The first is *Wealth in Families* (Collier 2008). The second is *Trustworthy: New Angles on Trusts from Beneficiaries and Trustees* (Goldstone and Wiseman 2012).

CHAPTER 18

PREPARE THE APPROPRIATE LEGAL DOCUMENTS

The documents described in this chapter are legal directives. They are instructions to someone to act for you in accordance with your wishes. A will instructs your personal representative regarding how to wind up your affairs after death. A special needs trust document directs a trustee how to manage assets held in trust for your child's benefit. A durable power of attorney appoints someone, called an agent or an attorney-in-fact, who can act for you when you are alive but unable to act for yourself. Medical directives are instructions to medical personnel or a healthcare proxy to make medical decisions when you cannot make your wishes known due to injury, illness, cognitive decline, coma, or persistent vegetative state. These are the documents needed by parents who have a special needs child. When you complete this chapter, please remember the following:

1. Both spouses should have wills. An important provision names a guardian for minor children or a child with special needs should something tragic happen to both you and your spouse.

2. You should establish a special needs trust if your child is receiving or will need SSI, Medicaid, or state disability services.

3. You should have your legal documents prepared by an elder law or a trust and estates attorney.

Wills

A will has three primary purposes with an important fourth purpose for parents of minor children or a child with a moderate or severe cognitive or mental disability. First, a will appoints someone to manage your estate and close your affairs after you die. That person is known as your personal representative, or executor in some states (executrix if female). Second, a will transfers your property—real estate and financial assets and other valuable assets—to those whom you wish to inherit them. Third, your will directs the payment of debts and taxes from the cash in your estate. Your personal representative takes all of these actions, under court supervision (called probate) per the provisions of your will. When the probate court agrees that your representative has satisfied all of the instructions in the will, it orders the estate closed. After that no creditor has any further claim against your estate or your family. One of the advantages of probate is finality.

The fourth purpose of a will is to appoint someone to be the guardian(s) of children who cannot take care of themselves. A probate or family court is not required to honor your wishes but it almost always will do so unless someone presents a convincing case to do otherwise. A problem arises if a successor guardian predeceases you and you have not named another. The court will then decide whom to appoint. It will likely turn to other family members in a legal line of preference which may not reflect your wishes, for example your ex-spouse who is the other biological parent. The court could decide that the child who has grown up since the will was drafted does not need a guardian. You should keep your will up to date, especially the provisions for a guardian. (Guardianship is treated in Chapter 20.) Both parents should have wills. Usually each spouse appoints the other to serve as the continuing guardian for their child if he or she dies. You should consider the possibility that you and your spouse could die together, or your spouse could die before you. Your wills should name a successor for this potentiality. I recommend two or three steps of succession to be safe. A person can refuse to serve or can resign from guardianship.

Provisions in a will can transfer real estate to a beneficiary, called a devisee, or direct the sale of property and the distribution of proceeds. However, if the title on the property—joint tenant with right of survivorship—already provides for transfer, the title takes precedence over the will. A will can transfer financial assets to someone unless you filed a beneficiary form with the bank or financial firm. Beneficiary forms override a will's provisions even if the will was executed later. Personal property, such as the family photograph albums, can be transferred by a personal memorandum attached to a will allowing one to conveniently update a list of possessions and the people to receive them. Wills usually have a residual property clause to transfer cash or property not explicitly mentioned in other provisions. When an estate plan is prepared or reviewed, someone should make sure the residual property clause is not a back door through which money or property passes inadvertently to a special needs child.

Minor changes to a will can be made by executing a document called a codicil. A problem with a codicil is the possibility it can get separated from the will or lost. Always make sure your personal representative has a copy of your current will and all codicils in force. A will should be replaced if you decide to make major changes, especially adding or removing devisees, or if several codicils exist that could create possible confusion.

Often overlooked is the need for an adult with a disability to have a will if competent to manage her affairs. She could need a will if she has real estate, significant financial assets, or valuable personal property. If she dies without a will, the court will dispose of property in accordance with state intestate laws, in which case her wishes may not be executed even if known.

Special Needs Trusts

A trust is a contract between a person creating a trust and a trustee to manage assets in the trust for the beneficiary's benefit. The legal origins of trusts go back to feudal England when landholders going on crusades placed their property and their families in the care of someone until their return. Their protection was to be assured by a person the landholder trusted, hence "trust." (The potential for mischief here is obvious and was the subject of much medieval literature.) In the US, trust law is in the state domain, not the Federal domain. Each state has laws governing trusts although most states are moving to adopt a uniform trust code to bring a general alignment of legal principles.

Trusts may be created in one of two ways. A trust may be created by an article in a will. This is called a "testamentary" trust. In this circumstance, the trust does not exist until the person dies and the will is probated. The personal representative of the estate ensures that the trustee is notified of the effectiveness of the trust and transfers cash or assets to the trustee when the court approves. The alternative is to execute a separate document called a trust agreement. The trust then exists when the agreement is signed and the initial assets (perhaps of nominal value) are transferred to it. This may be as simple as opening a bank account and making a deposit.

The person establishing the trust and providing the initial assets is called a "grantor" or "settlor." The grantor of a special needs trust is typically parents or grandparents. The trustee may be an individual (including the grantors), a professional fiduciary such as the family attorney, or an institution such as a bank. Generally a trust can have multiple beneficiaries but a special needs trust always has only one. Because of the importance of special needs trusts in planning for a person with a disability, trusts will be covered in more detail in Chapter 19.

Durable Power of Attorney

A power of attorney (POA) is a legal document that appoints someone to manage your affairs when you cannot. The person you appoint is called an agent or an attorney-in-fact. You, as the principal, have discretion to define the agent's authority as broadly or narrowly as you choose. An attorney should draft the POA document so the powers and restrictions are described in accurate and unambiguous language. The POA should be "durable," meaning it remains effective if you become disabled or unable to communicate. Without a provision for durability, a power of attorney ceases with your incapacity. A "springing" power becomes effective only when you are disabled. The power "springs" into effect when needed. A POA extinguishes at your death. At that point, the personal representative named in your will takes over. You can revoke a power of attorney at any time but you should recover and destroy all copies to prevent their continued use. Obviously, there is risk in granting someone power over your affairs. The appointee must be someone you trust to act conscientiously and ethically.

Why do you need a durable POA? If you have a special needs child in your care, you may need someone to take over if you are temporarily unable to perform your duties. However, the court will not allow you to permanently reassign or delegate your role as a guardian. If your disability is permanent, a court must appoint a successor. One of the powers you can give your agent is the power to petition the court to appoint a permanent successor if needed.

A durable, springing power of attorney is a useful legal arrangement for someone who is mentally ill and does not have a guardian. It gives someone the authority to step in and help if the person has a psychotic episode. However, the right of an individual to revoke a POA can defeat its purpose. A person who has a bipolar condition or schizophrenia may revoke the power when they most need help. A person who has a bipolar disorder may revoke the power in a manic phase believing he no longer needs an agent. A person with schizophrenia may erroneously believe the agent has the power to institutionalize him. A POA legally cannot give the agent that power—either the individual must consent or a court must order institutionalization. However, such legal niceties may be lost on someone who is psychotic. To deal with this problem, some states recognize an alternative form of agency called a Psychiatric Advance Directive (PAD) which cannot be revoked by a person needing psychiatric care.

Whom should you appoint? If the power is to manage your personal affairs, you probably want a spouse or a close family member. Your agent will not have any power to make medical decisions unless you include medical provisions in the POA document. Normally a separate medical power of attorney is used for medical decisions. If the power is for financial or legal affairs, the appointee may be an attorney, accountant, financial advisor, or anyone with the necessary skills. If the power covers managing a business one owns, a trusted business associate might be named.

One problem with a POA is the possible reluctance of a person or business to accept an agent's authority. Banks are notorious in this regard. Because you can revoke a power of attorney at any time, the bank is often wary of accepting the agent's authority until it can verify that the POA is effective. Unless the legal document was recently executed, typically within the past 12 months, the agent may be rebuffed. You can forestall this by notifying firms or individuals you do business with that an agent has been appointed with power of attorney. It may be wise to give the firm or person a copy of the document for their records. Banks and other institutions may require the use of heir own forms for appointing an agent, with standard authority for client accounts. Some states allow your agent to provide a sworn affidavit assuring the bank the POA is still in effect, the principal is alive, and the affiant is still the appointed agent for the principal.

Medical Directives

There are medical "advanced directives" to assure that your wishes for medical care are carried out if you have a critical or terminal medical condition and are unable to make your wishes known. The conditions when you cannot make your wishes known include brain injury, dementia, coma, or persistent vegetative state. The advanced medical directives are:

- a directive to medical personnel, commonly called a "living will," regarding medical or surgical treatment, pain relief, nutrition, and hydration, and withholding of treatment when prolonging life serves no purpose

- a medical durable power of attorney for someone you appoint to make decisions for you if you cannot make your wishes known

- a cardiopulmonary resuscitation (CPR) directive or Do not Resuscitate Order (DNRO).

A living will can fail to address unforeseen circumstances. To avoid this problem, you should appoint someone (called a healthcare proxy or agent with power of attorney for medical decisions) to make decisions for you when the living will is not conclusive as to your wishes. If you have a valid living will that clearly governs the circumstances, it will take precedence over the medical power of attorney. I suggest that you provide copies of your healthcare directives to your physicians and ask them to make sure the hospital to which you may be brought has copies on file.

The person appointed is often a close relative. It should be a person sufficiently familiar with your values to likely understand what you would have decided for yourself. Give careful consideration to whom you wish to give this potentially heavy responsibility. A spouse is most likely to know your values and religious convictions but may be too close emotionally. The proxy you name, especially a younger person, may be pressured by other family members to make the decision they want made. Talk to the individual you want to serve as your agent and confirm her willingness to serve. There is no legal obligation on anyone to serve, even spouses. Discuss your philosophic or spiritual values with the person who may someday have to make a heart-breaking decision. Make sure the individual does not have a conflict with your wishes and her own religious beliefs or personal convictions. Don't be reluctant to have this conversation or gloss over the implications. It can sound so theoretical until that awful moment comes when the physician hands the person you designated the papers to sign directing that all life-prolonging measures be discontinued.

Can You Do it Yourself? Should You?

People who have minimal possessions and no children do not need to have a will drafted by an attorney. Some people use form wills or software with standardized articles. Some states recognize handwritten wills, called "holographic" wills. People are tempted by this option to avoid attorney fees. They may have read a book of "do it yourself" law. Parents of a special needs child should not take a chance that a defective, handwritten will places their child at risk. There are several potential problems with handwritten wills. One is the failure to have them properly witnessed. Another is mixing handwriting and printed text. In many states, a holographic will must be completely handwritten. The will may be carelessly written, either ambiguous as to intent or incomplete as to terms. It may unintentionally or illegally disinherit a family member. A handwritten will can get lost or not recognized in a pile of papers by people trying to settle the deceased's affairs. Holographic wills are risky documents for taking care of your loved ones.

Handwritten medical directives will not be accepted by medical professionals and hospitals unless prepared using forms permitted by state statutes. Some states have a "fill in the blanks" form that is legal when properly completed and witnessed. However, the form may not anticipate all of the circumstances that can arise in individual situations such as a persistent vegetative state.

In short, I believe that families with a special needs child should not cut corners. Despite the cost of having an attorney prepare your legal documents, probably $2000 to $3000 for a complete set of documents for both spouses, you should engage an attorney. Never put a special needs child at risk to save money.

You should make sure key people have copies of your documents or know where to find them. Attorneys who prepare estate documents generally keep copies in their office files and handle necessary filing with government agencies, such as submitting first party trust agreements to the state's Medicaid authorities.

How to Choose an Attorney

You should have your estate documents—wills, trust agreements, power of attorney appointments, and medical directives—prepared by an elder law attorney or a trusts and estates attorney. I suggest elder law attorneys because they must know Social Security, Medicaid, and state disability regulations to practice in the field. Most trust and estates attorneys know these regulations as well, but some do not practice in this area. They practice in other specialties such as tax law, wealth protection, or estate planning for high net worth families. You should ask the T&E attorney about their experience.

Your search for an attorney should start by asking for recommendations from special needs families and non-profit organizations. Consider membership in National Association of Elder Law Attorneys (NAELA) or the Special Needs Alliance (SNA). State bar association websites have search capability ("Find a Lawyer") by practice specialty and city or county. They may have links to individual attorney websites.

There are two types of attorney. There are those who help families make their decisions by explaining options or things to consider. Then there are those who take the approach of using standard documents and boilerplate language—if you don't know you need something, you won't get it. I once asked an elder law attorney, "Why doesn't this trust have a trust protector article?" His answer: "They didn't ask for one." Obviously, you will be better served by the first type of attorney. This is also a reason to do your own research and consider what you want to happen before you see an attorney.

I am frequently asked to recommend attorneys. I know many from having been a member of the Colorado Bar Association's Elder Law Section as a non-attorney associate. I joined the COBAR as a way of keeping current with the laws and regulations that dominate special needs planning. I met many fine attorneys and had to decide which ones I would recommend to clients. I decided to give preference to attorneys who contribute in some way to the special needs community, attorneys who do *pro bono* work or provide public education, or serve on boards or as consultants to non-profit organizations. You too should give preference to attorneys who are in it for more than the money. With one exception (because he creates the most versatile and enduring special needs trusts I have seen) the attorneys I recommend to special needs families are the ones who give of themselves.

Where to Go for More Information

The websites of the two professional societies mentioned in this chapter are:

- The National Association of Elder Law Attorneys (NAELA), www. naela.org.
- The Special Needs Alliance, www.specialneedsalliance.org.

Both websites have attorney search capability.

CHAPTER 19

ESTABLISH A SPECIAL NEEDS TRUST

Trusts are legal agreements between a trust creator, called a "trustor," "grantor," or "settler" for the management of money or property by an individual or legal entity, called a trustee, for the benefit of the person or persons for whom the trust was created, called a beneficiary. A trust agreement is a contract between the trustor and the trustee. The trust agreement defines the duties, powers, limitations, and compensation of the trustee. A person creating a trust has wide discretion in structuring it to meet his or her objectives. Trusts can be used for almost any purpose except enabling a criminal activity.

Trusts are flexible, powerful, often-used estate planning tools. Our interest here is a particular type of trust—a special needs trust, sometimes called a supplemental needs trust. The most common type is a "third party" special needs trust established by parents to support a child with a disability. There are also three types of "first party" special needs trust. It is important to understand the difference between first and third party trusts.

Three things to take away after reading this chapter are:

1. A third party special needs trust allows parents to set aside money to support their child while preserving his eligibility for SSI, Medicaid, and state disability services. Trust assets do not count toward the $2000 asset limit to qualify for these programs.

2. You have family decisions to make regarding how the trust is to be managed. You should give them some thought before you see an attorney.

3. Special needs trusts should be drafted by an attorney with expertise in Social Security and Medicaid law, and with experience drafting special needs trusts. He or she should be an elder law attorney or a trust and estates attorney.

Types of Special Needs Trust

The purpose of a special needs trust (SNT) is to allow money to be set aside for a person with a disability without causing him to lose his eligibility for means-tested government assistance. Properly drafted, the money and property in the trust will not count toward the $2000 SSI and Medicaid asset limit. Government policy is to support a person with a disability at the poverty line. An SNT gives parents a way of lifting a child receiving government assistance out of poverty. A special needs trust is not needed if the child is not eligible for SSI or Medicaid, or does not need assistance, or if the parents choose to provide all of the support themselves.

The important legal requirement for a valid SNT is that the beneficiary can have no control over the trust or its assets. He cannot be able to withdraw money, compel a payment, replace a trustee or trust protector, or amend or terminate the trust. Because the beneficiary has no legal right to the assets, the government cannot count them in determining Social Security and Medicaid eligibility. In order to effect this, the trust agreement must give the trustee complete discretion whether or not to spend money for the beneficiary's needs, how much to spend, what to spend money on, and whether or not to give any money to the beneficiary. No outside party or trust provision can compel a payment or distribution. Language articulating the trustee's absolute discretion must conform to relevant articles in the Social Security Act.

Special needs trusts are intended to pay for goods and services the government does not pay for or provide. An SNT is intended to supplement and not replace government assistance and consequently such trusts are often called supplemental needs trusts. The purpose of an SNT is to provide a better quality of life for a person with a disability and not to pay for room and board (SSI's purpose) or healthcare (Medicaid's). The trust can allow a trustee to pay for food or shelter, but the trustee should have a compelling reason since doing so will reduce SSI payments and jeopardize eligibility. (See Chapter 9 for SSI and the In-Kind Support and Maintenance rule.)

There are three parties to a trust. The first party is the beneficiary. The second party is the trustee who owns and manages the trust assets for the beneficiary's needs. The third party is the settlor who created the trust and made the initial contribution. These definitions identify the two types of special needs trust: first party and third party trusts. The most common type is a third party trust (TPT) typically established by parents or grandparents. Once established, a TPT can accept contributions from anyone *except the beneficiary*. The first party of a trust cannot be the second party, or to put it another way, the beneficiary cannot be a trustee. This is true of both first and third party trusts. Serving as trustee violates the restriction that a beneficiary cannot control the assets. The third and second parties can be the same. Thus parents can establish and fund a third party trust and appoint themselves as co-trustees.

Sometimes, the person with a disability has assets of her own because she was awarded damages from a lawsuit, inherited a substantial amount of money, or was disabled as an adult after accumulating wealth. Other than spending the money down to below the $2000 limit, how can she qualify for SSI and Medicaid? Social Security Act §1917(d)(4)(a) allows her to transfer her assets to a first party trust to become or remain eligible for SSI and Medicaid. A first party trust (FPT) is also called a "self-settled" trust. There is a catch, though: a first party trust must have a Medicaid payback provision. Otherwise, a person could shield substantial personal assets to become eligible for benefits that were intended for the poor. When the beneficiary dies, Medicaid can claim (has a lien) on trust assets for reimbursement up to the value of services Medicaid provided. If the trust owns the beneficiary's home, Medicaid can, with some exceptions, require the property be sold to satisfy its claims.

Never commingle third party and first party money in the same trust. Medicaid can then treat the trust as a first party trust and attribute all of its assets to the beneficiary. Medicaid can claim the entire trust corpus at the beneficiary's death, including the parents' contributions. This mistake is correctible but an attorney and accountant will likely be needed to unwind the transactions to the satisfaction of Social Security and Medicaid authorities.

There are two other types of FPT. An SSA §1917(d)(4)(b) trust, also called a Miller trust or income trust, receives the income of a person who needs to remain eligible for Medicaid. It is useful in the situation of an elderly person with a pension who needs long-term care they cannot afford without Medicaid help. It is useful when a person receives payments from a lawsuit structured settlement. It can accept child support awarded by a divorce decree. Section 1917(d)(4)(b) trusts must have a Medicaid payback provision.

The third type of FPT is a charitable, pooled-asset trust authorized by SSA §1917(d)(4)(c). These trusts are trusts that pool the assets of beneficiaries to be commonly invested and managed. A (d)(4)(c) trust must be a charity. It can charge for services but income from investments and fees cannot be distributed to owners or directors. Each beneficiary has a sub-account for his needs. When his sub-account is exhausted, the pooled trust's responsibility ends. If the beneficiary dies before his sub-account is exhausted, the remainder in the account is retained by the charitable trust to support its mission. In contrast to the other two types of FPT, Medicaid has no claim to the residual in a decedent's sub-account. Charitable pooled trusts often offer other services such as case management, representative payee services, Medicare set-aside accounts, and third party trusteeship. Case management is a valuable service to beneficiaries who have no one to care for them. If a charitable pooled trust serves as trustee for a third party trust, its assets are kept segregated from first party pooled assets and from other third party trust accounts. Charitable trusts typically accept clients with modest assets, in contrast with bank wealth management departments and trust companies which prefer catering to affluent clients. Many of the true charitable trusts were established by state and local Arc chapters. However there are for-profit companies moving into the field, commercial companies that create a charitable subsidiary to collect assets for the parent to manage for lucrative fees. Make sure you are dealing with a true charitable trust or at least compare the fees of candidate pooled-asset trusts. (Some large metropolitan areas have more than one pooled-asset trust.) An elder law attorney will likely know whether a pooled-asset trust is a true charity. Charitable, pooled-asset trusts are often the best first party trust option: they usually have lower asset minimums and often lower fees than traditional banks and trust companies. If the charitable trust accepts third party trusts, it can be an excellent option for parents as well.

How is a Trust Created?

Before meeting with an attorney, you should give thought to the decisions shown in Table 19.1. The first two address the legal form of the trust. Your attorney will explain these options to you. The remaining eight are non-legal decisions, what I call the family decisions. A financial advisor knowledgeable in special needs trusts can help you with the first five. The last three are yours to make, perhaps with the advice of an attorney, financial advisor, professional advocate, knowledgeable family member, etc.

Table 19.1 Decisions in setting up and managing a special needs trust

Inter vivos versus testamentary Revocable versus irrevocable	An attorney will explain the options
Trust funding 　　How much 　　With what 　　When Investments Residential property Distributions Administration	A financial advisor can help with these
Trustee and successors appointments Trust Protector and successors appointments Remainder beneficiaries	You decide, perhaps with advice

A special needs trust can be established in two ways. A living trust, or *inter vivos* trust, is a stand-alone trust created by a living person who executes a trust agreement. A testamentary trust is established by provisions in a will. A testamentary trust does not exist until the deceased's will is validated by a probate court and the court authorizes the estate's personal representative to transfer assets to the trustee. If parents anticipate that a grandparent or someone else may contribute to their child's trust, they should establish an *inter vivos* trust. If a grandparent dies before the parent, a testamentary trust does not exist and there is no place for the money to go.

A revocable trust is a trust the trustor can amend or terminate as she chooses. She retains the right to withdraw trust assets at any time. Her right exists even if she is not the trustee. Irrevocable trusts are the opposite; the trustor cannot amend the trust and has relinquished rights to the assets conveyed to the trustee. They can't be taken back. A trustor can convert a revocable trust to an irrevocable one by amending the trust agreement. A revocable trust automatically converts to an irrevocable trust at the trustor's death or incapacity or if it receives contributions from someone other than the grantor. A testamentary trust is irrevocable by circumstance. The first or second paragraph of the trust document usually declares the trust to be revocable or irrevocable. If it does not, a knowledgeable person can tell by reading the document. If a trust is only nominally funded, it makes little difference whether it is revocable or irrevocable—if the trust is irrevocable, the trustee can painlessly distribute the small amount of money in the trust and terminate it.

The three bases for deciding between revocable and irrevocable are flexibility, taxes, and asset protection. A *revocable* trust provides more flexibility and control to the person creating it. As to taxes, the income of a revocable trust is grantor's income under the Internal Revenue Code. She reports the trust's income from assets on her personal income tax return. Revocable trusts are also called grantor trusts.

An *irrevocable* trust is a taxable entity with its own tax identification number. A Federal trust tax return, a Form 1041, must be filed annually with the IRS to report trust income taxes. An irrevocable trust pays income tax on its retained earnings (i.e. with some oversimplification, its income less its distributions to the beneficiary). Depending on the state where the trust is located, a state income tax return may be required as well. One does not want to retain earnings in an irrevocable trust; the tax bill can be punishing. Personal tax brackets are set at higher incomes than trust tax brackets (see Table 15.1).

If a trust will hold substantial investments and not need to make distributions until some time in the future, a revocable trust may be a better choice. (However, an irrevocable trust is more advantageous as an estate tax strategy.) Prematurely funding an irrevocable trust is usually unwise from an income tax standpoint since there may be a practical limit on how much money can be spent for the beneficiary, especially one who is very young. This is one reason irrevocable trusts are rarely fully funded for minor children. I have only touched on a set of considerations here that inform an important decision. You should get legal and tax advice as to the best option for you in your circumstances.

Asset protection is usually not given consideration by most middle-class families. It is, though, by wealthy and high-income professionals who are frequent targets of lawsuits, for example doctors. However, one should consider that a revocable trust's assets are marital property in a divorce. Trust assets intended for a child's support will be divided between the two spouses by a divorce decree unless both agree to exclude them. A child from a previous marriage can be particularly at risk.

Attorneys will, more often than not, draft an irrevocable trust unless the trustor instructs otherwise. (A first party trust must be irrevocable.) How do you decide which is better for you? A categorical statement cannot be made. When a trust is nominally funded, I prefer revocability. Settlors have the option to convert later. You should seek the advice of an attorney and weigh your options. If you are high income and high net worth, you should also consult with a tax attorney or certified public accountant.

A special needs trust is usually established by parents by executing a trust document naming themselves as trustees. They open a bank account registered to the trust and deposit enough cash so the bank waives its monthly fees. A trust now exists. It has trustees, a trust corpus, a beneficiary, and a governing document. A nominally funded trust is called a "shell" or "pour-over" trust. "Pour-over" refers to the fact that the trust will eventually be funded with money pouring over from an estate or life insurance. How a shell trust is funded is addressed in Chapter 13.

Choosing a Trustee

A trustee performs the following tasks:

- manages the investments and property held in trust

- makes payments or distributions for the benefit of the beneficiary

- seeks to minimize trust taxes and prepares tax returns or statements

- submits annual reports to the beneficiary, guardian, trust protector, designated family member, or advocate as required by the trust agreement and state statute

- understands Social Security and Medicaid regulations and manages the trust to maintain eligibility for public assistance

- carries out other responsibilities described in the trust agreement.

Parents usually appoint themselves as trustees when a trust is set up. If one parent dies, the other continues as the sole trustee. Parents should carefully consider whether they or another family member can perform the trustee's duties for a fully funded, operating trust. You must understand a trustee's fiduciary duties to the beneficiary. Trustees have two primary fiduciary duties: to act with *prudence* and *loyalty*. Taken together, prudence and loyalty means that a trustee must act diligently, competently, and in the best interest of the beneficiary. Fiduciary duties are defined in trust law and enforced by the courts. They are stringently enforced against corporate fiduciaries—banks and trust companies. These duties are also imposed on family trustees. Banks and trust companies understand these fiduciary obligations. Family trustees must know them as well and perform their duties accordingly.

There are four common trustee options:

- a family trustee

- a corporate trustee (bank, trust company, charitable trust, or financial firm)

- co-trustees with a family member making decisions for the beneficiary's care and a corporate trustee managing investments and administrative matters

- a family trustee hiring an investment manager, an accountant, attorneys, property managers, etc. to advise or perform delegated tasks.

Parents typically believe that they or another family member will better care for their child than a heartless bank. This assumption should not go unchallenged. Managing a high-value, fully funded, operating trust (one making distributions) requires sophisticated financial skills. Parents often lack the necessary skills, particularly skills in managing investments and taxes. A corporate trustee or co-trustee is an option that should be considered.

There are four types of corporate trustee: banks; trust companies; charitable, pooled-asset trusts; and financial firms such as broker/dealers and investment management companies. Financially sound banks and trust companies are solid options for you to consider. They have permanence and stability, expertise in managing trusts, and objectivity in balancing various needs. They are heavily regulated, subject to external audit, have deep pockets for lawsuits, and find unsympathetic judges and juries when they fail in their duties. Consequently, they are conservative in carrying out their responsibilities, which usually serves the beneficiary well. They usually have minimum asset requirements that must be met for them to accept a trustee apointment. Large national banks are increasingly turning away clients who do not have three-quarters to a million dollars in related accounts. The regional banks are in the three to five hundred thousand dollar range and trending higher. If this trend continues, middle-class families with modest trusts may find that banks and trust companies catering to the wealthy are not options for them. A charitable, pooled-asset trust is usually the acceptable alternative, particularly for small-to-medium value trusts.

Broker/dealers and investment management companies are possible options if you find the right financial advisor and if the firm is structured to manage trusts. It should have a trust subsidiary to take independent custody of the assets. Independent custodianship is very important. Broker/dealers and investment management companies are heavily regulated. However, financial advisors are usually not employees but independent representatives. They have a contractual agreement under which the financial firm provides services in return for a share of the advisor's fees. It is more difficult to conduct due diligence on independent advisors and broker/dealers and investment companies, one reason I feel more comfortable recommending banks, trust companies, and charitable trusts to financially unsophisticated parents. *It creates a fiduciary conflict of interest for a family's financial advisor or investment advisor to also serve as the trustee of a special needs trust for a family member.* There are individual, independent professional trustees but I consider them only for small accounts because there is less regulatory oversight. They are often appointed as conservators by courts. These professionals must be bonded.

Parents experienced in managing investments, or having the skills and diligence to oversee investment managers and accountants, can be effective trustees of large-value trusts. A family trustee can hire professionals to perform tasks for them, such as investing or managing property. This option, a family trustee who retains advisors or managers to work under his supervision, can be the least expensive option in terms of fees charged to the trust. However, a family trustee cannot assign or delegate his fiduciary duties to an outside party. Fiduciary responsibility remains with the legal trustee by law and he is liable for the failures of those he hires.

If you plan co-trustees, the trust agreement should be drafted by an attorney to define each trustee's role and responsibilities. There should be clear decisional rules to preclude an impasse where neither can act without agreement of the other. The family trustee usually has responsibility for decisions regarding the child's care. The corporate fiduciary manages investments, makes payments and distributions as directed by the family trustee, prepares trustee reports and tax returns, and handles administrative matters. Co-trustee arrangements can be sources of contention and litigation. A corporate trustee will not accept fiduciary responsibility for exhaustion of trust assets if the family trustee can cause it to run out of money prematurely. It will refuse an appointment if the language in the trust agreement creates for them a fiduciary risk they cannot control.

Corporate trustees must be compensated. One should consider whether a family trustee should be. The decision depends on the bond of love and loyalty weighed against the burden of time and responsibility the family member assumes. Whether compensated or not, the trust agreement should allow the family member to be reimbursed for professional advice and services including investment, tax, and legal advice. The family trustee should be reimbursed for all reasonable expenses.

Should a trustee be bonded? Family and individual trustees should be bonded except for trusted family or for small trusts (less than $25,000). Banks and trust companies carry fiduciary insurance and are heavily regulated; a bond is therefore unnecessary. However, there is a subtle issue with independent advisors affiliated with financial companies. The company will have errors and omissions (E&O) insurance covering its independent representatives but this is a group policy primarily designed to protect the company, not necessarily the advisor or his clients. The problem is the company's aggregate coverage which can limit the advisor's coverage if aggregate claims against the company exceed the policy limit. I recommend you require an independent advisor managing trust assets to be bonded or carry individual E&O insurance unless you have an attorney's opinion that the company's insurance offers you adequate protection.

The trust agreement should name successors for trustees and have a mechanism to appoint one if the last-named is unable to serve. An individual can refuse an appointment; time and events may prevent a trustee from continuing. I recommend a sequence of two named successors with language in the trust agreement authorizing the last-named to appoint his successor. If there is no trustee to serve and no mechanism for appointing one, someone can petition a court to appoint a trustee. One should be wary of potential conflicts of interest in special needs planning: there is a potential conflict when a trustee is also a remainder beneficiary. The conflict is related to the fiduciary responsibility for undivided loyalty to the beneficiary. I recommend you avoid this possibility.

What is a Trust Protector and Why Would I Want One?

A trust protector, in some states called a trust advisor, has the power to amend or terminate a trust or change a trustee in accordance with language in the trust document. I believe in checks and balances to protect a person with a disability. Consequently I recommend you have a trust protector article in your special needs trust. Many attorneys do not include this provision unless you say you want it.

The common power given to a trust protector is the authority to replace or appoint a trustee. The power to appoint becomes very important if an individual trustee can no longer serve and there is no named successor. The trust protector's power may be "for cause" or "at will." I recommend "at will." If the power is "for cause" the trustee must have breached its fiduciary duty as defined by law. A trust protector doesn't define "for cause," the law does. "At will" provides more flexibility. For example, if parents relocate to another state, they will probably want to take the trust with them. A trustee or trust officer should have a direct relationship with the beneficiary and the family, more likely if the trust officer is in the same city. One might want to replace a trustee because of poor investment returns or service problems. An at-will clause better serves the family. A trustee should be required to provide annual reports to the trust protector to enable him to evaluate the trustee's performance.

The powers of the trust protector should be carefully crafted for two reasons. First, a trust protector should not be able to interfere with or direct a trustee or in any way that relieves it of its fiduciary duties or prevents it from meeting them. Second, corporate trustees are wary of trust protector clauses, especially at-will clauses. You may find that a corporate trustee will not accept appointment if the trust protector's powers are too broad or vaguely defined. A family trust protector must be careful not to become a *de facto* fiduciary with the potential liabilities that go with it.

Whom should you consider for the role? Logical choices are a parent, guardian, family member, or an attorney. Although I believe a trustee should live or have an office in the same city as the beneficiary, a trust protector need not as long as he can oversee the trustee and monitor the beneficiary's welfare. You should name a line of successors; I suggest two successors in sequence after the initial appointee. The last successor should have the power, but not necessarily the obligation (in case the trust assets are largely depleted), to name his successor. Again, beware of a potential conflict of interest. Just as a remainder beneficiary should not be a trustee, nor should one be a trust protector.

Remainder Beneficiaries

Parents need to decide what happens to the money remaining in their trust after their child dies. A remainder beneficiary receives the remaining assets after the beneficiary's death which terminates the trust. Although special needs trusts always have a single beneficiary, they can have any number of remainder beneficiaries. Parents can designate their other children, other family members, a charity, a church, or anyone they choose. Parents can name themselves as remainder beneficiaries. I suggest you give consideration to individuals and charities that have helped you or your child. Parents can choose differing payments or percentages for the remainder beneficiaries. If the trust is revocable, a grantor can change remainder beneficiaries. If the trust is irrevocable, the remainder beneficiaries cannot be changed, although one can and should designate successors. I again raise a caution about potential conflicts of interest. In the circumstances of your family it may be appropriate to have a sibling serve as a guardian and be a remainder beneficiary. Nonetheless, I suggest thoughtfulness in this decision.

Asset Protection

Asset protection is an area of law where you should consult with an elder law or trust attorney. State laws vary and there are diverse case law interpretations and applications of general legal principles. Can the assets in a special needs trust be claimed by a creditor, successful plaintiff, or a hostile spouse in a divorce proceeding? In most states and in most circumstances, the answer is "no" if the trust is irrevocable; claimants against the grantor cannot reach the trust assets because the grantor gave up ownership when the assets were conveyed. The trust owns the assets. Ownership is the key. The exception is a fraudulent conveyance, a trust contribution made to defraud or deliberately defeat the claims of a third party. Transfers and contributions to a trust may be reversed by a court depending on facts and circumstances indicating intent on the part of the grantor to remove assets from the reach of his creditors. A revocable trust provides no protection from claims against the grantor since he or she can recover the assets. The creditor of a non-grantor contributor to a revocable trust has no claim because that contributor gave up ownership when the gift was made unless it was a fraudulent conveyance.

Where to Go for More Information

I again recommend the book *Planning for the Future: Providing a Meaningful Life for a Child with a Disability after your Death* (Russell and Grant 2005).

I mention again *Managing a Special Needs Trust: A Guide for Trustees* (Jackins et al. 2012).

For those interested in charitable, pooled-asset trusts I recommend *Pooled Trust Options: A Guidebook* (Lovelace 2010).

I suggest again *Trustworthy: New Angles on Trusts from Beneficiaries and Trustees* (Goldstone and Wiseman 2012). This book may give you some insights into best relations and best practices between trustees, families, and beneficiaries which might inform your perspective in selecting a trustee. It's also valuable for trust protectors and trust advisors.

CHAPTER **20**

OBTAIN GUARDIANSHIP OR IMPLEMENT ALTERNATIVE PROTECTIONS

Many people believe that guardianship is a parent's natural role. It is not. It is a legal concept under which each state oversees the protection of those who cannot protect themselves, typically a child who has not reached adulthood (in legal terminology, the age of emancipation). A child who is not a legal adult is a "minor." A guardian manages the personal, medical, legal, and financial affairs of a person called a "ward." The law assumes that parents are their minor child's appropriate guardians unless they are found unfit, so court appointment is unnecessary. Each state also protects adults who cannot care for their own needs due to a cognitive impairment or mental illness. Only a court of jurisdiction can appoint a guardian for an emancipated adult.

Guardianship takes away of some or all of a person's civil rights. In some states this includes the right to vote or marry. Guardianship is only appropriate when there are no adequate alternatives for an individual's protection. Possible alternatives are limited guardianship, conservatorship, a trustee for property or financial assets, an agent with power of attorney, a healthcare proxy (also called an agent with durable medical power of attorney), a representative payee, or an advocate empowered with privacy waivers.

The takeaways from this chapter are:

- Consider petitioning for guardianship or establishing alternative protections when your child turns 18.

- Have provisions for successors in case something happens to you.

- Choose the least restrictive option that ensures your child's protection.

Guardianship

A child becomes a legal adult on his or her eighteenth birthday in most states. Federal laws such as the Social Security Act generally assume age 18 as the age when a minor becomes an adult. Parents who have a child with a cognitive impairment or mental illness must make a decision whether to petition for guardianship or establish alternative protections when the child turns 18.

Although guardianship is a legal concept, one does not need an attorney to petition a court for appointment. Parents can do it themselves. The process takes a few months and costs a few hundred dollars in most states. In Colorado it's "3 and 3," three months and $300 if the court visitor recommends appointment and the petition is uncontested. Petitioning is straightforward but it does take time and personal attention. The process is designed to protect the civil rights of an individual and not to serve the convenience of petitioners. The process steps are:

1. Parents file the petition with the clerk of court and pay the required fee. A physician's statement of the medical condition justifying guardianship must be filed with the petition. The petition lists interested parties which usually include the child (legally termed the "respondent"), the child's physician, care givers, certain relatives, and those with whom the child is living.

2. Interested parties must be notified of the petition by the petitioners.

3. The court appoints a court visitor or *guardian ad litem* (GAL) who investigates the respondent's situation and advises the court in its decision. The GAL will meet with the child and others he thinks appropriate. The petitioner pays the GAL's fees.

4. After the GAL submits his report to the court, the court sets a hearing date and notifies the petitioner who must then notify the interested parties and show evidence to the court of having done so.

5. The parents and the child appear in court on the scheduled date unless the child's medical condition prevents his or her attendance. The judge will talk to the child to ask if he agrees with having a guardian and if he wants his parents to be his guardians. The hearing usually concludes quickly and the judge rules from the bench and signs the order.

6. Parents should keep copies of the guardianship order to show others that they have authority to act for their child's benefit if questioned.

7. Guardians are required to submit annual reports to the court regarding changes in situation, care provided, and the continued need for guardianship.

As a guardian, you must understand your duties and responsibilities and the legal limits of authority. In many communities there are non-profit organizations that can advise you on the appropriateness of guardianship and its alternatives, offer classes in a guardian's responsibilities, and help complete a petition. Arc chapters are common resources for information and education. You should consult with an attorney if an appointment is likely to be challenged. Why would guardianship for an adult with a condition such as Down syndrome be contested? It happens when the parents are divorced or divorcing. It also happens when the child has money which someone wants to control.

One can petition for full guardianship or limited guardianship. Full guardianship gives the guardian authority over almost all aspects of a person's life including the management of daily affairs, medical needs, money, and legal matters. If you petition for limited guardianship, you describe the authority you think you need in the petition. The court decides the scope of authority appropriate to the circumstances. Limited guardianship is typically sought for managing a person's financial and legal matters while she retains the power over her personal affairs.

Guardianship is not necessarily permanent. Failure to file annual reports can result in termination. A guardian can petition to have his authority amended, narrowed, expanded, terminated, or transferred to another. If the parents move to another state, they usually need to petition a court in their present state of residence for approval to move the child out of state. They will also need to petition a court for guardianship in the state to which they are moving. Parents who are guardians should designate successors in their wills to succeed them when they die. The court is not obligated to follow their wishes but will almost always do so unless someone contests or the GAL recommends against.

A problem that is often not anticipated arises when the guardian cannot fulfill his role because of injury or disability. The legal document needed here is a durable power of attorney appointing someone to act as a temporary guardian. In some states a guardianship order can designate an alternate or successor called a standby guardian. An emergency guardian can be appointed by a court within a matter of hours or days but the existence of a durable POA or a standby guardian makes the scramble for an emergency guardian unnecessary. If the guardian's disability is likely to be permanent or long-term, typically more than 60 days, the agent or someone should petition the court to appoint a successor if a standby guardian has not already been designated.

A guardian does not have complete authority over the ward. He cannot approve an abortion, an organ donation, sterilization, or institutionalization. He cannot appropriate money or property belonging to the ward, for example transfer money in a UTMA account to his own account or to a special needs trust. He cannot revoke the ward's appointment of an agent with medical power of attorney. Nor can a guardian choose to not comply with provisions of a divorce order in matters of custody, visitation, or other rights of the non-custodian parent.

When is guardianship appropriate? Parents seek guardianship when their child needs protection and alternative measures are inadequate or unreliable.

They seek guardianship to get a place at the table in decisions affecting their child with medical professionals, schools, government agencies, and service providers. They seek it for standing in legal actions such as a civil rights complaint on their child's behalf. Individual and family circumstances are unique and the appropriateness of guardianship must be determined in individual circumstances. Guardianship is not appropriate for those who are physically impaired with normal intellectual capacity. If the person is capable of living independently, full guardianship is not appropriate although limited guardianship for financial and legal affairs may be. If a person requires continuous care and supervision or is defenseless against abuse or exploitation, full guardianship is probably appropriate. In between independence and the need for continuous care, no inflexible guidance can be given. Disability rights advocates argue that guardianship is overused and that parents should err on the side of self-determination. Parents with a special needs child will usually err on the side of protection. It is always possible for a guardian to ask the court to rescind or reduce her powers if experience shows that full guardianship is unnecessary for the person's care and safety.

Conservatorship or a Trust to Manage Assets

Personal supervision and managing money are two different things. The courts in some states allow a guardian to manage only routine amounts of money. A "conservator," someone with financial management expertise, is appointed to manage significant amounts of money and property. Some states distinguish between a "guardian of the estate" for financial assets and a "guardianship of the person" for personal supervision and require separate appointments. There is no hard rule as to the value of assets that triggers the appointment of a conservator. If the money is of a sufficient amount to be invested, the court may well view appointing a qualified financial manager as conservator to be in the person's best interest. The process of conservatorship appointment is similar to guardianship.

A simple option is a joint bank account which one of the people on the account registration manages for the other person whose name is on the account who cannot manage money themselves. The bank account can receive direct deposits of Social Security payments with the first account registrant named as a Social Security "representative payee."

Another alternative is for the person to appoint an agent with durable power of attorney for his financial affairs. An individual appoints an agent by signing a power of attorney document (see Chapter 18). The power of attorney option preserves self-determination and does not require a court order. A person can define the responsibilities and limitations of his agent, which allows much more flexibility than the appointment of a guardian or conservator whose powers are defined in law and by court order.

Assets can be placed in a trust to be managed for the person's benefit. This option affords the greatest level of financial protection. However, there are considerations. A person cannot convey his assets to a trust without affecting eligibility for SSI and Medicaid unless the trust is a properly drafted, self-settled special needs trust. A trust can be more expensive to administer. You should get legal advice on the appropriateness of this option. A trust is often a good option for a person with mental illness for whom a guardian cannot be justified, and who may be too quick to revoke the appointment of an agent when he most needs help.

Appointment of an Agent with Power of Attorney

This is often an excellent alternative because POA documents can be written to address unique needs and circumstances. The person appointing an agent is called a "principal." The agent is called an "attorney in fact." One can have different agents for different decisions, such as an agent for financial and legal affairs and an agent for healthcare decisions. A springing, durable POA is an alternative to guardianship for someone with mental illness.

Representative Payee

A representative payee is someone authorized to receive Social Security payments for a Social Security beneficiary. A "rep payee" is appointed by the Social Security Administration. If the person receives state assistance, a state agency may also appoint a rep payee for state payments. If the person's only income is from public assistance, a representative payee may be the only protection required. SSA generally prefers a family member to serve as a rep payee. A rep payee can also be a guardian, conservator, agent, non-profit agency, licensed for-profit organization, or trustee.

Advocates with Privacy Waivers

This can be an excellent possibility for someone for whom guardianship is not appropriate. To say that state Medicaid or disability service agencies are not user-friendly is to put it mildly. Many people with a cognitive impairment are vulnerable if they try to encounter "the System" alone. However when a friend tries to help, the agency may refuse to meet with him, answer questions, or share records with the justification of protecting the individual's privacy rights. To empower the advocate, the individual must sign privacy waivers, also called HIPAA waivers, authorizing medical professionals, hospitals, service providers, state employees, etc. to disclose needed information to his advocate. Often government agencies and medical institutions require their privacy waiver form to be signed. Forms can be valid for a limited period of time. It can be a challenge to assemble the forms for many organizations and agencies and execute new forms as each expires.

The problem can be more than merely inconvenient—if there is no signed privacy waiver on record and the individual is not able to execute one when help is needed, a situation can be overtaken by events. I once had a client who had an advocate assisting with a Medicaid application. The applicant was hospitalized while the application was being processed. While in the hospital, the county human services agency asked for additional documentation to support the application. The advocate sought to respond but was refused a meeting by the agency because he lacked a privacy waiver. When the requested information was not forthcoming in its arbitrarily set response time, the agency did not simply place the application on hold, it denied it. Meanwhile the individual needed Medicaid to pay for the hospital!

Despite the limitations, advocates with privacy waivers can be a better option than guardianship. The person does not have his rights taken away. It honors the principles of self-advocacy and self-determination. It's cheaper and more flexible. The advocate needs to be available only when requested. However, an advocate's powers are more limited than those of a guardian or agent.

Concerns for People with Mental Illness

I have already mentioned that guardianship is not appropriate for someone who lives independently with a mental illness effectively controlled with medication. A court will not appoint a guardian for someone who has demonstrated a capability to manage his affairs. An agent with power of attorney, however, is an option. If the person has a psychotic episode, an agent can intervene if needed. A change in mental function can be caused by physical changes from aging, changes in body chemistry or metabolism, or a developing medical condition. (Parkinson's disease wreaks havoc with antipsychotic medications.) A person I have known for 20 years has bipolar disorder and functions reasonably well for six to eight years at a time. Unpredictably he deteriorates into a psychotic state. He then requires admittance to a mental facility until an effective adjustment can be made to his drug prescriptions. A springing, durable power of attorney can work in this situation. Someone can take over temporarily while the person is in the hospital to manage his bank account, receive income, pay expenses, take care of a pet, arrange for cleaning the residence, etc.

However, the individual with a mental illness may revoke his agent's powers when he most needs help, fearing institutionalization. (This fear can appear with paranoia or schizophrenia.) Recognizing this problem, some states recognize a legal document called a Psychiatric Advance Directive (PAD) which cannot be terminated by someone in a psychotic state. However, if you are an agent and the principal revokes your power, do not continue to serve even if diligently trying to help—you expose yourself to personal liability by acting without authority.

CHECKLIST
CREATING A LEGAL PLAN

		Yes/ Done	Action Req'd	Not Needed
	Estate Plan			
1	Have you decided on your estate planning goals?			
	(a) Care of spouse, children, special needs child, others			
	(b) Control of property or money for those not able to manage competently			
	(c) Steps to eliminate potential family conflicts			
	(d) Prearrangements while alive and bequests and insurance benefits at death			
	(e) Compliance with laws for required inheritance and spouse's elective share			
	(f) Minimizing transfer tax exposure (estate, gift, generation-skipping transfer)			
	(g) Are you a blended family with children from previous marriages?			
	(h) Are you and your partner not legally married or common law married?			
	(i) Are you a same-gender couple?			
	(j) Are you in a community property state?			
	(k) Are you a current or potential party in litigation?			
	(l) Do you own a substantial business with employees, inventory, or assets?			
2	Have you had a family discussion regarding your plans with adult children?			
	(a) How you addressed the question of fairness to each child			
	(b) Responsibilities for special needs sibling			

		Yes/ Done	Action Req'd	Not Needed
	Estate Plan (continued)			
3	If you are high net worth, have you engaged a professional team for planning?			
	(a) A trust and estates attorney			
	(b) An estate tax attorney or accountant			
	(c) An investment manager or wealth management office			
	(d) Specialists in business transfer planning			
4	How will protection and lifetime support be assured for a special needs child?			
	Legal Documents			
1	Have you executed the appropriate legal documents?			
	(a) Wills for both parents			
	(b) A power of attorney for both parents in case of disability			
	(c) Medical directives for both parents—living will, DMPOA, and DNRO			
	(d) A stand-alone or testamentary special needs trust			
2	Have you engaged an elder law or trust and estates attorney to draft documents?			
3	Have you selected a personal representative or successor to your spouse?			
4	Have you selected a successor guardian after you and your spouse pass away?			
5	Have you decided on the bequests in your will?			
	(a) Real estate			
	(b) Financial assets and other property			
	(c) Personal possessions to be distributed by memorandum attached to will			
6	Are there previous wills or codicils to be superseded?			
7	Have you accounted for all property to be transferred and dispositioned them?			
8	Have you decided on an agent with POA or successor?			
9	Have you decided who will hold medical power of attorney and a successor?			

		Yes/ Done	Action Req'd	Not Needed
Legal Documents (continued)				
10	Do you review your documents periodically for changes?			
	(a) Particular attention to named individuals no longer alive or available			
11	Are your legal documents described in your letter of intent?			
12	Are your documents stored where they can be readily obtained by your PR?			
13	Have you shared your decisions with your family, including adult children?			
Special Needs Trust				
1	Do you understand the purpose and characteristics of a special needs trust?			
2	Do you understand the difference between a third party and a first party trust?			
	(a) Are you aware you should never comingle first and third party money in a trust?			
3	Will the trust be a stand-alone, *inter vivos* trust, or a testamentary trust?			
	(a) *Inter vivos* trust if there are others who may contribute			
4	Before meeting with an attorney, have you considered the family decisions?			
	(a) Trustees and successor trustees			
	(b) Trust protector and successors			
	(c) Do you expect to co-trustee a family member and a corporate fiduciary?			
	(d) Remainder beneficiaries			
5	Will you initially set up a pour-over trust with you and your spouse as trustees?			
6	Will family trustees hire professional investment and tax advice?			
7	Are trustees required to file reports with parents, guardian, or trust protector?			
8	Will the trust protector have "at will" or "for cause" powers to remove a trustee?			
9	Do you understand the significance of revocability versus irrevocability?			

		Yes/ Done	Action Req'd	Not Needed
Special Needs Trust (continued)				
10	Have you engaged an elder law or trust and estates attorney?			
	(a) If a T&E attorney, have you confirmed experience with special needs trusts?			
11	Do you have a plan for what happens later after you set up the trust?			
12	If there is more than one trust for the child, have you named a common trustee?			
Guardianship or Alternative Protections				
1	Have you considered applying for guardianship when your child turns 18?			
2	Will you petition the court yourself or hire an attorney?			
	(a) Do you know how to file, and are you willing to take the time and pay the fees?			
	(b) Consult with an attorney if guardianship is likely to be contested			
3	Have you considered alternatives to guardianship?			
	(a) Limited guardianship for financial and legal affairs			
	(b) Trustee or conservator for financial assets			
	(c) Someone appointed as an agent for the child with power of attorney			
	(d) An advocate empowered with privacy waivers			
4	Are you aware that annual guardianship reports must be filed with the court?			
5	Do you know that you can petition to limit or remove guardianship later?			
6	Have you decided on successors to you and your spouse?			

CASE STUDIES
LEGAL PLANS

Let's meet again with Angel, Mike, Noelle, and Henry and see how their parents' legal plans are coming along, or in Henry's case, his plan.

Angel Herrera

John and Michelle Herrera have a set of legal documents including personal wills, healthcare directives, and a special needs trust drafted shortly after Angel was born. They have been largely forgotten amid all of the other distractions in the Herreras' lives. The law firm that drafted them no longer exists. They meet with the attorney, Gene Taylor, who co-presented at the Transitions Day workshop. He is an elder law attorney and a partner with a medium-sized firm with practitioners in family law, business law, elder law, and trust and estates law. After the preliminary consultation, Gene suggests he would like the Herreras to meet one of the firm's senior partners, Martin Robling, the senior estate attorney. What Gene sees is that the Herreras need more than an update or replacement of old legal documents. With their net worth and family situation, they need an estate plan that addresses family planning, wealth planning, and potential exposure to wealth transfer taxes. Mr. Robling is an elderly gentleman, now semi-retired, who continues to serve a modest number of long-term clients. The attorneys in the firm know that Mr. Robling (as everyone addresses him out of instinctive respect) takes only "interesting" new clients. "Wealth" is not a word in Mr. Robling's definition of interesting. Gene senses the Herreras fit his definition.

The conversation in Mr. Robling's office isn't what the Herreras expected. The talk is not about updating legal documents or estate taxes or Medicaid. Instead, Mr. Robling draws them into talking about family. He wants to know about Angel and about Jo and Paul. He wants to know not only about Jo's and Paul's relationship to Angel but also their relationship to each other. He wants to know about John's and Michelle's parents. At one point in the conversation, having learned that John has a sister and three brothers, he turns to John and asks, "Which one of you will take care of your parents when the time comes?"

The Herreras have never talked about that, figuring it to be a conversation to be had "when the time comes." All four parents have been prematurely aged by a lifetime of physical labor, John's dad as a construction laborer, his mother as a janitor, and Michelle's parents as farm workers. They have vaguely thought that their parents could come and live with them if necessary. Their house is larger than family need. Its spaciousness serves for John's entertainment of company executives and potential clients.

The Herreras' net worth is not high enough for exposure to estate taxes even with $2 million of life insurance. However, John is in his peak earnings years, and although 51, a promotion to vice-president could still come. The estate planning issue is not simply one of taxes. Family wealth, especially multi-generational family wealth, brings opportunities, challenges, responsibilities, and sometimes strife. Mr. Robson asks them, with a twinkle in his eye, "If you had $20 million, would it change anything—your goals, your values, what you do, who your friends are? How would it change your children?"

At a subsequent meeting, he works with them to develop a framework for family planning. He gives them two books to read, *Wealth in Families* (Collier 2008) and *Trustworthy* (Goldstone and Wiseman 2012).

Over a period of three months, multiple plans come together for John and Michelle. Gene Taylor has frequently worked with Sue Sundstrand, a financial planner, on client cases and they team on the Herreras' case. The Herreras' wills are updated to change the designation of the personal representative to one of the probate attorneys in the law firm. The attorneys design an estate plan with features for probate avoidance, lifetime prearrangements, and estate and gift tax management. The legal instruments include revocable living trusts and the common trusts used to maximize the use of the estate tax exemption, the so-called ABC trusts. I do not have space to explain these here. These three types of trust are known in legal terminology as a marital trust with power of appointment, a by-pass or credit shelter trust, and a qualified terminable interest property (QTIP) trust. Angel's special needs trust will be integrated into the flow of family wealth into the various trusts. The Herreras' life insurance policies will be placed in an irrevocable life insurance trust, also called an ILIT.

The special needs trust they have had for 20 years is fortunately revocable, allowing several changes to be made. A trust protector clause is added. The logical appointee is Jo since she is a CPA. Whether a trust protector is necessary is debatable with the careful selection of a corporate fiduciary but the appointment serves to begin knitting the siblings together in a common family purpose. Because Angel's trust will likely be substantially funded, Mr. Robling recommends that the trustee be a corporate fiduciary. John and Michelle need to take care in selecting the firm. Mr. Robling explains the legal, financial, and personal considerations involved. He recommends the trust company he has worked with extensively which he believes to be highly qualified, ethical, and committed to serving the needs and aspirations of its clients and beneficiaries.

However, he suggests they interview two or three firms. He provides them with a short list of fiduciaries.

The Herreras know that they should create a letter of intent for Angel's future. Under Mr. Robling's guidance, this expands into a larger family meeting with John, Michelle, Jo, Paul, and Angel. As part of this, Mr. Robling meets Jo and Paul individually and gets to know them. And of course, Martin Robling becomes Angel's friend too. (Angel is always ready to make a new friend.) It is noted that someday Angel may need a professional guardian. Mr. Robling suggests that Paul is the appropriate person to have responsibility to hire, oversee, and replace the guardian if necessary. The family meeting will eventually evolve into a family counsel that includes Mr. Robling, the Herreras' personal representative, the family trust officer, Angel's guardian, and either her live-in companion, support person, or manager of her community living residence. Most of the members of this family counsel will become Angel's circle of support.

Mr. Robling remarks that if John and Michelle have been well served by their financial advisor (who is a registered representative of a securities broker), he would not suggest they change. (However, unless the advisor has served the family very well in terms of investment performance and maintaining a personal relationship, he is likely to lose the business to the corporate fiduciary as its relationship develops with the family.)

There is a last piece of family business. It leads John and Michelle on trips to Tucson and Bakersfield. It's a visit to their parents, this time with an added purpose. It's to hear the parents' concerns and wishes for end-of-life care. John and Michelle have learned it's not simply a room in their home. They have done their homework about the services that can allow an elderly couple to maintain their independence for as long as possible and not be separated by different care needs. And one more thing. John and Michelle's visits are to express their gratitude and love and their assurance to their parents that they will live out their twilight years in the security and dignity they deserve.

Mike Olmstead

Sharon has a preliminary consultation with Virginia Moore, the attorney that her friend recommended. Ms. Moore practices in elder law, trust and estates law, disability planning, and guardianship. Sharon finds Ms. Moore to be understanding and empathetic to her situation. She listens to Sharon's concerns for her son, the uncertainty that clouds his future, and her worries for who will care for Mike if something happens to her. Finding a sympathetic ear, all of the fears and the frustrations and the stress and the psychological and physical burdens that Sharon has carried over all of the years of caring for her son alone tumble out in Virginia's office. Ms. Moore has heard it before, too many times before.

Given the fact that Mike's life can go down two very different paths—a life of independence or a life needing care and supervision—Virginia recommends that Sharon establish a revocable living trust with herself as trustee and the power to appoint her successor. Sharon's home will be the main asset conveyed to the trust. When she dies the trustee, who should also be the personal representative of her estate, has the discretion to take appropriate action. If Mike remains disabled and will need SSI and Medicaid, the trustee will sell the home and transfer the proceeds to a third party special needs trust, or sell the home, buy a condominium for Mike, and transfer the residual cash to the trust. If Mike is employed and independent, the trust will continue to hold the home with Mike having a life estate to live there, or the home may be sold to purchase a residence suitable for his circumstances. (His employment could be in another city or a smaller residence or condominium might make more sense.) Having the property and cash remain in the trust is a protection for Mike, particularly protection from financial exploitation. While alive, Sharon will be the beneficiary of the trust with Mike the remainder beneficiary. Should Mike predecease Sharon, Sharon's parents are successor remainder beneficiaries, and if they have also deceased, the trust will distribute its assets to charities named by Sharon.

Virginia recommends that a successor trustee be named in the document since the person will need to make critical decisions quickly after Sharon's death. Sharon knows no one to perform the duties required. Ms. Moore suggests an attorney who handles these matters. The successor trustee will step into the trustee role if Sharon is not mentally competent to serve as trustee, a potential issue as she ages into her senior years. Sharon would like Ms. Moore to serve as the trust protector if a successor trustee has taken over for her. Ms. Moore is willing to serve with compensation for her professional services.

Sharon does not anticipate anyone contributing to Mike's future support. Frank, her ex-husband, intends for his estate to go to his current wife and children. Given this, Ms. Moore recommends a testamentary special needs trust be incorporated into Sharon's will. This is needed if Mike's condition proves to be permanently disabling. The trustee will be the state's charitable, pooled-asset trust for people with disabilities. The personal representative of her estate, who is also the trustee of the revocable living trust, will execute the agreement with the trust when the estate is settled. The charitable trust offers case management and other services which Mike will need. When Mike dies, any remainder in the third party special needs trust will be left to the charitable trust company.

Sharon also needs to have a durable, springing power of attorney for someone to act for her if she is not mentally competent to manage her own affairs. The power of attorney document can empower her appointed agent to manage Mike's care and supervision should Sharon be unable to do so herself. This is useful if Sharon's disability is temporary. However, the agent should not be able to override or interfere with the decisions of a legal guardian. Sharon also needs a durable power of attorney for healthcare decisions and signed HIPAA waivers for her healthcare proxy. Sharon decides to name her closest friend as both her personal agent and her healthcare agent. Sharon also needs to execute a living will to make her wishes for medical care known.

Next, Sharon raises the question of guardianship for Mike. Virginia recommends that Sharon petition for guardianship so that she can intervene if Mike cannot cope with college. The court petition should request appointment of a standby guardian to ensure continuity in the event of Sharon's sudden death. Sharon does not know of anyone to take over the guardianship role. Ms. Moore advises that a professional guardian is a possibility, but Sharon will need to consult with a financial planner to ensure that there is money in her estate to pay a professional.

Ms. Moore notes that if Mike is successful at school and will seek professional employment, Sharon should petition the court to have guardianship terminated. Employers will likely not hire Mike if they know he is under the care of a guardian. Mike should execute his own power of attorney if legally independent, appointing whomever he wishes to serve as his agent. Sharon hopes that she will be the agent, but Ms. Moore points out that it will be Mike's decision. The attorney notes that if Mike is able to manage his affairs as an independent adult, Sharon needs to be willing to let go.

Ms. Moore's fee is $2700 for crafting the legal documents, including the revocable living trust, a will containing a testamentary trust, and healthcare directives. Ms. Mason recommends that Sharon inform her parents of her arrangements and will provide her with a letter to send them. She also recommends that Sharon write a letter of intent for others who might be involved in Mike's support after her death. She also notes that many of the elements of the plan interlock, and she must take care that the documents are uniformly updated. Last, Ms. Moore notes that when Mike is ready to embark on his journey into independence, she would like to meet him, and would be pleased to help him with his estate planning. As an independent adult, Mike will need a will, power of attorney, and healthcare directives of his own.

Noelle Williams

Robert and Dorothy have not executed legal directives in the event of their deaths or disability. As with many families, the needs of the moment have distracted them from taking care of the uncertainties of the future. One of the men in their church, Mr. Moses, is a lawyer and he prevails on them to address planning for their estates. One decision was simple and straightforward for the Williams'. Whatever they can leave to their children, they want Noelle and Robert, Jr. to share equally. The house is their most valuable asset and will be the primary component of their legacy. Robert's union pension has a spousal survivor benefit but there is no survivor benefit for children. Although Robert and Dorothy both come from large families, all of their relatives are working class and there is no expectation of an inheritance. Robert has earned the necessary work credits for Social Security retirement, disability, and dependent and survivor benefits.

The Williams' work with Mr. Moses to draw up wills. If one spouse dies, the other receives his or her estate. Each is also appointed the other's personal representative. They must make decisions relating to their dying together or one quickly after another. They trust one of the women in their church, Ms. Martin, to complete raising Noelle and Robert, Jr.; she is whom they will name to be a minor's guardian. They would like their home to be held for their two children until out of college and on their own but there will be no income to pay for the mortgage, taxes, and insurance if Robert dies. The home will have to be sold with the proceeds going to the daughter and son as adults or held for them by a trustee or conservator if they are still minors. The Williams' talk to the bank president about setting up a custodial account for either child until adulthood, but find that funds in the custodial account (a UTMA) must be turned over to them under state law at his or her eighteenth birthday. Robert and Dorothy prefer to have each child's legacy protected until he or she graduates from college. Mr. Moses suggests that a trust be set up by an article in their wills if there is no surviving parent. The proceeds from the sale of the house and property, held by the trust, can be used to pay for a child's college. When a child graduates and demonstrates to the trustee he or she is either employed full-time or is diligently looking for work, the remainder of his or her share can be distributed. This sounds like a reasonable plan to the Williams'. When the question comes as to who to appoint as personal representative of their estate and trustee of the testamentary trust, they decide to appoint Mr. Moses. A trust protector is probably not essential in this situation. If an advisor were to suggest appointing one, the Williams' would probably reject it as an insult to their friend.

Robert and Dorothy need to execute power of attorney documents in case either becomes mentally incapacitated. Each appoints their spouse as agent. The Williams' also complete and sign standard healthcare directives.

As a last step Mr. Moses offers to review Robert's union contract and his pension and health insurance documents. The review of the pension confirms that, although there is a survivor benefit for Dorothy and a modest death benefit to cover funeral and burial expenses, there is no survivor benefit for the children. Mr. Moses points out something to them that neither had thought about. Dorothy and the children are covered as dependents on Robert's health insurance but there is no coverage for any family member after his death. It is unlikely that Dorothy can get affordable health insurance for herself and probably not for her children. A health insurance exchange under the Patient Protection and Affordable Care Act might be the answer, but until the state sets up the exchange there is no certainty in this option. Another option is Medicaid planning. Mr. Moses admits he isn't an expert on Medicaid but he is aware of the income and asset limits to be eligible. He knows an attorney in the nearby city that specializes in Social Security, Medicare, and Medicaid. If Robert dies, Mr. Moses, as the personal representative of his estate and as a friend of the family, will help Dorothy decide on what to do about health insurance, visiting the Medicaid attorney together and checking the possibility of health insurance through a state exchange.

Health insurance is an easily overlooked aspect of financial planning because most people are covered by an employer or union plan. It is too often taken for granted. When a family or advisor is developing a plan, access to health insurance must be considered for the protection of all family members. It is increasingly important to give this area more emphasis. Many employers are cutting back on group plans or shifting a greater share of premiums to the employee. Medicare and Medicaid will remain hostage for some time in the national debate on deficit reduction. Health insurance exchanges under the Patient Protection and Affordable Care Act have yet to be established. Assuring access to healthcare is an imperative in legal and financial planning for an individual or family.

Henry Lowenstein

Henry would like to end reliance on government disability assistance and make it on his own. If he is successful in achieving his goal of meaningful employment, he could face a very difficult dilemma: how will he pay for his medications? Once his income exceeds Social Security's SGA of $1040 per month, he will no longer be considered disabled. Private group health insurance companies seek to avoid providing coverage for high-cost individuals and often refuse to write policies for small employers that have such an employee. Henry might get a job with a large employer where his medical costs will be insignificant relative to the size of the plan's premiums. However, the positions he is seeking will probably not be with large private companies. The state where he lives is important. If he lives in a state that uses "categorically needy" eligibility criteria for Medicaid, he will probably not get help paying for his prescriptions if his monthly income is much over $2000 per month. If he is in a state that uses "medically needy" eligibility criteria, he may be able to get help. This illustrates the huge obstacle that many people with mental illness face trying to raise themselves out of poverty. In any case, Henry will need to consult with a Medicaid attorney or health insurance consultant to understand how his goals for employment will affect his medical care.

It is easy to overlook that Henry needs his own set of legal documents. His only possession that carries an ownership title is his automobile. Assuming the car has value, it could be transferred to one of Henry's friends by a simple will. He probably can use a generic will generated by commercially available software. His personal possessions can be given to others by personal memorandum. If he wants to purchase a condominium, he should understand its treatment in Medicaid law. He will have to accept a Medicaid lien on the property or place the property in a Medicaid-payback trust. He should discuss this with an attorney prior to making an offer on a property.

In Henry's case, he should appoint someone to act for him with a durable, springing power of attorney. This person could be his friend Craig or his brother Alan. A potential problem with a power of attorney is the possibility that a mentally ill individual revokes the power because of fear of losing his independence. Some states recognize a legal document called a Psychiatric Advance Directive (PAD) that authorizes an agent to make decisions over the objections of the person needing psychiatric care. To protect the individual, these states impose specific and strict standards for how these documents are executed and the powers that can be delegated to an agent. Henry should consult with an attorney to determine if his state recognizes a PAD or if the common agency form is the one conforming to state laws.

Henry also needs the typical medical directives—a living will and a durable medical power of attorney, and possibly a Do Not Resuscitate Order or Cardiopulmonary Resuscitation directive. One can argue that these medical directives are even more important for a person with a mental illness than a typical person.

Henry should pay attention to the state-level implementation of the Patient Protection and Affordable Care Act. If attacks from the political right on the implementation of healthcare exchanges prevail, Henry will be out of luck once again. If the Act survives, it can be one of the most important enablers for him to earn a better life.

PART 5

SPECIAL CIRCUMSTANCES

CHAPTER 21

DIVORCE AND THE SPECIAL NEEDS CHILD

A special needs child can draw a family together. But the stress of being a parent or the avoidance of parental responsibility can break a fragile relationship. The needs of a child with a disability are inadequately addressed by the divorce laws in many states. Many judges and attorneys are not experienced in this area. There is a general sense that the child has extraordinary needs, but how to meet those needs and the implications of a permanent disability are often not well understood. The separation agreement or divorce decree must provide for and protect the child's lifetime support to the extent practical given the parents' financial resources.

In this chapter I will review some of the principles in divorce law regarding child support and spousal maintenance. Be aware that divorce law is promulgated by the states. There is general consistency but not uniformity from state to state. If you anticipate being a party in a divorce, you should consult with a divorce attorney and a Certified Divorce Financial Analyst (CDFA) in your state.

The Psychological Effect on the Child

Divorce is traumatic for any child but especially for the child with a significant disability. Children with disabilities have a sense of their vulnerability, though perhaps only an instinctive sense if they are cognitively impaired. They have a visceral psychological need for security. The younger the child and the more serious the disability, the greater will be this emotional need. The ending of the parents' relationship and the break-up of the family will be very stressful and very hurtful. The outcome of divorce, from the child's perspective, can be the loss of a parent, a parent they love and have depended on. It may be hard to recognize the trauma a child is experiencing if he is non-verbal or has poor expressive skills. His distress may be evident only from changes in behavior. A special needs child will likely need trauma or grief counseling before and after the dissolution of the marriage. This should be recognized in the separation agreement with provision for how the cost will be shared.

Some divorces are relatively amicable and some are bitterly hostile. The child's anxiety will be increased by parents' open animosity toward each other. It is best if they can avoid exposing the child to their antagonism. It is also cruel to put a child in the position, deliberately or effectively, of having to choose between parents if he or she lacks the intellectual capacity to understand what's going on and the emotional skills to cope. The child may also be exposed to one parent's disparaging and spiteful remarks about the other as he moves back and forth in shared custody. It does a child no good for a parent to try to take away the love the child feels for the other parent unless the relationship is being severed for his safety.

As awkward as it may be, parents should sit down with their child and explain calmly and in language the child can understand what is happening and what the future will be like. A child in need of security and protection will feel terrible anxiety when he begins to sense that the life he has known is coming to an end. He should be assured that the parents' separation was not his fault and that he is still loved and part of a family—albeit a changed family. Parents may need psychological counseling themselves to help them help their child.

Our legal system is structured on the principles of adversarial proceedings but mediated or negotiated divorce are well-established options which should be used if possible. A child's care and financial needs will likely be better met in mediation than in litigation. One thing lacking in the divorce legal system, something sorely needed, is an independent advocate for the children affected, similar to the role played by a *guardian ad litem* in a different domain of family law.

Spousal Support (Alimony)

Spousal support, also called spousal maintenance or alimony, is a series of cash payments or a lump sum payment made by the spouse with greater wealth or income to the other. (Alimony is the term used in the Internal Revenue Code.) Spousal support can be negotiated by the spouses or ordered by the court when they can't agree. *Spousal support is non-modifiable unless the parties agree that it can be modified later.* Support may be open-ended or fixed-term. Open-ended support is for an unlimited duration. It is used when there is likely to be a permanent disparity in the income or expenses of the ex-spouses. It is appropriate when a spouse takes a long-term care giver role for a child with a disability and cannot work due to the care giver role. Fixed-term support is payable for a defined period of time or until a certain dollar amount is paid. It is used to balance a property division, retire debt, pay for a child's education, or help a spouse become self-supporting. With either open-ended or fixed-term, the monthly or annual amount can be the same over all periods or it may be increased or decreased from year to year. The decree may provide for terminating support in defined circumstances such as a receiving spouse's remarriage. Spousal maintenance is tax-deductible to the ex-spouse paying it and taxable to the one receiving it.

Child Support

Parents have a legal obligation to support their minor children and they cannot negotiate that obligation away. Child support remains a parental obligation until the age of emancipation, which is the eighteenth birthday in most states or until the child completes high school. Each state defines the age through which child support must continue. In Colorado, it continues until the child's nineteenth birthday or until he graduates from high school. Parents can agree to extend support for a longer period. It must be extended for the lifetime of a permanently disabled child and must be so ordered by the court—the divorce legal system recognizes the appropriateness of extended support for a disabled child. The question that creates much controversy is the appropriate amount of support.

All states have guidelines that determine the parents' minimum support obligation and how that obligation will be allocated between them. Minimum support is for *basic expenses*. Typically the amount is determined from a table with rows for the parents' combined income and columns for the number of children. Each cell in a row-column intersection shows the amount of child support. The amount is allocated to each parent by the ratio of their incomes. Although this calculation is termed a "guideline," in practice the courts usually follow it for the basic expenses of a non-disabled child.

Most states recognize that a child may have *extraordinary expenses*. Extraordinary expenses and their allocation between the parents can be negotiated or a parent can petition the court to order support. *A child with special needs will have extraordinary expenses by definition.* Statutory laws and case law established by court decisions are not explicit regarding the definition of extraordinary expenses for a special needs child. Typically the law and the courts recognize work-related expenses, higher education expenses, healthcare, and health insurance as extraordinary expenses. The court may not recognize all of the needs a parent feels should be included. It may recognize expenses for medically necessary needs or needs caused by the disability but not expenses for quality of life. It can be important that the parents agree on extraordinary expenses and not leave the courts to apply a narrower definition.

The best possible estimate of a child's lifetime support should be prepared to help determine the amount of child support. Child support is always modifiable by the court if it is established the child's needs have substantially changed. It is a legal principle that the State retains authority to assure that the needs of minors and those legally "incompetent" are met. However, repeated trips to the court for increases in child support are rarely in the child's best interest. You should always start with the best possible estimate, recognizing at the outset that the financial support needed by a child with a permanent disability is likely to increase over time at a rate greater than inflation. A separation agreement can include language identifying milestones, circumstances, or ages when the child's needs will be re-assessed.

An estimate of a child's support should be based on the life plan. A problem arises when the parents cannot agree on the plan, in which case they will not agree on support. An agreement or decree may include language describing a life planning process such as PATH planning. If the PATH team includes independent people focused on the child's needs, particularly if suitably experienced (e.g. professionals involved in preparing IEPs), their consensus opinion regarding the child's needs may be persuasive to a judge when the parents can't agree.

Child support is neither tax-deductible to the payer nor taxable to the spouse receiving payment for the child. However, Social Security and Medicaid regulations treat child support as income in calculating SSI and in determining eligibility for Medicaid and state services. If the child is under age 19, two-thirds of the payment is considered unearned income. At 19 or older, all child support is considered income, reducing SSI dollar-for-dollar (after the $20 allowance if not already taken). Child support is similarly counted toward the income limit for Medicaid recipients. Social Security entitlement payments are not affected. The reduction in SSI and potential loss of Medicaid eligibility can be avoided by paying child support to a first party special needs trust. However, this is an awkward solution since control of trust assests must be in the trustee's sole discretion, and it is likely the support-paying parent will object if the custodial parent is the trustee.

Because of the tax deduction for spousal maintenance, the paying parent may wish to have child support included in spousal maintenance. This is never a good idea. Because child support is modifiable and maintenance is usually not, the child may not receive the support needed that emerges later in life. Children's needs should be met explicitly with child support.

Protecting the Child's Lifetime Support

The award of child support is only the first step in providing for a child's lifetime needs. The continuance of support must be protected. The obvious risk is the death or disability of a parent. Both parents should be required to have adequate life and disability insurance if insurable. It is possible to have the insurance policies owned by a special needs trust with money for premium payments paid to the trustee. If the child's disability is permanent, the insurance should be a type of permanent insurance—whole life, universal life, or variable life. Term insurance is often used because it is cheaper but it is not appropriate to protect a permanently disabled child, unless there are other resources to continue support when the insurance reaches the end of its guaranteed term.

The divorce decree should anticipate the parents' eventual retirement. When a parent experiences the drop in income at retirement, he may petition the court for a reduction in child support. However, the child has probably not had a reduction in her needs. This circumstance is foreseeable and the problem can be met by incrementally funding a special needs trust during the working years or by requiring financial assets be transferred to the trust at retirement.

Obviously, affordability may constrain what can be done to ensure a child's lifetime support. However, if the financial condition of one or both parents improves, needs that were previously not affordable can be addressed by a modified support order.

Coordinating the Estate Plans of Divorced Parents

The possibility of the child outliving either or both parents must be considered. The estate plans of the parents, taken together, should provide for the child's lifetime support needs and complete the funding of a special needs trust. A guardian's estate plan should designate a successor guardian.

If the parents are co-trustees of a special needs trust and are unlikely to cooperate in its administration, an independent trustee should be appointed. Similarly, if the trust has parental co-trust protectors, it is advisable to replace them with an independent party such as an attorney. If the special needs trust is irrevocable, these changes can be problematic and it may be necessary to petition a court to modify the trust agreement. One or both parents may want the property settlement to divide a special needs trust into "his" and "her" trusts. From the standpoint of efficient trust administration, this is a poor decision. A better option is to appoint a corporate trustee for the trust. If the trust is divided, a common trustee should be appointed for the two trusts.

A problem in a hostile divorce is the reluctance or refusal of parents to share their estate planning documents. The decree should require sharing the provisions each makes for the child's support.

Guardianship

One aspect of a separation agreement or divorce decree is the allocation of parental responsibilities for childcare, including custody and visitation rights.

This is not the same as adult guardianship. Future guardianship for a minor child with a permanent disability may get overlooked in the immediate proceedings, only to surface when she reaches the legal age of emancipation. Then a conflict erupts over which parent gets guardianship or a demand for shared guardianship by the parent paying child support, concerned that the guardian spouse will make unilateral care decisions and petition the court for increased support. The separation agreement or court order should anticipate the possible future need to appoint a guardian for an adult child with a permanent disability. One option to consider is giving one spouse the responsibility for day-to-day care with major life planning decisions subject to negotiation. This option won't work if the parents are unlikely to agree on the child's needs. Establishing a life planning process as described in Chapter 1 involving independent advocates can be a possible solution. Requiring mediation for life planning decisions and child support may be the best solution.

Common Law Marriage

Common law marriage is an area of family law where there is considerable variation from state to state. Some states recognize the validity of common law marriage with legal criteria for determining if such a marriage exists or if there is mere co-habitation. A special needs child may be vulnerable when an informal relationship ends. The issue is not child support. A biological parent has that obligation by the fact of being the parent. The issue is spousal support when one of the parents is the stay-at-home care giver. If the relationship between the two individuals does not meet the legal criteria for a common law marriage, the home-bound partner will not be entitled to support. She may face a dilemma of staying home to care for her child with no income to support herself, or taking a job and somehow finding affordable childcare. This can be a very difficult situation.

State law defines the criteria for recognizing the validity of a common law marriage. Typical criteria are: the couple must be living together, they must both be of minimum age, neither can be currently married, and they must have represented themselves as being married. They can represent their relationship as marital by using the same last name, by introducing a partner to other people as a spouse, by filing a tax return as a married couple, by having a joint bank account, or by one partner listing the other as a spouse on an insurance policy or an employee group benefit form.

One may not only need to satisfy the criteria for common law marriage, one may need to prove it to a court. I once had a *pro bono* client who was a stay-at-home mom, the full-time care giver of a two-year-old child with Down syndrome. The biological father claimed there was no marital relationship in his response to her petition for support. Because she had no income or assets to pay the upfront retainer ($5000) for a divorce attorney, she could not find an attorney to represent her. She went into court *pro se*, meaning she represented herself. She lost her case. I was unable to advise her in the petition because, not being an attorney, I am barred from giving legal advice. These things happen. If you are in a relationship that is not legally sanctioned as a marriage (i.e. no marriage certificate) and have a special needs child, you need to understand the risk you are running, and the risk your child is running with you.

Pre-nuptial Agreements

A divorced parent with guardianship or custody of a special needs child faces a diminished prospect of finding another life mate. But sometimes they do. In this circumstance, a pre-nuptial agreement is advised to protect the financial arrangements for the future support of a special needs child. A pre-nuptial agreement is a contractual agreement which describes the property separately owned by a person prior to the marriage and prevents his or her new spouse from claiming a share of those assets at divorce or death. The issue of death is relevant with remarriage because a current spouse is legally entitled to a share of a deceased spouse's estate. This is called an "elective share" in estate law. By signing a pre-nuptial agreement the new spouse waives his or her right to an elective share of the assets identified in the pre-nuptial agreement. The new spouse may also waive his or her right to a survivor benefit in an ERISA-covered retirement plan so the plan's assets can be set aside for a special needs child. Gifts and inheritances expected after the marriage can be addressed as well. There are legal requirements for a pre-nuptial agreement to be valid. One requirement is a full disclosure of all assets by the protected party before both parties sign the agreement. Another requirement is that both parties must be advised to obtain their own independent legal counsel.

The law recognizes post-nuptial agreements but a spouse's ability to obtain one may diminish after the exchange of vows.

Either or both of the partners may find the discussion of a pre-nuptial agreement distasteful, mercenary, or threatening. The parent of a special needs child can be reluctant to bring up the subject. (Strangely, high net worth individuals usually overcome this reluctance.) Nonetheless, the child's protection warrants it. There are alternatives to a pre-nuptial agreement such as transferring assets to a trust prior to the marriage. However, the trust must be irrevocable or the new spouse may be able to claim a share in a future divorce action or at the settlor's death.

Where to Go for More Information

I recommend *Friendly Divorce Guidebook for Colorado* (Hauer 2007). The book is intended for those in a negotiated or mediated divorce and takes great care in explaining the principles of divorce law. It only explains Colorado law, so you should be careful. After reading the book and understanding the general principles, seek the advice of an attorney in your state.

Another book is *Divorce and the Special Needs Child* (Price 2009). This book does not describe the law and court procedures in the depth of the Hauer book, and it curiously fails to address some important issues, for example the treatment of child support in calculating SSI payments.

When a divorce is contemplated or a spouse has been informed by the other of an intention to file, almost everyone knows to go see a divorce attorney. What is often not recognized is the need to see a financial planner. A competent financial planner is expert in projecting wealth accumulation, assessing tax liabilities, analyzing insurance needs, and in retirement and estate planning. Earlier in this book I encouraged you to work with a Certified Financial Planner (CFP). The domain of divorce is an exception. Consult with a Certified Divorce Financial Analyst (CDFA). A CFP may not understand the intricacies of divorce law, especially Qualified Domestic Relations Orders (QDROs). Seek the advice of a financial planner early in the process so she can advise in the negotiation of a separation agreement. A financial advisor may not be able to persuade the attorneys who have completed their work to reopen a negotiated agreement. If the advisor can get negotiations reopened, it will increase the client's fees, can create or exacerbate hostilities between the parties, and the other spouse may reopen his demands as well.

CHAPTER 22

DENIAL OF ELIGIBILITY FOR GOVERNMENT BENEFITS

Most parents of a special needs child experience no problems having the child's application approved for Social Security Disability Insurance benefit, SSI, or Medicaid. Some conditions such as Down syndrome, cerebral palsy, total blindness, or muscular dystrophy are presumed to be totally and permanently disabling. (One can still fail non-medical criteria.) When a condition is not presumed disabling, the assessment of eligibility looks at the severity and "residual functional capacity" of the condition. Some physical, genetic, or mental abnormalities cause functional limitations meeting the "residual functional capacity" threshold considered disabling. For example, autism is not a presumptive disability but it is Listing 112.10 in the regulations under the category of mental disorders. The listing provides guidance for assessing the severity and limitations of autism in adults and children. Questions of eligibility can arise when a physical or mental condition is not one of the diseases or disorders presumed disabling, does not fit any of the listed conditions, or the cause is not known, or the functional limitation cannot be clearly ascertained or verified. There is a possibility that eligibility will be denied in these gray areas. In this chapter I will cover some of the reasons why an application may be denied and how to appeal.

How Common is the Problem?

The Social Security definition of a disability, described in Chapter 8, is very narrow. This is the cause of most denials of benefit eligibility. Improperly prepared applications are another cause. A common problem is inadequate medical or psychiatric documentation of the severity and the limiting effects of the condition. There is another possible factor—"the System" seems to have a bias for denial of eligibility indicated by the success rate of appeals. What are the statistics? According to attorney Karl Kazmierczak, 65 percent of the applications for Social Security disability and SSI were denied in 2010. Of those who appealed the denial, about 62 percent won. Overall, slightly less than 60 percent of those who apply for Social Security Disability or SSI receive benefits. These are sobering statistics. The Social Security Administration used to publish the data on eligibility decisions on its website. It no longer does.

Documenting the Basis for Eligibility

One can apply for Social Security disability (including SSDI, dependent, and survivor benefits) by phone, on-line, by mail, or in person. One applies for SSI at a Social Security office. Like all government agencies, the operation of the Social Security system is forms-driven. The elderly, uneducated, or someone with a cognitive or mental impairment may require help with an application. A vulnerable individual should not try to encounter "the System" alone. Medical records are essential. One should alert one's doctor or psychiatrist that they will be asked to provide records in support of a disability application. The medical records must be provided by an "acceptable medical source," which Social Security defines as a licensed physician, osteopath, optometrist, podiatrist, speech-language pathologist, psychiatrist, or psychologist. An evaluation by an accredited occupational therapist, physical therapist, behavior analyst, or trauma counselor may be helpful in supporting an evaluation by an accepted medical source.

Social Security has a five-step procedure to evaluate a claim:

1. Is one capable of work that qualifies as a Substantial Gainful Activity (explained in Chapter 8)?

2. How severe are the impairments described if not caused by a condition presumed to be disabling (e.g. Down syndrome)? If judged "not severe as described," that is, should not prevent one from gainful employment, the claim will be denied.

3. If the impairment is potentially severe, is your condition found in the Listing of Impairments in the regulations? If the condition is not in the listing, are the impairments observed equivalent in limitation and severity to a listed condition?

4. Can you return to your prior work?

5. Can you do any other job? Note it is the theoretical physical and mental possibility of employment that is evaluated, not whether the individual can find a job.

After the Social Security Administration receives an application and completes an initial screening (steps 1 and 2), it sends the application to a state Disability Determination Services (DDS) office. This is a state agency, not a Social Security office. The DDS obtains the medical records and makes the determination of medical eligibility. It sends its decision back to the SSA. If approved, the SSA determines the amount of payment. The SSA sends the applicant or authorized representative a letter informing them of the dollar amount that will be paid or the reason(s) for denial of benefits. If denied, the letter will inform the applicant of the right of appeal and how to proceed if one wishes to appeal.

There are three things to keep in mind when applying. One, you must understand the stringent definition of a disability in the Social Security regulations. Two, if eligibility is questionable or you find the forms or procedures intimidating or confusing, seek expert advice. Three, make sure you have the necessary medical records and have alerted the doctor, psychiatrist, optometrist, etc. of the application. The DDS will request additional records from a doctor if necessary but it is not the responsibility of the SSA or the DDS to chase doctors. If a doctor does not provide the required documentation, the application will be put on hold or denied.

Common Reasons for Denial of Eligibility

In defense of the Social Security Administration and Medicaid administrators, many people who apply are not eligible. A common public misunderstanding is the criterion of duration. Social Security does not consider temporary or treatable conditions to be disabling. The disabling condition must be likely to last for longer than 12 months or result in death. Also, pain by itself is not a criterion. These issues will likely be irrelevant for most people with a cognitive or mental condition but someone who is physically disabled may face questions about the possibility of rehabilitation or whether the pain is debilitating.

High functioning individuals with a cognitive or mental impairment may have difficulty proving eligibility. Parents of a child with a mental disorder are more likely to have an application denied. Until about 15 years ago, Social Security didn't recognize that Asperger's syndrome could be disabling. Again, a common reason for denial is poor documentation of the severity of the condition and its effects. This can pose a problem for people who are disabled from an unknown cause. Persons who are not disabled because of a single condition but by the compounding of multiple conditions face a higher possibility of denial. If the applicant does not have a physician, Social Security will send the applicant to one of its consultative physicians to perform the evaluation. However, it is best to have one's own doctor provide the documentation. The consultative physician may not be as sympathetic and the law gives more weight to a treating physician's report.

If one is applying for dependent and survivors benefits on a parent's work record, proving that the onset of the condition was prior to the twenty-second birthday is necessary. Late diagnoses are not uncommon with some types of mental illness or conditions such as Asperger's syndrome. If the records of the initial diagnosis have not been kept and you wait until after the twenty-second birthday to file, you must reconstruct the medical history or face the likelihood of denial. If the diagnosis was made after the twenty-second birthday, eligibility may be denied if onset of the condition prior to the birthday could not be established with certainty.

There are a couple of uncommon reasons for rejection. The disability cannot have been caused by alcohol use or drug addiction. ("Caused by" does not mean "as a result of." Some people with physical disabilities become addicted to pain medication, which is not a reason for losing their benefits.) A failure to follow a prescribed treatment or therapy is also a reason to be denied a disability claim.

Never accept a verbal denial of eligibility or refusal to accept an application from an employee in a Social Security, Medicaid, or state office. (This rarely happens in an SSA office but does in state and county offices.) Ask the employee to put the denial or refusal in writing, citing the statute or regulation that justifies the rejection. If the employee refuses, ask to speak to a supervisor. If one is not allowed to talk to a supervisor or if one is not satisfied by the supervisor's response, take notes of the conversation and consult an attorney or non-profit advocacy organization for advice on how to proceed. Don't meekly accept a verbal denial or refusal of an application if the government employee will not put the rejection in writing with a regulatory citation.

Appealing a Denial

There are four levels of appeal of a denial of benefits. One level is disappearing.

The first level, which seems to be phasing out, is the Reconsideration level. The success rate of appeals at this level is only 13 percent, leading some to conclude that Reconsideration tends to rubber-stamp the original decision. Most states have dropped Reconsideration but if your state still uses this step, you must take it before you can appeal to a higher level.

The appeal following an application denial or a denial on Reconsideration is a hearing before an Administrative Law Judge (ALJ) in the Office of Disability Adjudication and Review (ODAR). The success rate at this level is about 62 percent.

If you are denied at an ODAR hearing, you may appeal to the Social Security Appeals Council. Only 2 percent of the appeals are won at this level. Twenty-two percent are remanded to the ODAR for reconsideration (usually by the same ALJ who heard the original appeal). This is the highest level of appeal within the SSA. If denied at this level, the last option is to file suit in a US District Court.

US District Court decisions rarely result in an award of benefits. Almost half of the cases are denied or dismissed. The other half are remanded to the SSA for further review.

If you receive a denial letter, take action immediately. Take the actions set forth in the determination letter. Hire an attorney experienced in Social Security and Medicaid appeals. You have 60 days to appeal. Untimely appeals are almost uniformly rejected. Note carefully the basis for denial in the determination letter. These are the findings you will have to rebut. Keep all correspondence from the SSA and a log of all phone communications. You may need them at the ALJ hearing.

A major criticism of the appeal process is the length of time it can take to reach an ALJ hearing—12–18 months, longer to reach the Appeals Council. This is a compelling reason to take due care with the initial application.

Medicaid is administered by the states and eligibility decisions are made at the state level. If you apply for stand-alone Medicaid with your state or county department of human services, it may be wise to understand the appeals process when you apply in case you are denied. Social Security allows you 60 days to appeal an adverse determination. State deadlines are often shorter; Colorado's deadline is 30 days. You may have as few as ten days to file and you should be prepared to act quickly to protect your rights.

Pro Se versus Hiring an Attorney

If your application is denied and you are considering an appeal, you have three options: handle it yourself, engage an attorney, or consult with a non-profit advocacy or parent support organization. You can appoint a non-attorney to represent you with a claim or appeal. Your decision as to who will appeal should give consideration to the cause, severity, and limitations of your child's condition, and the reasons for denial of the application. In the resource box below I recommend a book that describes Social Security's disability determination criteria for the listed conditions in the 14 categories in the regulations. Read the criteria for the condition and consider whether your child's eligibility is questionable. This may help you decide if you should seek expert advice or legal representation.

If you decide to appeal a denial, I recommend you to hire a Social Security or Medicaid attorney. If you are in a Reconsideration state, an attorney can help you fix an inadequate application in response to the reasons cited in the denial letter. If you are not in a Reconsideration state or have lost on reconsideration, recognize that the hearing before an ALJ is your best chance of success and you should take all prudent steps to win at this level. The chance of success before the Appeals Court or a US District Court is very low.

Where to Go for More Information

The website www.ultimatedisabilityguide.com has a wealth of information on the government's definition of a disability, guidance on preparing an application, common reasons for denial, the appeal procedure, guidance on whether to hire an attorney and more. The statistical data in this chapter was obtained from this website under the link "Denial Rates." The statistics were developed by Karl Kazmierczak, a Social Security Disability Attorney certified by the National Board of Social Security Disability Advocacy, an accrediting organization of the American Bar Association. His data was downloaded on June 24, 2012.

Nolo's Guide to Social Security Disability: Getting and Keeping Your Benefits (Morton 2012), also mentioned in the resource box in Chapter 8, is a helpful resource for those applying for benefits or wishing to appeal a Social Security denial. It has guidance for filling out the required forms, illustrations of completed forms, and a detailed description of the appeals procedures.

CHAPTER 23

MARRIAGE
CONSIDERATIONS FOR PEOPLE WITH DISABILITIES

Marriage for people with disabilities raises social, financial, legal, and moral questions. Some questions are straightforward and factual, such as the effect of marriage on government assistance. Some are practical, like how the couple can make the relationship work. There are also difficult questions about individual rights and social values. Few questions arise when the partners are physically disabled. Questions generally won't come up when only one of the potential partners has a disability. However, they will when both are cognitively impaired or have a mental illness.

How do we choose a life partner? We form relationships with people we have things in common with, people we have fun with, people we laugh with, and can cry with when we need to. We form our deepest relationships with people who understand us, appreciate us, and love us for ourselves. This is no less true for people with special needs than for anyone. It should not be surprising that two people with similar challenges and similar hopes for the future will turn to each other to satisfy the deepest of human needs, a partner to share a lifelong, loving relationship. Call it marriage; call it what you will. This is what this chapter is about.

The Right to Marriage

Four decades ago, most states had laws forbidding marriage of two people who were "mentally retarded." Those laws have been repealed but legal questions remain, questions related to one's mental competency to enter into a marriage contract, whether the appointment of a guardian establishes a lack of competency, and whether a guardian can prevent or annul a marriage. To discover possible legal impediments in your state, consult with a family law attorney. Family law includes laws pertaining to marriage, divorce, guardianship, and the protection of children. Guardianship law is easily overlooked. A guardianship appointment revokes certain personal legal rights. The right of marriage may be one. Even if the guardianship law itself does not deny the right, a guardian may have the legal power to forbid it.

If one accepts, as I do, that people with a cognitive impairment are human beings first, and that as human beings they have the same civil rights as other human beings which can only be overridden for compelling reasons of personal safety or protecting others, then the question is not whether to allow a marriage, but how to help make the relationship loving, caring, and meaningful. There are difficult ethical dilemmas such as the possibility of having children. Nonetheless, I believe that two individuals with an intellectual disability have a right to be married.

David Hingsberger said it as well as it can be said:

> I cry at every wedding of people with disabilities that I go to. I never cry at the weddings of my friends…primarily because they are on their third or fourth try. Why the tears? Well, I recognize the journey that they have traveled to get to that altar. It has been a long journey through prejudices, antiquated laws, smirking relatives, and disbelieving systems. There is no question that the triumph of love between people with disabilities is a significant one. (Schweier and Hingsberger 2000, p.158)

To find a life mate is an event of enormous significance. For someone with an intellectual disability it has significance for themselves, for our society, and for their peers. It is a blow against one of the last barriers of discrimination, the right of a person with a cognitive impairment to marry. There are three times in our lives when we are the center of attention: when we're born, when we die, and when we're married. The ritual and celebration of a wedding should be an option for our children. Against the legal impediments to a formal marriage, I do not accept that our society can deny two human beings an opportunity to have a committed and lasting relationship. Why should it not be so for our children? The solemnizing of such a relationship can be deeply moving and deeply meaningful.

If there are legal impediments to formal marriage there is an option. The three "Peace Churches"—Quakers, Mennonites, and Brethren—have a long history of resisting government laws that deny one's right of personal conscience and the right to practice one's faith. George Fox, the founder of the Friends, laid down the Quaker principle regarding marriage in 1669:

> For the right joining in marriage is the work of the Lord only, and not the priests' and magistrates'; for it is God's ordinance and not man's; and therefore Friends cannot consent that they should join together; for we marry none; it is the Lord's work, and we are but witnesses. (Religious Society of Friends 2005, Ch.16, para.16.01)

In Quaker practice, the couple seeking marriage writes a letter to the clerk of the Meeting (a Quaker term for its congregations) requesting their marriage be taken under the Meeting's care. The Meeting appoints a "clearness committee" to help them discern the depth of their love for each other, their understanding of the commitment they are making, and possible impediments that could prevent them from honoring their vows. If the Meeting decides to take the marriage under its care, there is no marriage ceremony as such. Simply, in a meeting for worship the couple stand and state their vows to each other in the presence of the community. Their vows may use the wording suggested by the Society of Friends or may be self-composed. The couple sign a document placed on a table in the center of the room that records their vows. After the meeting for worship closes, those attending sign as witnesses.

A Quaker marriage certificate is usually prepared by a professional calligrapher on heavy paper and is typically 24 by 36 inches. Most Quaker couples frame their certificate and hang it in their home. The clearness committee for marriage may continue to support the couple and nurture the relationship after the vows. This simple, deep procedure could easily be used by two people with Down syndrome, cerebral palsy, autism, or any other impairment who wish to marry in the face of obstacles, "…for we marry none; it is the Lord's work, and we are but witnesses."

Preparing for Marriage

Couples with a developmental disability may wish to marry because they have seen others marry, perhaps their brothers and sisters, but not understand the responsibilities of marriage or have the interpersonal skills for a long-term, mutually supporting relationship. As with any marriage, maturity and preparation are important to success. Parents should anticipate the possibility of marriage or an intimate relationship at an early age and teach the empowerment skills covered in Chapter 3 including healthy sexuality. If parents have not foreseen the possibility and now realize the child's desire to have a long-term relationship with someone he or she knows, they need to help the couple prepare by receiving counseling in sexuality, birth control, and issues surrounding parenthood. The couple will also need to be taught more mundane skills such as managing personal finances, managing a home, and taking physical care of each other. Despite my belief in the right of marriage, a relationship that can only founder or cause harm should not go forward. Like independence, getting to the point of embarkation will take whatever time is needed.

Is it advisable to have a trial period of living together? The idea may be anathema for traditionalists but it should be considered. People with a cognitive impairment are not abstract or theoretical thinkers. They learn by experience. It could be the only way they learn what a committed relationship means and the sexuality that goes with it.

How Marriage Affects Government Assistance

The SSI and Medicaid eligibility criteria for a couple are different than for individuals. The financial asset limit is $3000 for a couple versus $2000 for an individual. The income limit for stand-alone Medicaid is similarly 50 percent higher for a couple. The maximum SSI monthly payment is $1066 per month (2013) rather than $710. This is about 17 percent below the National Poverty Guideline. Financial support can be as necessary as social support.

Social Security Disability Insurance benefit on one's own work record is not affected by marriage. Dependent and survivor benefits can be. If an adult disabled child marries another adult disabled child, dependent or survivor benefits are not affected. If the adult disabled child marries someone who is not disabled, his or her dependent or survivor benefit will be terminated.

Supporting a Lifelong Relationship

When a person with a disability marries, there must be adequate income or financial support to cover the expenses of the household. It is likely that the couple will need advice and help managing their personal finances and the home. An uncommon but important issue arises in legal planning. Having a personal will may not have been important for a single person with a disability; it is for someone with a spouse. What happens to one's personal property should be addressed, including the property brought into the marriage and property acquired later by purchase or inheritance. It is a question that should be asked, which the individual probably will be eager to answer, "What do you want (*spouse's name*) to have when you die?" Few adults with disabilities own a condominium or house. If he or she does, the bequest to the spouse should be included in a will or the property must be conveyed by title (joint tenant with right or survivorship); or if the residence is owned by a first party special needs trust, the property should be transferred from the trust to the spouse or their trust as a remainder beneficiary. In most states, if a person leaves a residence to his or her disabled spouse, the property can be transferred without Medicaid repayment. The Medicaid lien remains with the property and is still enforceable when the surviving spouse dies.

We have all heard the statistics for the failure rate of marriage in our society. One would be naïve to ignore the risk with two people with disabilities. There is no statistical evidence to quantify the risk because such marriages are uncommon and there is no mechanism for collecting data. Setting aside one's personal idealism, there's no reason to suppose the risk is lower. Continued relationship and sexuality counseling should be available to the couple. Such help will also be important if one or both of the spouses have a mental illness.

If the adult child has the circles of support described in Chapter 2, the circles (hopefully two circles coming together) can provide precious support to the couple.

Relationship and sexuality counseling should be given by a psychologist experienced in counseling adults with developmental disabilities or mental illness, whichever is relevant. A typical married couple can be very helpful as role models and for advice and encouragement. I am skeptical whether on-going mentoring or counseling should be given by parents. The disadvantages include the possibility that the parents of each take sides or can't agree, the diminishment of the couple's independence from parental oversight, and the parental instinct to intervene.

What about Children?

There is without a doubt no area of special needs planning that is more fraught with passionate disagreement than the rights of people with an intellectual or mental disability to have a child. In no other area do we face a circumstance where what is best for two human beings (the parent and their child) can come into conflict. To begin with, we need to dispose of the myth that people with disabilities are asexual. This attitude is both patronizing and scientifically indefensible. Nor can one duck the question by assuming the person is infertile. It is common that fertility is diminished but childbearing is usually possible. It was not long ago that it was believed that adults with Down syndrome could neither father nor bear a child. Research has refuted that mistaken belief (Couwenhoven 2007). It is uncommon but not impossible.

As a society we are past the era when a government agency could sterilize a person without his or her consent. Nor can medical authorities unilaterally do so. Guardians do not have the legal authority to have their wards sterilized. A person must give informed consent to the procedure or it must be court-ordered. It is increasingly unlikely that a court will order sterilization unless childbearing would be life threatening. These comments apply also to abortion.

When the question of marriage of a person with a disability comes up, the question of childbearing must be raised with it. The answer to that question is anything but obvious. There are two issues. The first is the ability of the individual to be a good parent. The second, more difficult, is whether the child will be born with an inherited birth defect, suffer social stigma, or be adversely affected by a lack of adequate parenting. Many individuals with mild intellectual disabilities or mental conditions can make good parents with adequate preparation, advice, and support. The uncertainty increases as the seriousness of the impairment increases. Birth control is a topic that must be included in teaching healthy sexuality. Counseling should also be given on the responsibilities and skills of parenthood. If there is a possibility of an inherited genetic defect or mental illness, this concern needs to be faced with compassion and honesty.

The outcomes of child-rearing by a parent having a cognitive impairment or mental illness are difficult to predict. The question is not theoretical. There are concerns for a child's self-esteem who may feel embarrassed or defensive about his or her mother or father. There are questions about the adequacy of parental role modeling and nurturing. There may be questions of the quality of care and the possibility of neglect or abuse. It is not uncommon for a parent with a mental illness to have his or her children taken away by court order, especially when the individual is struggling to control their condition. The petition by a department of human services will always allege that is in the children's best interest. Once taken away, the children will not likely be returned. Child development is a fragile and elusive thing. As a parent I have felt the bewilderment of not knowing what to do or what went wrong, and so it is not surprising that there are concerns about parenting with a cognitive or mental condition. But I urge you not to ignore these questions because they are difficult, nor should you carelessly follow "conventional wisdom" which too often stereotypes people with disabilities.

Once the possibility of childbearing is raised, the issue of abortion comes right behind. Intense passions and deeply held moral values tend to overwhelm rational discussion, sometimes even common sense or human decency (as with advocacy for violence). I won't enter that debate here.

There is no more difficult dilemma in special needs planning than childbearing and child-rearing by a couple who are cognitively impaired or mentally ill. In other sections of this book I have made clear my passionate belief in the civil rights of people with disabilities. But in this, there are no easy answers. At the foundation these questions are moral as well as social. I have a deep respect for the exercise of personal conscience. I won't suggest what you should do. I do hope you will open yourself to conversations with others and be courageous enough to talk to someone who may hold different views than you. I plead with you that if your child can grasp the issues and has the maturity and unselfishness to make important decisions for themselves, give them a voice in the discussion and help them understand the concerns for the well-being of potential children.

Where to Go for More Information

The two books cited in Chapter 3, *Sexuality: Your Sons and Daughters with Intellectual Disabilities* (Schweier and Hingsberger 2000) and *Teaching Children with Down Syndrome about their Bodies, Boundaries and Sexuality* (Couwenhoven 2007), both treat the subjects of marriage, sexuality, and childbearing for people with disabilities.

Descriptions of Quaker marriage procedures are found in the books known as a "Faith and Practice" or a "Book of Discipline," which describe the spirituality, beliefs, organization, and procedures of the Society. Quaker meetings associate with one another in convocations called "yearly meetings" because they meet for business once a year. One of the largest is Philadelphia Yearly Meeting. Most yearly meetings have their own Faith and Practice or Book of Discipline. You can obtain Britain's Yearly Meetings (the quotation in this chapter was taken from it) or Philadelphia's from Friends General Conference Bookstore, www.quakerbooks.org.

CHAPTER 24

TWELVE THINGS
TO REMEMBER

My purpose in writing this book is to present the important principles and concepts in special needs planning with practical guidance on how to go about it. The "how to" ideas are offered as suggestions. I am not an expert in some areas, notably the topics in Part 1. I am a parent, with expertise in financial planning, who has spent a lot of time trying to create a better future for my daughter. You may find approaches or techniques that work better for you—parents can be very creative. Special needs planning is not post-doctoral physics, though it is complicated. Common sense, diligence, and the help of professionals in certain areas will be what you need.

One disadvantage of a "how to" book is that important principles can get lost in a welter of detail. So as I bring this to a close, I want to step back and leave you with 12 things to remember. These 12 principles are the essential elements of comprehensive special needs planning. If you take nothing else away from this book, hold on to these:

1. Start with a life plan. I can't stress this enough. Your and your child's vision will be the guide star and foundation for the resource, financial, and estate plans. The life plan is what it's all about; the rest is implementation.

2. Get serious about planning when your child is in his or her early teens. It takes time and persistence to teach an individual with a cognitive or an intellectual impairment the skills needed as an adult. The focus of high school and the transitions program should be on the child's life after aging out of school. You and the special education staff should be working on the empowerment skills for personal care management, social relationships, self-esteem, self-assertiveness, healthy sexuality, and safety awareness. Address the task skills for employment and independence if your child's abilities support these possibilities.

3. Understand eligibility and benefits of government programs for people with disabilities including the entitlement programs (Social Security and Medicare) and the means-tested programs (SSI, Medicaid, and state disability services).

4. Sign up for state services as soon as the regulations allow. Most states have a wait list for services due to inadequate funding. Some have a very long list. (Colorado has a die list.) The date you sign up determines your place in line. Many states allow signing up for services at an age earlier than the eligible age to receive them. Know what these ages are.

5. Create the network of supports to sustain your life plan. Identify the key roles and find good people to fill them. Pay particular attention to the guardian, care managers, fiduciaries, advocates, and companions. Obtain their commitments to serve. Decide how they will work together and include your plans and instructions in a letter of intent.

6. Consult with an attorney and a financial advisor with experience and expertise in special needs planning. The attorney should practice in elder law or trust and estates law. Financial advisors who practice in this field are rare. If you cannot find one, the best option is likely to be a Certified Financial Planner. They have expertise in creating comprehensive personal financial plans, including retirement and estate plans, and they commit to the highest fiduciary standards in the profession.

7. Execute the necessary legal documents—wills, powers of attorney, and healthcare directives for both parents. Establish a special needs trust for your child's financial support if he or she is to receive SSI, Medicaid, or state services.

8. Update the death benefit designations for all financial accounts, retirement plans, and insurance policies to implement your estate plan. Have a competent financial advisor trace the flow of bequests, distributions, and death benefits at the death of either or both parents. Verify that a special needs child does not inherit money or property causing a loss of government assistance unless you are wealthy enough to go it alone. Confirm the special needs or disability trust funds as intended.

9. Have a plan to open doors to employment, including higher education, vocational training, or job coaching. Do not underestimate the pride and self-esteem that a person with a disability feels holding a job. Individuals with special needs often place more importance on a job than typical adults who take employment for granted or as something to endure.

10. Consider the range of residential options available. If affordable, consider a private pay residence given common problems with access, control, quality, and reliability with state residential services. A place in the

community, especially a home of one's own, are powerful manifestations of relative independence.

11. Prepare a letter of intent to guide those who will come after you. The most important element is your personal family narrative, what you know as a parent, what you have learned as a parent, what you wish as a parent, and what your child wishes too.

12. Keep your plan current, review it periodically, and update it when needed.

One last thought to leave with you. I am not naïve about this nor should you be. Creating the best possible life for a person with significant special needs is not easy and it can be quite hard. Your task is to create a system of supports to last a lifetime. This network may need to function for decades, perhaps for many, many years after you're gone. It must be strong and flexible, capable of renewing itself, and capable of redesigning itself as life unfolds. You will need diligence and persistence, probably a financial commitment, and perhaps more than a little luck. It is not easy, and for some, limited by economic circumstances and insolvable constraints, their hopes and dreams for their child may not be possible.

When our daughter was born, the Mile High Down Syndrome Association paired me and my wife with a couple who had an older child with Down syndrome to help us through our first year, to help us overcome the fear of the unknown, to help us with the grieving and healing and strengthening we would need to face a future we had not anticipated and were ill-equipped to face. I will never forget something that Bill said to us one evening: "It will never be as good as you hope, but it will never be as bad as you fear." This is the most profound wisdom anyone gave to us. It has never been as bad as we feared. It has been quite a journey over 26 years. It has been a spiritual journey. But there are hopes built into our daughter's life plan. Some of those hopes may prove to be…a bridge too far. Nevertheless, we go forward. We cherish the triumphs that come along the way, like the day Meg came home with a job offer from a local department store. You should have seen her. She was so thrilled. She was so proud. And sometimes things don't work, like the day she lost her job. Well, what's Plan B? Plan C? It is discouraging sometimes, but it has been immensely rewarding. So we persist, taking it one day at a time, one task at a time. We learn by doing. We learn as we go along. We do the best we can with what we have to work with. It's a labor of love. It's a love for someone who has given more to me than she will ever be able to understand. And it's a project I will never finish.

My prayers and best wishes go with you, and your precious, special child.

LIST OF ACRONYMS

AAMS	Accredited Asset Management Specialist
ADL	Activity of Daily Living
ALJ	Administrative Law Judge
AMT	Alternative Minimum Tax
AWMA	Accredited Wealth Management Advisor
BCBA	Board Certified Behavioral Analyst
BPD	Borderline Personality Disorder
CCC	Certificate of Clinical Competency
CCM	Certified Care Manager
CD	Certificates of Deposit
CDFA	Certified Divorce Financial Analyst
CDR	Continuing Disability Review
CFA	Chartered Financial Analyst
CFP	Certified Financial Planner
ChFC	Chartered Financial Consultant
CIMA	Certified Investment Management Analyst
CLU	Chartered Life Underwriter
CMFC	Chartered Mutual Fund Counselor
CMS	Centers for Medicare and Medicaid Services
CNA	Certified Nurse Assistant
COLA	Cost of Living Adjustment
CPA	Certified Public Accountant
CPI	Consumer Price Index
CPR	Cardiopulmonary Resuscitation
CRC	Certified Rehabilitation Counselor
DD	Developmental Disability

DHHS	The United States Department of Health and Human Services
DI	Disability Insurance
DNI	Distributed Net Income
DNRO	Do Not Resuscitate Order
DS	Down Syndrome
DVR	Department of Vocational Rehabilitation
E&O	Errors and Omissions
EFC	Expected Family Contribution
EIA	Equity-Indexed Annuity
EIC	Earned Income Credit
ERISA	The Employee Retirement and Income Stability Act of 1974
ESA	Education Savings Account
ETF	Exchange-Traded Fund
FAFSA	Free Application for Federal Student Aid
FBR	Federal Benefit Rate
FERS	Federal Employee Retirement System
FICA	Federal Insurance Contributions Act
FINRA	Financial Industry Regulatory Authority
FPA	Financial Planning Association
FPT	First Party Trust
GAL	*Guardian ad litem*
GSTT	Generation-Skipping Transfer Tax
HCBS	Home and Community Based Services
HCVP	Housing Choice Voucher Program
HIPAA	Health Insurance Portability and Accountability Act of 1996
HOA	Home Owners Association
HSA	Health Savings Account
HUD	The United States Department of Housing and Urban Development
IAA	Investment Advisors Act
IC	Incentive Compensation
ICF/MI	Intermediate Care Facility for Individuals with Mental Illness
IDD	Intellectual or Developmental Disability
IDEA	The Individuals with Disabilities Education Act of 2004

IEP	Individualized Education Plan
IKSM	In-Kind Support and Maintenance
ILIT	Irrevocable Life Insurance Trust
ILP	Individual Life Plan
IRA	Individual Retirement Account
IRC	The United States Internal Revenue Code
IRS	The United States Internal Revenue Service
IRWE	Impairment-Related Work Expenses
ISP	Individualized Service Plan
ITP	Individualized Transition Plan
JTWROS	Joint Tenants with Right of Survivorship
LCSW	Licensed Clinical Social Worker
LMHC	Licensed Mental Health Counselor
LMSW	Licensed Master Social Worker
LOI	Letter of Intent
LPN	Licensed Practicing Nurse
LTCI	Long-Term Care Insurance
MHDSA	Mile High Down Syndrome Association
MI	Mental Illness
NAELA	National Association of Elder Law Attorneys
NP	Nurse Practitioner
NPA	National PLAN Alliance
NPG	National Poverty Guideline
NPV	Net Present Value
OASDI	Old Age, Survivors and Disability Insurance
ODAR	(Social Security) Office of Disability Adjudication and Review
OT	Occupational Therapist
PAD	Psychiatric Advance Directive
PASS	Plan for Achieving Self-Support
PATH	Planning Alternative Tomorrows with Hope
PCA	Personal Care Alternative
PEBES	(Social Security) Personal Earnings and Benefits Estimate Statement
PFS	Personal Financial Specialist

PHA	Public Housing Authority
PLAN	Planned Lifetime Advocacy Network
PLR	Private Letter Ruling (IRS)
POA	Power of Attorney
POD	Pay on Death
PPACA	Patient Protection and Affordable Care Act
PR	Personal Representative
PT	Physical Therapist
QDRO	Qualified Domestic Relations Order
QTIP	Qualified Terminable Interest Property
RLT	Revocable Living Trust
ROR	Rate of Return
RRT	Registered Respiratory Therapist
SGA	Substantial Gainful Activity
SLP	Speech and Language Pathology
SNA	Special Needs Alliance
SNT	Special Needs Trust
SSA	The Social Security Administration
SSDI	Social Security Disability Insurance
SSI	Supplemental Security Income
TIC	Tenants in Common
TOD	Transfer on Death
TPT	Third Party Trust
TTW	Ticket to Work
TWP	Trial Work Period
UTMA/UGMA	Uniform Transfer (Gift) to Minors Act
VUL	Variable Universal Life (Insurance)

DEFINITIONS OF
IMPORTANT TERMS

Agent with Power of Attorney—Someone you have empowered to act for you by signing a legal document known as a Power of Attorney (POA). An agent with a POA is also known as an attorney-in-fact. (See Power of Attorney Document.)

Advanced Directives—Legal documents which inform medical professionals, family, and healthcare agents or proxies of your wishes for medical care if you are unable to make your wishes known. The typical advanced directives are a living will, a medical power of attorney, a cardiopulmonary resuscitation (CPR) directive, and a Do Not Resuscitate Order (DNRO).

Age of Majority (or Emancipation)—The age when a minor becomes an adult and can legally manage his or her affairs. In most states this is on the person's eighteenth birthday.

Agent—Someone appointed to act for another (called a Principal) in accordance with a legal document called a Power of Attorney (POA). Another term for an agent is an attorney-in-fact.

Aging Out—A person with a disability reaching the age when his or her entitlement to a public education ends under the Individuals with Disabilities Education Act. It is age 20 in most states but some states extend the entitlement through age 21.

Assets—Assets are cash, cash equivalents, financial accounts, or entitlements in a person's name or possession. The assets of a person with a disability are counted by Social Security, Medicaid, and State disability service agencies in determining eligibility for means-tested government assistance.

Beneficiary—One who is entitled to receive a bequest, trust distribution, or insurance policy death benefit. A beneficiary may be primary or secondary (also known as a contingent beneficiary). A secondary beneficiary receives the bequest or distribution if all primary beneficiaries (and their heirs if *per stirpes* distributions are elected) predecease.

Bequest—A provision in a will that leaves cash, property, or assets to an individual, trust, or legal entity such as a charity.

Bridges Program—A Special Education Program for students age 19 through age 20 (21 in some states) to prepare the student for adult living after aging out of school. Also called a Transitions Program.

Care Manager—A person who coordinates and manages all care for a person with a disability, both government-provided and privately contracted services.

Case Manager—An employee or contractor of a government agency who coordinates and manages services provided by that agency.

The Centers for Medicare and Medicaid Services (CMS)—The Federal agency within the United States Department of Health and Human Services that administers Medicare and sets Federal policy for Medicaid.

Certified Financial Planner (CFP)—The highest professional certification earned by financial planners and advisors. CFPs accept a fiduciary duty to advise clients in their best interest. The certification is administered by the Certified Financial Planner Board of Standards, an independent entity. To receive a CFP designation a person must complete prescribed college-level courses and pass a rigorous, two-day exam. There is a requirement for continuing education to maintain one's CFP certification.

Codicil—A legal addendum to a will that changes the will's provisions. A codicil is used for simple changes to avoid rewriting the will. It must be signed and witnessed.

Common Law Marriage—A co-habitation arrangement which in some states has legal status equivalent to a formal marriage. Certain criteria must be met. Typically, both parties must be legal adults, not currently married to anyone else, living together, and identifying themselves as spouses (for example, by using the term spouse on forms). Common law marriage is defined by state law or courts.

Conservator—Someone appointed by a court to manage significant financial assets for an individual who is not competent to do so. A guardian is usually allowed to manage routine amounts of money. If substantial money is involved, the courts will appoint someone it determines to have the necessary financial competency as a conservator.

Death Benefit Designation Form—An insurance or annuity company or retirement plan form that names who is to receive death benefits if the owner of the account, contract, or plan dies. An individual, trust, or entity (e.g. a charity) can be a beneficiary.

Deed—A document that designates who holds legal title to real estate.

Deeming Rule—A rule used by Social Security and Medicaid that counts the income and assets of parents as the income and assets of their minor child for purposes of determining eligibility for means-tested government assistance. This policy reflects the legal obligation parents have to support their children until the age of majority.

Devisee—A beneficiary who inherits something per the terms of a will, in contrast to an heir who inherits as a result of intestacy law.

Durable Power of Attorney—A power of attorney that becomes or remains effective if a person is disabled. It allows someone to act for them if he or she cannot make the decisions described in the document for themselves.

Entitlement Programs—The Social Security OASDI Program for income payments and Medicare for health insurance. Contrast entitlement with means-tested programs—SSI, Medicaid, and state disability services which have income or asset limits to qualify. One who meets the eligibility criteria for an entitlement program is entitled to benefits, as well as one's eligible spouse and children, because one paid FICA (Social Security) or Medicare taxes. Moreover, the benefits were promised at the time the taxes were collected. Thus retroactive reductions to benefits already earned and paid for break a social contract between the government and its citizens.

ERISA-covered Retirement Plans—These are employer-sponsored retirement plans. They are so called by the section of the Internal Revenue Code that governs the tax treatment of contributions and withdrawals. Common types are 401k, 403b, and 457.

Estate—All of the property and assets you own when you die—money, investments, personal property, real property, debt owed to you, etc.

Executor/Executrix (male/female)—The personal representative of your estate appointed in your will to carry out the terms of the will after you die.

Federal Benefit Rate (FBR)—The maximum monthly payment that an SSI beneficiary can receive from Social Security. A few states supplement the FBR because the Federal Benefit Rate is less than 75 percent of the national poverty level.

FICA Taxes—Social Security OASDI payroll taxes. FICA is an acronym for Federal Insurance Contributions Act.

Fiduciary—An individual or legal entity (e.g. a bank trust department) that takes responsibility to act on behalf of another with loyalty and prudence. A fiduciary may be a personal representative, trustee, guardian, conservator, agent, attorney, advisor, or someone who holds themselves out to be acting as a fiduciary.

Generation-Skipping Transfer Tax—One of the three transfer taxes (along with estate and gift transfer taxes) triggered when a bequest is made to someone two generations below the deceased, e.g. a grandchild.

Gift—Almost anything valuable given to someone or something is a gift. Above a generous exclusion amount, a gift is taxable unless made to a spouse or charity. Contributions to a special needs trust are potentially taxable gifts.

Gift Tax—One of the three transfer taxes (along with estate and generation-skipping transfer taxes) that is owed if one makes gifts above an exclusion amount to anyone or anything other than one's spouse or a charity.

Grantor—A person who creates and transfers money, property, or assets to a trust, also called a settlor or trustor.

Guardian—Someone appointed by a court to be responsible for the affairs of someone who cannot manage for themselves, for example minors under age 18 if the parents are unable or unfit to serve, or someone with mental incapacity. A guardian may have full or limited powers. Full powers cover all matters of a person's life. If limited, the court will specify the powers granted, usually management of financial and legal affairs.

Guardian ad litem—A guardian appointed by a court in a legal proceeding to protect the interests of someone the court judges to need assistance. In a guardianship proceeding, it is someone appointed to protect the person for whom guardianship is sought.

Health Care Power of Attorney (HCPOA)—A legal document that authorizes the person named in the document to make decisions for your medical care if you cannot make such decisions yourself or make your wishes known (e.g. if you are in a coma).

Health Insurance Portability and Accountability Act (HIPAA)—A broad act primarily intended to allow people to change jobs without unreasonable exclusions for prior medical conditions by the new employer's group health insurance plan. An important set of provisions in the Act protects the privacy of adults in matters of physical, medical, psychological, or mental conditions. Parents who are not guardians, agents with power of attorney, or named in a privacy waiver signed by their adult child have no right to know the contents of their child's medical records or have their child's condition discussed with them by medical, government, or other professionals.

Healthcare Proxy—Another term for an agent holding a durable power of attorney for healthcare decisions.

Heir—A beneficiary who inherits something in accordance with a state's intestacy laws, in contrast to a devisee who inherits by the terms of a will.

HIPAA Waiver—A privacy waiver conforming to the Health Insurance Portability and Accountability Act.

Home and Community Based Services (HCBS) Programs—Medicaid services for an eligible beneficiary to support them in the community as an alternative to receiving institutional care. The policy recognizes the cost-effectiveness of community services in comparison with the high cost of institutional care.

Housing Choice Voucher Program—Payments by the United States Housing and Urban Development Department that can be used by a low-income person or a person with a disability for apartment rent or mortgage assistance. Also called the Section 8 Voucher Program.

Impairment-Related Work Expense (IRWE)—Expenses that allow a person with a disability to work. A person's income is reduced by these expenses when computing the SGA or SSI payments.

Income—Social Security and Medicaid considers almost all money that lands in the bank account or pocket of an SSI or Medicaid beneficiary to be his or her income whether taxed or not, and whether earned or unearned, for example from gifts, investment income, SSDI payments. There are special rules for counting child support.

The Individuals with Disabilities Education Act (IDEA)—Entitles a person with a disability to a public education until his or her twenty-first birthday in the least restrictive environment, often interpreted to mean in a mainstream public school. It also requires that school professionals work with the parents to develop an Individualized Education Plan (IEP) describing the support the child needs and will be provided to receive an appropriate education.

Individualized Education Plan (IEP)—A plan of educational support for a student with a disability cooperatively prepared by a school's teaching staff and parents.

Individual Life Plan (ILP)—A life plan prepared for a person with a disability after aging out of public school. It is a best practice not mandated by law.

Individualized Transition Plan (ITP)—The equivalent of an IEP for someone in the 18–20 age group to prepare him or her for life after aging out of the school system. The primary emphasis is often employment and personal management skills.

In-Kind Support and Maintenance (IKSM)—SSI is intended to pay for a person's room and board. If someone else provides room and board without charge, this is defined as IKSM and monthly SSI payments will be reduced by one-third of the Federal Benefit Rate (FBR). In effect this lets the government off the hook for the support it is required by law to provide. This can affect parents whose SSI-receiving child is living in their home rent-free. The SSI payment reduction can be avoided if parents charge their adult child fair rent for room and board. (See also the One-third Reduction Rule.)

Intestacy—A problem that arises when someone dies and has made no provision for the transfer of money, assets, or property in a valid will or a trust. Intestacy can apply to the entire estate or to specific items that have been forgotten and omitted. Intestate assets are distributed to next of kin in a hierarchy defined in state law. This can result in a special needs child receiving an unintended inheritance that eliminates his or her eligibility for government assistance until the assets are spent down.

Inter vivos **Trust**—A trust established during a person's lifetime by executing a legal document called a trust agreement. Contrast this with a testamentary trust.

Irrevocable Trust—A trust that a grantor cannot change, such as changing a beneficiary or terms of distributions. The grantor cannot reclaim any of the assets or money he or she gifted or transferred to the trust. Contrast this with a revocable trust.

Joint Tenant with Right of Survivorship (JTWROS)—A form of joint property ownership. When one owner dies the other automatically acquires sole title.

Letter of Intent (LOI)—A set of documents which make known the wishes of parents for their child, describes the arrangements that have been made, and the actions that should be taken upon their death or incapacity. It consists of a personal narrative, a summary of the parents' wishes and files of documents. It is a guidance document and not legally binding on others.

Limited Guardian—A guardian appointed with limited powers, usually for an individual's financial and legal affairs leaving him or her to manage their daily lives.

Living Will—An advance directive prepared for healthcare providers expressing a person's wishes not to be kept alive by artificial means if he or she cannot make such wishes known due to mental incapacity or inability to communicate.

Means-tested Government Programs—SSI, Medicaid, and state disability service that have income and asset limits to receive benefits. These programs are for those who live in poverty. It is the policy of the government only to take care of the life-sustaining needs of a person with a disability while providing cash assistance that, at best, supports an individual at the national poverty level.

Medicaid—A complex program with three aspects. One, it is the national health insurance program for families or individuals who live below the poverty line. Two, it is the largest payer in the nation for assisted living or skilled nursing care for the frail elderly who have inadequate income and assets to afford their own care. Three, it is a block-grant program to states for Home and Community Based Disability Services.

Medicaid-Waiver Programs—This is a synonym for Home and Community Based Services programs. It reflects a history that Medicaid paid for institutional services for the mentally ill, people with a disability, and the frail elderly. When it became apparent that community based services cost less than institutionalization, a policy allowing payment for services outside of an institutional setting was developed.

Medicare—The national health insurance entitlement program for those who have paid Medicare taxes and who are age 65 or older, have Amyotrophic Lateral Sclerosis (Lou Gehrig's disease), end stage renal disease (kidney failure), or who have received Social Security Disability Insurance (SSDI) benefit for 24 consecutive months.

Minor—One who has not reached the legal age of adulthood, age 18 in most states.

One-third Reduction Rule—If an individual receives IKSM (in-kind support and maintenance, i.e. free room and board from someone else), his or her SSI payments will be reduced by one-third of the Federal Benefit Rate (FBR).

QDRO (pronounced Quad-Row)—A divorce court order that orders an ERISA-covered retirement plan administrator to divide the assets of the plan between divorcing spouses. It also terminates the right of a spouse to a future survivor benefit on the ex-partner's plan.

PATH Planning—A structured process for annual life planning.

Pay on Death (POD) Beneficiary Designation—A designation used by banks, on a form they require, that designates to whom the account is to be transferred at the owner's death.

Per capita—In wills, trusts and death benefit designations, a *per capita* distribution is a distribution in equal shares to living, eligible beneficiaries named in the will, trust agreement, or beneficiary designation form.

Per stirpes—In wills and trusts, a *per stirpes* distribution allows the heirs of a deceased beneficiary to inherit his or her share.

Personal Representative—The person appointed in your will to carry out the terms of your will when you die. Also called an Executor/Executrix (male/female).

Pooled Trust—A charitable, pooled-asset trust authorized by the United States Code §1396(d) (4)(c). It is a first party special needs trust but exempt from the requirement to have a Medicaid payback provision. The residual in a beneficiary's sub-account is retained by the pooled trust at the beneficiary's death to further its charitable purpose.

Pour-over Trust—A trust that is established with nominal funding. Full finding is planned to occur when death benefits or bequests "pour over" into the trust at someone's death. This is a common, though sometimes inappropriate, strategy to fund a special needs trust.

Power of Attorney (POA) Document—A legal document that appoints an agent to act for you in specific circumstances and with specific powers described in the document. Often courts will refuse to appoint a guardian for a person with mental illness if the person's drug regimen allows them to function normally. A POA is used instead to allow someone to intervene if the person becomes incompetent to make his or her decisions. The document does not empower an agent to institutionalize the individual for whom they are acting. Only a court can institutionalize an individual without his or her consent.

Psychiatric Advanced Directive—A type of medical advanced directive which gives the agent the power to make decisions for someone whose mental state does not permit them to make rational decisions regarding their treatment or safety.

Privacy Waiver—A legal document signed by an individual authorizing an individual, company, or government entity to disclose information about a person's physical, medical, psychological, or mental history or condition. It is used to allow the named third party to be informed of a person's condition and assist or advise in decisions for his or her care. A full guardian does not need a privacy waiver. Court-ordered guardianship pierces the veil of privacy.

Private Pay Services—Services that are privately contracted for by an individual, family, or other person to provide assistance, care, and support for someone with a disability. Contrast this with government services.

Program Operating Manual System (POMS)—The policy and procedures manual of the Social Security Administration.

Real Property—Land, buildings, and improvements thereon, also known as real estate. Contrast with personal property, which is the movable possessions of an individual.

Representative Payee—A person or organization authorized to receive, deposit, and cash Social Security payments, including SSI payments, for a person who cannot manage his or her own money.

Residual Beneficiary—A trust beneficiary who receives the assets or money remaining in the trust when the primary beneficiary dies.

Revocable Trust—A trust that can be changed or terminated at will by the grantor. Contrast this with an irrevocable trust.

Section 8 Vouchers—Payments by the United States Housing and Urban Development Department under the Housing Choice Voucher Program that can be used by a low-income person or a person with a disability for apartment rent or mortgage assistance.

Self-settled Trust—A term for a first party special needs trust.

Settlor—Also called a grantor or trustor, the person who establishes the trust.

Shell Trust—A trust to be funded in the future, for example a pour-over trust.

Social Security (OASDI)—The Federal program for retirement (Old Age), survivor (S), and disability insurance (DI).

Social Security Dependent Benefit—Benefits paid to a dependent of someone who receives Social Security retirement or disability benefits on his or her work record.

Social Security Disability Insurance (SSDI) Benefit—Payments for an individual with a disability who has paid Social Security taxes, has met the required number of work credits, makes less than the SGA, and who medically qualifies as disabled. SSDI payments are also made "to adults disabled since childhood" who are the children of a parent receiving a Social Security benefit or who was eligible when deceased.

Social Security Spousal Benefit—The benefit received by a spouse of a Social Security eligible person who meets the eligibility requirements. The Social Security eligible person does not have to be receiving benefits for his or her spouse to receive a spousal benefit and there are special rules for divorced spouses.

Social Security Survivor Benefit—The benefits received by a spouse or dependent, who meets certain eligibility criteria, of a Social Security eligible person who dies.

Special Needs Trust (SNT)—A trust established for the benefit of a person with a disability that allows money or assets to be set aside for his or her support while maintaining eligibility for means-tested government assistance provided certain provisions of the Social Security Act are met. If the trust is structured properly, trust assets are not counted as assets of the beneficiary for determining eligibility for means-tested government assistance. Also called a supplemental needs trust. There are three types of special needs trust: first party, third party (most common), and charitable pooled-asset trusts. (See Trust Parties.)

Spend Down—Depleting the assets of a person with a disability by spending money for their benefit until the assets fall below the asset eligibility limit to receive SSI, Medicaid, or State disability services. If substantial money is involved, an alternative is to establish a first party special needs trust with a Medicaid payback provision.

Springing Power of Attorney—An appointment of an agent with POA that takes effect if and when a person is incapacitated and unable to act for themselves.

Successor—Someone who takes over for another in roles such as a personal representative, guardian, trustee, trust protector, care manager, or fiduciary.

Supplemental Security Income (SSI)—A Social Security means-tested program for income assistance for a person with a disability.

Supplemental Needs Trust—Another name for a special needs trust.

Substantial Gainful Activity (SGA)—An economic eligibility requirement for Social Security disability benefits. It is the maximum amount a person can earn and still be eligible. By coincidence, the SGA is approximately the earnings for a full-time job at minimum wage and only slightly above the national poverty guideline.

Surety Bond—Also called a performance bond, a surety bond pledges an amount of money to assure performance by a fiduciary, such as a trustee. The bond is forfeited if the fiduciary fails to perform his or her duties.

Tenants in Common (TIC)—A form of joint ownership that permits the owner to gift or bequest his or her interest in property to whomever they desire. The ownership share can be any percentage. The share percentage is stated in the property deed.

Testamentary Trust—A trust created by a provision in a will. A testamentary trust does not exist until the creator dies and his or her will is probated. Contrast this with an *inter vivos* trust established during one's lifetime.

3-Bed PCA—A common type of residence for people with disabilities provided by states through a Home and Community Based Services program. It is typically a four-bedroom house—three client bedrooms and one bedroom for staff.

Transfer of Death (TOD) Beneficiary Designation—A designation used by investment and financial firms that designates to whom the account is to be transferred at the owner's death.

Transfer Taxes—Estate, gift, and generation-skipping transfer taxes, dishonestly called death taxes by conservatives who want their repeal. The term "death tax" is inaccurate because few people who die pay these taxes due to generous estate exclusion amounts. These taxes are more accurately termed wealth taxes.

Transitions Program—A Special Education Program for students age 19 through age 20 (21 in some states) to prepare the student for adult living after aging out of school. Also called a Bridges Program.

Trust—A legal entity established to allow money or assets to be managed for a beneficiary. It is a contract between a grantor or settler who establishes and funds a trust and the trustee who will manage the assets in accordance with the terms of the trust agreement.

Trust Agreement—A legal document that establishes a trust specifying the purpose of the trust, the beneficiary, the powers and limitations of the trustee, and how the trust is to be managed.

Trustee—An individual or entity (such as a bank trust department or charitable pooled trust) that manages trust assets for the benefit of the trust beneficiary.

Trust Parties—There are three parties to a trust. The first party is the individual for whom the trust is established to benefit—the beneficiary. The second party is the trustee, who owns and manages the assets for the benefit of the first party. The third party is the individual forming the trust. If the beneficiary establishes the trust, it is called a first party or self-settled trust. If any other party establishes the trust, it is called a third party trust.

Trust Protector—An individual or entity who is given powers defined in the trust agreement which may include powers to terminate the trust or change its provisions. Two powers often given are to amend a trust document to keep the trust in compliance with laws and regulations, and to replace the trustee, either for cause (the failure to discharge one's fiduciary duties as defined in law) or at will, depending on the wording of the trust provisions.

Trustor—The person who establishes a trust, also called a grantor or settlor.

Uniform Transfer (Gift) to Minors Act Accounts—The Act allows custodial accounts to be established for minors. The assets in a UTMA/UGMA account are considered by Social Security regulations to be the property of the child for whom the UTMA/UGMA was established. These accounts can render an individual with a disability ineligible for means-based government assistance until the assets are spent down.

Ward—A person for whom a guardian has been appointed.

REFERENCES

Berman, D. and Matthews, J. (2012) *Social Security, Medicare & Government Pensions.* Berkeley, CA: Nolo.

Choate, N. (2011) *Life and Death Planning for Retirement Benefits* (7th edition). Boston, MA: Ataxplan Publications.

Clifford, D. (2012) *Plan Your Estate* (11th edition). Berkeley, CA: Nolo.

Collier, C. (2008) *Wealth in Families* (2nd edition). Boston, MA: Harvard College.

Commito, T. (2012) "The IRS Data Book Yields Interesting Information." *Journal of Financial Services Professionals 66,* 4, 13–14.

Couwenhoven, T. (2007) *Teaching Children with Down Syndrome about their Bodies, Boundaries and Sexuality.* Bethesda, MD: Woodbine House.

Etmanski, A. (2000) *A Good Life.* Vancouver, BC: Planned Lifetime Advocacy Network.

Goldstone, H. and Wiseman, K. (2012) *Trustworthy: New Angles on Trusts from Beneficiaries and Trustees.* Denver, CO: Trustscapes, LLC.

Hauer, M. (2007) *Friendly Divorce Guidebook for Colorado.* Denver, CO: Bradford Publishing.

Jackins, B., Shulman, K., Onello, H., and Blank, R. (2012) *Managing a Special Needs Trust: A Guide for Trustees* (2012 edition). Brookline, MA: DisABILITIES Books.

Landis, A. (2012) *Social Security: The Inside Story, an Expert Explains Your Rights and Benefits* (2012 edition). Lexington, KY: Thinking Retirement.

Lovelace, R. (2010) *Pooled Trust Options: A Guidebook.* Round Lake, NY: Mélange Press.

Lucia, R. (2004) *Buckets of Money: How to Retire in Comfort and Safety.* Hoboken, NJ: John Wiley.

Mannix, D. (2009a) *Social Skills Activities for Secondary Students with Special Needs.* San Francisco, CA: Jossey-Bass.

Mannix, D. (2009b) *Life Skills Activities for Secondary Students with Special Needs.* San Francisco, CA: Jossey-Bass.

Morris, W. (ed.) (1981) *The American Heritage Dictionary of the English Language: New College Edition.* Boston: Houghton Mifflin.

Morton, D. (2012) *Nolo's Guide to Social Security Disability: Getting and Keeping Your Benefits.* Berkeley, CA: Nolo.

O'Brien, J., Pearpoint, J., and Kahn, L. (2010) *The PATH and MAPS Handbook: Person-Centered Ways to Build Community.* Toronto, ON: Inclusion Press

Price, M. (2009) *Divorce and the Special Needs Child.* Chicago, IL: American Bar Association.

Religious Society of Friends (2005) *Quaker Faith and Practice: The Book of Christian Discipline of the Yearly Meeting of the Religious Society of Friends (Quakers) in Britain.* London: Quaker Books.

Russell, L. and Grant, A. (2005) *Planning for the Future: Providing a Meaningful Life for a Child with a Disability after Your Death.* Palantine, IL: Planning for the Future.

Schweier, K. and Hingsberger, D. (2000) *Sexuality: Your Sons and Daughters with Intellectual Disabilities.* Baltimore, MD: Paul H. Brookes Publishing.

Specialized Housing (2010) *Passport to Independence: A Manual for Families.* Boston, MA: Specialized Housing.

FURTHER READING

Atwood, T. (2007) *The Complete Guide to Asperger's Syndrome*. London: Jessica Kingsley Publishers.

Begley, T. and Canellos, A. (2012) *Special Needs Trust Handbook*. New York: Aspen Publishers.

Braddock, D., Hemp, R., Rizzolo, M., Haffner, L., *et al.* (2013) *The State of the States in Developmental Disabilities 2013: The Great Recession and Its Aftermath*. Boulder, CO: University of Colorado.

Department of the Treasury Internal Revenue Service (2013) *2011 Internal Revenue Service Data Book, October 1, 2010 to September 30, 2011*. Washington, DC: USDOT.

Dukeminier, J., Johanson, S., Lindgren, J., and Sitkoff, R. (2005) *Wills, Trusts and Estates* (7th edition). New York: Aspen Publishers.

Grandin, T. (2011) *The Way I See It: A Personal Look at Autism and Asperger's* (2nd edition). Arlington, TX: Future Horizons.

Greenbaum, J. (2007) *Life Planning for Adults with Developmental Disabilities: A Guide for Parents and Family Members*. Oakland, CA: New Harbinger Publications.

Hale, N. (2010) *Managing My Money: Banking and Budgeting Basics*. Bethesda, MD: Woodbine House. (A book for people with an intellectual disability.)

Heiser, K. (2007) *Medicaid Secrets*. Superior, CO: Phylius Press.

Hughes, J. (2004) *Family Wealth: Keeping It in the Family*. Princeton NJ: Bloomberg Press.

Hull, J. (2001) *On Sight and Insight: A Journey into the World of Blindness*. Oxford: Oneworld Publications. (Originally published in 1990.)

Jamison, K. (2012) *An Unquiet Mind: A Memoir of Moods and Madness*. New York: Vintage Books. (Originally published in 1996.)

McGuire, D. and Chicoine, B. (2006) *Mental Wellness in Adults with Down Syndrome*. Bethesda, MD: Woodbine House.

Meyers, J. (2008) *How to Teach Daily Living Skills to Adults with Developmental Disabilities*. Lincoln, NE: iUniverse.

Miklowitz, D. (2011) *The Bipolar Disorder Survival Guide*. New York: The Guilford Press.

Nadworney, J. and Haddad, C. (2007) *The Special Needs Planning Guide: How to Prepare for Every Stage of Your Child's Life*. Baltimore, MD: Paul H. Brookes Publishing.

Scherer, M. (2012) *Assistive Technologies and Other Supports for People with Brain Impairment*. New York: Springer.

INTERNET RESOURCES

The Centers for Medicare and Medicaid Services website has information on the two Federal healthcare programs, Medicare and Medicaid. Because Medicaid is state-administered, the CMS website has information by state as well as topic. The website is www.cms.gov.

Inclusion Press is a publisher of books and materials on PATH Planning. Its website is www.inclusion.com.

The Social Security Administration's website is www.ssa.gov. It has an extensive library of current information on Social Security OASDI benefits and SSI. The website is well organized and the Social Security Administration typically produces well-written publications.

The Ultimate Disability Guide website, www.ultimatedisabilityguide.com, is a website managed by a Social Security disability attorney. It has information about applying for Social Security disability benefits and appealing an adverse SSA decision.

The United States budget can be obtained from the website www.whitehouse.gov/omb/budget. The document *The President's Budget for Fiscal Year 2011* contains the enacted budget for Government Fiscal Year 2011 (October 2010 through September 2011) and the proposed budgets for GFY 2012 and GFY 2013. (At the time the 2013 budget was being prepared, Congress had not enacted the 2012 budget. It did so in December, 2011.)

INDEX